Literatures in the Digital Era:
Theory and Praxis

Literatures in the Digital Era: Theory and Praxis

Edited by

Amelia Sanz and Dolores Romero

(LEETHI Group)

CAMBRIDGE SCHOLARS PUBLISHING

Literatures in the Digital Era: Theory and Praxis, edited by Amelia Sanz and Dolores Romero
(LEETHI Group)

This book first published 2007 by

Cambridge Scholars Publishing

15 Angerton Gardens, Newcastle, NE5 2JA, UK

British Library Cataloguing in Publication Data
A catalogue record for this book is available from the British Library

Copyright © 2007 by Amelia Sanz and Dolores Romero and contributors

All rights for this book reserved. No part of this book may be reproduced, stored in a retrieval system, or transmitted, in any form or by any means, electronic, mechanical, photocopying, recording or otherwise, without the prior permission of the copyright owner.
ISBN 1-84718-291-7; ISBN 13: 9781847182913

TABLE OF CONTENTS

Introduction 1
Amelia Sanz and Dolores Romero

Part I: Hyper-Paradigm 17
María Goicoechea

Chapter One 23
Comparative Literature From Text to Hypertext or What do Electronic Media have to Offer the Discipline?
George Landow

Chapter Two 41
Always Already-Known Hypertexts: a Recent Debate in Old Terms
Apostolos Lampropoulos

Chapter Three 51
Ludology meets Hypertext
Susana Pajares Tosca

Chapter Four 61
Actualizing Allusions: Hypertext and Cognitive Literary Research
Ziva Ben-Porat

Part II: Hyper-(W)reader 81
María Goicoechea

Chapter Five 85
The Boundaries of Digital Narrative: a Functional Analysis
Juan B. Gutiérrez

Chapter Six 103
Some Notes on the Reading of Digital Literary Works.
Alckmar L. Dos Santos

Chapter Seven 123
"Lector in machina": towards an Erotic of Reading
Laura Borrás

Chapter Eight 151
Reading Guidelines For Electronic Literature
Alexandra Saemmer

Part III: Hyper-Editing 167
María Goicoechea

Chapter Nine 171
Aspects of Scholarship and Publishing in the Age of New Media Technology
Steven Tötösy de Zepetnek

Chapter Ten 185
A Dynamic Authenticity of Texts in E-Archives: On Digitized Cultural Resources in Comparative Literary Studies
Jola Skulj

Chapter Eleven 201
Postmodernity and Critical Editions of Literary Texts: Towards the Virtual Presence of the Past
Marko Juvan

Chapter Twelve 221
The Hypertextual Structure of Writing Processes
Dirk Van Hulle

Chapter Thirteen 235
Digital Text: Conceptual and Methodological Frontiers
María Clara Paixão de Sousa

Part IV: Hyper-Praxis 253
María Goicoechea

Chapter Fourteen 257
The *Hyper* in Calligraphy and Text
Marie-Thérèse Abdel-Messih

Chapter Fifteen 267
Hypertext: An Alternative Route to Short Stories Theorizing
Anastasia Natsina

Chapter Sixteen 277
The Echo of Narcissism in Interactive Arts
Lee Scrivner

Chapter Seventeen... 289
Hypertext and Collective Authorship: The Influence of the Internet
on the Formation of New Concepts of Authorship
Florian Hartling

Chapter Eighteen 297
Hypermedia Narratives: Paratactic Structures and Multiple Readings
Ana Pano Alamán

Chapter Nineteen 305
"Salaam Baghdad": Warblogs in the Textual and Social Economies
of the Internet
Priscilla Ringrose

Chapter Twenty 319
From Hypertexts to Blogs: 'El primer vuelo de los Hermanos Wright'
and 'Más respeto que soy tu madre'
Perla Sassón-Henry

Chapter Twenty One.. 329
Spanish Literature in the Digital Domain: Culture, Nation and Narrations
Dolores Romero López

Contributors.. 343

INTRODUCTION

AMELIA SANZ AND DOLORES ROMERO (LEETHI GROUP[1])

Hyper-technologies

Technologies, ideologies and cultures have been linked throughout the history of humankind. Nowadays, the Global South sees the so-called "West" not only as a physical place but as a virtual space; it is not so much a geographical or political division, but a social one, depending on class and generational boundaries: a working place, a space created by ICT. Statistics on the number of Internet users worldwide show the Global Digital Divide between those with regular effective access to digital technologies and those without, which puts into question the democratic venue for the globalization of knowledge and knowledge transfer. While we wait for this potential to be realized, at the present time just 16,6% of the world population has Internet access, ranging from 3,5% of the population of Africa to 69,4% in the United States. Any discussion on closing the Digital Divide deals fundamentally with both the impoverishment and empowerment of people; it is the key to both social equality and mobility and to economic equality and growth.[2] To be or not to be (dis)connected

---

[1] L.E.E.T.Hi. (*Literaturas Españolas y Europeas del Texto al Hipertexto/Spanish and European Literatures from Text to Hypertext*) is a research group based at the Complutense University, Madrid, whose projects have focused on the teaching of literature from an intercultural perspective while simultaneously helping to develop competence in information literacy following the impact of entrepreneurial activities on the academic research system. We are particularly grateful to María Goicoechea's contributions and Valery Stacey's corrections to this volume.

[2] Craig Warren Smith. *Digital Divide.org*, http://www.digitaldivide.org, [accessed March 10, 2007] and "Internet Usage Statistics. The Big Picture". In *Internet World Stats*, http://www.internetworldstats.com/stats.htm. More information in

from one's own society or from virtual societies—that is the question.

The same question could be asked of the Humanities. Writers and intellectuals are often cautious about new media technology in general and online scholarship in particular, perhaps because the Humanities are very much the culture of the solitary scholar. Any utterance of the word *hyper* means *danger*! They feel threatened and intimidated by these new kinds of commercial wars for the control of information and access to knowledge (e-reviews, data bases, free books, etc.), by new virtual services which become more highly valued the more they are shared by virtual scientific communities (the *Google Library Project*), and by new communication structures based on collaborative human expression (such as *Wikipedia*). And this is all taking place against a background of language "confusion" (the "Global English Babel" that has arisen from the homogenization of cultures through media convergence), of legal disorder (the copyrights debate) and of a dramatic reduction in lexical resources, which benefits sign codes other than the written language. At the same time, the idea of a professional instrument providing entertainment for the rest of us is discomfiting.

The debate about relations between literature and technology is now over. Only in the field of literary studies does this antagonism between the two still persist; in the other arts, such discussions are already part of the past; Humanistic Informatics is no longer an oxymoron these days.

Books may be endangered, but not so verbal communication, since we have never had so many opportunities to express ourselves and read what others express. What is happening is that the heritage from literary traditions based on authors, books and, for the most part, paper, is also playing a major role in *hyper*text, which is an actual referent and not just a metaphorical one. Scholars such as MacLuhan, Bolter or Chartier have demonstrated that books are first and foremost a kind of technological artefact—a machine to be used and a product to be bought and sold; this is the economic dimension of text-supporting materials.

If books, on the one hand, are indeed teaching and communicating *machines* (see Landow), then the "electronification" of universities and research institutions does not imply technologizing them or applying further technology to them in some way alien to their essential spirit. The future will, in fact, be collaborative, because new media can support or facilitate the traditions of scholarship in the humanities, which are, namely, those of reflection and reflective reading (see Tötösy). This is the reason why the most prestigious institutions, conscious of their past and future role

---

Internet Society, http://www.isoc.org/isoc/, [accessed March 10, 2007].

in the sharing and distribution of knowledge, have invested time and financial resources in organizing sources to provide users and clients with easily-accessed data networks, including bibliographical data in virtual libraries, network encyclopaedias[3], digital periodicals and magazines and online data banks. We are reminded of the decline of the monasteries when they lost control of the process of reproducing written work, and the success of the alliance between universities and printers. Nowadays, if technological domination and control by new managers of information and knowledge is to be avoided, certain precautions and initiatives should be taken (such as Open Access for scientific publications).

On the other hand, traditional humanistic scholarship has always involved networks that existed in the minds of scholars. Texts have never in fact existed in isolation but form part of a diachronic and synchronic series of texts; we have always been tempted to expand the text by supplementing our reading and writing with such activities as adding notes, glossaries, illustrations and indexes, to shape a network, traditionally on printed sheets and nowadays on screens. Electronic hypertext—a recent form of prosthetic memory—can create new forms of writing, just as the Humanists did with their notations.

Traditionally, the mobility and storage capacities of supporting materials have been a key factor in the adoption of writing technologies. The consequence of technologies that have accelerated the diffusion of writing and reduced the time between production and consumption has been to succeed in modifying the mental processes involved in communication, information and education. Nowadays, this acceleration is taking place along a low-cost superhighway that results from electronic technology, and we cannot stop it.

The contributions we present in this volume analyse some of the social, cultural and cognitive transformations involved in new writing technologies and the generation of new models of reading literatures.

Hyper-identities

As the speed of communications across geographical space increased throughout the twentieth century, space became de-territorialized. More recently, with the introduction of networking technologies, it has been replaced by a kind of non-geographical space: *cyberspace* or *hyperspace*.

---

[3] See our contributions to the *Comparative Literature in the Age of Global Change*. In *Encyclopaedia of Life Support Systems (EOLSS)*, Oxford, Eolss Publishers, UNESCO, http://www.eolss.net.

Diasporic movements resulting from the expansion of global economies are able to share interests and common culture through computer-mediated communication. The immediate effect has been to create a sort of illusion of participation as both physical and hierarchical distances between communicators have been removed. But this is just an illusion, a *simulacre*.

In the past, of course, it was the advent of the printing-press that had such a defining impact on our individual and social structures; in present times, electronic technologies have produced a similar effect. Nowadays, networking technologies provide new ways of organizing our knowledge and our communicative capacities. Different kinds of written technologies allow us to communicate rapidly and non-presentially, liberated from the restrictions of time and space. As a result, space, time and knowledge are all managed by electronic tools.

The truth is, we have always been involved in some situation or other in which cross-cultural communication takes place: in former times, it might have been the wholesaler negotiating bundles of books in the port, the monk copying oriental manuscripts in the monastery, the humanist fingering the latest work printed in Italy, or a group discussing a new translation in a society salon. Nowadays, such communication takes place at a much faster pace, twenty-four hours a day: we answer e-mails in three or four languages, work on the same screen with colleagues located all over the world in different time zones, consult documents stored on the other side of the planet, and so on. Everything is being done at a more rapid pace and our lives have become ever more hectic. With this constant "cultural clicking", in what kind of culture can we feel rooted?

Indeed, we could be defined by the sedentary lifestyle we have adopted, with nomadism belonging to a previous stage of evolution, though still a constituent one in human memory. We are both sedentary *and* nomadic. The change from a way of life based on hunting (in the Palaeolithic period) to an urban culture (in the Neolithic period) was a crucial time in human evolution: the wider world was not only situated on a horizontal plane (geographical and physical and always at a distance), but also, to a large extent, on a vertical one (temporal, metaphysical and transcendental). It was the time when human beings began to dig graves they could revisit again and again, days, months or years afterwards. By using and extending these images and the metaphors they support, it may well be that virtual space requires a new definition of the horizontal and vertical dimensions of inter-subjective identities, in accordance with current technological and social changes. For, paradoxically, we can move, surf, navigate, roam and cross all kinds of frontiers by staying at home and sitting still in front of our screens. Moreover, in a literary context, we are able to explore archives and penetrate deeper and more thoroughly into the strata of hypertext.

In short, nowadays minds tend to be nomad and bodies tend to have a sedentary lifestyle. We may dare formulate another paradox: if orality went together with nomadism, and writing with sedentarism, perhaps that is the reason why e-writing is using orality as a model for communication. In any case, we should be aware of metaphors we use.

Since Kerckhove (1997)[4], it has been noticed that web technologies produce the sensation of loss of our own personal and defined limits as we digitally project ourselves outwards. The first comparative international study of a variety of communities in different geographical locations [5]shows that there is a move away from densely-knit tightly-bounded groups to diffuse loosely-bounded networks. The Internet is not a self-contained world; it is being used in much the same way in many parts of the globe. New technologies, and the Internet in particular, are reshaping the geography of communities, especially dispersed ones, by providing them with the means for inexpensive and convenient communication; at the same time, there is a shift away from the group towards networked individualism, which complements, rather than replaces, traditional communities: e-citizenship has both a local and a global dimension.

All identifications are technologized, that is, achieved by means designed to secure the subject in relation to something other than itself: a photograph, a publication or a web-page. With the proliferation of e-mail addresses, public distribution lists, personal data protection and processing, open or closed hot lines, real or pseudo-weblogs, etc., both private and public boundaries are being redefined, as happened in the past at certain crucial junctures of history; we are reminded of the transformations of private and public boundaries implemented by the absolutist monarchy in France during the so-called *Ancien Régime,* and those brought about by the French Revolution for the *Nouveau Régime.* Blogging, for instance, both as a cultural genre that has *retooled* the traditional diary, and as a social action, is also reacting to the shifting demarcations of the boundaries between private and public domains, and is an indication of the way technology both limits and opens up readers'

---

[4] Derrick de Kerckove, *Connected Intelligence. The Arrival of the Web Society.* Toronto: Somerville House Books, 1997.
[5] B. Wellman et al., "The Social Affordances of the Internet for Networked Individualism", *Journal of Computer Mediated Comunications*, 8 (3) April, 2003. http://jcmc.indiana.edu/vol8/issue3/wellman.html.

choices, as Ringrose and Sassón-Henry demonstrate in this volume. Warbloggers themselves may also derive personal gratification from the risks involved in politically subversive acts of self-disclosure in the context of an emerging model of Internet-based economic production that is peer-driven or based on common behaviours. Thus, the appearance of computer-mediated or virtual communities is providing a crucial area of research in the Humanities, particularly in certain literary domains.

On the other hand, at the same time as our sense of identity begins to unfold, there is a weakening of the structure and concept of the nation[6]—that fixed product of the printing-press era. Books, as a technology, served nation-states through the use of national and unified languages; moreover, even nowadays, our very conceptions of what literature is are linked more to writing, print and European nations, than to orality, manuscripts and the Romanic era. Nevertheless, things are changing.

Electronic technologies, however, are serving other kinds of communities that are not so much multilingual as Global English-speaking, a phenomenon reminiscent of the *koïné* that substituted Latin prior to the formation of nation states. Returning to the data on Internet use, we note that at a global level this shows that 35,8% of the online population use English, 64,2% are non-English-speakers, and 37,9% use a European language other than English.[7] But this is a significant paradox because more and more countries are developing models for information literacy as an integral part of their education curricula.

We may ask ourselves if the Internet is likely to become the steamroller of globalization for languages and their literatures in the same way as minority languages in some European countries were to a large extent steamrollered by the advent of television. It may be possible to "regionalize" Internet services on the basis of linguistic and cultural criteria, but the fact remains: neither the 300 million Spanish-speakers nor the approximately the 300 million people in the Eurozone are sufficient in number to set up their own markets and supply them with their own products.

But establishing an identity does not only depend on language. Literatures, as bearers of cultural memories, form an integral part of our cognitive universe and play a significant role in making our everyday experience of the world an aesthetic one. But literatures cannot be

---

[6] See Dolores Romero and LEETHI Group (eds.). *Naciones literarias*. Barcelona: Anthropos, 2006.
[7] "Global Internet Statistics (by Language)" in *Global Reach*: http://globalreach. biz/globstats/index.php3, [accessed March 10, 2007].

assimilated exclusively and out of necessity to bounded and monolithic national units. This has always been a singular error. What is more, in the digital era, in virtual spaces with electronic technologies, national boundaries have neither an epistemological framework nor social validation. Our new global cultural economy can no longer be understood in terms of centre-periphery models. Notions such as reception, mediation, hybridity and cultural identity will no longer be functional for the understanding of virtual migrations, which need to be understood as a complex disjunctive order. From now on, we should be attentive to all kinds of virtual migrations and phenomena related to transfer and translatability: *Hyper* is *trans*.

Hyper-literatures

Within this process of converting the digital medium to a privileged space for information, communication and culture (in this sequence), we observe that two of the greatest impacts on literature arising from technology have been, in the first place, electronic editions for didactic and scientific purposes, and, secondly, the advent of digital literature, that is, literary works that have been created specially for the computer.

E-editions, in fact, have generally been widely accepted by mainstream literary scholars, who were otherwise far more sceptical about the relevance of other major aspects of the digital humanities, such as computer-assisted stylistics, authorship studies and learning activities. The critical archiving of texts using electronic media is the implementation of an underlying philological model of the systematized collection of literary documents and related data, with the object of preserving the text as a semiotically-transmitted *reality* and making it available for further use, not only for literary studies and other interests related to the humanities, but also as a ready source of information for other less exclusive publics (see Skulj). The analysis of writing processes and literary geneses, or comparative genetic criticism, could be one of the most useful applications of digital media in literary studies, which, by their very nature, are essentially organized in a plurivocal, inconclusive and multi-linear way (see Van Hulle). Moreover, according to post-modern textology (which presents literary texts not as static, self-enclosed monads but as an open-ended writing and reading process in which meanings and subjects are articulated dialogically), scholarly editing by electronic tools may manipulate the historical profile and relevance of past literary works and secure their permanent presence in ever-changing reading repertories (see Juvan). It may seem paradoxical that it is computer-generated *virtual* cyberspace that meets post-modern efforts to restore the *concreteness* of historical presence. In fact, in the search for text-centred editions and text stability, scholars have discovered multimedia editions and a multiplicity of hypertexts. However, certain precautions should be taken: there is always the risk that a kind of cacophony of e-archive data may overshadow what is supposed to be of real importance, namely, the effect of the text's historical presence.

In fact, it seems that there are two main demands from scholars. First, we need a clear and consensual definition of what is an e-edition. Even if texts on screens look alike, there are profound differencies in quality and, even worse, standards and tools for e-editing are so different that a full-scale electronic comparatist editions is not possible. Strictly speaking, there never was a specific standard of editing in the realm of Comparatism, but it is time to gather the fruits of expanding and expanded electronic textualities and to look for compatible interactive tools and basic markup standards.

Second, scholars are demanding for each reader a more personalized and better adapted working area on the screen for the sake of creativity, diversity and dynamicity. In open-ended electronic editions, text control should be passed to its users, according to the readers' work and interests, readers' responses, readers' local notes, links and quotation. A paradigm shift is affecting not only literary criticism, but also more particularly textual criticism, focusing on readings rather than on authors or texts' motions.

Electronic editions for scholarly purposes involve specialized knowledge of text editing and electronic language processing. In digital text production, an unprecedented stage is introduced into the chain of information processing: the mediation of codification by mathematical programming—the double dimension of process and product (see Paixao). As we start to work with digital processing, layers of information acquire enhanced technical possibilities in the intersections between code and presentation. This is because the methods for codifying language vary considerably in spirit, and they are not based purely on immediate visual correspondence.

Digital literature, however, has its own characteristics: firstly, virtual text can be multi-linear, multimedia, multiple in content and in form, dynamic, and connected (linked), unlike other texts which, although edited in digital or electronic format, are created simply to be reproduced by printing. Secondly, a virtual text is not created for paper but for the screen and, as such, is constructed on at least two levels (the programming language and the operating system). So, unlike printed text, the text we see on the screen is not the text as it is written. Furthermore, it can be rewritten, reorganized, linked, provided with graphical designs, pictures and even sounds.

How do we account for the innumerable possibilities of juxtaposition and interference of codes, the imminence of plurality, the prodigious and somewhat awe-inspiring impression produced by electronic textualities? We have a first page—or screen—that we may call visible, with its languages of forms, its interactions, its iconic denseness, its movements of transformation, adaptation and interactivity; in another space, that of the programmers (space of another visibility), we have the source-code, which is precisely what makes that first page visible, manipulatable and, as a consequence, endowed with a degree of coherence. This duplicity between the two spaces is not reduced to manichaeist dichotomies; one does not have priority over the other (see Dos Santos).

Scholars seem to be in trouble. There was a time when criticism made use of linguistic tools to analyse new media such as cinema or television, simply because they were available and familiar, with no consideration given to the novelty of codes and materials. In the same parallel way, early hypertext enthusiasts rallied behind them postmodernist theorists, claiming they subverted the tyrannies of linearity in old-school left-to-right print, fixed meanings and one-way flows of signs from subject-author to object-reader. It is time to create more specific tools for electronic environments, and, as Lampropoulos proposes, the toolkit we are in need of should be made up of several critical genres, all equally appropriate.

In order to understand this new process of reading and writing, early scholars of ICT resorted to the critical tools and metaphors available to them at the time. These were mainly post-structural conceptions, focusing on intertextual relationships as key concepts for defining literaty in the twentieth century. The very notion of hypertext is indebted to these a priori definitions of literature.

In this context, notions such as collaborative writing, the rupture of linearity, demystification of the canon, the democratization of art, new humanism, interactivity and open-endedness in literary works have gained popularity with the incursion of the concept of hypertext in the field of literature created specially for the hypermedia. However, there is a lack of unanimity with respect to their meanings, due to the multiplicity of co-existing definitions. These notions are discussed critically in several contributions to this volume.

In particular, according to literature theoreticians in the euphoria of the early stages of the process, the Internet appeared to bid a final farewell to authorship. The conceptions of collaborative writing convert the already-discussed dictum of *death of the author* to *the birth of the reader*, in an oscillating movement, in much the same way receiver and empirical criticism did. More recent positions are definitely more differentiated and have also (re-)accepted the author online (see Hartling) as new forms of authorship being created on the Internet *dispositif*: the new "sharing economy" refers to large-scale Internet-based projects resulting from the participation of large numbers of individuals. Nevertheless, there are apparently more literary-critical and academic texts *on* collaborative projects than there are projects themselves.

Furthermore, because of the lack of concepts and definitions, metaphors could take us a long way. For instance, the spatial metaphor of the network used for defining text as a hypertextual system has been used to represent other spatial metaphors inherited from intertext definitions[8], such as archive, archaeology or series. That is to say, a collection of horizontal spatial images (synchronic, such as *navigating, surfing, linking, jumping on the screen*) have translated a diachronic (vertical) conception of literatures.

Suddenly, as if by a miracle, a very abstract, theoretical and not so easily-handled concept such as intertext could be (re)presented in an actual/virtual mode by means of electronic technologies. Going with the flow, Landow and Ben Porat have explored all manner of associative multi-media cultural possibilities in hypertext form by studying how readers move by way of arbitrarily chosen links towards unrelated segments that do not easily yield an interpretative hypothesis. For Ben Porat, the aim is to gain an understanding of the cognitive processes involved in the actualization of mass media/literary canon intertextuality in its many forms, with the focus on sharing information and facilitating interaction between readers and texts as a part of literary hypertext theory

---

[8] Some of these were used as starting points for exploratory and premonitory works about hypertext. Theoreticians like George Landow took theses such as: "*Il n'y a pas d'énoncé qui n'en suppose d'autres, il n'y a pas un qui n'ait autour de soi un champs de coexistence, des effets de série et de succession, une distribution de fonctions et des rôles.*" (Michel Foucauld. *Archéologie du savoir*. Paris: Gallimard, 1969: 131); "*Il n'est de texte que d'intertext.*", (See Charles Grivel. "Thèses préparatoires sur les intertextes" in Renate Lachmann. *Dialogizität*, München: Fink, 1982: 327-48); "No text is read independently of the reader's experience of other text." (Umberto Eco. *The Role of the Reader*. Bloomington: Indiana University Press, 1984: 21); "Reading a text is necessarily the reading of a whole system of texts, and meaning is always wandering around between texts." (Harold Bloom. *The Anxiety of Influence. Towards a Theory of Poetry*. Oxford & New York: Oxford University Press, 1973: 107-8)

and cognitive studies.

However, one paradox stands out: the supposedly solid ground of post-modern theory that seemed to coincide with the fluidity of cyber-realities has gradually led to cybercriticism becoming, in part, a kind of easy theory. The critics' attention has primarily been focused on a theoretical reflection on the consequences of applying ICT to the processes of composition, reception, distribution and teaching of literature. At the same time, however, development itself and the actual implementation of the possibilities have been drawn-out and slow, and this has had the effect of moderating and delaying the course of events (see Borràs).

If we take the story of Echo and Narcissus as a possible paradigm for the relationship between text and reader and the mutual inclusiveness of the audio and visual image (see Scrivner), we soon see limitations in hyper-systems over which we have complete control: interactive art, it seems, does not allow for any less tyranny or any more conceptual freedom than do standard, non-interactive media, since art only exists as the conceptions of it that we hold in our heads. Furthermore, some scholars are beginning to wonder if digital literature might remain in an epigonal situation, comparable to that of the literary *avant-garde* of the twentieth century, since this was particularly noticeable in the early days of textual experiments on electronic supports.

In a certain way, many of the tendencies of classical and traditional literature are continued in the Internet *dispositif*; authors reconsidering the pre-modern and post-modern divide in this volume have observed the presence of a kind of hypertextual structure, even a kind of virtuality, in other supporting materials originating from different cultures or earlier periods of history: these range from manuscripts from the European Middle Ages that require a significant heightening of sensory activity as the essence of the work as a whole is regained through electronic textuality (see Borràs) to Arabic calligraphy as a writing system that avoids linearity, includes pictographic elements and re-processes a pre-written text in a new space (see Abdel-Messih).

Indeed, electronic textualities are characterized by new kinds of connectivity. Links and lexias create a networked structure (link-and-node hypertext, made familiar by the World Wide Web, blogs and Wikis), while other kinds of link allow texts to expand, revealing additional information hidden in their midst—Ted Nelson's *Stretchtext,* for example (see Landow). With a more precise focus on connectivity between paratactic structures or variations in hypermedia narratives, it is possible to analyse the resurgence of new rhetoric figures that contribute to the volatility of meaning and the constant reconfiguration of the narrative sequence (see Pano), or the consequences of hypertext and animation on the meaning of text, using the principles of narratology for classifying links (see Saemmer), or even the relationships between hypertexts and short story collections (see Natsina).

In other words, we should consider digital texts from a strictly material perspective in order to understand their significance in the material transformation of the production of written language: the shift from tactile to digital, from physical to code, from hard to soft media, producing text with distinctive qualities (see Paixao). C-books are not merely vehicles for linguistic signs; because of their content and physical properties, they play a crucial role in structuring knowledge systems, co-determining generic identities and shaping writing and reading.

Rather than an incremental point in the evolution of text-production techniques, digital text is perhaps a watershed in the history of text diffusion (see Borràs). In any case, we are lacking, firstly, a unified theory of electronic textualities and electronic editing that assembles a wide spectrum of critical tools, and secondly, a common well-established and sufficiently complex standard for e-editions, e-books and e-literatures. We keep on searching for the literary specificity of all "virtual" texts.

Hyper-worlds

The word *virtual* comes from the Medieval Latin *virtualis* or *virtus*, meaning force and potency, something that is not yet actual but tends towards it. Thus, the virtuality characteristic of cyberspace not only has negative connotations ("appearance", "illusion" or "deception"), but also positive ones ("potentiality", "productive capacity").

All information, particularly written information, is a virtualization of memory actualized by reading. It could be said that a kind of virtual *hyper-reality* is made actual by being read according to subjective inferences, personal necessities and cultural references—a construction that is both social and personal. A poem, a novel and a play are all different kinds of alternative fictional worlds, built up artificially by words. But, like technology, virtualization, from the well-known myth in Plato's *Phaedrus* to the present day is often considered to be an artificial process alien to humanity and therefore not only inhuman but dehumanizing.

While it is a constant source of amazement to see our hyper-readers surfing attractive and ever-changing environments, we might do well to ask ourselves if hypertexts are being substituted in the users' minds by hyperworlds, or whether, on the contrary, hypertextual structures are always useful for understanding how virtual realities function in computer games, learning activities or different kinds of literary performance. The two approaches have much in common and deal with similar problems.

For example, as a representational technique, cyberfictional bridges or metalepsis in literary texts are perfectly indicated for identifying fictional as well as actual realities, with neither of them having any ontological priority. An assortment of instruments facilitates the fictional immersion of readers/users, both in literary realities and virtual ones, because these are possible worlds to be explored from the positions of the narrator or the narratee: they should be indexed and analysed in order to discover any similarities and particularities which might help us re-design and re-define our electronic tools for reading and writing. As we do this, we venture to change our definition of literariness, narrativity and poeticity as a plurality of worlds. Perhaps we should go not from intertext to hypertexts, but from possible worlds to *hyperworlds*.

This is the reason why, instead of commending the miracle of hypertext and interactivity, some of our contributors have been seduced by the graphic and plastic aspects of on-screen text. Borràs, for example, focuses on the physical, authorial, typological and perceptual complexity of digital literatures that have established links with space and form; novelty would form only a part of their evolution—the written word becoming physical image. Reading based on a race for information and frantic surfing is often regarded as unpleasant by scholars, but we could consider it an immersive and intuitive activity, in which the reader is also sensitive to the graphic and plastic dimensions of the texts. All things considered, reading has always been an erratic, randomized, fragmented and non-sequential activity: these qualities are the readers' rights.

In contrast, ludology-narratology wars could be considered as a symptom of the struggle to define a new discipline that is completely removed from the predominant hypertextual or cinematic digital paradigms of the time (see Pajares). This debate actually mirrors some of the deepest theoretical concerns held in this field, such as the difficulty of integrating interactivity with narrativity. It might look as if ludology has killed the hypertext star of the nineties, when theorists rejected the Internet because it was not *really* hypertextual. In fact, not everything taking place on the Web adjusts to the classic definitions and expectations of hypertext; reader interaction may be kept at an external level, where no real changes to the story can be made Ludologists prefer real interaction and therefore favour games, in which emergent structures mean that no playing sequence is pre-fixed.

Meanwhile, there will always be a gap to bridge: literature mainly involves words and texts. Considering the decline of television and broadcasting in educational domains, we wonder if there will be an opportunity for electronic supports to create and share knowledge through private initiative and concentration of production, beyond the mere entertainment and information offered by television.

To start with, we have not only visual but interactive development, in which a keyboard, not a remote control, is required for reading and writing. Even though the links between language proficiency, intelligence and reasoning are far from clear, early reading seems to be the best predictor of later reading comprehension and other cognitive abilities. As Gutiérrez's assessment below shows, the processing of language takes place principally in the frontal lobe, as does analytical thinking, whereas images are processed elsewhere.

Although Internet devices seem to be the cause of a decrease in the rate of reading, the demographic group with the highest reading rates is also the group with the highest use of the Net; at the same time, the accelerating decline of readers of printed books has been compensated by an increase over the same period in the number of people practising creative writing. It could be that we are becoming illiterate just at the time when there is an unprecedented amount of textual information freely available, and people are starting to use digital media not only to read everything from news to fiction, but also to write. How can the Internet be used to foster reading habits in the population? How can it attract established authors from the world of *printed narrative*, and motivate new writers to make a living writing *digital narrative*? These are some of the questions developed by Gutiérrez. A clear differentiation should be made, however, between different types of users (domestic and institutional) and different types of reading (primary texts and scholarship), and between the nineties (see Tötösy) and the twenty-first century (see Gutiérrez).

As a hypothesis, our present-day *wreaders* could well be changing in much the same way as the type of "intensive" reader, devoted almost exclusively to a limited text corpus, was supplanted during the Enlightenment by the modern "extensive" reader who consumed a variety of printed genres.

Decoding a manuscript, taking down and unrolling a scroll, looking at a codex and comparing two versions on a desk, reading a large number of books and searching for a specific quotation, opening a hyperdocument and jumping from link to link on a personal computer... Each activity has its own *tempo*, demands its own cognitive resources, creates a life world, a mental geography, a culture—and we are all involved.

To be or not to be *hyper*

We are a long way from *hyperutopias*. Looking at the data, we can no longer trust the liberating and exhilarating picture that has been painted of new technologies: hypermedia are not really free and neither are exchanges absolutely free; web structures are not in themselves emergent, but are designed and planned, just as gas, telephone and rail networks were designed in the nineteenth century. In spite of technological achievements, we are always waiting for an *actual*, immanent and transcendental cyberspace and its virtual reality, those technological myths inspired by gothic and neo-romantic influences that were promised by post-industrial societies. The failure of e-books and the complexity of e-editing have demonstrated that our anxiety for perenniality only produces anguish for the ephemeral. In the meantime, scholars are looking for a new *text-appeal* for a generation of clickers and browsers (see Ben Porat): *hyper*-research for *hyper*-learning.

This volume consists of a selection of contributions from among those who took part in the International Seminar on *Literatures: from Text to Hypertext* in September 2006, which was held at the Philology Faculty of the Complutense University of Madrid and organized by the LEETHI Research Group at the same university and the International Comparative Literature Association (ICLA/AILC) Committee. It was an initiative entrusted to us by the then president of the ICLA/AILC, Tania Franco Carvalhal who was destined never to give us her opening talk. We have compiled this book in her memory and dedicated it to her name in grateful appreciation of the trust she placed in us.

As we vertically face our screen—the horizontal desktop of the word—we will continue to ask: open access or subscription; printed or virtual literatures; intended or unintended readings. To be or not to be (dis)connected.

PART I

HYPER-PARADIGM

MARÍA GOICOECHEA

The massive irruption of information technology in our lives has, as Marshall McLuhan already prophesized in *The Gutenberg Galaxy*, transformed the way we perceive the world around us. We could say that the mechanisms used by popular culture to assimilate the changes denote certain primitivism, as the new milieu created by digital technology is "read" in the form of myths: the myth of the cyborg, the global village, hackers rebelling against the Olympus of Microsoft, etc. For the intellectual, however, the manner in which computer science and its concepts (programming, language, feedback, interactivity, memory, reading, hard disk, etc.) infiltrate every field of knowledge needs to be thoroughly assessed, since it has taken on a dimension that seems to call for a revision of previous paradigms.

As the title of this section makes apparent, the use of the word "paradigm" and the prefix "hyper" already connote our willingness to debate the existence of a new paradigm in the field of literary studies, one that has to do with most things "hyper", including hypertext, hypermedia and the hyper-threading technology of advanced processors. But does Jauss' idea of a change of paradigm really apply to the field of literary studies? And if this were so, is the hyper-paradigm taking the lead? In any case, what does the hyper-paradigm have to offer the study of literature?

As a conceptual frame, a paradigm not only constitutes a referent, a set of criteria that readers use to judge the literariness of texts, but also a set of questions, questions that a specific situation makes possible to pose, as they emerge from the comparison between structures belonging to the "already-known" and the new cultural products. So it is a debate between the past and the present, conditioned by the cultural context in which the reader finds him- or herself. In this debate, we identify two positions or tendencies, which we are going to call the technophile and the bibliophile positions. The technophile point of view defends computer technology in its role as generator of new forms of knowledge and cultural formations, which will give rise to a new interpretive paradigm, a new way of reading that will incorporate not only the written language but also other forms of semiosis. The bibliophile perspective, however, does not believe that the culture of the book will ever be substituted by the culture of the computer. What is a fact, however, is that information technology has had the power to make literary critics revise their old presuppositions, reread the past in the light of new interests promulgated by the new paradigm and rediscover works of literature that appear to fit better than others with new trends in electronic media, such as intertextuality or interactivity. According to George Landow, we have reached a point in which literary theory and computer programming converge and can be mutually useful: hypertext can serve as a laboratory for the testing of theory, while theory can give the programmer ideas with respect to the design and the cultural effects of computer technology.[1]

The four essays presented in this section offer different glimpses, from very varied perspectives and locations, of the present state of affairs in relation to the changes introduced by digital technology in the field of literary studies. Their writers come from the Mediterranean (Cyprus, Israel, Spain), and from the US, all nomad minds that at some point exchange places: the periphery for the centre, the new world for the old world. A dis-location also takes place in their critical stances. As we will see, the digital medium has decentred criticism and everyone has a free voice—a dislocated voice.

On the technophile side of the critical spectrum, we can situate the work of George P. Landow. In his article "Comparative Literature From Text to Hypertext", Landow explores the advantages of digital textualities for the study of literature, focusing in particular on scholarly and critical hypermedia. An important difference between scholarly hypermedia, and literary or artistic hypermedia is that in the first case the author must find ways to orient the reader, whereas in the second case disorientation of the reader is often a goal in itself. Disorientation is reduced, according to Landow, by the use of stretchtext, which expands the text while retaining the original text on the screen, allowing it to serve as a context or anchor even after the reader has activated the link.

Landow provides a practical example of the new possibilities and advantages for the study of comparative literature offered by the hypermedia, and of the appropriateness of a combined use of stretchtext

---

[1] See "What's a Critic to Do?: Critical Theory in the Age of Hypertext", in *Hyper/Text/Theory*. Baltimore: Johns Hopkins University Press, 1994: 1-48.

and the habitual node-and-link. He analyses the new possibilities and modes of reception introduced by a hypertextual version of a scholarly article written originally for a print format. He asks himself the following question : "What happens when we reify the links that make it, like any scholarly or critical text, a node in a network?" In Landow's opinion, whereas in print the article stands by itself, with the exception of a few gestures that take the reader beyond it in the form of citing other texts and providing additional information in footnotes, its hypertextual form approaches Roland Barthes' ideal text: a text full of interacting networks, "a galaxy of signifiers", without a beginning or a predetermined order, without a hierarchical structure...

He concludes that hypermedia "offers a much more accurate picture of the nature of scholarly collaboration, sources, and confluences than print does", but his argument that "more is better" is debatable. Landow argues that "the electronic version makes far more information readily available than before, thus producing a richer, better scholarly work", even if this easy access to additional information makes the article less central and easier for the reader to abandon for other texts. Landow projects onto this apparent paradox of hypermedia his own notion of the ideal text, at once both rich and anti-hierarchical.

Apostolos Lampropoulos offers us a particularly meta-reflexive article, "Always Already-Known Hypertexts: A Recent Debate in Old Terms." This article could instead be entitled "What do We Actually Do When We Theorize?" as Lampropoulos uncovers the theoretical manoeuvres behind three "snapshots" of cybercriticism.

Lampropoulos' position is more critical than Landow's with respect to the hyper-paradigm and its theoretical foundations. Whereas for the latter, hypertext and computing have the power to make the avant-garde seem old-fashioned, for Lampropoulos cybercriticism runs the risk of becoming too complacent. He examines three instances of cybercriticism in which concepts from French theorists Michel de Certeau, Michel Foucault, and Jacques Derrida are applied to the study of cyberspace and hypertext. These applications—which follow a series of operations in which concepts are appropriated by analogy, de-contextualized, or taken as a hypothesis of the real to be confirmed rather than as vacuous categories—blunt the theories, emptying them of their previous provocation and subversion, and making them appear self-evident where they were once ground-breaking. In his own words: "Cybercriticism does not seem to breed serious critical doubt vis-à-vis these well-known theoretical propositions. On the contrary, it leads to willing acceptance, promotion and even celebration of yesterday's contested and controversial issues."

With his intelligent remarks, Lampropoulos does not intend to discard all cybercriticism but to alert the cybercritics of the "potential deceptiveness" of certain critical moves, and to encourage them to take advantage of the field opened up by cybercriticism, which boosts a rethinking of older theories and becomes a site of debate and awareness of difference.

In her article "Theory of Hypertext: a Cognitive Approach", Ziva Ben-Porat illustrates other forms of integrating the hyper-paradigm in literary studies. Ben-Porat uses a type of hypertext which works as a prosthetic literary memory in a series of experiments designed to test readers' cognitive habits of text interpretation, in particular, their ability to process intertextual allusions. Ben-Porat shows us how hypertext can be used, not only to trace the reader's interpretative activity, but also to "gain understanding of the cognitive processes involved in the actualization of mass media/liteary canon inter-textuality in its many forms".

Ben-Porat's hypertext is a multimedia cluster of texts linked on the basis of explicitly-defined inter-textual relations. By providing readers with an actualized associative net, she pretends to fill the gaps of the educative system, especially with respect to the knowledge of canonical literary texts, and to improve the processing and interpretation of allusive texts. These educative hypertexts have also been used to research readers' abilities to identify and interpret intertextual allusions. What she found is that exposure to hypertext is already affecting our reading habits: "It seems that the need to retain a number of vaguely formed interpretative hypothesis in limbo might develop a competence that could be an important addition to our arsenal of reading strategies."

In this case, hypertext comes to the rescue of an endangered canon that has fallen from grace for a generation of "clickers and browsers", but that, thanks to a hypertextual makeover, can again be endowed with "text-appeal".

Susana Pajares' contribution, "Ludology meets Hypertext", could be already situated in some "beyond-hyper" paradigm. It shares with Lampropoulos' its meta-reflexiveness, since it is a comparison at theoretical level of two of the paradigms (if the idea of one paradigm sharing space with another is indeed possible...) in the study of digital texts: hypertextual theory on the one hand, and ludology on the other.

According to Pajares, the hypertextual paradigm is already dead, since most digital scholars are turning their attention to other objects of study, such as computer games, blogs, or social software. If Lampropoulos denounces the easy safe-theorizing of cybercritics with respect to their use of French theory, Pajares exposes the mistakes of this theoretical appropriation, which functioned well as a publicity stunt that made room for them in literature departments, but failed to account for the real trends within the web. According to Pajares, the theoretical emphasis should have been not so much on metaphors of infinity but on metaphors of organization; not on the dissolution of the author but on author control; not on the reader as author, but on the reader as searcher, etc.

Pajares presents ludology as a theory of the new century whose evolution has many points in common with that of hypertext. Ludologists are trying to find a role in the actual division of intellectual labour by separating themselves from early attempts at theorizing computer games, many of which, like with hypertext, came from literature. But this move away from textual theories, Pajares concludes, runs the risk of becoming an all-excluding formalist approach, which can miss "the most interesting aspects of games as cultural objects".

CHAPTER ONE

COMPARATIVE LITERATURE FROM TEXT TO HYPERTEXT OR WHAT DO ELECTRONIC MEDIA HAVE TO OFFER THE DISCIPLINE?

GEORGE P. LANDOW

Hypertext has the potential not only to enable standard approaches employed by the comparatist but also to offer a means of remedying one weak point of comparative studies. Comparative literature is often criticized, sometimes validly, by specialists in individual national literatures with proceeding with inadequate awareness of local contexts, including political and social contexts, traditions, and changes of reference. Hypermedia offers a means of both carrying out traditional comparative studies while also rooting texts in a wider range of contexts than ever before possible. Of course, realizing such potential does not happen automatically if one uses the World Wide Web or other hypermedia environment: scholars must self-consciously write with an awareness of the presence of other texts, which means that in practice they will find themselves working with new forms of collaboration, both intended and unintended. These new forms of writing and collaboration remind us that both digital information technologies and that particular form of them known as hypertext offers the possibility of entirely new forms of both literature and ways of writing about or *within* it.

Forms of Comparative Studies Involving Digital Media

Considering the relationship of digital textuality and the technologies that support it, one realizes that it can take at least half a dozen forms:

1. Linguistic corpora, dictionaries, encyclopaedias, concordances, *rimarii,* and other tools and references works in digital form, whether or not they originally appeared in print and were later

translated into digital form. Such electronic reference works—whether one of the many dictionaries and encyclopaedias written originally for a print environment available on the net or new forms, such as *Wikipedia*, offer one undeniable advantage over their print counterparts—amazingly fast access to large amounts of often unwieldy information.

2. Digital versions of primary texts as well as scholarly and critical commentary originally written for print that preserve as much as possible of the original form of the print work. Project Gutenberg is the best-known source of such texts. At best, such works employ markup languages, such as combinations of XML and the TEI (Text Encoding Initiative) standards adapted to the individual text. Here the value of digitalization appears in the economy and convenience of storing, sharing, and searching texts. Such digitization of print works has special value for rare and difficult-to-obtain texts. To cite one example of a pioneering project: The Brown University Women Writers Project, which proposes to preserve and mark-up all writing by women in English from its beginnings to 1830, has already had a marked effect on literary history.

3. Studies of non-hypertextual digital literatures, including (a) static text with moving images, such as Christy Sheffield Sanford's *Safara in the Beginning* (1996); (b) animated text, ranging from Maxine Fung's animated versions of Brecht's "My Brother Was a Pilot" (1994) and Kate Pullinger and Talan Memmot's elegant *Branded* to Philadelpho Menezes and Wilton Azevedo's *Interpoesia: Poesia Hipmedia Interativa* (1998) and Camille Utterbach's *Text Rain*; (c) text that readers' actions caused to appear, disappear, or be replaced with other text, such as Robert Kendal's *A Life Set for Two,* Don Bosco's *Fast City,* and Stephanie Strickland's *Vniverse;* (d) timed text, such as Stuart Moulthrop's *Hegirascope;* (e) computer-generated text; and (f) text, moving, and interactive in virtual reality environments, such as Noah Wardip-Fruin, Andrew McClain, Shawn Greenlee, Robert Coover, and Josh Carroll's *Screen* (2005).

4. Moving on to hypertext: hypertext editions and archives of both primary and secondary texts of printed texts ranging from the two dozen hypertextual translations of scholarly

books on the *Victorian Web* to Jerome J. McGann's *Rossetti Archive,* Massimo Riva's *Boccaccio Web,* and Phil Gyford's translation *of Samuel Pepy's Diary* into a blog with multi-authored annotation.
5. Studies written in hypertext of print works. These range from Barry Fishman's pioneering 1990 thesis written in IRIS Intermedia to my essays on Thomas Hughes and Thomas Arnold in the *Victorian Web* (2006).
6. Studies—articles and books—intended initially for print publication on digital literatures in two or more languages, such as the chapter "Reconfiguring Narrative" in various versions of my *Hypertext 3.0* (1992, 1997, 2006).
7. Digital but non-hypertextual studies published in either transfer media (floppy disc, DVD) or the Internet about digital literatures in two or more languages, such as sections of the *The Cyberspace, Hypertext, and Critical Theory Web* devoted to discussions of Michael Joyce's *afternoon* and Shelley Jackson's *Patchwork Girl* (1990 to present).
8. Studies composed in hypertext about digital literatures in two or more languages. These may consist of either separate hypertext essays—that is, those not available from within the text discussed, such as Steve Cook's *Inf(l)ections: Writing as Virus, Hypertext as Meme* (1996)—or those linked to and from within the text being discussed. (Since the dominant form of hypertext is the World Wide Web, which, like printed text, is read-only and not the read-write form envisioned by Nelson and others, few examples of such writing criticism within another text exist, though as early as 1990 my students created them in Intermedia, Storyspace and HTML as critiques of works by others in classes structured as writing workshops.)

Link-and-Node Versus Stretchtext

This form of electronic textuality has two chief forms with particular relevance to comparative and other literary studies. The first is composed of links and lexias that create a networked structure (link-and-node hypertext familiar from the World Wide Web, blogs, and Wikis) and, in the second, texts expand, revealing additional information hidden in the midst of the text (Ted Nelson's Stretchtext). In either case, new kinds of connectivity characterize this mode of textuality, which therefore has special value for comparative literature, a discipline whose defining procedures involves connecting texts, genres, modes, and movements from different literatures.

Four Hypertext Modes or Genres

If one considers hypermedia not from the vantage point of software design but from that of its use or application, one sees at least four fundamentally different forms:

1. Reference hypermedia (e.g., dictionaries, encyclopaedias, repair manuals) in which linking can be almost entirely automatic or computationally driven. These are also essentially fixed, and complete when done.
2. Language-instruction hypermedia.
3. Scholarly, critical, and instructional hypermedia in which (a) linking offers much more than search tools can because it often involves specialized knowledge, (b) much of the linking is subjective (i.e. not capable of being automatically generated, (c) it is always open-ended and changing, a living developing form of text, and (d) one must find ways for the reader to avoid getting lost in e-space.
4. Literary and artistic hypermedia, which is experimental and may make extensive use of disorientation. It is almost entirely different from scholarly, critical, and pedagogical hypermedia, though some works like Shelley Jackson's *Patchwork Girl* include substantial lexias that consist of quotations from print-published scholarly works.

Our topic today concerns the third form, that is, scholarly and critical hypermedia, which includes both electronic editions of print texts and its frequent use in instruction. I propose to begin with a few remarks on what aspects of digital media and digital text differentiate these from print technology and the thought world (or worldview) that printing created, and continues to support. Next, I shall discuss two notably relevant kinds of hypermedia, observing how each relates to the study of comparative literature as scholarly and critical disciplines. Comparative Literature, like interarts criticism, would seem to be a discipline particularly well-suited to that form of digital media known as hypertext, for Comparative Literature, like other comparative studies, interarts criticism included, demands connectivity—in other words, the characteristic feature of hypermedia.

Whenever comparative studies take three or more texts as their subject, scholarship necessarily encounters textual relations that take the form of a network, and the network lies at the heart of both stand-alone hypermedia, which resides in individual machines—hypertext documents and environments on isolated computers—or wide area hypermedia, such as we find in the World Wide Web.

First, a crucial parenthetical remark: We have to remind ourselves that if, how, and whenever we move beyond the book, that movement will not embody a movement from something natural or human to something artificial—from nature to technology—since writing, and printing, and books are about as technological as one can get. Books, after all, are teaching and communicating *machines*. Therefore, if we find ourselves in a period of fundamental technological and cultural change analogous to the Gutenberg revolution, one of the first things we should do is remind ourselves that printed books are technology, too.

We find ourselves, for the first time in centuries, able to see the book as unnatural, as a near-miraculous technological innovation and not as something intrinsically and inevitably human. We have, to use Derridean terms, de-centred the book. In other words, we find ourselves in the position of perceiving the book as technology. The great value of such a recognition to our project here lies in the fact that it reminds us that electronifying universities does not take the form of technologizing them or adding technology to them in some way alien to their essential spirit. Digital information, in other words, is only the latest technology, to shape an institution that, as Carlyle reminds us, is both itself a form of technology—a mechanism—that has also long been influenced by those technologies on which it relies.

Returning to hypertext: Link-and-node hypertext requires two basic features—digital text (which encompasses both word and image) and a network. This information technology has special importance to humanistic scholarship for the simple reason that it has always involved networks. Thus, readers comparing Milton's *Paradise Lost* to other epics and to both predecessor and later texts, carry in their minds, say, the way the poet's calling upon the muse commingles instances of inspiration from the Old Testament with traditional invocations from Homer, Vergil, and Dante. Presented in the form of a diagram, this one example already takes the form of a network, which becomes increasingly complex as more juxtapositions and linkings take place. But where is this network? Like a document on the World Wide Web that readers experience as a nexus with links to many other texts, this traditional scholarly network is virtual. It exists in the mind of scholar, whereas electronic hypertext, a recent form of prosthetic memory, exists in electronic space as easily reproducible computer codes that create a new form of writing. Hypermedia is a form of writing that includes both the texts of earlier writing and a means of graphing—writing—the connections among them. It is nexographic, and writing in and with this medium can therefore be thought of as nexographic. Vannevar Bush, who conceived what Ted Nelson has taught us to call hypertext in the mid-1930s, did not emphasize links and nodes as much as many later thinkers on the subject do. Instead, he proposed that by reading text in what was then the latest, most-cutting edge information technology—microfilm—the knowledge worker (he was an engineer by trade) would make a record of the connections discovered among different texts and different portions of the same text. That record, like some later sophisticated hypermedia systems, such as Intermedia and Multicosm, stored these reading paths in a separate place outside the text. Such a so-called open hypertext system has two characteristic features: first, it permits authors to record and share these reading paths (or chains of links) with others who possess the same texts. Secondly, it permits an indefinite number of readers to record and share their own readings of the same text in the form of such reproducible paths. Scholarly or expert writing, according to Bush, therefore, takes the form a record of connections. Bush has added a new dimension to writing, one that boils arguments down to the chains of connections.

Scholarly and other forms of hypermedia require two things: digital virtual text, and networks, which take the form of a collection of links that connect the machines in which this digital text resides. The characteristic effects of computing upon the humanities all derive from the fact that computing stores information in electronic codes rather than in physical marks on a physical surface. For the first time, writing, which had always been a matter of physical marks on a physical surface, instead takes the form of electronic codes, and this shift from ink to electronic code—what Jean Baudrillard calls the shift from the "tactile" to the "digital" (115)—produces an information technology that combines fixity and flexibility, order and accessibility—but at a cost. Using Diane Balestri's terminology, we can say that all previous media took the form of hard text (cited in Miles' "Softvideography"); computing produces soft text, and this fundamental change, like all developments in infotech, comes with gains and losses. For example, although electronic writing has the multiplicity of print, it does not have the fixity—and hence the reliability and stability—of either written or printed texts.

This fundamental shift from tactile to digital, physical to code, and hard to soft media produces text with distinctive qualities. First of all, since electronic text-processing is a matter of manipulating computer-manipulated codes, all texts that the reader-writer encounters on the screen are virtual texts. According to the *Oxford English Dictionary*, "virtual" is that which "is so in essence or effect, although not formally or actually; admitting of being called by the name so far as the effect or result is concerned," and in computing, the virtual refers to something that is "not physically existing as such but made by software to appear to do so from the point of view of the program or the user". All texts encountered on a computer screen by the reader and the writer exist as a version created specifically for them while an electronic primary version resides in the computer's memory. One therefore works on an electronic copy until such time as both versions converge when the writer commands the computer to "save" one's version of the text by placing it in its memory. At this point the text on screen and in the computer's memory briefly coincide, but the reader always encounters a virtual image of the stored text and not the original version itself; in fact, in descriptions of electronic word processing, such terms and such distinctions do not make much sense.

Another parenthesis: Having pointed to the fundamental importance of dematerialized virtuality to the nature of digital text, one must emphasize that our experience of it *always* involves the physical, material conditions of the computer devices we need to read it. The size of monitors, the change from bitmap to greyscale to colour displays, the portability of computers, and our physical distance from computer screens make dramatic differences in kinds of texts we can read and write ("What's a critic to Do?" and "Connected Images," 82).

Returning to the subject of electronic text: The code-based existence of electronic text that makes it virtual also makes it infinitely variable. If one changes the code, one changes the text. Digital text can be infinitely duplicated at almost no cost or expenditure of energy. Duplicate the code, duplicate the text—this is true for both images (including images of text, as above) or alphabetic text. Because the codes that constitute electronic text can move at enormous speed over networks, either locally within organizations or on the Internet, they create the conditions for new forms of scholarly and other communication. Before networked computing, scholarly communication relied chiefly upon moving physical marks on a surface from one place to another with whatever cost in time and money such movement required. Networked electronic communication so drastically reduces the time scale of moving textual information that it produces new forms of textuality. Just as transforming print text to electronic coding radically changed the temporal scale involved in manipulating texts, so too has it changed the temporal scale of sharing them. Networked electronic communication has both dramatically speeded up scholarly communication and created quickly accessible versions of older forms of it, such as online, peer-reviewed scholarly journals, and new forms of it, such as discussion lists, chat groups, blogs, and IRC (Landow, "Electronic Conferences," 350). In networked environments, users also experience electronic text as location independent, since wherever the computer storing the text may reside in physical reality, users experience it as being here, on their machines. Finally, electronic text is net-work-able, always capable of being joined in electronic networks—hence, hypertext and the World Wide Web.

A full hypertext system, unlike a book and unlike some of the first approximations of hypertext available—Hypercard™, Guide™, and the current World Wide Web (except for blogs)—offers the reader and writer the same environment. Therefore, by opening the text-processing program or editor, as it is known, you can take notes, or you can write against my interpretations, against my text. Although you cannot change my text, you can write a response and then link it to my document. You have thus read the readerly text in several ways not possible with a book: you have chosen your reading path, and since you, like all readers, will choose individualized paths, the hypertext version of this essay would take a very different form, perhaps suggesting the values of alternate routes and probably devoting less room in the main text to quoted passages. You might have also have begun to take notes or produce responses to the text as you read, some of which might take the form of texts that either support or contradict interpretations proposed in my texts.

When one considers the history of both ancient literature and recent popular culture, the figure of the reader-as-writer hardly appears at all strange, particularly since classical and neo-classical cultural theory urged neophyte authors to learn their craft by reading the masters and then consciously trying to write like them. Anyone who has taken an undergraduate survey course will know that Vergil self-consciously read and rewrote Homer, and that Dante read and rewrote both Homer and Vergil, and Milton continued the practice. Such very active readers appear throughout the past two centuries: Graham Swift's *Waterland* (1983) and Peter Carey's *Jack Maggs* (1997), for example, both rewrite Dickens's *Great Expectations*. (A World Wide Web version of this essay would link to a series of essays by several authors on these relationships.)

Translations into hypertextual form already exist in poetry, fiction, and other materials originally conceived for book technology. The simplest, most limited form of such translation preserves the linear text with its order and fixity and then appends various kinds of texts to it, including critical commentary, textual variants, and chronologically anterior and later texts.

Hypertext corpora that employ a single text, originally created for print dissemination, as an unbroken axis off which to hang annotation and commentary, appear in the by now common educational and scholarly presentations of canonical literary texts. One may consider the products of this use of hypermedia to be a transitional form, most useful for making print works searchable and easily read—but not very hypertextual, since they do not take advantage of the fundamental qualities of the medium.

Examples of Hypertextualized Comparative Literary Studies

Let us compare a standard scholarly article with what a hypertextual version might look like. Almost four decades ago I published "Ruskin and Baudelaire on Art and Artist," an essay whose most obvious point of interest appears in that fact that two such completely different men should have independently created identical portraits of an impassive artist and poet as a means of solving problems that romantic emotionalism and egotism produce for poet, painter, and critic. A second point of interest appears in the equally unexpected sources of both men's ideal artist and poet: Ruskin's unpublished notebooks show that he first came upon the idea in Balzac while Baudelaire cites Emerson! This unlikely exchange of ideas serves as an excellent advertisement of the comparative method, since it demonstrates that critics who confine themselves to a single national literature create a very distorted view of the development of individual authors. Now this essay of mine makes a good place to begin because it takes the form of a simple binary opposition. So what, therefore, does a hypertextualization of it look like? What happens when we reify the links that make it, like any scholarly or critical text, a node in a network. In print this rather ordinary article stands by itself, and the only gestures beyond it take the form of naming other texts and footnotes that provide additional information. It hypertextual form, however, it approaches Barthes's ideal text in which:

> the networks (*réseaux*) are many and interact, without any one of them being able to surpass the rest; this text is a galaxy of signifiers, not a structure of signifieds; it has no beginning; it is reversible; we gain access to it by several entrances, none of which can be authoritatively declared to be the main one; the codes it mobilizes extend **as far as the eye can reach**, they are indeterminable. . . ; the systems of meaning can take over this absolutely plural text, but their number is never closed, based as it is on the

infinity of language" (emphasis in original; *S/Z*, 5-6 [English translation]; 11-12 [French]).

Ruskin and Baudelaire's Romantic Interarts Theories

George P. Landow, Professor of English and the History of Art, Brown University

[Part one of "Ruskin and Baudelaire on Art and Artist," which originally appeared in the *University of Toronto Quarterly*, 37 (1968): 295-308. ⊡ indicates linked materials not in the original print version.]

he parallels, the convergences, what Henri Lemaitre, an editor of Baudelaire, calls the "résonances analogues" [lxix] in the art criticism of Ruskin and Baudelaire are many and interesting. To begin with, Ruskin and Baudelaire each defend a great colourist, ⊡ Turner and Delacroix. Each sees his favourite as the perfect artistic representation of the age. Each sees himself as the interpreter of an artist who, isolated by genius, is so original that few can understand or appreciate him in his own time. Ruskin begins *Modern Painters* in 1843, as Baudelaire begins his *Salon de 1845*, to defend his favourite painter against the malice and ignorance of periodical critics. Each proceeds to formulate as part of his defence a theory of art; and to create this theory of art each transfers the criteria, methods, and emphases of ⊡ romantic poetic theory to the criticism of painting (my discussion of painting romantic critical theory is, of course, dependent upon M. H. Abrams). Each as a result independently creates a romantic version of the principle of ⊡ *ut pictura poesis*. And, having formulated a romantic theory of painting emphasizing the role of emotion, each is so troubled by the potentially distorting effects of emotion that he draws a portrait of an ideal artist-poet, who, though deeply emotional, can yet paradoxically remain impassive when moved.

John Ruskin, *Self-portrait*. Watercolor on paper, 1874

[Not in print edition; click on picture for larger image.]

Both critics accept the notion of *ut pictura poesis* as a first principle. Not only do they believe that painting and her sister art, poetry, share the same emotional nature, treat the same subjects, and create the same effects, but they also hold that the critic can profitably use the terms painting and poetry, painter and poet, interchangeably. Ruskin and Baudelaire base their conception on the belief that the two arts share a common nature and function — to express the thoughts and feelings of the artist-poet. According to Ruskin, the basic fact about painting is that it "is properly to be opposed to speaking and writing, but not to poetry." Both painting and speaking are meanings of expression. Poetry is the employment of either for the noblest purposes.... Great art is produced by men who feel acutely and nobly; and it is in some sort an expression of this personal feeling" (5.31-2). And since Ruskin and Baudelaire focus their aesthetic theories upon the creator, and are most concerned to describe the nature and process of expression, they characterize the artist, like the poet, primarily not by his ability to imitate, but by his ability to express himself. Baudelaire, for example, epitomizes painters as "des hommes qui sont voués à l'expression de l'art" (329), and throughout Ruskin's works, he, even more than Baudelaire, emphasizes that this notion of expression is a key to art and its appreciation. Ruskin, for example, concludes the final volume of *The Stones of Venice* with this remark on the importance of this idea of expression: "[W]hatever may be the means, or whatever the more immediate end of any kind of art, all of it that is good agrees in this, that it is the expression of one soul talking to another, and is precious according to the greatness of the soul that utters it. And consider what mighty consequences follow from our acceptance of this truth! what a key we have herein given us for the interpretation of the art of all time!" (11.220) See also: 5.69, 11.201, and 3.135. [295/296]

The digital (not the hypertextual) nature of the article allows the insertion of images, such as a portrait of Ruskin or the paintings discussed, that had been economically impracticable in the print version. Hypertextual links, however, permit the reader near-instant access to material on J. M. W. Turner, including reproductions and John Ruskin's discussions of his work. Similarly, when coming upon the statement that each man formulated "a romantic version of the principle of *ut pictura poesis*, readers—*if they wish*—can leave the essay about Ruskin and Baudelaire and read an extensive history of earlier interarts theory, and the same is true of topics, including "sublimity," "sympathy," and the "pathetic fallacy," all of which become the anchors or endpoints of paths to essays on these subjects. In addition, if one had the texts cited in the course of the argument available in electronic form, one could quickly and easily examine the original context of quotations, reading, for instance, the sentences immediately before and after what I cited.

Comparative Literature from Text to Hypertext

Hypertext and Comparative Literature

Dante Shakespeare Homer

Balzac   Emerson

Royal Academy   Paris Salon

Ruskin   Baudelaire
defends Turner   defends Delacroix

Wordsworth   colorists (Venetian painters)
Coleridge

Edinburgh school of Moral Philsophy
Adam Smith et al

This simple exercise of translating a print article into hypermedia—hyper*media* because it also includes images—has several obvious results; the first of which is that, although its electronic version makes far more information readily available than before, thus producing a richer, better scholarly work, access to additional information paradoxically decentres it and makes it both less important and easier for the reader to leave for other texts. One may, for example, begin with my quotation from Baudelaire, follow that to the complete text from which I took the quotation, and then find Baudelaire more compelling than Landow and, perhaps without making a conscious decision, end up reading Baudelaire closely instead of my essay. Hypermedia versions of conventional articles and essays written originally in electronic form both offer the possibility of providing multiple-stage quotations—that is, one can quote, as one does now, a word, phrase, or passage and then provide at the end of link those paragraphs that function as its immediate context, after which one can use another link as a doorway into the entire text. One can also easily link both to one's own earlier work and that of other scholars, thus firmly locating an argument in the context of contemporary and earlier scholarly discourse. In so doing, one provides a more accurate, if obviously less self-centred, picture of the relation of one's own texts to those by others. Hypermedia, in other words, offers a much more accurate picture of the nature of scholarly collaboration, sources and confluences than print does.

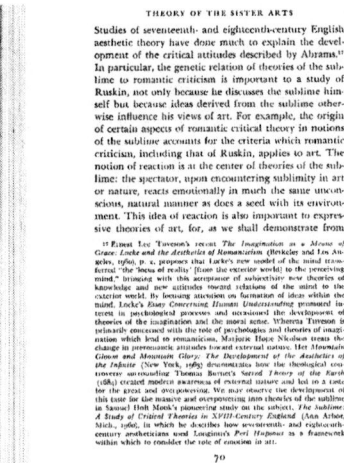
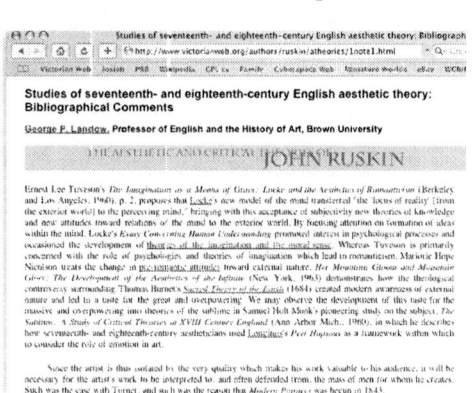

Stretchtext

Having looked at the relation of by now conventional link-and-node hypertext to comparative studies, let us examine a less common form and look at its potential use in comparative literature. Ted Nelson proposed what he called *Stretchtext* as an alternative to the node-and-link form. According to Nelson's *Computer Lib/Dream Machines* (1974), "this form of hypertext is easy to use without getting lost... Gaps appear between phrases; new words and phrases pop into the gaps, an item at a time... The stretchtext is stored as a text stream with extras, coded to pop in and pop out at the desired altitudes" (315). Compare a reader's experience of stretchtext to that of reading the Web. When one follows a link on the World Wide Web, one of two things happens: either the present text disappears and is replaced by a new one, or the destination text opens in a new window. Most web browsers follow the potentially disorienting replacement paradigm, whereas other non-web hypertext environments, such as Intermedia, Storyspace, and Microsoft, emphasize multiple windows. Stretchtext, which takes a different approach to hypertextuality, does what its name suggests and stretches or expands text when the reader activates a hot area. By way of an example, let us look at a single sentence as it appears in a document based on passages from my essay on Ruskin and Baudelaire that I made using Nicholas Friesner's web-based stretchtext. One first encounters the following: "The parallels, the convergences, what Henri Lemaitre, an editor of Baudelaire, calls the '*résonances analogues*' (lxix) in the art criticism of Ruskin and Baudelaire are many and interesting. To begin with, Ruskin and Baudelaire each defend a great colourist, Turner and Delacroix". Clicking on "Turner" stretches the text, that single word, producing "Turner, who was one the most attacked and yet, paradoxically, the most economically successful painter of his age," and clicking on this last clause makes it expand to "including his conception of painterly genres working in several styles, some conservative and others radical, so that wealthy collectors with vastly different tastes purchased his work". If one wishes to examine another part of the discussion one clicks upon the expanded text, returning it to its former state, at which point one can read more deeply, as it were, about Ruskin.

Before continuing this narrative on reading a stretchtext translation of an essay originally written for print publication, let us pause to look at the implications of what we have encountered thus far. As I explain in *Hypertext 3.0*:

> One of the most important distinguishing characteristics of stretchtext follows from the manner in which it makes new text appear framed by the old: Stretchtext does not fragment the text like other forms of hypermedia. Instead, it retains the text on the screen that provides a context to an anchor formed by word or phrase even after it has been activated. Stretching the text provides a more immediate perceptual incorporation of the linked-to text with the text from which the link originates. In effect, the text with which we began becomes context, or always demonstrates that it is context, as new text is added; or rather, the previously present text remains while the new text appears and serves as its context. This conversion of text to context for other texts may be seen more abstractly in any textual medium, but stretchtext takes this notion quite literally.

The experience of using this web-based implementation demonstrates that in certain situations stretchtext has advantages over link-and-node hypertext; in other uses the link-and-node form works better. One strong advantage of stretchtext derives from the fact that hidden text and images are already present, though not visible, when the web browser loads the HTML file, and they therefore appear instantly when the text expands. In comparative studies it has the advantage of conveniently and unobtrusively providing a means for the reader to have access to translations of quoted text, the passage in the original language of translate passages, and parallel examples.

In addition, the newly revealed passage revealed by stretchtext also contracts instantly, thus providing two real advantages: first, because the newly appearing text appears in immediate physical proximity to the text one was reading before activating the stretchtext, readers experience none of the disorientation that may occur when following a link. Secondly, the very speed with which the stretchtext appears encourages readers to check stretchable areas to see if they in fact want the additional information on offer, the effect here being that readers feel they have more control over obtaining information.

This form of electronic text obviously offers a way of incorporating definitions, brief explanations, and glossary-like annotations. In fact, a second or even a third layer of stretchtext works better than the replacement-window paradigm for more detailed information directly related to the original anchor. Of course, this approach also has disadvantages and situations or uses to which it does not seem well suited. The one disadvantage not faced by the more clearly atomizing link-and-node hypertext appears if one expands ancillary information: reading a succession of increasingly more detailed stretchtext passages of the main topic can make the reader feel disoriented when returning to the passage in its original form by shrinking the text. Here the occasionally criticized atomizing effect of link-and-note hypertext in fact proves a major advantage, because when readers follow a link they know they have moved to someplace new. The gap that always plays an essential role in linked hypermedia here has an orienting, rather than disorienting, effect.

One obvious way to draw upon the special strengths of each kind of hypertext is to include links at appropriate points within the stretched text ("appropriate" here being defined as those places at which further expansion of the original text makes returning to the original contracted text confusing). For an example, let us return to that stretchtext version of the Ruskin-Baudelaire essay, this time clicking upon *Modern Painters*, which expands to create the following:

Modern Painters, a multi-volume study that changed during the first years of its composition—its five volumes took seventeen years to complete, during which he wrote a series of other books—from a polemical defence of a few contemporary artists to a full-blown theories of aesthetics, imagination, representation, iconography, and interpretation.

Clicking upon "aesthetics" next demonstrates another capacity of stretchtext—its ability to incorporate standard kinds of linking. (As I demonstrate in *The Aesthetic and Critical Theories of John Ruskin* (1971), which is available in the *Victorian Web*, Ruskin began with a *theocentric theory of beauty* that permitted him to defend all art as moral, and then moved, after his loss of belief before completing his five-volume study, to very modern approaches to *iconography and iconology*.)

1 The parallels, the convergences, what Henri Lemaitre, an editor of Baudelaire, calls the "résonances analogues" (lxix) in the art criticism of Ruskin and Baudelaire are many and interesting. To begin with, Ruskin and Baudelaire each defend a great colourist, **Turner** and Delacroix. Each sees his favourite as the perfect artistic representation of the age. Each sees himself as the interpreter of an artist who, isolated by genius, is so original that few can understand or appreciate him in his own time. Ruskin begins Modern Painters in 1843, as Baudelaire begins his Salon de 1845, to defend his favourite

2 The parallels, the convergences, what Henri Lemaitre, an editor of Baudelaire, calls the "résonances analogues" (lxix) in the art criticism of Ruskin and Baudelaire are many and interesting. To begin with, Ruskin and Baudelaire each defend a great colourist, **Turner** who was both one of the most attacked at yet, paradoxically, **the most economically sucessful painter of his age for several reasons** including his conception of painterly genres working in several styles, some conservative and others radical, so that wealthy collectors with vastly different tastes purchased his work inspired Ruskin to write ***Modern Painters*** and **aesthetics**, and Delacroix. Each sees his favourite as the perfect artistic representation of

3 The parallels, the convergences, what Henri Lemaitre, an editor of Baudelaire, calls the "résonances analogues" (lxix) in the art criticism of Ruskin and Baudelaire are many and interesting. To begin with, Ruskin and Baudelaire each defend a great colourist, **Turner** who was both one of the most attacked at yet, paradoxically, **the most economically sucessful painter of his age for several reasons** inspired Ruskin to write ***Modern Painters*** and **aesthetics**. (As I demonstrate in _The Aesthetic and Critical Theories of John Ruskin_ (1971), which is available in the *Victorian Web*, Ruskin began with a theocentric theory of beauty that permitted him to defend all art as moral, and then moved, after his loss of belief before completing his five-colume study, to very modern approaches to iconography and iconology.) and Delacroix. Each sees his favourite as the perfect artistic representation of the age. Each sees himself as the interpreter of an artist who, isolated

The underlining represents the presence of links to entire chapters of the book whose title I mention at the beginning of this passage—to material, in other words, far too long to access via stretching text.

Web-based stretchtext also works well with images and hence proves itself to be a form of hypermedia that provides authors with new options. Web-based hypermedia has three main ways of incorporating images: (1) Placing images at the end of the link whether or not they appear alone or within text containing explanatory information; (2) Placing images within a Javascript-created pop-up window that is usually smaller than the document it overlays; (3) Placing thumbnail images within a text, often at the right or left margin, which can link to larger images (a simple use of align = "left" or "right" plus hspace = "10" within the image tag provides an easy way to flow text around an image, providing an aesthetically pleasing border that separates them). Stretchtext offers a fourth way to handle images, and like its purely text-based form, it has some particularly effective applications. A lexia chiefly devoted to discussing one painting most effectively includes the image of it as a linked thumbnail within the text, but passing mentions of details, sources, or analogous paintings work better as stretchtext presentations, for they are non-intrusive, quickly viewed, and quickly closed and left behind. Thus, stretchtext image presentation seems particularly well suited for presenting images to which one may wish to refer.

The appearance of any new information technology like hypertext provides conditions both for major societal change and change within a discipline, though it may take a very long time for any change, such as the democratizing effects of writing, which took millennia, to take place. Such changes of information regimes always produce both losses and gains. In fact, let us propose a fundamental law of media change: No free lunch, in other words, there is no gain without some loss. Thus, if writing offers us the ability to contemplate information and respond to it at our leisure, thereby permitting personal reflection and considered thought, it also lacks the immediacy of the spoken voice and the clues that we receive while observing the person to whom we are speaking. Similarly, if we gain large audiences, new forms of text preservation, and standardization of the vernacular from print, we also lose what Benjamin termed the "aura" provided by the unique object. When people find that any particular gain from a new information technology makes up for the corollary loss, they claim it represents progress; when they feel loss more than gain, they experience the new information technology as cultural decline. If I am right, students of comparative literature will find much to celebrate in and with hypermedia and other forms of new media.

Bibliography

Barthes, Roland. *S/Z*. Paris: Éditions du Seuil, 1970. *S/Z*. Translated by Richard Miller. New York: Hill and Wang, 1974.

Baudrillard, Jean. *Simulations*. New York: Semiotext(e), 1983.

Bush, Vannevar. "As We May Think". *Atlantic Monthly* 176 (July 1945): 101- 8.

Carlyle, Thomas. "Signs of the Times". *Collected Works*. London: Chapman and Hall, 1858. 98-118.

Derrida, Jacques. *De la Grammatolgie.* Paris: Les Éditions de Minuit, 1967. *Of Grammatology.* Translated by Gayatri Chakravorty Spivak. Baltimore: Johns Hopkins University Press, 1976.

—. *La Dissemination.* Paris: Éditions du Seuil, 1972. *Dissemination.* Translated by Barbara Johnson. Chicago: University of Chicago Press, 1981.

Forss, Pearl. *Authorship.* http://www.cyberartsweb.org/cpace/theory/authorship/pearl/index.htm

Gunder, Anna. "Aspects of Linkology: A Method for Description of Links and Linking". *CyberText Yearbook 2001.* Jyväskylä: Research Centre for Contemporary Culture, University of Jyväskylä, 2002. 111-39.

Hayles, N. Katherine. *How We Became Posthuman: Virtual Bodies in Cybernetics, Literature, and Informatics.* Chicago: University of Chicago Press, 1999.

Landow, George P. "Electronic Conferences and Samszdat Textuality: The Example of Technoculture". *The Digital Word: Text-Based Computing.* Ed. George P. Landow and Paul Delaney. Cambridge: Massachusetts Institute of Technology Press, 1993. 237-49.

—. "What's a Critic to Do? Critical theory in the Age of Hypertext". Ed. Landow. *Hyper/Text/Theory.* Baltimore: Johns Hopkins University Press, 1994. 1-50.

—. ed. *The Victorian Web.* http://www. victorianweb.org/

Marshall, Catherine, and Frank M. Shipman III. "Spatial Hypertext and the Practice of Information Triage". *Hypertext 97.* N. Y.: ACM, 1997. 124-33.

McLuhan, Marshall. *The Gutenberg Galaxy: The Making of Typographic Man.* Toronto: University of Toronto Press, 1962.

Miles, Adrian. "Softvideography: Digital Video as Postliterate Practice" in *Digital Tools and Cultural Contexts: Assessing the Implications of New Media.* Ed. Brian Hawk, James A. Inman, and Ollie Oviedo (pre-publication PDF copy).

Nelson, Theodor H. *Computer Lib/Dream Machines.* Seattle, Wash.: Microsoft Press, 1987.

—. Selection from *Computer Lib/Dream Machines. The New Media Reader.* Ed. Noah Wardrip-Fruin and Nick Montfort. Cambridge: MIT Press, 2003. 301-38.

Nyce, James M., and Paul Kahn (eds.). *From Memex to Hypertext: Vannevar Bush and the Mind's Machine.* Boston: Academic Press, 1991.

Ong, Walter J. *Orality and Literacy: The Technologizing of the Word.* London: Methuen, 1982.

Chapter Two

Always Already-Known Hypertexts: A Recent Debate in Old Terms

Apostolos Lampropoulos

Theory nowadays tends to take the form of a *fin-de-siècle* discourse insisting on "after theory" or even its "end". This is meant to indicate both a turning point and a spectacular flop: theory is supposed to change, then disappear. But, for the time being, this very talk of post-theory fills the space of activity previously opened up by theory itself. In this context, French Theory is perhaps the most obvious example of what one might call theory in use, or theory practised, or even theory that invigorates the seriousness and validity of critique. In a way, French Theory profits from the place it occupies in the history of theory in general. It has long been considered as a starting point and a constant reference for cultural studies; as such, it maintains some of its "authenticity" and "authority", which nevertheless do not necessarily go with its initial vital force. French Theory has been gradually taken out of the prison house of language and adapted to a more political terrain. In the criticisms that followed French Theory, or stemmed from it, one of the main concerns was to make it abandon its inbuilt hermeticism and put out roots to the "out there". The more implicit agenda, though, consisted of healing its annoying difficulty: bringing French Theory into touch with reality would not only prove it to be useful, but would also unpack it.

When it comes to the presence of French Theory in cybercriticism, there is an outstanding paradox: the supposedly solid ground of reality coincides with the fluidity of cyber-realities; what was supposed to facilitate one's contact with French Theory is, in the same way, itself indecipherable. What should also be taken into consideration is the fact that cybercriticism is a flourishing field that has developed very quickly over the last decade and is in need of both an unyielding theoretical base and some catchy link with the critical past. In what follows, I intend to take a look at the way French Theory has functioned in a different demanding situation and go on to examine how, gradually, it has partly become a kind of "easy theory". My intention is to elaborate on three "snapshots of cybercriticism" which I perceive as theoretically significant, and to elucidate the foundations of the practices mentioned above.

1. Snapshots of Cybercriticism

1.1. "Natural" Analogies and "Safe" Theorizing

The initial statement of Diana Saco (2002, 7, 8, and 28) about cyberspace reads:

> Michel de Certeau tries to get at the same point with his aphorism "*space is a practised place*" [...] Or similarl ', a written text is "a place constituted by a system of signs" but a "space produced" by readers in that the activity of reading those signs conveys a meaning [...] By analogy, computer network sites are *places* ordered by certain imperatives (physical and technological), but the space of networking is produced by, for example, the act of surfing the Internet. [...] then hacking is one of several computer activities that have served further to redefine networking as a kind of space, i.e. to *respatialize* cyberspace according to a particular kind of spatial order.

The procedure followed here is quite obvious: the parallelism capitalizes on a lexical coincidence, that is, the concept of "space" as the object of spatial criticism and "cyberspace" as an already fixed way of describing what happens within the realities set up by new technologies. This parallelism depends on the metaphorization of the text as space, that is, as a semiotic place practised through reading. What is surprising is, firstly, the ease with which this seemingly "natural" analogy is established, and, secondly, the possibility of a genuinely Certeauian respatialization of cyberspace in terms of "electronic frontiers" and "information superhighways" being accepted. Manifestations of this insightful "spatial thinking" form one of the pillars of post-modern thought. In view of this, de Certeau's work gained much of its popularity by contradicting the rigid "objectivism" of the finished city and by introducing a respectable amount of flexibility in the exploration of fossilized objects; it therefore activated a whole range of productive reactions to a customary way of thinking, and often functioned as a lens through which a number of cultural phenomena could be re-examined. Theoretical as it was, this project questioned a certain mode of criticism and proved to be quite influential. The passage above applies de Certeau's solidified success to a new reality empirically named space.

What I find significant here is the fact that an analogy is almost "automatically" established. The form of this analogy is just as important: it is neither between common sense and criticism (no everyday notion is transported into the critical jargon), nor between old and new theories (it is not about the numerous re-configurations of a certain idea); it is an analogy established between a theoretical concept and an accurate description of reality. On the one hand, a negotiable and potentially divisive construct preserves a theoretical flavour, and is still named after theory, while on the other hand, it asserts an authority rooted in its pragmatics. What was functioning up to now as a refreshing way of thinking, now becomes a "naturalizing" representation. This is what I would dare to call a shift in the role of a text belonging to "theory": the provocative starting point becomes "safe" theorizing, and the ground-breaking becomes "self-evident" or common language. The almost routine move from an undiagnosed reality to its conceptual filter tends to be recognized as an itinerary leading to theorization. The automatic repetition of well-known or "used" concepts seems to consolidate them and "elevate" them to the status of supposedly proved data.

1.2. "Realized" Concepts

Let us take a look at the confident remarks on authorship by Silvio Gaggi (1997, 108, my italics):

> *Hypertext and electronic networking seem to respond to the call for an alteration of the role of the "author" that Foucault made. For Foucault the "author function" acts as an ideological constraint on the reading of texts, and he argues for a loosening of that authorial hold* [...] Viewing the author-function as historically contingent, he is able to envision a time when it might be different [...] [Foucault's] ideas could easily be taken to apply to other forms of textual ownership. [...] experience in working in hypertext can provoke a Foucauldian *realization* that notions like authorship and intellectual property, as natural and self-evident and just as they seem to be, are constructs that are historically specific. In different historical situations there might be different understandings of the proper relationship of an individual to his or her discourse and the discourse of others.

Re-using, or actually "using" theory to describe new realities undeniably remains an issue here: Foucault's "author function" and the subsequent liberation from the stifling author-figure seem to be a very convenient scheme which accounts for authorship on the Web. However, what needs our attention is the historical dimension of the remark mentioned above. For Gaggi, as opposed to the more "solid" and almost "undeniable" author-figure, author function is history dependent: this source of coherence necessarily varies with time and the construction of an author is inescapably liable to be imprinted by its context. But the fundamental difference lies elsewhere: both the concept of "author function" itself and many of its structuralist and post-structuralist transformations highlighted the relativization and abandonment of the traditional author-figure; in fact, they attacked authorship in order to show that such a concept can no longer hold. As I conceive it, author-function was not expected to show off a series of successive historicizations—in other words, become a list of alternative descriptions of what an author has been or may eventually become. Such an attempt would more probably result in a stunning history of authorship, making its diversity much more obvious than before. The very concept of authorship would nonetheless remain intact, even if it were somehow disguised. The core of the author-figure would be waiting to be both transformed and discovered.

But if authors throughout history were able to share a minimum role, the Foucauldian project would then have failed entirely. Instead of being diluted, authorship would have been reinvigorated and put back on its throne, whereas the aim of author-function was authorship's potential decentrement. Actually, at the centre of this project was the replacement of the author as source of unity with the reading's *hic et nunc* as a guarantee of its potential coherence. Instead of multiplying the conceivable author-figures, they were to be abandoned altogether. In other words, this kind of work was based on the harsh critique and radicalization of a notion, rather than on suspicion, hypothesizing and the expectation of a corroboration. Moreover, it was born out of the strong epistemological desire to know what one does when one refers to an author. In Gaggi's text, however, it is retrospectively seen as mere speculation: what was a Foucauldian hypothesis is now supposed to have led to a "Foucauldian realization". The opening of author-function to historical variation turns out to be an experiment in need of its empirical data; what is more, theory is seen as something to be confirmed and, once this is done, it can almost be seen as a solid theory-come-true. Or, to be more precise, it is a low expectation—almost un-theorized—version of theory that is celebrated.

1.3. "Apodictic" Theory

In a sophisticated study of the Internet, Mark Poster (2001, 144) discusses several ways to the conceptualization of the virtual. A passage concerning Derrida reads as follows:

> In his review of *Specters of Marx*, Jameson raises this question in a particularly acute manner: "Whether the new figurality, the figured concept of the ghost or specter, is not of a somewhat different type than those that began to proliferate in Derrida's earlier work, beginning most famously with "writing" itself and moving through terms like "dissemination", "hymen". Does the introduction of the ghost in the *mise-en-scène* of deconstruction cause an alteration in its theoretical composition? Jameson reasons that it does because Derrida's messianism harkens to the "post-modern virtuality" of new communications technology, in other words to a reconfiguration of materiality. And I agree. To the extent that the mode of information restructures languages and symbols generally into a configuration that is aptly termed *virtual reality*, the particular form of the messianic, of our hope for justice, must go through this technological circuit and must account for the difference between writing and e-mail, dissemination and the Internet, the parergon and the World Wide Web. Unless such an account is provided, deconstruction may return to its minimalist position of critique as critique, as disavowal of ontology, forever incapable of an affirmative sentence.

This passage is part of a chapter in which Poster discusses Derrida's analysis of the virtual; he points out that even when Derrida mentions contemporary technological apparatuses this seems to be an accessory or incidental move. Poster then evokes Jameson when he claims that the introduction of the ghost constitutes a major evolution of deconstruction as it associates it with the broader notion of virtuality re-developed to cover new technologies. He then expands on Jameson's remark to talk about and redistribute Derrida's messianism, something that at first glance resembles an attempt to think of Derrida as a political scholar and to build on what seem to be two simultaneous reconfigurations of materiality. The position that deconstruction occupies as a critique of a critique is condemned to be considered as minimalist: the fact that deconstruction is neither immediately nor obviously politicizable is thought of as a sign of non-radicality, an unbearable restriction that has to be treated in order to be exorcised.

It would perhaps be too much to expect a detailed explanation to the questions of how minimalism is combined with messianism and how the total and innate absence of affirmation can be healed. But one can easily discern here a rushed move of anti-deconstructive critique, based on an inadequate discussion of what could be a promising coincidence between the Marxian ghost and the technological virtual. Actually, this attempt gets trapped in its desire to find the essential link between the basics of deconstruction (such as writing, hymen, dissemination) and what Poster terms "technological circuit". Despite the fact that Derrida's direct references to cyber-realities are rather rudimentary, therefore hardly conceivable as a focused cultural analysis, Poster clumsily drags deconstructive theory into the terrain of cultural criticism. What is at stake is the feasible extension of traditional deconstructive concepts in order to render them productive in this new context, but in a surprisingly fast and unmediated way. Deconstructive discourse on the virtual is to alert cybercriticism to the "hauntology" of an undifferentiated virtuality. If the metaphysical way of thinking has been the major enemy of deconstruction over the last decades, it is not easy to understand how Poster condemns the transcendentalism of literary studies while requiring deconstruction to discard its main task and no longer act as a safety valve. In brief, by calling upon deconstruction to abandon its intrinsic "messianism", he asks it to function both descriptively, with respect to cyber-realities, and apodictically, with respect to itself; deconstruction should grasp a unique chance and go on talking cyber-realities while looking for its own confirmation within them. Again, theory has suddenly to be related with proof.

2. Cybercriticism as a Symptom of Critical Complacency

In remarks such as those mentioned above, one can easily identify several underlying theoretical issues that have been on the critical agenda for some time. To mention only an influential few, one could refer to: the end of authorship through the distinction both between analogue-traditional authorship and digital authorship, and between the "bodiliness" of the analogue author and the "bodilessness" of the digital author (cf. Bordo 1997, 181-182), the openness of the text, "intended" or "accidental" intertextuality, the sacralization of writing, and so on and so forth. In my opinion, all these issues should be seen in the light of theory, both as a flux and as a habit. In this sense, the classics of theory would be a happy moment in the history of ideas, rather than a perpetually ground-breaking, pioneering, almost imperishable, concept; what is more, theory would be conceived as a constant urge to question what it has already done and a steady reluctance to take this for granted, rather than the will to enjoy the stir it has caused.

Hence, cybercriticism does not seem to breed serious critical doubt *vis-à-vis* these well-known theoretical propositions. On the contrary, it leads to willing acceptance, promotion and even celebration of yesterday's contested and controversial issues. In fact, cybercriticism tends to revive numerous theoretical utopias, such as the unfinished or the writerly text, unlimited intertextuality or the death of the author. It dares to appropriate the vacuous and often non-applicable categories that have been proposed by theory as a critique of the critique, and then treat them as practisable notions that can be implemented and directly put on the cybermap. It is therefore mainly the "oldies-but-goodies" of French Theory that are often reactivated by cybercriticism and used as multi-purpose methodological tools. The whole setting is much more likely to be seen as a porous area into which "skimmed" theories or ex-theories can easily slip, co-exist and interact, than as a blatantly anti-theoretical front. It is in this sense that cybercriticism is understandable as a new theoretical map in the making. If my argument has any validity whatsoever, many thematic areas, as well as almost any of the x, y, z studies and several critical genres, would be equally appropriate for the same study.

I believe that within cultural studies cybercriticism might be a part of the broader use of theory (or at least of past theory that is no longer *à la mode* but is still recognizable, workable and pliable). In this sense, cybercriticism is conceivable both as a locus onto which concerns about theory could eventually be projected, and as a kind of exploitable and trustworthy critical cartography. In my view, this is a matter of theoretical self-awareness; struggling for the theoretical avant-garde seems to be have been partially replaced by the digital euphoria that makes the struggle sound commonsensical. "Hypertext and computing in general have the (apparent) power to make those who position[ed] themselves as the advocates of the new appear to themselves and others as old-fashioned" (Landow 1997, 273). That is why one can imagine a theoretical disappointment and a theoretical delight at the same time: what was once the fascinating "theoretical impossible" or the welcome "theoretical extreme" now becomes customary and trivialized. Such uses of theory seem to make the most of the fact that, for them, theory predicts only what will happen several years later; and, more importantly, that it is justifiable for theory to query old convictions, mainly because it will thus proceed to speculations which might be "realized" in the long run; in other words, the continuity between theory and the "out there" that I brought up at the beginning of my paper will be piously respected.

The apparent danger in my venture is oversimplification. Nothing would be easier than ridiculing cybercriticism and turning it into a medley of concepts and quotations, deprived of any resourceful complexity or freshness, predestined to reproduce commonsensical ideas and reach anticipated conclusions. In addition to this, nothing would be more comforting than an *ex cathedra* disapproval of systematic under-theorization in present-day cultural studies, or even of a conservative turn in the humanities. Considering either component as simply problematic would thwart our understanding of the phenomenon. In fact, it would fall back to the same vulgate of theory that it seems to decline: if it rejected what happens in the name of theory just because it deviates from the old theory-as-usual and replaces it with a new one, it would inevitably reproduce the same weaknesses. In that sense, my approach neither refers to the entirety of contemporary theory, nor pretends that all theoretical activity has taken the form described above. What is more, it does not call for underestimation of the possibility of a coincidence between theory and reality, but warns against its potential deceptiveness. Based on a theoretical precedent (namely French Theory), it focuses on some cases of theoretical mastication and rumination, explores some of the basic mechanisms and hints at some reasons why cybercriticism might offer some ground for such experimentations. In other words, I did not endeavour to talk about all theory or all cybercriticism. The aim of my deliberately cyclopic reading was to survey the co-existence of the corpse and the hale and hearty body of theory; my intention was to see not only how one of the most vibrant thematic studies can partly become an instance of mortifying and posthume resistance to French Theory, but also how the overall procedure can mark one's conception of it, demystify it and increase its popularity by reducing its risks.

In any case, cybercriticism can proffer both an opportunity for critical introspection and a booster for updated theoretical activity. From a meta-theoretical point of view, cybercriticism is interesting, not because it outlasts and prolongs the older theory's usefulness, but because it offers itself to rethinking—both retrospectively and prospectively—the essential nerve of theory. Within this, there is much greater potential than what is put to work at a first level: what, for some, is "new-technologies-and-theory", has become for me "revisiting-theory". It might be less important to discover exactly what cybercriticism is, and more interesting to see that it is a "site of debate, awareness of difference, and tentative exchange" (Bal 2002, 13). In other words, cybercriticism seems to be a crossroads of discourses describing cyber-realities; it can thus be considered as a discourse summarizing both cyber-cultures and past theories. What is more, it might follow the destiny of obsolete theories when reborn, as well as the idea that a theoretical inquiry "confirmed" a posteriori might be an indication of theoretical reluctance which may thus lead to (undesired) critical complacency.

Bibliography

Bal, M. "Travelling Concepts in the Humanities". Green College Lectures. Toronto: University of Toronto Press, 2002.
Bordo, S. *Twilight Zones*. Berkeley-Los Angeles: University of California Press, 1997.
Gaggi, S. "From Text to Hypertext". Penn Studies in Contemporary American Fiction. Philadelphia: University of Pennsylvania Press, 1997.
Landow, G.P. *Hypertext 2.0. (Parallax: Re-Visions of Culture and Society)*. Baltimore-London: Johns Hopkins University Press, 1997.
Poster, M. *What's the Matter with the Internet? (Electronic Mediations)*. Minneapolis: University of Minnesota Press, 2001.
Saco, D. *Cybering Democracy*. (*Electronic Mediations*). Minneapolis: University of Minnesota Press, 2002.

CHAPTER THREE

LUDOLOGY MEETS HYPERTEXT

SUSANA PAJARES TOSCA

1. Introduction

This chapter is an introduction to ludology. It also attempts to compare two of the most popular paradigms in the study of digital texts to see how they differ from and are similar to each other. Although it might seem that ludology has killed the hypertext star of the nineties, the two approaches have a lot in common and deal with similar problems.

This is a comparison at theoretical level, which I call a *meta-chapter*. To my mind, introducing the subject of ludology at a hypertext volume is interesting because it gives us a better idea of what has been going on recently in the digital arena. It can help us understand why some things go out of fashion and others take their place, but it also argues that the gap between the two fields is not as wide as some would hold. It may also be helpful for today's ludologists to understand the mistakes of hypertext theory so that they can try to avoid them and adapt their paradigm to an ever-changing digital world.

2. Hypertext is Dead – Long Live Hypertext

In the context of this volume the object of hypertext need not be defined. Rather, I will use this space to reflect on its life as a discipline. Hypertextual theory has an interesting history in that it was the predominant paradigm of the nineties[1] in the field of digital textuality and digital aesthetics, but all but disappeared after the turn of the century,

---

[1] For a history of the term, its use and its theory see Tosca, 2004.

when most digital scholars seemed to turn their sights to other objects of study (computer games, blogs, social software) or other digital text properties that have nothing to do with the structural emphasis brought about by hypertext (remediation, multimodality, dynamics, etc.). However, while the visibility of hypertextual theory has decreased enormously, hypertext understood in a structural way as *text plus links* has become ubiquitous, and every user of the Web is naturally hypertext-literate in a way that has obliterated the early theorists' fear that hyper-readers would not be able to make sense of fragmented text. The average Internet user shifts between pages, topics and modes of expression with an ease that was difficult to predict in the early nineties.

Hypertext theory was derived from post-structuralist literary theory (most notably seen in Landow, 1992 and subsequent editions). As Robert Coover put it in "The End of Books"(1992): "Hypertext is truly a new and unique environment. (...) Fluidity, contingency, indeterminacy, plurality, discontinuity are the hypertext buzzwords of the day, and they seem to be fast becoming principles". The first theorists were not very web-friendly. They mostly built their apparatus using *Storyspace*, the popular hypertext writing tool produced by Eastgate, the company that also published the most quoted hypertexts of all times, for example, *Afternoon*, by Michael Joyce, and *Patchwork Girl,* by Shelley Jackson. For early theorists, such as Bolter, Joyce, Landow or Yellowlees Douglas, hypertext embodied all the symbolic fragmentation of text pointed out by deconstructionists and other post-modernists. It was a brilliant publicity stunt that had the virtue of making hypertext palatable and interesting in literature departments, but at the same time it overloaded the new concept with an impossible weight, where hypertext was associated with ideologies of liberation from the tyranny of linear text and rigid social structures. Many early authors built their arguments for hypertext as opposed to text, characterizing "text" with all sorts of negative features which hypertext liberated us from. It is obvious that a text like *Ulysses* in hypertext poses the same kinds of problems as it does in print text (I would go further than this and maintain that it *only* makes sense as print text), but here, the two levels—material and phenomenological—are confused. Arguments on embodiment helped to legitimize the study of hypertext (and new media) in humanities departments by linking them directly to the great contemporary philosophical traditions, but did not really help the new form, which could not live up to expectations.

Although hopes were high, liberation never happened; the production of literary hypertext was never more than a small series of experiments without wide reader appeal. The embodiment of intertextuality and the link as a simulated connection of minds between author and reader should have remained inspiring metaphors instead of a guiding principle that made a lot of theorists reject the Internet because it was not *really* hypertextual.[2] The Web was ripe with examples of interesting educational, journalistic, fictive and personal attempts at non-linear writing, but many theorists ignored them. The theoretical stress on metaphors of infinity, never-ending text, dissolution of the author, reader as author (which were part of the manifesto of the few hypertext fictions) was damaging to the discipline. If the stress had instead been on metaphors of organization (encyclopaedias, newspapers, databases), readers as searchers, or strong author control—which defined the real Web—a lot of opportunities would have emerged. Not everything happening on the Web adjusts to the classic definitions and expectations of hypertext, but hypertext is everywhere.

The truth is that we, the theorists, have for too long been concentrating on a very small part of the picture: a few very experimental hyperfictions produced mainly by Eastgate. Moreover, in privileging the hypertextual over any other characteristic of electronic text we have ignored other interesting properties, such as its dynamism (temporal and spatial dimensions), its ergodic properties, the possibilities of multimedia, the collaboration of authors on weblogs, for example, or social software, as well as many other aspects to come which are still being researched.

3. Ludology: A Short History

In contrast to hypertext, ludology is a theory of the new century, appearing at the same time as the first attempts at theorizing computer games, many of which, like hypertext, came from literature. Some of these early approaches were centred on the representational quality of computer games, and authors were thus able to apply literary models to the description and cultural understanding of their object (Murray, 1997; Ryan, 1991, 2001; Laurel, 1993; Aarseth, 1997).[3] However, these attempts have been vehemently rejected by one group of researchers, identified by

---

[2] My critique of some aspects of hypertext theory should not be interpreted as an attempt to diminish the importance of the works by the first wave of theoreticians, whose work I deeply admire. They created the field and their books are important landmarks in the study of new media.
[3] Jesper Juul relates this to the extension of the concept of narrative after modernity: "The narrative turn of the last 20 years has seen the concept of narrative emerge as a privileged master concept in the description of all aspects of human society and sign-production". (2001).

the name of "ludologists",[4] whose aim is that computer games should be considered *as games* and not as narratives, or anything else for that matter. The formal properties of computer games would thus be more important, more *intrinsic*, than the stories in them. The debate has raged on for the last several years, with ludologists attacking the supposed colonization of the new field of game studies from "alien" disciplines such as literature. Controversy is sometimes good, and we could say that this discussion has helped considerably in bringing the study of computer games into the spotlight.

The ludologists' argument against the comparison of computer games and stories is that literature is not the only appropriate paradigm for approaching the new field of computer games. They mainly identify narrative with *narratology*, which is a particular sub-field of literature, and, arguably, a favoured approach by those interested in computers and narrative, due to its focus on the formal properties of literature.

We could relate narratology to the above-mentioned attempts at talking about computer games and stories by Ryan, Murray or Laurel, but we should not think that narratology is all there is to literary studies. As Marie-Laure Ryan herself explains, it is meaningful to use narrative to study computer games, because it is also an essential part of the player's experience:

> Many people will rightly argue that computer games are played for the sake of solving problems and defeating opponents, of refining strategic skills and of participating in on-line communities, and not for the purpose of creating a "trace" that reads as a story. Yet, if narrativity were totally irrelevant to the enjoyment of computer games, why would designers put so much effort into the creation of a narrative interface? Why would graphics be so sophisticated? Why would the task of the player be presented as fighting terrorists or saving the earth from invasion by evil creatures from outer space rather than as "gathering points by hitting moving targets with a cursor controlled by a joystick"? The narrativity of action computer games functions as what Kendall Walton would call a "prop in a game of make-believe". It may not be the *raison d'être* of computer games, but it plays such an important role as a stimulant for the imagination (…) (Ryan: 01).

---

[4] See Frasca, 2003, for a history of the use of the concept. *Ludus* means game in Latin, therefore *ludology* would be the study of games. Researchers identified as ludologists are Markku Eskelinen, Gonzalo Frasca, Aki Jaarvinen, Jesper Juul and Espen Aarseth.

Kendall Walton[5] is certainly no narratologist. It actually becomes extremely difficult to identify the literary/narratologist side of the debate, as the first ludological articles, although confrontational, do not really identify their "enemy". For example, Jesper Juul's article, "Computer Games Telling Stories? A Brief Note on Computer Games and Narratives", starts by stating the three common arguments for computer games being narrative; but who does he refer to? Who has used these "common arguments"? The whole article seems to be fighting an unnamed phantom. Markku Eskelinen's article, *"The Gaming Situation"* (2001), also refuses to name opponents employing the "wrong" arguments.

For ludologists, there are several reasons why subsuming computer games under the title of narrative is a bad idea, particularly the fact that this could lead us to overlook the intrinsic properties of computer games. As Eskelinen forcefully puts it:

> The old and new game components, their dynamic combination and distribution, the registers, the necessary manipulation of temporal, causal, spatial and functional relations and properties, not to mention the rules and the goals and the lack of audience, should suffice to set games and the gaming situation apart from narrative and drama, and to annihilate for good the discussion of computer games as stories, narratives or cinema (Eskelinen, 2001).

We find a similar, if less radical, perspective in Jesper Juul's article "Computer Games Telling Stories?", in which he argues that part of the problem arises from the indiscriminate use of the word narrative. If everything is a narrative, it is, of course, not very useful to say that computer games can also be described as such. Juul tries to find other reasons why some theorists might be tempted to take the comparison too far:

> 1) The player can tell stories of a game session.
> 2) Many computer games contain narrative elements, and in many cases the player may play in order to see a cut-scene or realize a narrative sequence.
> 3) Computer games and narratives share some structural traits (Juul, 2001).

His arguments against this comparison refer mainly to the impossibility of translating computer games into stories and vice versa,[6] to

---

[5] She refers to Walton's extensive book on representation in visual arts and fiction, *Mimesis as Make-Believe. On the Foundations of the Representational Arts* (1990).
[6] Although he does not mention adaptation of fictional universes, which is

an understanding of narrative as a re-telling of events, and to the fact that the experience of playing a game is very different from that of reading a story (Juul, 2001).

Not surprisingly, this debate is still alive in the public consciousness of computer games research, and the first DIGRA[7] conference in 2003 included a number of papers on topics related to computer games and narrative, where presenters felt the need to position themselves in relation to ludology before starting their talks. It also included Gonzalo Frasca's paper, "Ludologists Love Stories Too: Notes from a Debate that Never Took Place", in which he comes out in defence of ludology and rejects the most extreme critiques by arguing that ludology's *raison d'être* is not at all to reject stories, but to focus on games. For other theorists, however, ludological arguments are quite dangerous, even though their rhetorical purpose is understood and accepted; Rune Klevjer has warned against the ideological dangers of confusing games as discursive modes with computer games as cultural products (2002: 193). A too tight focus on the formal structure (rules) of computer games could preclude other kinds of study, such as games as social artefacts. It remains to be seen if ludology will continue to be defined negatively, that is, in opposition to narratology, instead of as a general term applied to the study of computer games themselves, as their promoters intended. Misunderstanding is bound to continue as long as both groups talk about different things as if they were the same. When ludologists talk about *narrative*, they usually refer to a fixed sequence of events, and when their opponents use the same term, they refer to a story—a fictional world. The ludology-narratology wars are a symptom of the struggle to define the new discipline of game studies outside the hypertextual (see, for example, Landow, 1992, 1997, 2006) or cinematic (Manovich, 2001) which dominate the digital paradigms of the times. The debate is interesting because it actually mirrors some of the deepest theoretical concerns about the field, such as the difficulty of integrating interactivity and narrativity.

4. Ludology meets Hypertext: Conclusions

So how do the two theories compare to each other? Due to the limitations of space in this paper, I will summarize some of the issues that were expanded on in my presentation:

---

certainly possible even though the same sequence of events is not maintained.
[7] Digital Games Research Association.

HYPERTEXT	LUDOLOGY
Establishes itself as a discipline by opposition to the concept of *text*.	Establishes itself as a discipline by opposition to the concept of *narrative*.[8]
Points to post-modern literary theory as a source of legitimacy.	Rejects literary theory and considers games the only valid approach to games.[9]
Favours a formalist approach by focusing on structure.	Favours a formalist approach by focusing on rules.
Considers that hypertexts are different from traditional narratives.	Considers that games are different from traditional narratives.
The problem with trying to tell stories in hypertextual form is that the reader's choice will necessarily mean worse stories.	The problem with trying to tell stories in game form is that the player's choice will necessarily mean worse stories (and boring games).

Apart from comparisons at a meta-level, that is, of theories as rhetorical operations, we can see that hypertext and game researchers have a topic in common. Authors like Landow (1992) or Douglas (1992) have wondered about the break with traditional narrative brought about by hypertext narrative. Ludologists also deal with this problem (Aarseth (1997), Eskelinen (2001) or Juul (2001)). A common interest, for example, is the structural techniques that would allow for integration of story and interactivity, such as branching. How can a designer/writer tell a good story/game if readers are to be allowed real choice? Both paradigms propose different solutions that are actually not so far from each other as would seem at a first glance. Hypertext authors talk about ways of giving more authorial control without seeming to constrain the reader experience: for example, by using what Mark Bernstein calls the split/joint pattern of hypertext (Bernstein: 98), which is a common device in adventure games to guide the player through multiple options. Game designers[10] use a narrative model that is very similar to that of a hypertext with controlled branching or split/joint pattern:

---

[8] In games.
[9] This is a tautology, but they want to focus on the need to discover the essence of the new medium of games.
[10] Of narrative games such as adventure games.

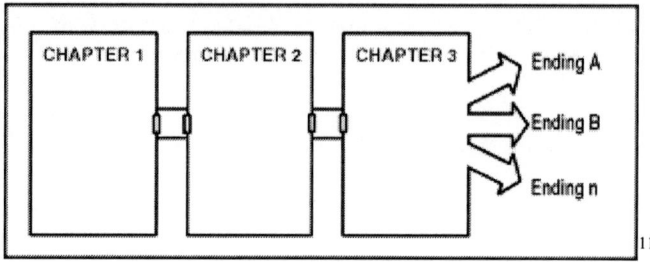

In this kind of fiction the player has to solve puzzles in each chapter, usually with some flexibility as to which puzzle goes first, so that some feeling of freedom is achieved. There is not a continuous emotion curve; rather, designers rely on the "unambiguous sense of victory" that solving the puzzles gives the player (Smith 2000). But ultimately, the player is "solving a story" instead of actively creating it, even if his actions provoke a variety of endings (for example, *Myst*). This is the model that most adventure and action-adventure games follow, and successive chapters can work in a cumulative way so that at the end some kind of climax or resolution is provided, usually preceded by a difficult "boss fight" to give a greater sense of achievement. This is also what a lot of hypertexts do, keeping the interaction of the readers at an external level where no real changes to the story can be undertaken.[12] But ludologists prefer real interaction, and thus favour games where emergent structures mean that no playing sequence is pre-fixed, something which occurs in multiplayer games, or games with good AIs or efficient object-oriented programming. None of these solutions is viable in hypertext, but the two media have different strengths, and while I would say that computer games do well in exploiting their potential for free player-action, hypertexts can make use of a more limited kind of interactivity to tell stories that are not as fixed as printed ones, but should not aspire to total reader liberation either.

To conclude, ludology has an advantage over hypertext in that the available objects of study (games) are much more abundant and popular than hypertexts. This means that there is a huge user-base to conduct empirical studies, and a vast library of titles to choose from when trying to dissect and understand the medium. Hypertext theorists have not been so lucky, but then again, maybe they should have looked to the Web instead

---

[11] Graphic by Jonas Heide Smith (2000).
[12] This is what Marie-Laure Ryan would call external exploratory, although the games that let players change the story would ultimately belong to the internal exploratory group and therefore offer more interaction (2001).

of to the few Eastgate hypertexts that have concentrated most of the criticism. On the other hand, while it was a wise move to distance themselves from textual theories that cannot possibly explain the new medium without making it flat, ludologists should be wary of an all-excluding formalist focus that could hide the most interesting aspects of games as cultural objects.

The game is not over yet.

Bibliography

Aarseth, Espen. *Cybertext. Perspectives on Ergodic Literature.* Baltimore: Johns Hopkins University Press, 1997.
Bernstein, Mark. "Patterns of Hypertext". In *Hypertext'98 Proceedings*, N.Y.: ACM, 1998: 21-29.
Coover, Robert. "The End of Books". *The New York Times Book Review*, 21-1 June 1992: 23-24.
Douglas, J. Yellowlees. *Print Pathways and Interactive Labyrinths: How Hypertext Narratives Affect the Act of Reading*, (doctoral thesis). New York: New York University, 1992.
Eskelinen, Markku. "The Gaming Situation". *Computer Gamestudies*, vol. 1, issue 1, July 2001. http://www.computer gamestudies.org
Frasca, Gonzalo. "Ludologists Love Stories Too: Notes from a Debate that Never Took Place". In *Level-Up* Conference Proceedings. Edited by Marinka Copier and Joost Raessens. Utrecht University, 4-6 November 2003: 92-99.
Juul, Jesper. "Computer Games Telling Stories? A Brief Note on Computer Games and Narratives." *Computer Gamestudies*, vol. 1, issue 1. July 2001. http://www.computer gamestudies.org
Klevjer, Rune. "In Defense of Cut-Scenes". In Mayrä, Frans (ed). *CGDC02 Conference Proceedings*. Finland: Tampere University Press, June 2002: 191-202.
Landow, George P. *Hypertext. The Convergence of Contemporary Critical Theory and Technology.* Baltimore: Johns Hopkins University Press, 1992.
Laurel, Brenda. *Computers as Theatre.* Readings, MA: Addison-Wesley, 1993.
Manovich, Lev. *The Language of New Media.* Cambridge MA: MIT Press, 2001.
Murray, Janet. *Hamlet on the Holodeck. The Future of Narrative in Cyberspace.* Cambridge, MA: MIT Press, 1997.
Pajares Tosca, Susana. *Literatura Digital. El Paradigma Hipertextual.*

Cáceres, Spain: Universidad de Extremadura, 2004.
Ryan, Marie-Laure. *Possible Worlds, Artificial Intelligence and Narrative Theory*. Bloomington: Indiana University Press, 1991.
—. "Beyond Myth and Metaphor. The Case of Narrative in Digital Media". In *Computer Gamestudies*, vol. 1, issue 1, July 2001. http://www.computer gamestudies.org
Smith, Jonas Heide "The Dragon in the Attic". *Game Research*, 2000. http://www.gameresearch.com/art_dragon_in_the_attic.asp

CHAPTER FOUR

ACTUALIZING ALLUSIONS: HYPERTEXT AND COGNITIVE LITERARY RESEARCH

ZIVA BEN-PORAT

Theories of hypertext were born in relation to cognitive theories: implicitly, already at the moment of inception, when in 1939 Vannevar Bush—universally acknowledged to be the chief precursor of hypertext—presented his vision of machine-enhanced memory ("Mechanization and the Record") to President Roosevelt, and explicitly, in his famous 1945 essay ("As we may think").[1] In this seminal work Bush establishes the relationship in mostly negative terms:

> The human mind does not work that way [indexing and fixing items and links]. It operates by association. With one item in its grasp, it snaps instantly to the next that is suggested by the association of thoughts, in accordance with some intricate web of trails carried by the cells of the brain. It has other characteristics, of course; trails that are not frequently followed are prone to fade, items are not fully permanent, memory is transitory. Yet the speed of action, the intricacy of trails, the detail of mental pictures, is awe-inspiring beyond all else in nature.

But he then goes on to say:

> Man cannot hope fully to duplicate this mental process artificially, but he certainly ought to be able to learn from it. In minor ways he may even improve, for his records have relative permanency. The first idea, however, to be drawn from the analogy concerns selection. Selection by association, rather than by indexing, may yet be mechanized. One cannot hope thus to

---

[1] Information on Bush and "Memex", as well as on Ted Nelson and "Xanadu" is easily accessible on the web. Enlightening discussions of the history of Hypertext can be found in Bolter (1991), Landow (1992), Floridi (1999), Gillis and Cailliau (2000), Naughton (2000), and many more books and articles.

equal the speed and flexibility with which the mind follows an associative trail, but it should be possible to beat the mind decisively in regard to the permanence and clarity of the items resurrected from storage (Bush 1945, 101).

This article is devoted to the presentation of a particular type of hypertext which, although as far removed from anything Bush had in mind as today's World Wide Web is from "Memex" and Nelson's "Xanadu", is in some ways a "Bushian" attempt to improve human memory by enhancing and reactivating forgotten associative trails and cultural entities. I employ this associative multi-media cultural unit in hypertext form in order to research one particular aspect of the processing of a literary text—the actualization of an allusion. This is, perhaps, the prototypical (in the sense of "best example") meeting point: it is here that Bush's original approach to hypertext (namely, the mechanical linking of text segments, associated by the individual for easy retrieval and guaranteed permanent storage) and the later technical emphasis on sharing information and facilitating interaction between readers and texts (for example, the purchase of flight tickets on the Internet) converge with literary hypertext theory (the non-linear "reading" of a text, the materialization of the open inter-textual nature of texts according to post-structural semiotic theories of language and literature, and so forth), cognitive studies of reading and learning from traditional printed texts (Mandl, Stein and Tabasso 1984, van Dijk and Kintch 1983, Britton and Graesser, 1996), and theories of relevance (Wilson and Sperber, 1986) and of cultural contexts as cognitive factors (Sperber 1996, Ben-Porat 2001, Nisbett, 2003).

The hypertext that I use in the experiment is a multimedia cluster of texts linked on the basis of explicitly defined inter-textual relations—an actualized associative net. The idea was developed during work on a European Commission project, CULTOS.[2] Situated in the field of cultural heritage, CULTOS was aimed at counteracting the damaged accessibility to (or simply lack of familiarity with) past canonic works in contemporary cultural memory (knowledge actively shared by members of a cultural community)—damage caused by changes in school curricula, the diminished social status of the humanities, the political critique of past

---

[2] CULTOS (Cultural Units of Learning Tools and Services) is an international European endeavour co-funded by the European Commission under the IST Program. EC: 5th frame, 6th call, IST (Information Society Technologies): http://www.cordis.lu/ist/. The two-year project ended successfully on Oct.31, 2003, with the design of an authoring tool for such units and an ontology of inter-textual relations.

canons, and the many transformed—even distorted—representations of canonic works in the mass media. The original idea was to harness the digital revolution, new literacy, and the new mode of acquiring knowledge to reactivate the major canonic texts that are still pertinent to active cultural memory. Technically speaking, this approach was intended to develop inter-textually related clusters (or threads) of various canonic traces in popular texts pertaining to the mass media—the most powerful player in the field of actual cultural memory—and to link them with canonic works that could qualify as their "origins". We assumed that in this way we could endow the endangered canon with "text-appeal" for a generation of clickers and browsers (Ben-Porat 2003).

By way of example, the next few pages show screens from a cluster designed to capture not only the wealth of associations but also the history of uses and interpretations surrounding the "tilting at windmills" episode from Cervantes' *Don Quixote*.[3] The obvious constraints of length mean that the richness of the cluster cannot be demonstrated from the few illustrations shown. Their task is limited to presenting the structure of this particular type of hypertext.

Illustration 1

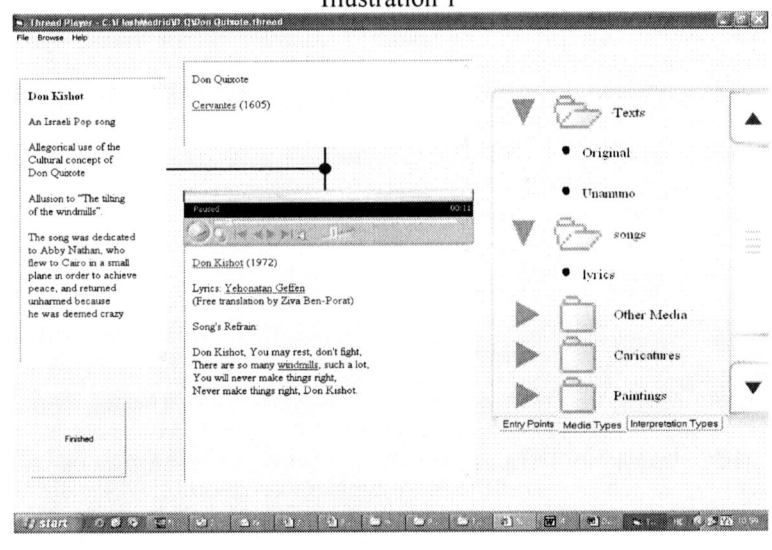

---

[3] These screens, as well as others included in this paper, have been designed specifically for my research and constructed on a different platform unrelated to CULTOS. The developer, Ziv Ben-Porat, would be happy to let other people use the software. If you are interested, please contact the author of this article, Ziva Ben-Porat.

Illustration 2

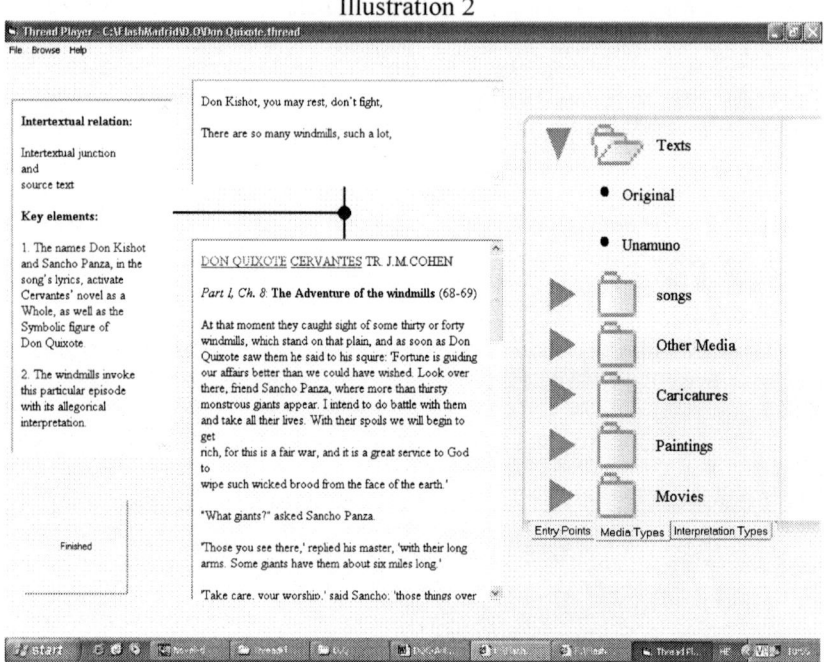

All screens have exactly the same formal design. At the centre are two text boxes, containing the linked nodes: segments or whole texts. The latter can be represented (by a title or the title page of a novel, for example), or presented (e.g. a picture).[4] Text boxes can function as list boxes when the same inter-textual junction can activate more than one associative trail, linking the triggering segment to more than one other text (or segment). The location of a segment in either box is insignificant in terms of the writing history (i.e. which text was published first and can be considered as source text) and in terms of the reading history (i.e. which is the triggering text). The lack of customary spatial significance (the top indicating priority) should not harm the optimal processing of the information contained on screen, since the nature of the inter-textual relation is explicitly stated in the left-hand box. The top box may contain either the activating or the activated node. In the illustrations, the

---

[4] There is no real size constraint on the presentation of even a long novel, since a text can be rolled if a box is not big enough to contain it, but we aim at constructing screens that can be comprehended as one whole; we do not expect viewers to read the two volumes of *Don Quixote* when it is the activated text.

caricature (Illustration 3) is both a parodic representation and a satiric manipulation of the scene that precedes it historically and is referenced in the top box. The pop song alludes to the "tilting at windmills" episode (Illustration 2) which chronologically precedes it, but is situated in the lower box; when it is shown using the cultural concept of "Don Quixotism" allegorically (Illustration 1), the source text (represented by its title, the publication date of its first part and name of its author) is situated in the top box. The menu on the right shows the wealth of multimedia materials and entities contained (and linked) in this cluster. The full menu cannot be presented in the illustrations because many of its items contain lists of entities, and the category labels need to be clicked on and opened in order for the full content of the cluster to be seen.

Different links have different colours:[5] one colour indicates out-going trails—links connecting a node to a site that would provide the browser with information on the node's subject, be it the name of an author, a performer or a text. For example, a coloured *Don Quixote* may be linked to one (or a number) of the many websites devoted to the novel, while a coloured "Cervantes" would be linked to one (or a number) of the many biographies. Differently coloured nodes take the browser into different screens within the cluster. Different screens can also be reached by using the menu.

Obviously, control over the links gives the author of a cluster some control over the browsing process. The ability to hide (or deactivate) some of the links (e.g. the menu) makes it possible to tune the cluster to the needs of different user groups. After all, the needs of a professional cultural critic are different from those of university or high school students, or from those of our originally-targeted fun-loving browser. It is, of course, the same for different learning situations (such as formal and informal) and it is crucial for the use of such hypertext clusters in any kind of experimental study.

Although these clusters have been constructed for other purposes, the built-in activity log (the browsing history option that tells us which links have been activated, how long the browser has stayed in each of them, and in what order they have been pursued) makes them potential tools for cognitive literary research. They can be used to study problems such as the ability to transform data into organized knowledge, or to construct a story on the basis of non-linear readings of its components, or to find out the necessary conditions for successful cognitive processing of materials introduced in an apparently disordered manner, and so forth.

---

[5] The different colouring is not reproduced in the illustrations.

Illustration 3

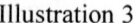

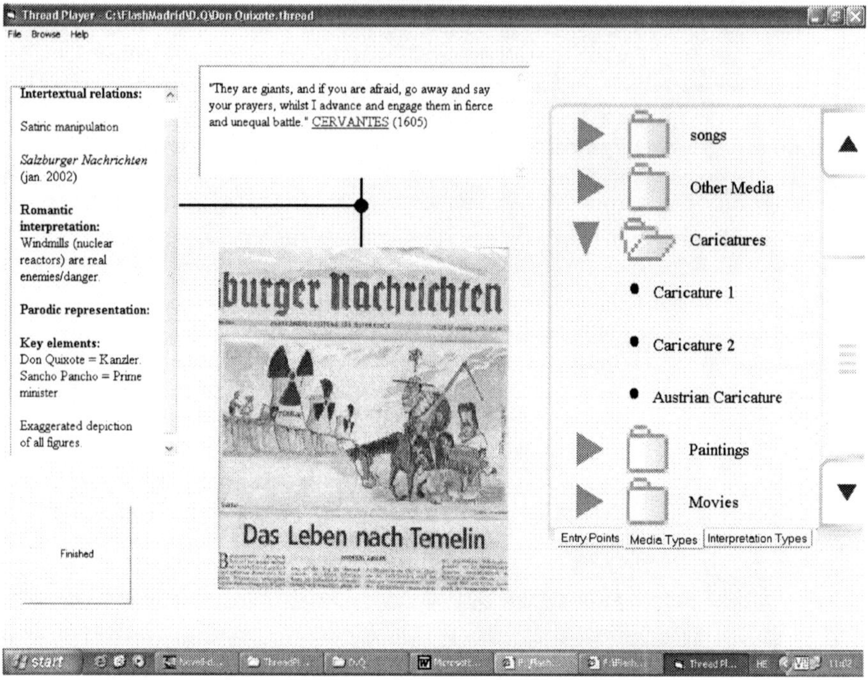

For example, people who had browsed through the Don Quixote Cluster might be asked questions that would indicate their ability to point out the interpretive change originating from the Romantic view of the text (not directly presented in the illustrations), or to create a story based on the chronology. Questions might be either open or closed. Participants might be asked to judge if the statement "Through allegorical interpretation, Romantic critics could claim that Don Quixote is the ultimate idealist" is correct or incorrect; or they might be asked to trace the history of interpretations of *Don Quixote* from comic to serious. They might respond to the latter with something like: In 1605, Cervantes' novel was basically perceived as humorous and parodic. At some time in the nineteenth century it was allegorized. The allegorical Romantic interpretation allows twentiesth century manipulations of the text in which original items can carry opposite meanings: the windmills can be either real or imaginary enemies or both; Don Quixote can be either a madman or a hero or both. Sometimes, as in the Austrian caricature (Illustration 3), the text exhibits the complexity of the relations obtaining between conflicting interpretations: the nuclear reactors are real enemies because of the risk involved in their use; they are ridiculed by being portrayed as windmills (dated-to-obsolete technologies), but, at the same time, they can have the same symbolic-metaphoric function that the novel's windmills had for Unamuno (1905): they represent the technology that overcomes humanism. Ultimately, the protagonists are made laughable, even while their enterprise could be fully justified.[6]

The analysis of navigation trails in relation to the interpretative achievements of different browsers should provide us with insights that concern not only the mechanisms of constructing knowledge structures—clearly a major cognitive input—but also the ways of evaluating hypertext structures with respect to didactic goals and informal teaching: a direct contribution to hypertext theory of the kind sought by designers and programmers.[7] More specifically, it might explain some intriguing findings concerning two seemingly unrelated problems: the limited way most readers actualize allusions when reading literature, and the disappointing response of most readers to the interactive co-authoring option that hypertext fiction offers.[8] In view of my major research interests, I'll deal systematically, and in some detail, with the first problem

---

[6] This derision is the combined effect of the nature of caricatures and the evocation of the novel with its opposite interpretations.

[7] See, for example, this piece of evidence:
   From: jorn@MCS.COM (Jorn Barger)
   Subject: A fresh start for hypertext theory?Date: 7 Feb 1996 12:39
   Summary: tying design theory to cog sci
   [...] mostly all I'm after is some decent hypertext theory, that WWWeb designers
   can agree on, and seek guidance from [...]
   Theoreticians do not give us the needed framework. They don't see the relationship between their claims and actual hypertext engineering. So who needs them? [...]

[8] Contrary to the interest and love that likely readers of this article may have for hypertext fiction, and even to their experiences as enthusiastic teachers of the subject, the fact is that it didn't catch on. Michael Joyce has moved to writing print fiction, and young readers prefer games in which they become characters or write episodes to the problematic interactivity characterizing co-authoring through predetermined arbitrary browsing. On this point see Chaouli, 2006. Also, in spite of successful efforts to treat hypertext fiction as complex literature (e.g. Van Looy and Baetens, 2003), not one text has been received as "great" literature. Perhaps hypertext fiction needs to be evaluated and judged as a new art form, but this, of course, is beyond the scope of this paper.

area, and refer to the second in a few relevant places. This I'll do by presenting my current project from its roots in an earlier project.

With the way open for constructing inter-textually linked cultural clusters in hypertext form, I decided to replicate and upgrade an experiment that I had conducted thirty years ago (Ben-Porat 1978), and whose findings, I suspected, were strongly influenced by the constraints of sequential presentation. As part of a comprehensive study on allusions and readers, carried out in 1976, I presented participants with literary passages whose significations depended to some extent on the actualization of the allusions they contained. By actualization I mean the realization of the inter-textual relation obtaining between two texts and the ensuing potential for semantic transfer from the triggered text to the triggering one.[9] In the case of allusions, the obligatory use of a specific referenced text makes it possible to judge the validity of a particular interpretation in exact terms, and to find out a reader's cultural knowledge and procedural equipment: their familiarity with various literary canonic texts as well as their awareness of linguistic potentialities and literary devices on the one hand, and the ability or willingness to process such complex material in as exhaustive a manner as possible on the other.

The experiment was conducted in four stages. In the first, participants were given the passages and asked to answer a simple interpretative question: "What does the narrator feel or think about the subject matter of the passage in front of you?" In the second, participants were asked explicitly about the presence of expressions known to them from other literary sources and were requested to indicate these expressions and identify them as fully as possible. In the third stage, the initial question was repeated in order to find out if and what improvement had been brought about by raised awareness. In stage 4 (which took place at a different sitting one or two weeks later), all the relevant information concerning the allusion was given to the participants and the first stage was repeated.

The passage cited below turned out to be the most appropriate choice for this type of inquiry. A correct answer to the interpretative question depends almost completely on full actualization of the allusion. This passage comes from a story that describes a horse running away from work near a construction site. Although published in the early 1960s, the story is associated with the author's childhood and is almost always read with reference to the pioneering period of the Jewish community in Eretz-

---

[9] It is enough to recall what the use of *Don Quixote* adds to the depiction of the Austrian Kanzler and his war against the Czech nuclear reactors to understand what I mean.

Israel. Moreover, the passage is taken from the description of a ploughing scene at the beginning of the story, before the horse runs away and musters the reader's sympathy:

> And here all this time a certain rectangle keeps growing up, loose and future-pregnant. It is the same in our yard and across the street from us, nearby, around the house of our lately arrived neighbour, Arieh, which stands in the vast opening that surrounds it all around. One yard, and yet another yard, and more layers of earth, saved from its meaninglessness, enclosed by a crust growing thorns and insignificant wild flowers, in order for the ultimate establishment of good order for the sake of the good future, in preparation for the days-to-come, about which songs are being sung, when, Amen and Amen, a dense community will grow here, *a house joined to a house, a field added to a field*, a tree to a tree, dense and orderly and closed.
>
> S. Yizhar: *The Runaway* (1964) [my translation]

The key element, indicated in bold script, contains an allusion to a theoretically well-known (studied at least twice in Israeli schools) source text:

> *Woe to those who join house to house, who add field to field*, until there is no room, and you are made to dwell alone in the midst of the land. The Lord of hosts has sworn in my hearing: Surely many houses shall be desolate, large and beautiful houses, without inhabitant, for ten acres of vineyard shall yield but one bath, and a homer of seed shall yield but an ephah.
>
> Isaiah V: 8-10

Without actualizing the allusion, and because of the historical context, it is possible to attribute to the narrator a positive attitude towards the depicted future, even though there are enough stylistic features that would make it at least ambiguous for a sensitive reader. And indeed, during stage 1, 70% of the participants (109) misread the passage in this positive way. Three of them (roughly 3%) mentioned the allusion. Only 20% (31) interpreted it correctly, pointing out the narrator's negative attitude, with three of these (10%) mentioning the allusion. The rest gave neutral answers, attributing an ambiguous attitude to the narrator. To our great surprise, there was little improvement between stage 1 and stage 3, regardless of the participants' achievements in stage 2 (noticing the allusion and identifying its source). The activated material was not perceived as relevant. Unfortunately, only 57 (out of the 124) participants who gave wrong or neutral answers in stages 1 and 3 participated in stage 4, where they were given the Biblical passage. The results are still highly significant. Not only did the participants receive all the relevant information, but it could even be argued that by then they were "led by the nose" toward interpretative realization of the negative attitude clinched by the allusion. Yet, although this time there was a marked improvement—10 of the 57 participants now gave correct answers—there was still a remarkably large group (47) that insisted on holding on to their original mistaken interpretative hypothesis.[10] It is this finding which is most closely related to the limiting constraints of sequential reading on the one hand and, on the other hand, to questions concerning the inevitable deferral of constructing a dominant integrative hypothesis in reading fictional hypertexts. Cognitive reading models teach us that the processing of a text is done in stages. The first step in the interpretation of a text is the construction of an interpretative hypothesis as soon as enough material is processed from reading the text. This hypothesis becomes a sort of matrix for the construction of meaning. The following stages involve the mapping of added information onto that hypothesis and adjusting it to account for elements that would not fit in. For various reasons, not least among them cognitive economy (the need to save mental energy), readers tend to keep their original hypothesis as long as possible and use various reading strategies to do so. More often than not, new data requires reorganization of the knowledge structures constructed thus far, and a new hypothesis replaces the first (or current) one. Nevertheless, the need to have an interpretative hypothesis even when holding other options in limbo remains a major constraint of the process of interpretation.

---

[10] The most stubborn interpreters were participants with backgrounds in literary studies. They could use the professional conceptual arsenal (e.g. paradoxically, ironically, in opposition to) to deal with the gap between their positive interpretation and the negative thrust of the allusion. They might have also been trained to believe that interpretation is only signification and depends on the reader more than on the writer or the text. Whatever the explanation, this finding sheds interesting light on contemporary debates about culture and cognition, which cannot be elaborated here. On this issue see Nisbett, Peng, Choi and Norenzayan, 2001 and Nisbett, 2003. On the related issue of the effect of ideological and psychological factors on cognitive processing of ambiguous texts see Zwaan and Graesser, 1998 and also Ben-Porat, 1996. The findings support many cognitive reading models, such as those that claim that readers are self-motivated and self-directed (Fielding and Pearson, 1994), and the search-after-meaning theory (Graesser et al., 1994).

This constraint is challenged by fictional hypertexts in which readers move by arbitrarily chosen links towards unrelated segments that do not easily yield an interpretative hypothesis. Being disconnected in terms of the temporal and spatial dimensions of the fictional world, often in terms of (unidentified) speakers, the linked segments do not allow a reader to activate existing knowledge structures (frames or scenarios, genre models, previous reading experiences) and form the desired hypothesis. And yet, this is not a universal biological constraint on cognition. It has been found that experienced readers of hypertexts or of modern poetry (not to mention individuals who seem to be naturally so inclined) perform much better than novices and even enjoy reading a text without a dominant hypothesis guiding their process of interpretation. It seems that the need to retain a number of vaguely-formed interpretative hypotheses in limbo might develop a competence that could be an important addition to our arsenal of reading strategies. The testing of the assumption that exposure to different inter-textually-related textual segments in hypertext form would improve the processing and interpretation of allusive texts is one of the major goals of my present research project, to which I now turn.

This new project aims to study and re-contextualize some of the literary, cultural, educational and ideological problems surrounding the West European component in Israeli cultural memory (or memories), and hence in multi-cultural Israeli society *from the inter-textual perspective*, using the methods of Empirical and Experimental Studies of Literature. The main objectives of this re-contextualization are: to establish the cultural viability and significance of West European canonic literary texts with respect to distinct cultural communities in Israel; to find out the role played by the mass media with respect to canonic components of cultural memory, in particular their equalizing impact, with reference both to various cultural communities and to traditionally distinct and hierarchical cultural strata; *to gain understanding of the cognitive processes involved in the actualization of mass media/literary canon inter-textuality in its many forms, in relation to the double-edged significance of the mass media and popular culture that keep past canonic texts alive and simultaneously distort them*; to develop a model for the study of Israeli cultural memory in relation to any past canon which still has identifiable traces in the culture; and *to devise modes of enhancing and reactivating effaced canonic elements wherever necessary*. Successful use of CULTOS-type digitized inter-textual clusters by various distinct groups of Israelis will validate the claim that an inter-textual cluster is a useful tool in the service of cultural memory because of its attractiveness to and concordance with the age of digital culture, as well as its culturally hybrid nature and explicit (tagged) inter-textual links.[11]

In the experiment, alongside the Don Quixote "tilting at windmills" Cluster, and other clusters constructed around well-known texts, ranging from *Hamlet*'s famous soliloquy ("To be or not to be") to *The Little Prince*'s "draw me a sheep", we decided to use a cluster centred on the Biblical story of Jacob and Rachel. In accordance with the policy of including as many popular traces of a particular canonic text when constructing a thread around it (explained above), this cluster contains a number of songs that present, refer to, or otherwise activate the Biblical story. The text (lyrics in the song system) of one of them was included in the 1976 "allusion processing" experiment described above. In this, participants received two versions of Rachel's "Sad Song", a lyric poem from the 1930s which became extremely popular when set to music in the 1960s (it has stayed in the popular system ever since):

Rachel: A Sad Song's closing stanza (manuscript version)

The last day of my life may soon transpire
Soon it will be time for parting tears;
I'll wait for you till my life expires
As Solveig has waited for so many years.

Rachel: A Sad Song's closing stanza (published and performed version)

The last day of my life may soon transpire
Soon it will be time for parting tears;
I'll wait for you till my life expires
As Rachel has waited for so many years.

These segments were presented to the participants in reverse chronological order: the published version preceded the manuscript. The motivation for this order was the assumption that the actualization of the allusion to Solveig would alert participants to the weakness of reading the simile as an allusion to Rachel, the matriarch. Although the Bible tells us nothing about Rachel's love for Jacob, and although she waited for him only seven years and one week (which would make her twenty years old at the most), her story is most often mentioned as the text that the simile

---

[11] In spite of the different wording of the project's goals, quoted from the project proposal, I trust the reader to see how "allusion processing" actually underlies the experimental part of the project. The methodology of studying this cognitive aspect will be spelled out later on.

alludes to. Our experiment was no exception. We hoped that after becoming aware of the content of the referenced text, Ibsen's Peer Gynt, in which the loving Solveig waits for Peer, who returns when she is very old, participants would reconsider their immediate identification, and that this would lead them in another direction, or would at least allow them to improve their comments on the function of the allusion when they returned to the interpretation question in stage 3, but this did not happen.[12] In the new experiment, however, the mode of presentation is different and varied because of the hypertext form and additional research questions.

All the participants in the experiment, from the innocent browser searching for songs performed by "The High Windows," to the Junior High student looking for material about the poet Rachel, encounter, at some point in their browsing, a screen with the whole text in which the title "Sad Song" is marked as a linked node. Clicking on this node takes them to a screen presenting segments of the two versions (manuscript and published), together with information about the inter-textual relation that links the two texts (Illustration 4). Moreover, the annotations ("published" or "manuscript version") make it possible to perceive the chronological order of the two texts, as does the commentary (in the text box on the left) that defines this inter-textual relation as "conversion", thereby implicitly suggesting the potential dis/similarity between the two comparisons.

---

[12] Here too, as with the primary interpretative hypothesis in the previous example, the initial identification, solidly grounded in the cultural context surrounding the poem (the poet's name, other poems in which she identifies with the matriarch, popularity of a cultural love myth inaccurately based on the biblical story, etc.), has not been changed, even in stage 4 when all the necessary information was clearly presented.

Illustration 4

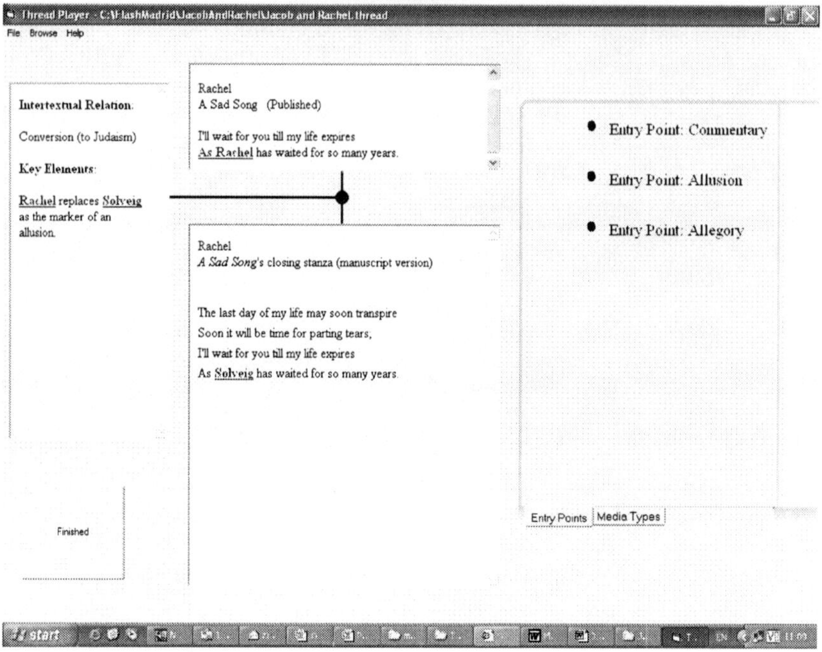

Participants can now continue to click on internal links, move out of the cluster or choose items (hence screens) from the menu. Within the framework of the experiment, they are divided into groups whose ability to navigate will be controlled differently. One group will not have access to the menu; another will not be able to leave the cluster; the third group will have only one clicking option on each screen, while another will have several options, including list boxes. Furthermore, there will be control groups that will work outside the clusters altogether. Such a group may, for example, receive a screen with the two versions followed by the questions, and instructed that it can use the Internet to search for any information it may need in order to answer them. Another group may not even have the questions; these will be given after the browsing time (not yet decided) is over. These groupings should allow us to judge the efficiency of the hypertext form and the effect of different hypertext structures on the process of interpretation.

Actualizing Allusions: Hypertext and Cognitive Literary Research   75

Illustration 5

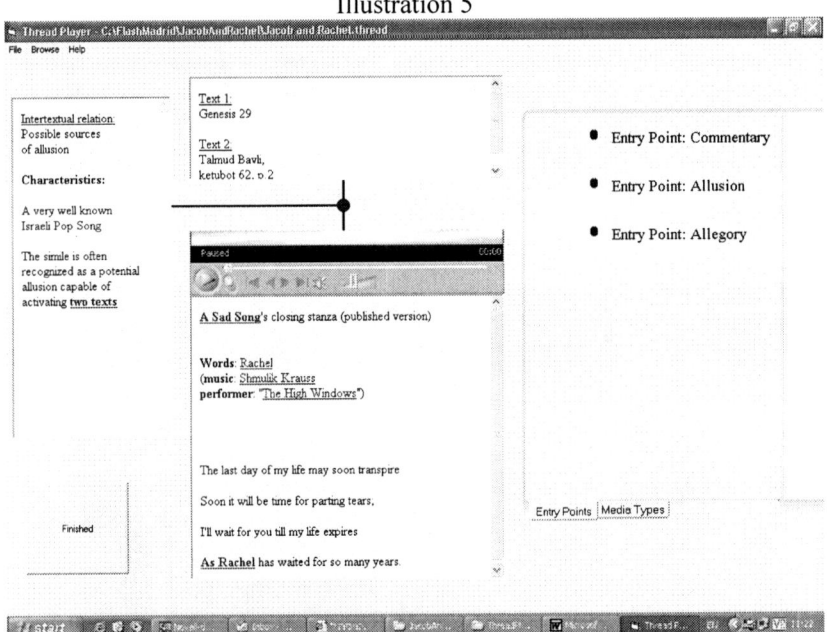

In the most closely controlled browsing option, participants click on "as Rachel", and the list box familiarizes them with two potential source texts for the allusion (Illustration 5). We assume that this form of alert might destabilize the typical automatic identification of "Rachel" as the matriarch and leave the participants open to consider the Talmudic story (Illustration 7), read before or even after the Biblical story (Illustration 6), as a more appropriate interpretative option for the simile. To give the Talmudic allusion even more strength, this highly predetermined navigation trail will take participants through the "back" command button (situated at the bottom left side of the screen) to the screen with two versions, from which they can access the Solveig screens (not included in the illustrations). Easy access to the play's final scene, in printed and performed versions, will provide the users of the cluster with the necessary information about the semantic content of the reference to Solveig. Even if they have no prior knowledge of the play, users should now have enough information to answer the attached interpretative questions of the experiment correctly.

Illustration 6

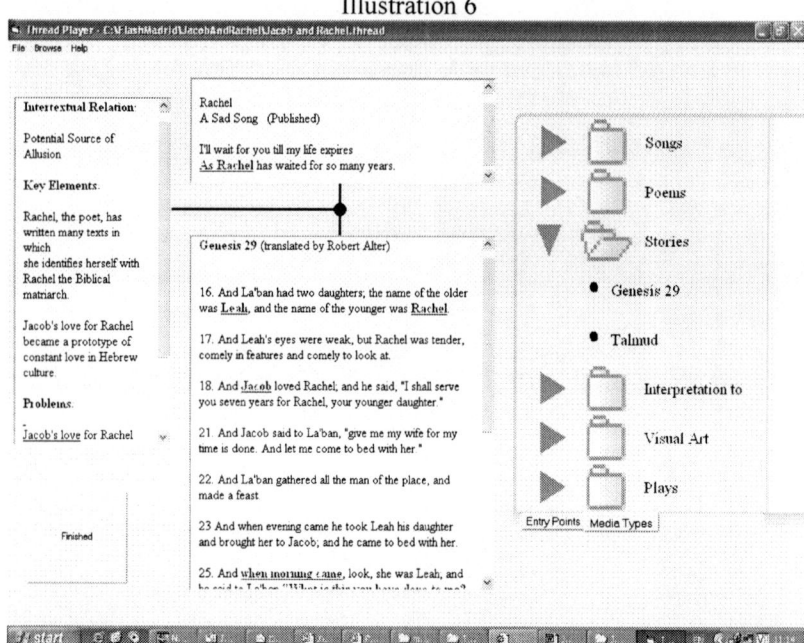

For example, after writing a short answer to the open question, copied—with the necessary adjustments—from the first experiment (i.e. What does the narrator feel or think about the subject matter of the two segments from Rachel's "Sad Song" that you have encountered while navigating the cluster?), participants have to answer a number of closed questions, such as:

I. Which of the following statements is incorrect?

1. The matriarch Rachel resembles Solveig in having to wait a long time for her lover.
2. The matriarch Rachel resembles Solveig in taking her lover back with love when she is already an old woman.
3. Kalba Savua's daughter (the Talmudic Rachel) resembles Solveig in taking her husband back with love when she is already an old woman.

(The correct answer, of course, is 2).

Actualizing Allusions: Hypertext and Cognitive Literary Research

Illustration 7

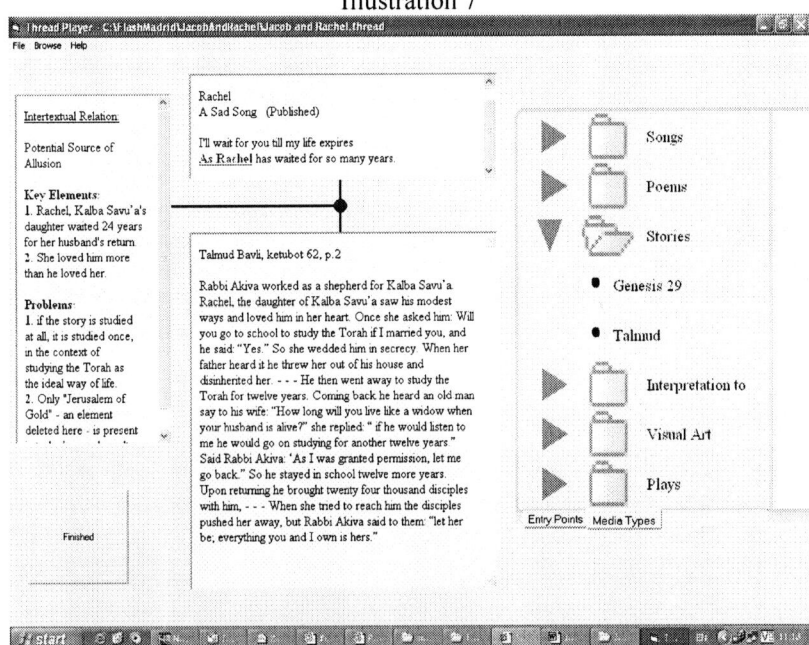

II. Which of the following statements fits more accurately with the interpretation that the poem reads as a hopeless love song?

1. The speaker identifies herself with the Biblical Rachel.
2. The speaker identifies herself with the Talmudic Rachel.
3. The speaker identifies herself with Solveig.

(The correct answer here is 3).

These examples should suffice as an illustration of the methods by which we plan to study the effects of non-sequential reading on the possibilities of constructing knowledge from discrete pieces of information in relation to reading habits, the presence of conflicting potential sources for the allusions contained in the similes, and the role of suspended hypothesizing in comprehending the text.

Our expectations are quite obvious and may even seem trivial. We would expect the participants working with the highly-controlled and most informative cluster to do much better than members of the other groups and participants in the fourth stage of the 1976 experiment. The comparative study of the findings of the two experiments is not a trivial matter. Because of the different way the information is handed to participants, this comparison is crucial for assessing the role of suspended hypothesizing. The situation is different for clusters built around texts that were not included in the earlier study. In these cases, differences in achievements between the various groups should come to the fore and provide pertinent insights. For example, the correspondences between specific levels of organization or controlled navigation and the ability to combine unrelated pieces of information into a story might help us to construct a model hypertext for either formal or informal education. Unfortunately, although the few results of sketchy pilot studies seem promising, we have to wait until the completion of the project before we can formulate and publish any conclusions. Even our certain contribution to the task, implicit in the claim that "a comprehensive model of reading hypertexts should integrate basic text comprehension mechanisms with the specific strategies required by this [hyper-textual] presentation" (Rouet, Levonen, Dillon and Spiro, 1996), will have to wait. For the moment, we have to be content with demonstrating the potential of hypertext for cognitive literary research.

Bibliography

Books

Bolter, J. D. *Writing Space: The Computer, Hypertext, and the History of Writing*. Hillsdale, N.J.: LEA, 1991.

Britton, B., and A.C. Graesser. *Models of Understanding Texts*. Mahwah, N.J.:L. Earlbaum Associates, 1996.

Floridi, L. *Philosophy and Computing–An Introduction*. London: Routledge, 1999.

Gillies, J., and R. Cailliau. *How the Web was Born*. Oxford: Oxford University Press, 2000.

Landow, G. *Hypertext: The Convergence of Contemporary Literary Theory and Technology*. Baltimore & London: Johns Hopkins University Press, 1992.

Naughton, J. *A Brief History of the Future: The Origins of the Internet*. London: Phoenix, 1999.

Nisbett, R.E. *The Geography of Thought: How Asians and Westerns Think Differently... and Why*. New York: Free Press, 2003.

Rouet J-F, J.J. Levonen, A. Dillon and J.R. Spiro (eds.). *Hypertext and Cognition*. Mahwah, N.J.:L. Earlbaum Associates, 1996.

Sperber, D. *Explaining Culture: A Naturalistic Approach*. Oxford: Blackwell, 1996.

Sperber, D. and D. Wilson. *Relevance: Communication and Cognition*. Oxford: Blackwell, 1986.

Van Looy, J., and J. Baetens. *Close Reading New Media: Analyzing Electronic Literature*. Leuven: Leuven University Press, 2003.

Zwaan, R.A., and A.C. Graesser (eds.). *Constructing Meaning during Reading*. Mahwah, N.J.:L. Earlbaum Associates, 1998.

Compilations

Ben-Porat, Z. "Cognitive Poetics and the Experimental Study of Literature". *Language and Literature Today: Proceedings of the XIX Congress of FILLM (Brasilia 1993)*, Neide de Faria (ed.). Brasilia: Universidade de Brasilia, 1996, 818-829.

—. "Sad Autumn and Cultural Representations: A Comparative Study of Japanese and Israeli *Autumn*". *The Psychology and Sociology of Literature*. G. Steen and R. Schram (eds.). Amsterdam: John Benjamins, 2001: 243-260.

Articles

Ben-Porat, Z. "Reader, Text and Literary Allusion: Aspects in the Actualization of Literary Allusions". *Ha-Sifrut* 26 [in Hebrew. English summary i-v] (1978): 1-25.

—. "Cultural Memory, Cultural History, and Cultural Canons in the Third Millenium". *Arcadia* 38, 2 (2003): 339-342.

Bush, V. "As We May Think". *Atlantic Monthly*, 176, July (1945): 101-8.

Chaouli, M. "How Interactive Can Fiction Be?" *Critical Inquiry* 31, 3 (2005): 599-617.

PART II

HYPER-(W)READER

MARÍA GOICOECHEA

The faculty of reading, which is at once a technological improvement and a cultural practice, becomes a rich field of study for the analysis of the intersection between technology and culture in the digital era. The act of reading, an activity affected by the evolution in both spheres, acquires diverse meanings, often in confrontation, ranging from the automatic decodification of text to a complex interpretative network where multiple dimensions (cultural, technological, social, historical and personal) fuse together and form various horizons of expectations with respect to the text and its value. The meaning attributed to the act of reading is placed under new scrutiny from the perspective of digital technology, igniting a revision of its history as well as an assessment of its present and future conditions.

The hyper-(w)reader constitutes one of the axes of the hyper-paradigm. For many, however, it is a foundational myth, an ideal reader yet to come, rather than an actualized function. According to Landow, computer technology transforms readers into reader-authors (or "wreaders"), since any contribution to the text can immediately be read by other readers, transforming footnotes or marginal commentary into public texts, with a subsequent democratizing effect.[1] Landow's statement triggers a series of responses, some of which are collected under this rubric. For some, the idea that in digital textuality the boundaries that previously separated readers from authors are blurring emerges as another digital utopia that has proved false; for others, it has become a reality, with other unsuspected ramifications.If previously-established notions of author, reader, literary canon and text as intellectual property have not been inevitable but are the result of an accumulation of social and political choices, the options made

---

[1] See "What's a Critic to Do? Critical Theory in the Age of Hypertext" in *Hyper/Text/Theory*. Baltimore: Johns Hopkins University Press, 1994: 14.

available by computer technology also confront us with crucial questions that have to be carefully reconsidered, as they will have a powerful effect in the future. Changes introduced by digital technology are not aleatory. It is therefore important to be aware of the ideological context in which they evolve, since they eliminate certain hierarchies but also establish new ones. The question is: who will benefit from the reconstruction of our culture by computers? Computer technology has already radically altered the concept of the book as a legal object. It is altering methods of publication and distribution, and is decentring access to information previously controlled by governments, educational institutions and libraries. However, the most fundamental changes we are facing have to do with the power of computer technology to alter the nature of texts and our relationship with them.

In his article, "The Boundaries of Digital Narrative: A Functional Analysis", Juan B. Gutiérrez tries to find a middle ground between the technophile and bibliophile perspectives. Classifying digital narratives as a separate art form from printed narratives, he nevertheless defends a compromise that would please readers and authors alike, and that will make digital narratives more attractive for both. He propounds a digital text that exploits the essence of digital media (for which he proposes the use of artificial intelligence to provide the text with autonomy through the manipulation of logic rules), and at the same time preserves the essence of narrative in the classical sense, that is, it allows the reader to experience immersion in the fictional world. Digital narrative, according to Gutiérrez, belongs to a paradigm that is separate from printed narrative, but which is still too young to have an established set of conventions. These conventions are necessary to permit readers and authors to concentrate on reading and writing and not on the constant exploration or creation of the interface (a movement that for dos Santos, as we saw previously, is an essential component of reading digital text).

When the hyper-(w)reader meets cyborgic text, a number of things can happen, and, as most of the authors in this section observe, the complexity of the reading activity is exponentially increased. The second article, "Some Notes on the Reading of Digital Literary Works" by Alckmar L. dos Santos, focuses on the double layer of the digital text, the programming code and the resulting text on the screen, and the exponential increase in complexity this duplicity entails for the analysis of the reading activity. For dos Santos, the ideal reader of the digital creation will need to have more than an average notion of computers and webs; he or she will have to cultivate a sensibility for reading the source-code as well, to "roughly comprehend the strategies and aesthetics of programming, thus opening up a path for their own interferences and effective understanding of the work." This sophisticated reader will be the perfect candidate for tempting into becoming a (w)reader. For this (w)reader, the text will open up like a toy, inviting him or her not just to inspect such code lines passively but to alter them at will. Double-layered text and its interstices reveal the infinitude of languages and their combinatory, chaotic, complex logic.

The last two articles of this section deal with the pleasure of reading in the digital media. Laura Borràs Castanyer (*"Lector in Machina*: Towards an Erotic of Reading"*) establishes an analogy between manuscript codices and computer screens, two spaces occupied by textuality at different times in its history. Through this analogy, she exposes the hidden corporeality and materiality of texts, and the cultural history that connects textuality with the five senses. Digital textuality is thus inscribed as another step in the history of creation and experimentation with words, sounds, images and different mediums—a history of creative tension between the creator and the materials.

The complexity inherent in digital textuality is circumvented by a nurtured sensibility that precedes the digital medium, a sensibility trained in reading illustrated manuscripts or visual poetry, led by a wandering eye which is free to rest anywhere on the page, enter the text through the back door, read it backwards, enjoy a panoramic view of it, or fix its attention on a small detail. In any case, the pleasure of the text relies more on an aesthetic, intuitive, direct perception of it than on "a cerebral discovery of sense".

Alexandra Saemmer further elaborates on Borràs' idea that texts on electronic supports are read more like images while conserving their meaning. In "Reading Guidelines for Electronic Literature", she explores the effect of hypertext and animation on the meaning of texts. Coinciding with Gutiérrez' thesis, Saemmer has observed several tendencies in a new generation of creators using electronic supports. A return to narrativity (in opposition to the fragmentation of non-linear texts) is one of them, as well as the exploitation of the autonomous function of "programmed literature". Providing concrete examples of the concepts explored in Borràs' article, Saemmer offers a detailed "phenomenology" of link processing and reception. Finally, she takes the discussion one step further by focusing on "animated" calligrams, which "break the 'simultaneity' of drawings and inscribe them into the logico-temporal process of reading". According to Saemmers, it is in interactive and animated poetry, rather than in hyperfiction, that the new qualities of text on electronic media are to be found.

CHAPTER FIVE

THE BOUNDARIES OF DIGITAL NARRATIVE:
A FUNCTIONAL ANALYSIS

JUAN B. GUTIÉRREZ

1. Introduction

A study conducted by the National Endowments for the Arts (NEA, 2004), "Reading At Risk: A Survey of Literary Reading in America", reports a drop in levels of reading of *printed narrative* in all groups studied between 1982 and 2002, with the steepest rate of decline in the youngest age group (18-24, 28%). While the report shows an accelerating decline of 10% in readers of printed books, it also mentions an increase of 30% in the number of people doing creative writing during the same period. The rate of decline tripled during the nineties, which corresponded historically to the popularization of personal and networked computing. The Internet seems to be the cause of this decrease in the rate of reading, since the demographic group with the highest reading rates is also the group with the highest use of the net. It is unlikely that America is becoming illiterate, precisely when there is an unprecedented amount of textual information freely available. Additionally, it is counter-intuitive that there are more writers and fewer readers. What is most likely happening is that we are in the middle of a shift from printed media to digital media; people are starting to use digital media to read everything from news to fiction, and also to write.

While reading some narrative pieces in digital devices is practically the same as reading them on paper, the focus of this paper is on those narrative pieces that are designed specifically *for* the computer. In this paper, I will refer to narrative pieces mediated *by* and designed *for* digital media as *digital narrative*, as opposed to the traditional *printed narrative*.

The first question at this point is: If reading of *printed narrative* is decreasing and Internet use is increasing, are readers switching to narrative originally written for printed media but delivered through an electronic device? This question is particularly difficult to answer because there are no studies that explore this type of reading in a statistically significant population. We can observe the known facts, if only to realize how difficult it is to conduct a reliable analysis. First of all, *printed narrative*, comprising novels, short stories and plays, attracted 47% of those American readers 18 or older in 2002 (96 million people), down from 56% in 1982 (NEA, 2004). Secondly, electronic books, which most of the time correspond to electronic versions of printed pieces, or electronic pieces faithful to the printed text paradigm, have seen a steady two-digit annual market growth during the last few years (IDPF, 2005); however, the size of their annual market ($11M) is negligible compared to the market size of the printed book. Finally, at this point it is not possible to consolidate readers' use of the Internet as a source of *printed narrative*, because there is an ever-growing list of distribution channels (e.g. practically all major libraries, Project Gutenberg, etc.) as well as distribution channels that are unaccounted for.

The next question is: Are readers being attracted to online reading of literary pieces designed *for* the computer, i.e. *digital narrative*? Fiction for digital media, initially named literary hypertext or hyperfiction, experienced significant theoretical development during the nineties, which was not followed by the proportional development of a market. It was proposed and widely accepted that: (i) reader's choice, intervention and empowerment were the key elements of literary hypertext[1] (Landow, 1997), (ii) hypertext reading fostered both passive and active reading where links provided decision points (Snyder, 1999), and (iii) the suggestive power of literary hypertext lies in the lyric quality of links; lyric because of its particular intensity when searching for meaning, similar to the way we read poetry (Tosca, 2000). While it is impossible at this point to tell with certainty how many readers have switched from reading *printed narrative* to reading *digital narrative*, anecdotal evidence suggests that such a change is not occurring. The level of consumption of *digital narrative* seems to be a far cry from that of *printed narrative*.

There is experimental evidence reported by Gee (2001) that refutes the premises described above regarding literary hypertext. According to her experiment: (i) multi-linearity causes disorientation and results in readers skimming rather than reading, (ii) readers want a single starting point, (iii) they prefer more or less linear narrative structures with moderate branching, and (iv) they do not seem to be clamouring to be co-authors or

---

[1] This is a utopian assumption from the early nineties that has been challenged many times. It basically points out that links can give readers more control than printed text does.

become empowered. The work by Gee has special significance because it seems to be the only empirical study on readers of *digital narrative*; however, these results might not be accurate because only one tool was used (Storyspace) and generalization to other systems of reading might not be valid. Since most of the web systems used to compose literary hypertext work with client-side technology, and those working with server-side technology do not seem to track user interaction, there is no way to consolidate users' behaviour beyond anecdotal and subjective information. The scenario laid out shows a decrease of reading rates in *printed narrative*, and uncertainty about whether *digital narrative* has captured these readers or not. The question at the core of this paper is: How could we write fiction in digital media so that it is attractive to readers and a viable option for authors?

This paper is organized as follows: Section 1 (Introduction) describes the problem of uncertainty about the current levels of reading in digital media. Section 2 (Video Games versus Literature) presents the cognitive differences between different formats used to present narrative and emphasizes the need of semiotic elements specific to *digital narrative*. Section 3 (Fabula, Plot and Rhizome) describes the time-dependence of the reading process, and relates the classic concepts of fabula and plot to the concept of rhizome. This step is considered necessary to establish a clear distinction between *printed narrative* and *digital narrative*. Section 4 (*Digital Narrative* as a Cybertext) presents the analysis of the reading process as a 3-tier system with a feedback loop, connects the concept of cybertext's feedback with the concepts of plot and fabula and contextualizes the concept of cybertext in *digital narrative*. Section 5 (Artificial Intelligence) defines the scope of intelligence in *digital narrative* systems, and defends the position that in cybertexts mediated by the computer some level of autonomy in necessary to produce feedback loops. Section 6 (Discussion) explores the importance of narrative in cognitive development and the importance of finding appropriate forms of expression of narrative in digital media.

2. Video Games versus Literature

Defining the object of study of *digital narrative* is not an easy task. What is *digital narrative*? What is new media? These are the questions that continue to plague this discipline, which tries to contain everything from Michael Joyce's *Afternoon* to Jaime Alejandro Rodriguez Ruiz's *Golpe de Gracia*. The boundaries of the discipline are not yet clearly defined, and they probably do not need to be. The only distinction that must be established for the purpose of this article is that of the use of interactivity, multimedia and text as narrative devices. The discussion necessarily passes through the field of video games, since some narrative pieces have incorporated these, e.g. *Golpe de Gracia*, and, at the same time, some video games have complex narratives, e.g. *Oblivion*.

Emphasis on the use of multimedia and interactivity is common in this discipline. While there is little debate as to whether interactivity and multimedia can make a piece of narrative more attractive, richer and/or more meaningful, such improvement is limited by the way information is processed in the brain. There is a big physiological difference between video games and literature as narrative devices. A gentle introduction to brain functional analysis (on which the argument below is based) is the now classic book by Carter (1999).

The brain is a complex organ that is functionally divided into zones. These zones are more or less the same in all individuals; however, there is some variation due to the brain's high plasticity and adaptability. Some parts are in charge of motor coordination, others of speech, others of language, etc. Every second, the brain receives through the bloodstream a limited amount of oxygen and glucose. When certain regions are used intensively, other regions decrease their activity in order to compensate for the demand in energy. This is easily seen when a person tries to execute several activities involving different parts of the brain; it would be physiologically impossible for the average person to do simultaneously such tasks as listening to a complex piece of music, reading a complicated book, performing some difficult movement and engaging in a conversation full of twists and turns.

Literature, as a linguistic activity, is processed in superior temporal lobe and the frontal lobe of the brain; it is here where superior cognitive processes, such as analytical thinking, mathematical ability and language processing, i.e. what defines us as humans. Video games, on the other hand, depend on eye-hand coordination, sound processing and spatial processing, which occur in the cerebellum, temporal lobe and visual cortex respectively. Since video games in general stimulate more the posterior zone of the brain, thus requiring glucose and oxygen, some higher cognitive processes located in the frontal lobe decrease in activity during a video game session. What happens then is lack of development of the language and thought centres through loss of opportunity.

It has been proposed that video games can have a positive effect on the development of certain cognitive abilities. In particular, it has been suggested that action video games modify visual selective attention and spatial processing ability (Green and Bavelier, 2003), that is to say, they further develop an area of the brain that is already highly evolved and specialized (the visual cortex). The diversity in video game paradigms further complicates analysis, since there are games that allegedly require analytical processing (e.g. strategy games).

The connection between higher cognitive processes and brain activity is complex and relatively unknown; it is currently the subject of intensive research. While individual analysis is very difficult, epidemiological analysis with large segments of the population might provide clues. Psychometricians are aware of a phenomenon called the Flynn effect, a tendency for scores on certain tests of intelligence to rise over time. It was reported by Sundet et al. (2004) that during the first two decades of the period 1950-2002, tests given to Norwegian conscripts produced increasingly better results, consistent with the ubiquitous Flynn effect. Gains began to slow in the 1970s and '80s, and the increase in scores for general intelligence stopped after the mid-1990s. Scores on tests of arithmetic skills in particular began to decrease after that time.

There are many factors that could influence the phenomenon reported by Sundet. A simple hypothesis that could explain it is the generalized decrease in development of the language centres that occurs when children and adults alike engage in activities that favour the use of zones of the brain that are *not* responsible for higher cognitive abilities. The influence of video games and other media were mentioned by Sundet as possible causes. The decrease in reading could also play a role; while there are no studies in Norway comparable to the NEA report, it can be inferred that a process similar to that in the US might have been present, since both nations are affluent and technologically advanced, and digital media has had a high penetration in the population.

Reading in general and reading narrative in particular have been considered a cornerstone of public education. For example, US Federal Law "The Goals 2000: Educate America Act" (Public Law 103-227) and its continuation, Federal Law "No Child Left Behind Act of 2001" (P.L. 107-110), with its "Reading First" initiative, emphasize the role of reading in the formation of citizens. While there was a politicized controversy about the implementation of these laws,[2] there was general agreement about the importance of the reading component. But not all reading is the same. There have been reported differences between reading narrative and

---

[2] "The Board of Directors of the International Reading Association (IRA) deplores the intentional mismanagement that occurred in the administration of the Reading First program by the U.S. Department of Education [...]" *International Reading Association. On Reading First.* First accessed on December, 15, 2006: http://www.reading.org/resources/issues/positions_reading_first.html

other types of books, what Mar et al. (2006) call *bookworms* (fiction readers) versus *nerds* (non-fiction readers). The latter show a lower level of development in emotional intelligence. Early reading is the best predictor of later reading comprehension and other cognitive abilities; specifically, it has been found that frequent readers of *printed narrative* are more critical of the world, more engaged in community activities and less likely to accept erroneous or biased information (NEA, 2004). The function of *digital narrative* seems to be the natural continuation of the role played by the printed book in the past and, so far, in the present.

We can place a *boundary condition* on the definition of narrative. While it might be very difficult to define what narrative *is*, we can define with less difficulty what it is not (still a formidable task): *a digital object is not a piece of digital narrative if it does not make use primarily of the frontal lobe*. I acknowledge the fuzzy boundaries of this definition, but it corresponds to the fuzzy boundaries of *digital narrative* itself. I must emphasize that this biological analysis is not reductionism, since it does not try to explain all processes that take place during reading. It is reductionism, however, to ignore the biological component in the analysis of the complex processes involved in reading narrative.

In the age of multimedia, *printed* and *digital narrative* seem to be inevitably destined to lose ground to multimedia and video games. While multiple media elements could enrich the reader's experience, it must be stressed that we do not know anything else that could replace reading as an enhancer of language development and therefore, in most people, an enhancer of intellectual ability. A study conducted by Cunningham and Stanovich (1998) showed that while the rank[3] of a median word in a normal conversation between college graduates, as well as in TV shows, is nearly 500, the rank of the median word in an adult book more than doubles that number. Even a children's book has a median word (627) with a higher rank than normal speech between educated adults. It is immediately evident that most speech is lexically impoverished, as compared to written language.

Written text delivered through a computer with moderate multimedia elements seems to be a viable option for producing narrative for digital media in a way that preserves the cognitive development fostered by *printed narrative*. At this point it is necessary to raise the question: What makes narrative delivered through a computer something specific to digital media, i.e. *digital narrative*? The answer to this question in this

---

[3] Rank is defined as the position of a word in a list of all words of a specific language, the list being sorted by word frequency. The most common word has rank 1.

paper will be geared towards finding the elements of *digital narrative* that preserve the cognitive function of *printed narrative*, but in a format appropriate for digital media.

3. Fabula, Plot and Rhizome

In *Mille Plateaux (A Thousand Plateaus)*, Deleuze et al. (1987) explain their image of the rhizome, a metaphor for various invisible connections. They contend that "The rhizome is altogether different, a *map and not a tracing*". Thus, as opposed to hierarchical or deterministic structures, such as trees, which have starting and ending points, the rhizome is a spatial metaphor that does not favour a particular path but offers instead a milieu for traversal.[4] While the rhizome has been identified with a geometrical construct, it is the reader, during the reading process, who makes the rhizome come to realization.

It is convenient to differentiate between the story told as a linear sequence of temporal episode-based moments and the way that story is told, not necessarily as a linear sequence, i.e. *fabula* and *plot*. Sometimes the distinction is difficult because of phenomena such as *analepsis* or the explanation of events that happened in the past but have not yet been discovered, and *prolepsis* or the anticipation of events still to happen (Genette, 1997; Calvi, 1999). Given a set of pages in a piece of *digital narrative*, the *plot* corresponds to the sequence of pages the reader selects among many options. The *fabula* does not depend upon the development of the reading process in time; it remains unchanged. The *plot* is time-dependent and corresponds to the way the reader explores the *narrative space*. Readers in Gee's experiment indicated that they preferred a linear story; in fact, they were complaining about the difficulty of building a *plot*.

When we consider the *fabula* as a *rhizome*, it becomes the map of a *narrative space*. The *plot* is the temporal fulfilment of the rhizome, or the development in time of a set of possibilities. The covering of the *rhizome* is mediated, in the case of *digital narrative*, by the computer. Therefore, the *plot* is the result of the interaction in time between reader and computer.

The classical approach to analysing a *plot* suggests that it is comprised of five basic parts: (i) introduction, (ii) rising action, (iii) climax, (iv) falling action, and (v) resolution. These sections are well defined in the paper universe and correspond to the initial chapters (i), the intermediate

---

[4] Mark Marino, personal communication.

chapters (ii, iii & iv) and the final chapters (v). These five parts still exist in *digital narrative*, but they do not depend on the order the fiction work is read; they depend instead on the knowledge readers acquire about the *fabula*. Therefore, introduction is the *period* in which readers familiarize themselves with the *narrative space*; rising action, climax and falling action are the *periods* in which readers comprehend what the tensions are and how conflicts develop in the *fabula*; resolution is the *period* in which readers finish the reading, either because they have read all the available text or because they have abandoned it. It is crucial to emphasize that these reading stages of the *plot* are displaced from the *spatial realm*, i.e. a book's page sequence, to the *temporal realm*, i.e. the order in which the fiction is read. It is the temporal dimension that allows us to have multiple *plots* in a *fabula*.

A natural question at this point is: Can a computer help in the discovery of the *narrative space*, i.e. the construction of the *plot*? There are several approaches to this question. First of all, it is possible, in principle, to build a device that creates narratives automatically—dialogues, actions, etc.—in such a way that they respond to user interaction (Bolter and Joyce, 1987). However, in practice this type of algorithmic literature has been more focused on interactive fiction,[5] one of the most recent examples being *Façade*.[6] Secondly, significant work has been done by proponents of *adaptive literary hypertext*, i.e. the dynamic creation of links on each page, based on previous choices a reader made. Mostly, it can be divided into two types of system (Calvi, 2004): (i) conditionality-based systems: certain rules are triggered when specific conditions are met. Examples of conditional systems are *Storyspace* (Bernstein, 1998) and *Connection Muse* (Kendall, 2000); some variations around this theme are what Bernstein et al. (2002) call calligraphic versus sculptural hypertext, that is, hypertext built by the addition of links between episodes, or by their removal. (ii) Adaptivity-based systems: the choice of which conditions to meet depends on the reader's interaction. An example of an adaptive system, though not literary-oriented, is *AHA!* (de Bra et al., 2003). A system that helped readers in the construction of the *plot* would exhibit a fundamental characteristic: it would adapt itself to the readers' interaction and, as a consequence, would provide each one of them with a potentially unique reading experience, i.e. a potentially unique *plot*. Before delving into the adaptivity capacity of the computer, it is

---

[5] Interactive fiction refers to software containing simulated environments in which players use text commands to control characters.
[6] *Façade, a one-act interactive drama*. URL: http://www.interactivestory.net. First accessed 06/2006.

necessary to explore the concept of cybertext and the feedback loops that occur between reader and computer.

4. *Digital Narrative* as **Cybertext**

The term *cybertext* is derived from the word *cybernetics*, coined by Norbert Wiener in his book *Cybernetics, or Control and Communication in the Animal and the Machine* (1948), and comes from the Greek word *kybernetes* - helmsman. The fundamental idea in the development of the theory of *cybernetics* is the concept of *feedback*: a portion of information produced by the system that is taken, totally or partially, as input. *Cybernetics* is the science that studies control and regulation in systems in which there is both flow and *feedback* of information. The term *cybertext* was brought to the literary world's attention by Aarseth (1997); his concept of cybertext focuses on the organization of the text in order to analyse the influence of the media as an integral part of literary dynamics. According to Aarseth, cybertext is not a genre in itself; in order to classify traditions, literary genres and aesthetic value, we should inspect texts at a much more local level. The concept of cybertext offers a way to expand the reach of literary studies to include phenomena that are perceived today as foreign or marginal (Aarseth, 1997). In Aarseth's work, cybertext denotes the general set of text machines which, operated by readers, yield different texts for reading. In the case of *digital narrative*, this means that multiple *plots* are created for different readers. The only difference between different *plots* would be user interaction, i.e. the system would be adaptive.

Cyber has become a prefix that loosely means "through the use of a computer". Words like cyberspace, cyberphobia, cybersex, etc. have appeared in the last two decades. Cyberspace, coined by William Gibson in 1982, became a metaphor for the Internet. However, the prefix *cyber,* if derived correctly from the original meaning of *cybernetics,* is device-independent since it implies a *process* within a system. While popular culture usually adopts terms of imprecise meaning, the academic community should not. Reportedly, Markku Eskelinen at Digital Arts and Culture'99 in Atlanta declared the death of hypertext literature (Montfort, 2001): "In the meantime, please forget hypertext fiction. It stayed static and cybertext fiction replaced it." Likewise, Nick Montfort declared in a provocative essay that "cybertext killed the hypertext star" (Montfort, 2001). What these declarations indicate is that some forms of text offer greater loops of *feedback* than others.

In order to understand the connection between *cybernetics* and the reading of narrative, it is convenient to analyse the reading process as a 3-tier system (Gutierrez, 2002), as shown in Figure 1:

Figure 1. Three-tier decomposition of the reading process.

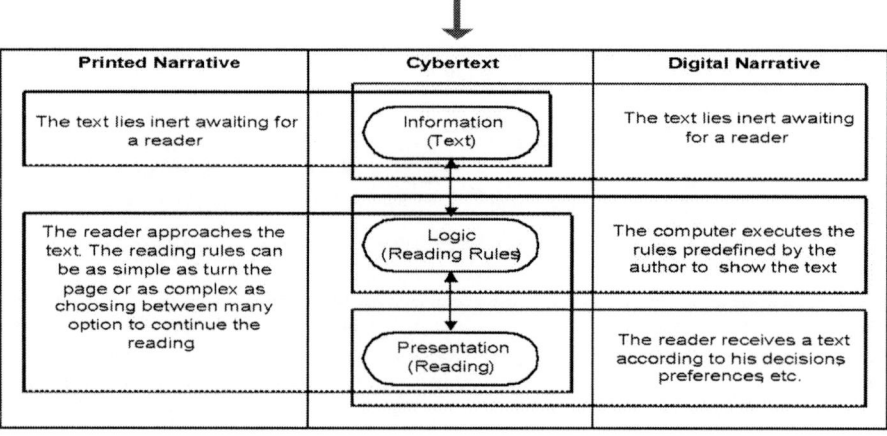

1. **Presentation Layer**: This is the physical rendering of the narrative piece, such as a sequence of physical pages or the on-screen presentation of the text.
2. **Logic Layer**: It is here that the rules necessary for reading a text lie. A reader of the Latin alphabet in *printed narrative*, for example, must scan the text from left to right, from top to bottom and turn the page after the last word of the last line. In *digital narrative*, this layer could contain the rules programmed in a computer for building a text output.
3. **Information Layer**: This is where the text itself lies. It is the set of words, images, video, etc., which form the *narrative space*

In this 3-tier system there are *feedback* and information loops. *Feedback* in a *printed narrative* is the information acquired by the reader as the text is read, which makes possible its subsequent understanding; in this case *feedback* is produced between the presentation layer and the information layer, which lie within the reader. In the case of *digital narrative*, the *feedback* is not only produced within the reader, but also in the interaction with the computer *if* the computer is involved in the construction of the *plot*. From the perspective of cybertext, the main difference between *printed narrative* and *digital narrative* is that of who executes the rules defined in the logic layer. Printed books place all the load of reading logic on the reader. Clearly, it is possible to do the same on a computer, and this seems precisely to be the complaint of those who say that hypertext is dead; in essence, their complaint is geared towards demanding greater autonomy from the computer.

In the proposed 3-tier model, the *feedback* of the system is not only possible, but is also a *sine qua non* condition for literary exchange. It is the continuation of McLuhan's asseveration that: "the media is the message". In *digital narrative, the media acts on the message.* The cycle of *feedback* in *digital narrative* is: (*i*) Readers receive a piece of information and, based on this, they execute a new interaction with the system, (*ii*) The computer then takes that input and applies logic rules that have been programmed into it by the author. (*iii*) The computer takes content from the information layer and renders it to the reader in the presentation layer, and (*iv*) the first step is repeated. Steps (*i*) through (*v*) describe a complete cycle of *feedback*, that is, the maximum realization of a cybertext.

It is a consequence of previous reasoning that *printed narrative* as well as *digital narrative* can be classified as cybertext. Therefore, the word cybertext should not be used to name a *digital narrative* subset. A word that describes *digital narrative*, that is, narrative designed *for* the computer, is *literatronic*. It comes from the Latin word *litera* (letter) and the Greek word that gave birth to the word electricity, *electron (*amber). Literatronic means a letter that requires electricity, or by extension, a letter that requires a computer. *Literatronic* works could not be reproduced on paper except, perhaps, as a reading path at a given moment. That is to say, a *literatronic* piece is a *fabula* or *map*, i.e. a *rhizome*, whereas its printed representation is a *plot*, i.e. a *tracing*.

5. Artificial Intelligence in *Digital Narrative*

By considering the computer as capable of participating in a feedback loop, we have to acknowledge its certain capacity for autonomy, i.e. a specialized artificial intelligence component. Artificial Intelligence (AI) is such a broad concept that it is very difficult to use it for describing something. It implies *perception, adaptation, behaviour*, and/or *learning* in computer systems. AI is a venerable field with active research and results from many directions, e.g. expert systems, fuzzy systems, case-based reasoning, etc. Tasks commonly thought to require intelligence in people were the focus of early AI research. A landmark paper by Turing in 1950 argued for the possibility of building intelligent computing systems, and proposed a test consisting of an independent observer trying to distinguish responses from two individuals, a computer and a person. If the observer could not identify the computer, it passed the test and was then considered to be intelligent.

A computer system does not need to have human-like intelligence in order to be considered intelligent. Ford and Hayes (1998) illustrated this point with an analogy between the development of mechanical flight and AI. Early efforts at mechanical flight were based on the noticeable features of birds, such as feathers and mobile wings. Successful mechanical flight, however, depended on understanding the underlying principles of flight and applying them to mechanical devices. Likewise, it is not necessary to reproduce, for example, human creativity in a computer in order to have AI. Although the underlying principles of human intelligence are not clearly defined, it is possible to build computer systems that exhibit some "intelligent" features.

From the perspective of a *digital narrative*, the computer that mediates the reading has:

1. **Perception**: This is given by the reader's input as a selection of options. Clearly, there is nothing wrong if only two options are offered to the reader, like "Next Page" and "Previous Page". A reader may also have several options available: for example, selecting the next page from a list of possibilities.
2. **Adaptation**: This can be understood as behaviour, and consists of adapting the text to the reader. Adaptivity may be time-dependent, user-dependent or group-dependent, etc. It becomes the author's role to decide what type of behaviour the system would exhibit.
3. **Learning**: The system could use past experiences to model future responses. This is closely related to adaptivity, but is not necessarily the same. For example, a system could have time-dependent adaptivity without ever considering user interaction.

From this point of view, an adaptive literary system could be considered a form of specialized AI engine that aims to optimize the *plot* for the reader. The level of autonomy described is what I call the *digital author*: the role of the computer in *digital narrative* when it builds links between pages in a way that corresponds to user interaction, i.e. when the computer completes a *feedback* loop with the reader. Adaptive *digital narrative* pieces reconfigure themselves for the reader, leading to a potentially unique read each time.

This behaviour has been reported in a *digital narrative* system (Gutierrez, 2006) in which adaptivity is achieved by an algorithm that approximates to a Hamiltonian cycle on a weighted graph, with weights varying in time according to a coupled set of ODEs, i.e. a non-linear dynamical system. The solution of a multi-terminal network flow on such graphs solves the optimization problem of minimizing hypertextual attraction (a measure of narrative continuity) and hypertextual friction (a measure of the risk of losing the readers' attention). This system stresses the importance of the temporal dimension of the *plot*, since this is what allows us to analyse reader-computer-author interaction with the powerful tools of dynamical systems.

6. Discussion

Since its inception *digital narrative* has been a field fraught with myths. These misconceptions were caused by poor knowledge about the underlying processes of reading and its associated cognitive developments. In particular, the early development of literary hypertext did not follow the scientific method in which (i) a hypothesis is established, (ii) an experiment is conducted to validate the hypothesis, and (iii) the hypothesis is validated or adjusted in the light of experimental evidence. In literary hypertext, the hypothesis was validated with little experimental evidence, practically derailing the field for a decade. The Internet could be fostering reading habits in the population. Popular tools like blogs, online news, online magazines, etc. are massively used. We simply do not know the extent of narrative consumption in digital media. The Internet is not attracting established authors from the world of *printed narrative*, and it is making it difficult for new writers to make a living writing *digital narrative*. A possible path is a symbiosis between *digital narrative* and *printed narrative*. One example of this is the *blogonovela— Más respeto que soy tu madre*—by the Argentinian Hernán Casciari. It started out as a blog, winning the Deutsche Welle Blog Prize in 2005. It then became a printed best-seller in Spanish. Essentially, it was first a piece of *digital narrative* that later became a piece of *printed narrative*. What is more, one is the image of the other. This does not necessarily indicate that *digital narrative* is popular among Internet users; however, it indicates that it is possible to write attractive narrative for the digital media.

One of the main arguments against hypertext put forward in the past by its opponents is the fragmented nature of the story offered to the reader. By incorporating basic AI behaviour it is possible to produce a feedback loop in the *cybertext*, such that the reader receives a *plot* that is optimized from the narrative perspective. That is to say, not only the reader receives a linear text most of the times but also a text that has narrative continuity. This raises a question: Are multi-linearity and fragmentation the goals of hyperfiction, or are they the product of the state of the art when the first literary hypertexts were produced? Is fragmentation a paradigm that we want to preserve? My intention is not to answer these complex questions here. However, I want to indicate that we have the ability to produce a text that exploits the essence of digital media, and at the same time preserves the essence of narrative in the classical sense: immersion.

Only when there are narrative pieces that make use of the digital media, i.e. pieces that could not exist otherwise, will we truly have *digital narrative*; otherwise, narrative on screen will be a super-extension of *printed narrative*. This raises another issue: Does *digital narrative* fall within the same category as *printed narrative*? Or is it something totally different, just as cinema is different from *printed narrative*? Rodríguez (2003) proposed that *digital narrative* is, in fact, essentially different from *printed narrative*.

It has been proposed in this paper that specialized AI could play a role in the field of *digital narrative*. However, it must be stressed that even though it is *possible* to use AI, it is not *necessary*. Undoubtedly, there are and will be many pieces of *digital narrative* that do not exhibit AI, not even in its most basic forms. The drive behind proposing AI is geared toward exploiting some of the main characteristics of digital media: autonomy and the manipulation of logic rules. The interdependence between medium and message still holds some surprises for us, as Morienau et. al (2005) discussed, with respect to the electronic book:

> ...because the electronic book is functionally closer to a computer than a traditional book (because of the support's inherently multi-functional nature) it does not provide the external indicators to memory that the classical book does, in that it does not serve as an unambiguous index to indicate a field of knowledge on the basis of its particular physical form.

The paradigm of *digital narrative* is different from the paradigm of *printed narrative*. In *digital narrative* we have to find what the conventions are. As described in Paul Saenger's *Space Between Words*,

The Origins of Silent Reading, over the course of the nine centuries following the fall of Rome, the task of separating words in continuous written text became a labour of professional readers and scribes, instead of the half-millennium tradition of using the individual reader's mind and voice for that purpose. That is how the space between words appeared. Such an elemental change, which has seemed so natural to all readers since first grade at school, took almost 4.000 years to develop. Other conventions in the printed media, such as page numbering, title pages, prefaces, tables of contents and indexes, appeared within a period of two centuries after Gutenberg's Bible; in other words, these elements took 4.500 years to develop.

What are the "conventions" in *digital narrative*? We have to start by mentioning that there is no *de facto* convention. Creators and editors have not reached consensus, in many cases because of the generalized belief that every work of *digital narrative* has to be new, thus the very idea of "convention in electronic literature" seems to be an oxymoron. Conventions, however, are needed because they permit the separation between presentation and content during the reading process, allowing readers to focus on what is being said, not on how it is being presented. Likewise, conventions help authors to focus on producing content, not on reinventing an interface every time. I propose that the minimum conventions in *digital narrative*, all of which can be automatically managed by an information system, have to do with: (i) volume indication, (ii) a map showing the structure of the information, (iii) an indication of what has and has not been read, and (iv) an ability to reset the reading on the reader's request.

The discussion on *digital narrative* necessarily passes through fields that leave the realm of classic literary studies, even in the sense of recent "classic" hypertextual theory. The study of the cognitive processes involved in narrative and human-computer interfaces becomes central, without reducing the importance of the classic aspects of literary studies. The influence of these previously unaccounted for elements is simply too big to be ignored. Understanding *digital narrative* and finding the way to make it attractive to authors and the greater public is a goal with a marked social dimension.

Bibliography

Aarseth, Espen J. *Cybertext: Perspectives on Ergodic Literature.* Baltimore: Johns Hopkins University Press, 1997.

Bernstein, Mark. "Patterns of Hypertext". In *Proceedings of the Ninth ACM Conference on Hypertext and Hypermedia*. ACM Press, 1998: 21–29.
Bernstein, Mark, David E. Millard, and Mark J. Weal. "On Writing Sculptural Hypertext". In *Hypertext '02: Proceedings of the Thirteenth ACM Conference on Hypertext and Hypermedia*. New York: ACM Press, 2002: 65–66.
Bolter, Jay David, and Michael Joyce. "Hypertext and Creative Writing". In *Hypertext '87:* In *Proceedings of the ACM Conference on Hypertext*. New York: ACM Press, 1987: 41–50.
Carter, Rita. *Mapping the Mind*. Berkeley: University of California Press, 1999.
Calvi, Licia. "'Lector in Rebus': The Role of the Reader and the Characteristics of Hyperreading". In *Proceedings of the Tenth ACM Conference on Hypertext and Hypermedia*. New York: ACM Press, 1999: 101–109.
—. "Adaptivity in Hyperfiction". In *Proceedings of the Fifteenth ACM Conference on Hypertext and Hypermedia*. New York: ACM Press, 2004: 101–109.
Cunningham, Anne E., and Keith E. Stanovich. "What Reading Does for the Mind". *American Educator/American Federation Of Teachers*, 1–8, Spring/Summer 1998. http://www.aft.org/ pubs-reports/american educator/spring sum98/ cunningham.pdf (First accessed June 2006).
De Bra, Paul, Ad Aerts, Bart Berden, Barend De Lange, Brendan Rousseau, Tomi Santic, David Smits and Natalia Stash. "AHA! The Adaptive Hypermedia Architecture". In *Proceedings of the Fourteenth ACM Conference on Hypertext and Hypermedia* . New York: ACM Press, 2003: 81-84.
Deleuze, Gilles, and Felix Guatarri. *A Thousand Plateaus: Capitalism and Schizophrenia*. Minneapolis: University of Minnesota Press, 1987.
Ford, J., and P. Hayes. "On Computational Wings: Rethinking the Goals of Artificial Intelligence". *Scientific American*, 9 (4) 1998: 78–83.
Gee, Kim. "The Ergonomics of Hypertext Narrative: Usability Testing as a Tool for Evaluating and Redesign". *ACM Journal of Computer Documentation (JCD)*, 25(1) 2001: 3–16.
Genette, Gerard. *Paratexts: Thresholds of Interpretations*. New York: Cambridge University Press, 1997.
Green, Shawn and Daphne Bavelier. "Action Video Game Modifies Visual Selective Attention". *Nature*, 423(29) 2003: 534–537.
Gutiérrez, Juan B. "Literatrónica - sobre cómo y porqué crear ficción para medios digitales." In *1er Congreso ONLINE del Observatorio para la*

CiberSociedad, Barcelona, Spain, 2002. Observatorio para la Cibersociedad.
http://cibersociedad.rediris.es/congreso/comms/g04gutierrez.html
(First accessed January 2003).

—. "Literatronic: Use of Hamiltonian Cycles to Produce Adaptivity in Literary Hypertext". *Proceedings of the Bridges Conference: Mathematical Connections in Art, Music, and Science*. Institute of Education, Uni-versity of London, August 2006: 215–222.

IDPF. *Industry eBook Sales Statistics 2005*. International Digital Publishing Forum:
http://www.idpf.org/doc_library/statistics/2005.htm
(First accessed December 2006).

Kendall, Robert. "Toward an Organic Hypertext". In *Proceedings of the Eleventh ACM Conference on Hypertext and Hypermedia*. New York: ACM Press, 2000: 161–170.

Landow George P. *Hypertext 2.0*. Baltimore: Johns Hopkins University Press, 1997.

Mar, Raymond A., Keith Oatley, Jacob Hirshaand, Jennifer de la Paz, and Jordan B. Peterson. "Bookworms versus Nerds: Exposure to Fiction versus Non-fiction, Divergent Associations with Social Ability, and the Simulation of Fictional Social Worlds". In *Journal of Research in Personality*, 40(5), October 2006: 694–712.

Montfort, Nick. "Cybertext Killed the Hypertext Star". *Electronic Book Review*, January 2001: http://www.altx.com/ EBR/ ebr11/ 11mon/ (First accessed June 2006).

Morineau, Thierry, Caroline Blanche, Laurence Tobin, and Nicolas Gueguen. "The Emergence of the Contextual Role of the E-book in Cognitive Processes through an Ecological and Functional Analysis". In *International Journal of Human-Computer Studies*, 62, 2005: 329–348.

NEA. *Reading At Risk: A Survey of Literary Reading in America*. National Endowment for the Arts, 1100 Pennsylvania Avenue, NW. Washington, DC 20506-0001, 2004.

Pajares Tosca, Susana. "A Pragmatic of Links". In *Proceedings of the Eleventh ACM Conference on Hypertext and Hypermedia*. New York: ACM Press, 2000: 77–84.

Rodríguez, Jaime Alejandro. *Teoría, Práctica y Enseñanza del Hipertexto de Ficción: El Relato Digital*. Bogotá, Colombia: Pontificia Universidad Javeriana, 2003.
http://www.javeriana.edu.co/relato_digital/ (First accessed September 2003).

Sundet, Jon Martin, Dag G. Barlaug, and Tore M. Torjussen. "The End of the Flynn Effect?: A Study of Secular Trends in Mean Intelligence Test Scores of Norwegian Conscripts during Half a Century". *Intelligence,* 32(4) July-August 2004: 349–362.

Snyder, Ilana. *Hypertext: The Electronic Labyrinth.* New York: New York University Press, 1999.

Turing, Alan. "Computing Machinery and Intelligence". In *Mind* (49), 1950: 433–460.

CHAPTER SIX

SOME NOTES ON THE READING OF DIGITAL LITERARY WORKS[1]

ALCKMAR L. DOS SANTOS

> Un livre ne commence ni ne finit : tout au plus fait-il semblant.
> —Mallarmé, *Le Livre*.

António Vieira spoke of sugar mills as a "sweet hell". Frequently, the reading of works in the digital medium makes us think of both the readings and the medium as an *exciting hell* because of the legion of signifiers, movements, gestures, images and interactions we are called upon to search, explore or propose. This plurality of possible significations, interpretations and meanings, which in the written and printed traditions was implicit information that remained as background to any reading, has broken its bounds, multiplying the instances of signification, the fields of sensible sedimentation and even the very signifiers. In other words, the digital medium, as is already well-known, has altered the materiality of the works we read both qualitatively and quantitatively. We are not talking here about the constant negligence of visual programmers, committed to the *ad nauseam* multiplication of figures, icons, interactions, plug-ins and PHP fields, etc. Extreme cases such as these merely illustrate slips that occur due to excesses inherent in the digital media and in literary works developed in this medium.[2]

---

[1] Translation by Otávio Guimarães Tavares.
[2] In this case, it is important to understand the distinction between excess and excessive that I consider in *Leituras de Nós*. São Paulo: Instituto Itaú Cultural, 2003. Excess would be the way to take advantage of the excessive characteristics that are frequently found in the digital medium; if it were not like this, we would be overwhelmed by informational hyperinflation and hindered from an effective appropriation of the digital medium and the works interacting with it.

We may take as an example an automatic generator: Pedro Barbosa's *Sintext* (accessible at http://cetic.ufp.pt/sintext.htm). By launching the automatic generation of *Didática*, we obtain:

>Vai ler uma sucessão automática de aforismos
>e
>fórmulas publicitárias experimentais em modo de demonstração.
>O texto será gerado electronicamente sem qualquer interrupção...
>Se pretender gerar o texto em ciclo infinito active o botão respectivo
>
>**
>
>Texto generativo
>concebido e realizado por
>Pedro Barbosa
>utilizando o Sintetizador de Texto Automático:
>versão Web - 1.1
>desenvolvida por José Manuel Torres
>1999
>(Centro de Texto Informático e Ciberliteratura
>)a partir do SINTEXT para DOS criado anteriormente
>por Abílio Cavalheiro & Pedro Barbosa
>(1995)
>
>*****
>
>"DIDÁTICA"
>(variações electrónicas)
>
>Para perguntas arrogantes, perguntas em êxtase .
>Quem faz perguntas cansadas, recebe respostas submarinas.
>A excelência do saber está na paixão de saber perguntar .
>O aluno faz perguntas exactas, o professor remói respostas na água.
>Grande é o saber do mestre que aprende o que não se pode aprender.
>Quem faz perguntas impertinentes, recebe respostas iracundas.
>O aluno faz perguntas exactas, o professor remói respostas impertinentes.
>Grande é a sapiência do mestre que aprende o que não se pode ensinar.
>A excelência do saber está na arte do interrogar .
>O aluno faz perguntas vomitadas, o professor remói respostas terrestres.
>Grande é o saber do mestre que ensina o que não se pode aprender.

The generation of phrases can be stopped by one click on "Parar Geração de Texto". Above the frame containing these automatically-generated phrases, there is another frame in which the programming that originates this automatic generation of phrases can be read:

{--------------------------------lexico-------------------------------}
[frase["O aluno faz perguntas "[1["cansadas "]1]", o professor remói respostas "[2["distraídas "]2]". "]frase]

[frase["Quem faz perguntas "[1["cansadas "]1]", recebe respostas "[2["distraídas "]2]". "]frase]
[frase["Para "[3["perguntas "]3][1["cansadas "]1]", "[3["respostas "]3][2["distraídas "]2]". "]frase]

[frase["Douto é "[nom1["o professor "]nom1][atr1["que ensina "]atr1][atr2["pelo prazer "]atr2][atr3["de aprender"]atr3]". "]frase]

[nom1["o mestre "]nom1]
[atr1["que aprende "]atr1]
[atr2["com a paixão "]atr2]
[atr3["de ensinar"]atr3]
[atr3["de interrogar"]atr3]

[frase["Grande é "[nom2["o saber d"]nom2][nom1["o professor"] nom1] [atr1 ["que ensina "]atr1][atr4["o que não se pode ensinar"]atr4]". "]frase]

With this, we already have at least two sets of signifiers that may be read. And reading, in the case of the programming lines, can only be a confirmation of what was done by the programmers, in other words, an inspection of such lines. But this reading can also be carried out in a more active way, undergoing direct interference from us as we modify elements or change programming sequences. But in this case, would not reading be turned into writing? Would not passive observation be turned into direct authorial interference? And yet, how do we account for the innumerable possibilities of juxtaposition and interference between: 1) automatically generated aphorisms; 2) interpretations we allow ourselves to make of them; 3) the lesser or greater understanding of the programming logics; 4) the modifications we can make to this programming; 4) the interpretations we make of the signifiers generated by our own programming?

Otávio Guimarães Tavares[3] has carried out a series of exercises in reading and reprogramming in *Sintext*. In one of these, he uses verses from Milton's *Paradise Lost,* with the following results:

---

[3] Member of the Núcleo de Pesquisas em Informática, Literatura e Lingüística (NUPILL).

Chapter Six

\<IN SEARCH OF PARADISE\>
(with fragments of the same)

Of all those myriads which we lead the chief;
Driven by a keen north-wind, that, blowing dry,
Left him at large to his own dark designs,
With floods and whirlwinds of tempestuous fire,
And after him, the surer messenger,
Pavilions numberless, and sudden reared,
Thy sleep dissent? New laws thou seest imposed;

Of unblest feet. Him followed his next mate;
Prone on the flood, extended long and large,
With ever-burning sulphur unconsumed.
In billows, leave i' th' midst a horrid vale.
Thus Satan, talking to his nearest mate,
Breaking the horrid silence, thus began:--
Would never from my heart: no, no! I feel

He looked, and saw the ark hull on the flood,
Bad influence into the unwary breast
With floods and whirlwinds of tempestuous fire,
On the other side Adam, soon as he heard
Quaff immortality and joy, secure
From standing lake to tripping ebb, that stole
Cast out from God and blessed vision, falls

The command lines entered in Sintext's programming field were:

[texto]In one moment, Paradise was lost
Lost beyond the reaches of man
Kept before the stars of his dreams

But, in an age where technology heaves with undying strength,
awaiting to consume all humanityperhaps, within the fragment of a moment
we may find a piece of what was lost

\<IN SEARCH OF PARADISE\>(with fragments of the same)
"
"
[ciclo000x7[
[frase["Of Man's first disobedience, and the fruit"]frase]
[tira-frase[
"
"

]ciclo000x7]
]texto]

[frase["Of that forbidden tree whose mortal taste"]frase]
[frase["Brought death into the World, and all our woe,"]frase]
[frase["With loss of Eden, till one greater Man"]frase]
[frase["Restore us, and regain the blissful seat,"]frase]
[frase["Sing, Heavenly Muse, that, on the secret top"]frase]
[frase["Of Oreb, or of Sinai, didst inspire"]frase]
[frase["That shepherd who first taught the chosen seed"]frase]
[frase["In the beginning how the heavens and earth"]frase]
[frase["Rose out of Chaos: or, if Sion hill"]frase]
[frase["Delight thee more, and Siloa's brook that flowed"]frase]
[frase["Fast by the oracle of God, I thence"]frase]
[frase["Invoke thy aid to my adventurous song,"]frase]
[frase["That with no middle flight intends to soar"]frase]
[frase["Above th' Aonian mount, while it pursues"]frase]
[frase["Things unattempted yet in prose or rhyme."]frase]
[frase["And chiefly thou, O Spirit, that dost prefer"]frase]
[frase["Before all temples th' upright heart and pure,"]frase]
[frase["Instruct me, for thou know'st; thou from the first"]frase]
[frase["Wast present, and, with mighty wings outspread,"]frase]
[frase["Dove-like sat'st brooding on the vast Abyss,"]frase]
[frase["And mad'st it pregnant: what in me is dark"]frase]
[frase["Illumine, what is low raise and support;"]frase]
[frase["That, to the height of this great argument,"]frase]
[frase["I may assert Eternal Providence,"]frase]
[frase["And justify the ways of God to men."]frase]
[frase["Say first--for Heaven hides nothing from thy view,"]frase]
[frase["Nor the deep tract of Hell--say first what cause"]frase]
[frase["Moved our grand parents, in that happy state,"]frase]
[frase["Favoured of Heaven so highly, to fall off"]frase]
[frase["From their Creator, and transgress his will"]frase]
[frase["For one restraint, lords of the World besides."]frase]
[frase["Who first seduced them to that foul revolt?"]frase]
[frase["Th' infernal Serpent; he it was whose guile,"]frase]

However, it is not only in *Sintext* that these possible and innumerable confrontations with instances submitted to our readings appear (the signifiers resulting from programming, the programming itself, the logics and strategies of interaction with the object, etc.). In any digital creation, these interventions may become the main focus of the readings, depending, to a greater or lesser degree, on the strategies of the programmer-creator, and also on the knowledge and ability of the reader.

It is precisely on this basis that Xavier Malbreil suggests that the reading of literary compositions created on the Internet should also pass through HTML source code analysis.[4] This demonstrates that, for these digital creations, it is not enough to be literate and have an average notion of computers and webs. There is a complexity to be developed and a sophistication to be cultivated by readers when they venture into digital space. Although there is no need for them to be programmers or specialists in visual programming, or to know the HTML command lines and syntaxes obligatorily, they have to develop and specialize their sensibilities and abilities to be able to examine the code lines and roughly comprehend the strategies and aesthetics of programming, thus opening up a path for their own interferences and effective understanding of the work.

We notice, therefore, a certain duplicity: in one space, where the work is displayed on the computer screen, we have a first page (or screen) that we may call visible, with its languages of forms, its interactions, its iconic denseness and its movements of transformation, adaptation and interactivity; in another space, that of the programming line editors (space of another visibility), we have the source code, which is precisely what makes that first page visible, manipulatable and, consequently, endowed with some coherence. This duplicity between the two spaces is not reduced to Manichaeist dichotomies, or anchored in immobilized and immobilizing fissures (translated idiomatically as "entrelugar"); neither does it resolve itself with dialectics, be they Platonic or Hegelian. As happens with the majority of duplicities in the digital medium, it cannot even be organized into a diachrony with a single and permanent meaning; from one to the other, or the other to one, it is not possible to impose a single temporal meaning. In effect, this undecidability is of the same order as the indefiniteness between 0 and 1 in binary language: the one does not have priority over the other. Respecting the creator, when effects, appearances, disposals and strategies are programmed, or when signifiers and interactivity strategies are accumulated, one can never determine if the written programming space—the source code—is the inaugural instance of the screens that will follow; there will always be leftovers and gaps that originate complex relationships of separation and contiguousness between the visible page (to be subjected to the manipulation of some reader) and the lines of programming. In the same way, the reader will never be far enough removed from the programming lines; in all reading of the visible

---

[4] In the conference entitled *Méthodologie d'approche critique de oeuvres de littérature informatique,* in the colloquium *L'internet littéraire francophone* that took place in the *Centre Culturel International Cérisy-la-Salle*, from 13 to 20 August, 2005.

page, in any interaction—sliding the cursor across the screen, dragging the icons from one point to another, the insertion of data, the gestures of clicking and letting go—in the trajectories of our decisions and indecisions, in the space between the lines of our movements, we always drag with us the command lines, the choices of programming language, the impositions of the compilers and the restrictions of the machine languages. In other words, the source code is at the same time contiguous to and away from the visible pages. And yet, the way these contiguities and distances are drawn up will not only depend on how the visible pages are constructed and how the programming lines are written; it will also depend on the ability of each reader to create spaces and passages of relations between the visible and programming pages.

Mallarmé's *Livre* gives some interesting indications on how to attempt movements of reflection and comprehension in this plurality of innumerable signifiers and significations of digital space, in the hesitations between a signifier-generating program and the signifiers generated. Although this approach between the *Livre* and digital space is not new, some interesting and even surprising conclusions can be drawn from it. Jacques Schérer affirms, in the edition he prepared of Mallarmé's works,[5] that:

> La dualité est l'indice et le moyen de l'ordre qui se construit à partir du chaos. (...) les constantes réduplications du Livre veulent être démonstratives et créatrices. Ce n'est un vain souci esthétique que le Livre confronte si souvent « deux poèmes ».[6]

In our case, this duality of the *Livre* (as presented by Schérer), and also a series of dualities drawn from readings of the digital work, could come to impose order on our computational chaos: work and text; production process and elements produced; generation and reading of signifiers; use of programmings and readings of the programming commands; programmer and creator; reader and author etc. In fact, the list seems interminable. Nevertheless, they are not dualities that confront and resolve themselves in a world where "everything exists to arrive at a book" (for this would give the illusion of being the point of arrival, the asymptotic limit, the supposed final synthesis of these dualities). Perhaps we are dealing precisely with dualities that should not be resolved, nor submitted to any unifying principle; any attempt at dialectical reduction would be as aporetic as the Cartesian substantial union between body and soul. In

---

[5] *Le «Livre» de Mallarmé*. Paris : Gallimard, 1977.
[6] Id. p. XVIII.

digital works, there seems to be no union, nothing of a single substance. Thus, instead of the *Livre's* "double *trompeur*",[7] we would in fact have revealing dualities—not revealers of a reduction in the principles of rational order or metaphysical necessity but revealers of a chaoticity that closely resembles the science of chaos, in which the world would be the result of determinism without predictability.[8] Schérer, still speaking of Mallarmé's *Livre,* gives a good description of the dynamics of dualities:

> ...le terme de dualité (...) n'est ni une identité ni une contradiction de deux objets. La meilleure formule, sinon pour la définir, du moins pour l'approcher, est une image mallarméenne : celle du pli. Un pli ne divise pas une feuille en deux moitiés identiques, ni même distinctes. Il sépare sans séparer. Il inaugure des éléments qualitatifs, puisqu'en créant au moins deux rectos et deux versos il est le point de départ d'une différenciation qui en se répétant peut, par une suite arithmétique rapide, mener très vite à des nombres très grandes. C'est bien pourquoi l'image du pli est centrale dans la thématique mallarméenne comme dans la structure du Livre. Elle respecte la réalité (la feuille pliée reste intacte) mais en permet l'évolution : le livre et le Livre naissent du pli. En d'autres termes, elle repose sur une notion dialectique.[9]

It should perhaps be stressed that the adjective "dialectic" at the end seems to conflict with what Schérer says above when discussing dualities that are not resolved with habitual syntheses. I shall explain: when he mentions *fold,* he talks about that which "separates without separating", immediately recalling the Moebius strip. In this strip, the undecidability of space—what is outside and what is inside?—is accompanied by a temporal indefiniteness—where is the beginning and where is the end? The strip is, in fact, an artefact of astonishing simplicity: a small twist (or *fold*), it seems to break any barriers between times and spaces, and between time and space. In this sense, it closely resembles various mechanisms in the digital medium. As with the Moebius Strip and Mallarmé's *Livre* (in Schérer's description), this medium also seems to make definitive synchronies and diachronies presenting a single meaning

---

[7] Schérer affirms that *Si tout est double, tout est trompeur et le « deuxième fond » évoqué plus loin, s'il n'est celui d'où le prestidigitateur tire un lapin de son chapeau, est du moins le point de départ d'un espace où retentit un écho—double par définition—et qui est décrit contradictoirement comme le théâtre le plus traditionnel.* Id. p. XXI.
[8] Alain Boutot. "La Philosophie du Chaos". *Revue Philosophique de la France et de l'Etranger*, n° 2, avril-juin, (1991): 171.
[9] Op. cit. p. XXII.

impossible; it repels any and all irrevocable hierarchies between its elements and operations and does not accept dialectical syntheses.

In other words, we are trying to describe a negative ontology, a series of impossibilities for digital space: 1) there seems to be no time nor place in it for a synchrony of unique *meaning* between its various elements; 2) there is no *prominence* of one element in relation to others; 3) there is no diachrony that imposes an invariant and rigid *sequence* between the various elements and operations that cannot be taken up again or altered once it has been established ; 4) one cannot impose a definitive *precedency* of one element in relation to the others. It is a fact, however, that nobody will have any difficulty associating *meaning, prominence, sequence* and *precedency* with both the creation and with the reading of digital works. To do this, it is enough to thrust your references of time or space to some point of the object or the reading to establish that the choice of permutation and combination techniques, for example, in *Sintext,* seem to have been the starting point of the creation; this is because they impose choices of languages and programming environments, and predetermine strategies ranging from the construction of logical elements to the choice of certain words and phrases (to the detriment of others). It is perfectly legitimate for the reader to determine his or her anchorage in the text being read, prioritizing the empty fields to be filled (by the reader and the system) and the instructions being followed, thereby determining the genesis of the meaning, the beginning of the sequence, the prominent element and the instance that precedes all the rest. This appeal to the empiric seems to contradict what was said at the beginning of this paragraph. However, let us examine this more closely.

Starting from this perspective, there are questions that cannot be answered in a clear and immediate way: up to what point are meanings, prominences, sequences and precedencies associated with digital work and text always the same (referring to both the object produced and its production)? How can one affirm that, in each rereading, meanings, prominences, sequences and precedencies stay inalterable to the work or to the text? Furthermore, what assurances are there that what we establish from the reading of the text that has appeared and is appearing is the same thing we will encounter in the work? None of this can be guaranteed, of course, in any artistic work, above all in digital works! We have, in fact, an undecidability that, inaugural in every text, fully affects the digital work (or rather, its materiality), an undecidability that prevents us from proposing the solution to the innumerable dualities of digital space by means of a supposed substantial union, a convenient dialectic synthesis or a final hierarchization.

What most disturbs these searches for order and attempts to reconcile the various dualities of digital space, is precisely the association between quantitative and qualitative. In the fragment transcribed above, Schérer says that the *Livre "inaugure des éléments qualitatifs, puisqu'en créant au moins deux rectos et deux versos il (...) peut, par une suite arithmétique rapide, mener très vite à des nombres très grandes."* When associating qualitative and quantitative, however, one does not do an *Aufhebung* of the one to arrive at the other. Both in the *Livre* and in digital space, quantitative and qualitative can coexist, each in its own sphere of signification, without one being reduced by the other, but in such a way that one does not cease influencing, altering, reducing or expanding the other. They are like vectors that can only be added in the intermediate space between them, as shown in the image below (simplified to two dimensions):

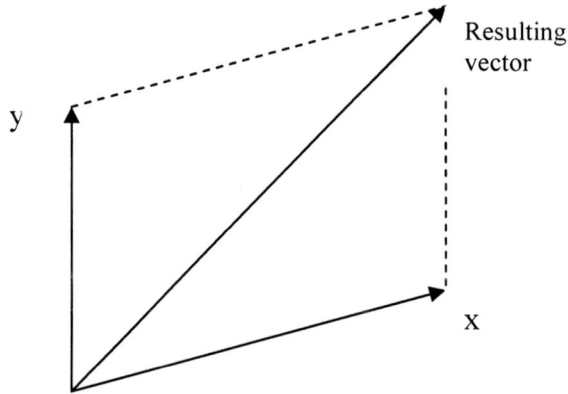

In fact, at each moment that we inspect the strategies of the production of signifiers and the signifiers themselves, quantitative and qualitative aspects appear under different but always contiguous perspectives. It is as if, in each short phrase emerging from *Sintext*, this limitation of words finds a reverse echo in an *imminence of plurality*. This imminence projects itself in the lines that accumulate, fitting into the tight, restricted space of the field destined for them, but no longer fitting into this same space as the phrases above are imperatively expelled for the lines below to be occupied. It is as if we had epigrams whose terms were not words, but entire dictionaries, as can be seen in Pedro Barbosa's generator:

Para perguntas arrogantes, perguntas em êxtase .
Quem faz perguntas cansadas, recebe respostas submarinas.
A excelência do saber está na paixão de saber perguntar .
O aluno faz perguntas exactas, o professor remói respostas na água.

In each one of these lines, the feigning of closed meaning, the obstinacy through shortening and the inclination to the epigrammatic insinuate or echo phrases already shown below and phrases that have not yet appeared on the screen—and will possibly not appear at all. The minimum as an echo of the maximum (and vice versa, the maximum as a repercussion of the minimum) seems to be one of the dominant points of E. M. Melo e Castro's poem *O Eco e o Ícone* ["The Echo and the Icon"]:

não recobrem as coisas as palavras
que se dizem de si arbitrárias e vagas
oceânicas em contra tempo e luz
só descobrem ruídos onde o som
electrónico infiltra uma frequência
de imagens hiperbólicas suspensas
em nada que se veja
o que se vê não pensa não produz
estas estereofluências só o sonho
é mais palavra que objecto por
isso é mais do som do que do tacto
mas a palavra é mais palavra que a palavra
e assim se descobre no reverso
o que diz a palavra está a ver-se

Words and things do not recover or substitute one another; they incessantly unfold: word into words, thing into things, words into things, things into words. With a word, an infinitude of things already appear, and vice-versa, in a never-ending process. However, this process may be given some temporary respite, a momentary suspension of this incessant pluralization, when it is observed: *e assim se descobre no reverso / o que diz a palavra está a ver-se*.[10] Sílvia Laurentiz transformed this poem by E.M. Melo e Castro into a VRML creation.[11] The first difference to be mentioned and explored is the fluidity of movements permitted by the view of the immobile page (or paper) that allows us to pass our eyes quickly over each verse, from top to bottom, from bottom to top, as opposed to the difficulty of making the elements in virtual reality move

---

[10] "And thus is uncovered in the reverse/what the word that is seeing itself says."
[11] Accessible at http://www.pucsp.br/pos/cos/interlab/in4/entrada.htm.

across the computer screen. In fact, the majority of VRML plug-ins still bring problems, ranging from the need to learn how to manipulate them (not always evident at first sight for the average reader) to halting interactivity, divided into a series of icons that separately encompass distinct possibilities of interaction or movements. As a result, we fall into a space of fragmentary displacements in which a certain movement is never carried out to completion; it is always the result of a combination of two or more others: going from top to bottom, at the same time coming closer to one of the phrases, demands, at the very least, a combination at distinct instants of the icon commanding vertical movements and the one commanding horizontal lines. In a beautifully-written essay entitled *Le langage indirect et les voix du silence,* Merleau-Ponty speaks of Matisse's paintings and points out that the gestures of the painter with the brush cannot be movements that are thought out, rationalized and chosen from other possible combinations of movement:

> Une caméra a enregistré au ralenti de travail de Matisse. L'impression était prodigieuse (...) Ce même pinceau qui, vu à l'oeil nu, sautait d'un acte à l'autre, on le voyait méditer, (...) tenter dix mouvements possibles (...) et s'abattre enfin comme l'éclair sur le seul tracé nécessaire. Il y a, bien entendu, quelque chose d'artificiel dans cette analyse (...) Il n'a pas tenu, sous le regard de l'esprit, tous les gestes possibles, et pas eu besoin de les éliminer tous sauf un, en rendant raison de son choix. C'est le ralenti qui énumère les possibles.[12]

Nevertheless, the movement actually carried out would not be on the same plane as the possible movements; the latter would be a background, or:

> ...conditions éparses sur le tableau, informulées, informulables pour tout autre que Matisse, puisqu'elles n'étaient définies et imposées que par l'intention de faire ce tableau-là qui n'existait pas encore.[13]

What stands out in the reading of Laurentiz's digital creation is precisely the fact that there is an inversion: the movement that leads directly to the desired point on the screen is the one that stays as background, while the possible and calculated movements are the ones that appear. What is more, between the former and the latter some kind of articulation becomes possible; a correspondence between them can be

---

[12] *Signes*. Paris: Gallimard, 1960: 57.
[13] Ibid., 58.

established as a vector, where real quantities (the composition of effectively carried out movements) and imaginary ones (the intuitive and direct movement) are somehow brought together.

On the other hand, a delaying effect is created, analogous to the *ralenti* mentioned above by Merleau-Ponty; it is as if each verse was in isolation, demanding greater effort and a series of operations to pass from one to another—as if they were all removed from each other by a distance much greater than the gaps between the lines of the printed version. In consequence, it is slow-motion that, strangely, becomes the immediate and natural way to establish movements and develop gestures on the computer screen. However, in contrast with the limited space of the printed version, which fits comfortably into the field of vision, the depth of the dark empty space of the VRML screen, that at the same time gives form to the words, brings to the field of immediate experience a sensation of the unlimited, the innumerable and the indefinable. In other words, this emptiness translates into vertigo in the form of three-dimensional illusion, caused by the horizon of sensations (encountered in the origin of every signifier and signified). This vertigo is closely related to another: the sensation that we have to deal with an infinity of possibilities, a sensation that becomes ever greater as it becomes more explicit. It is the *impression prodigieuse* mentioned by Merleau-Ponty—prodigious and awesome in that it makes us think that all movements, all gestures, all expressions are found in a infinitude of possibilities, an infinitude that always exceeds us, of course, and is beyond any of our possibilities. This could explain the attempt to incorporate chance in all contemporary artistic expression: without this, there would never be any hope of finding the adequate movement, the fitting gesture, the possible expression. However, from Mallarmé we learn that it is exactly the opposite. Schérer affirms that:

> Il faut éliminer le hasard des mots, dont chacun est constitué par une alliance contingente, et parfois perverse, entre un son et son sens.[14]

In the *Livre*, it seems that through excessive multiplication of this very chance Mallarmé justly seeks to eliminate it. In contrast to avant-garde and contemporary art—with their cultivation of casualness—or the surrealists with their *objective randomness*, Mallarmé's *Livre* is:

> ...abolition du hasard par son projet même. [...] il montre que le hasard n'y a point sa place habituelle. Pour l'éliminer plus radicalement encore, le

---

[14] Op. cit. p. XVI.

> Livre refuse la passivité de la continuité unilinéaire et se développe dans un hyper-espace à un grand nombre de dimensions comme en ont imaginé les géométries non euclidiennes. Ces nombreux ordres ont pour fonction de soumettre à leur ordre la contingence qui est le péché du langage.[15]

"Sin of the language"—or, put another way, the sickness caused by the infinitude of possible sensations experienced by the slow-motion effect of incursions in space with Sílvia Laurentiz's VRML creation.

Returning to the slow-motion mentioned above, in this digital recovery of Melo e Castro's poems we have a strange inversion that makes the pondered, planned slowness the less strenuous gesture and the most immediate movement; in contrast, the fluidity of direct movement would seek the most difficult and exacting passage. However, if we cannot escape the first possibility, we should not ignore the second, even if it never materializes. In fact, even when unaccomplished, the latter (that is, direct and fluid movement) remains as a horizon of possibility. It is as if our immediate exercise of digital space and VRML commands demanded the distant—we could almost say absent—presence of this movement that, on the screen and through available commands and interactions, is incapable of being accomplished effectively. In other words, it can only be executed as the indirect exercise of an impossibility. Between the two movements—those we try and then do, and those we attempt but do not carry out—there is coexistence at a distance, a mutual interference, a return to the vectorial scheme displayed some pages back. If an analogy is made with complex numbers, accomplished movement would be on the real numbers axis, while non-effective movement would be situated on the axis of imaginary ones.

Nevertheless, as mentioned above, these dualities are innumerable and it is clear that some can still interfere with others, which would result in a complex schema if we wished to show it in a two- or three-dimensional drawing. We would quickly arrive at a point where no graph or schema would be able to reproduce the most important elements and operations, and would have to resort to mathematical equations, which would take us too far from our original intentions. We should therefore think in terms of reducing these dualities to those which are most significant, while still trying to account for everything of importance that we have attempted to discuss so far. The result is a more or less simplified (and simplifying) schema that brings together work, text, readings, signifier producers,

---

[15] Ibid., XVII.

produced signifiers and significations. It would have the following appearance:

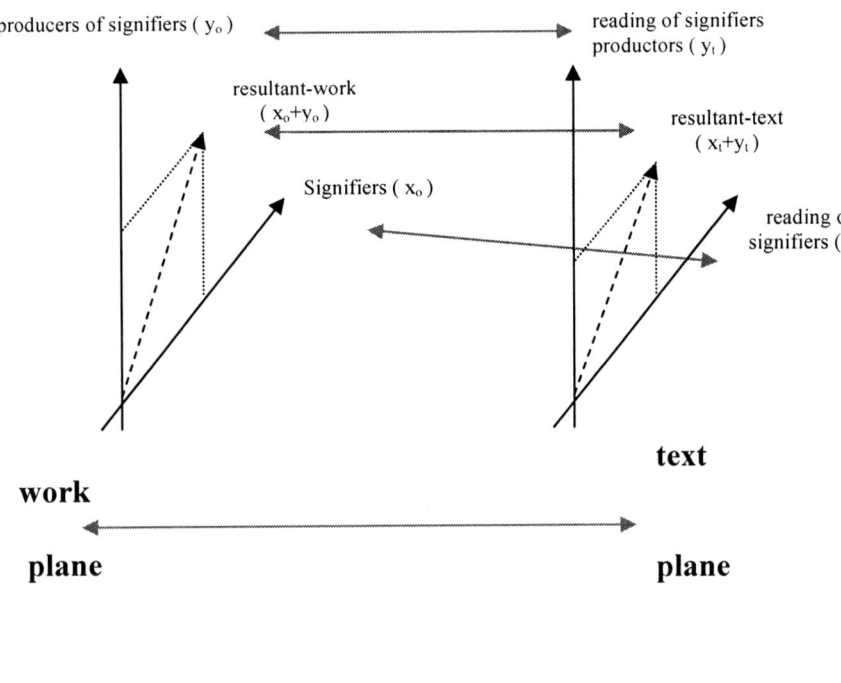

In the plane of the work, that is, its materiality, we have a conjunction (or vectorial sum) between the signifier production mechanisms, y_o (in *Sintext*, these are the programming strategies and lines) and the signifiers themselves, x_o (the phrases being generated). It cannot be said that the work is simply one or the other; it is a resultant-work ($x_o + y_o$) that will be in the intermediate space between producers and signifiers. In the plane of the text, that is, the result of the readings, we see another conjunction, this time between the reading we do of the producers of signifiers (y_t) and that of the signifiers themselves (x_t). Again, it cannot be affirmed that the text is a resultant of only one or the other, or of one and the other; the text will be in the intermediate region between one reading and another, in what we call resultant-text ($x_t + y_t$). However, the dualities do not cease there; from the mapping of these two planes (work and text), it is possible to propose exercises of significations (that is, vectorial sums) that begin precisely on the axis corresponding to each one. Thus, we would be discussing possible meanings from this line (or the vectorial sums) that leads from the signifier producers (y_o) to their reading (y_t), from the signifiers produced (x_o) to their reading (x_t), from the resultant-work ($x_o + y_o$) to the resultant-text ($x_t + y_t$), and, finally, from the plane of the work to the plane of the text. We can make the schema even more sophisticated (and complicated, of course), if we introduce another duality: the one between author and reader. In this case, a three-dimensional schema would not be able to represent all the possibilities, even precariously; we would have to make use of a simulation in four dimensions, which would only be possible using mathematical equations (as mentioned above).

We do not go so far as to propose that the issue of reading artistic works in digital space should be decided by resorting to vectorial calculations, or even that we should set out to accomplish such calculations. These schemas, paradoxically, try to give a less schematic image of very complex questions and indicate some possibilities for treatment of the elements and operations involved. In fact, this attempt to place everything, elements as well as operations, on co-ordinate axes and in vector spaces seem to lead us in the direction of a kind of topologization, as simple as this may be. In this case, we suggest that it may be interesting to start thinking of them in terms of neighbourhoods or limited areas. Nonetheless, such vectorization and topologization are not intended to turn themselves into a machine generating strategies, tools and results of reading. Nor are they intended to insinuate that topologization, schematization or vectorization give origin to concepts from which any digital works are read, comprehended and classified. In other words, the vectors signification, suggested in the schema above, is not manufactured by another machine—one producing concepts[16]—that we would put above the computer. In any case, it is important for us not to think of concepts as ready and conclusive, or definitive in their actions of giving goals to reflections, but to think of them as conceptual operators. Through these, an attempt is made to account for the movements and gestures of thought. Therefore, instead of concepts that are always ready and conclusive, what is desirable is the expression of conceptual movements in a spacialization-vectorization of thought that is also the spacialization-vectorization

---

[16] To paraphrase Oswald de Andrade, one might say that a concept-creating machine is not being made; we already have the writers of postmodern essays.

associated with any expressive gesture.[17] Thus, when dualities were mentioned, rather than seeking their resolution in simplistic syntheses, or fixing them in an irreducible Manichaeism, there was a wish to multiply such instances of duplicities to the maximum, pluralizing the resulting dissonance of this multiplication of dualities in each element and process.

It could be said in conclusion that we have tried to suggest some conceptual movements for the reading of digital artistic works, starting from elements and processes of digital space. The use of the vectorial schema above, even to account for the simpler dualities, already involves too many complications, which hinders effective understanding and experimentation of the digital artistic object. The key could be in metaphorization and this has habitually been done from images of the labyrinth and the rhizome. However, both seem to have depleted a good part of their potential for sharpening the spirit and renewing sensibility. That is why we are searching for a position that is removed from any metaphorization (although this does not cease to be a process that always involves the development of concepts with a minimum of reflective coherence, argumentative validity and formal finishing). Instead of labyrinth or rhizome, what would be considered would not be the image itself but the topology of the Moebius Strip. It would be the appearance of these movements of conceptual operators in three-dimensional space that we try to describe and explain here: in the same way as the strip passes from plane to space and space to plane (and from time to space and space to time), the conceptual operators allow the passage, also in two directions, from one term to another of the different dualities composing digital space, without establishing any priority or anteriority between them. From its beginning, the *Livre* seems to me a proto-space for experimentation in all these conceptual movements: how to think of an expressive gesture that does not completely abolish its contingency or

---

[17] In this in case, literature would be in an uneven position for sharpening the space of language through folds of language (in this case, the "parole" would be the conceptual operator acts within the "langue"). Literature would then be the privileged space where such operators are generated and used (processes, operations). In short, literature itself has always been a conceptual movement (never with ready conclusive concepts, but always constant on the side of concepts and ideas; this is the reason why the ideological history of literature always comes up against some impossibility or other). Movements, or, put another way, conceptual operators, such as the ones suggested here, are not, therefore, concepts. The moment one passes from movements to concepts, one is already out of the arts. It is from the former that one can, eventually, arrive at the latter, along a course in which the privileged space is that of the arts, with literature being the most important of these.

randomness, but reduces them to its own elements, strategies and processes, through reversibility. This is precisely what interested me about Mallarmé's creation and digital space: a closed contingency and an absolute randomness that reveal themselves as illusions; in other words, an exteriority that never stops reaffirming itself in the same movement and moment in which it reduces itself to interiority (and vice versa). We could even risk saying that the *Livre*, the Moebius Strip and digital space are direct confirmations or experiences of what Merleau-Ponty, in *Le Visible et l'invisible*, calls *chiasma* or reversibility. But to me this seems to be going too far, certainly beyond what the exiguity of this space allows. To finish, or rather momentarily suspend this discussion, let us return once more to what Jacques Schérer said of Mallarmé's *Livre*:

> Comment prouver le Livre ? Il ne peut ressembler à rien qui lui soit extérieur. Ce n'est qu'en lui [...] qu'il trouvera sa propre preuve. Elle est parfaite et totale, puisque rien de la contingence extérieure, qui pourtant alimente le Livre, ne peut parvenir jusqu'à son cœur et le vicier. C'est pourquoi le monde existe pour aboutir à un Livre. Il ne peut aboutir à rien d'autre qu'à un Livre, et à ce Livre même de Mallarmé.[18]

Schérer goes on to speak of a ritualizing, in a sense almost religious, dimension to the *Livre*, which leads him to propose a dramatization of Mallarmé's work. Also of interest to me are the characteristics of direct experience and secularized ritual, as they give another facet to the old metaphor of the world-as-book. This now evolves in the direction of another metaphor of the world-as-theatre. If the world exists to end up in a book, it also exists to be put on stage. Nevertheless, in contrast to other times (we might mention the Renaissance in relation to the first metaphor and the Baroque period in relation to the second), in the *Livre*, book and theatre do not exclude or nullify each other. Both compete for an extremely complex topology in which work and text feed each other and provoke each other, becoming more and more complex, in a game of mirrors whose infinite depth is not seen but presumed. Is this not a description of digital space, when inhabited and magnetized by artistic creation? As in the *Livre*, it is also possible for digital creation to be the occasion of a *coniunctio* between book and theatre, work and text or hypertext and ritual, as was the case between work and text or producers and signifiers mentioned above. And these dualities do not cease; they feed off one another, awaken one other and reach out indefinitely to one another. In fact, between a work that never becomes a text and a text that

---

[18] Ibid., XVIII.

never fixes itself in a work, only the staging of Book and Work can result in effective reading. As quoted in the epigraph to this essay, Mallarmé argues that something that neither begins nor finishes can only exist if it turns its beginning and its end into pure staging, even if it is a certain staging of concepts, as we have attempted to show here.

CHAPTER SEVEN

LECTOR IN MACHINA:
TOWARDS AN EROTIC OF READING

LAURA BORRÀS

A condition for the assessment of the tools that ICTs provide in the area of literary creation is that we first enter into a theoretical reflection on the consequences of their application for the processes of the composition, reception, distribution and teaching of literature. (We should in any case not attempt definitive assessments since this is an area that is evolving at great speed.) Consequently, in order to analyse some samples of electronic textuality, I intend to reconsider the very concept of textuality and our textual heritage. I would like to claim a certain erotic in digital reading, and to this end I will go back to the medieval discourse of the senses to recover the sensations of the page and transfer them to what should now perhaps be called "screen sensations". I will then present various samples of literary creation on the Internet, thus expounding certain reading practices so as to emphasize the "erotic" concept from the point of view of research, investigation and evocation of the pleasure that enhances the will to explore and discover within a new reading space.

A Prior Reflection

There are theorists and essayists who, often with as much vehemence as ignorance, have devoted ever more space to denouncing the cultural and artistic decline that follows the appearance of "pseudo-", "para-" or "contra-" literary forms, such as electronic literature. It is true that this denunciation is consonant with the volume, also on the increase, of declarations stemming from various academic and critical circles, which, especially towards the end of the eighties, turned hypertext into the latest of the "new media" revolutions. It is also true, however, that all of this is related to certain expectations, some of a particularly redemptive kind, that were stirred up towards the end of the twentieth century, but which have now been laid to rest. In general, in articles such as these, concerning the possibilities of an artefact that is claimed to be "radically new", there is usually a serious discrepancy between the headlines and the small print, so to say. Thus, even the most serious theorists heralded spectacular effects for the near future, while both development itself and the implementation of possibilities were long-drawn-out and slow, moderating and delaying the course of events. Overall, however, the message was optimistic: we were informed of the changes that had taken place, and changes that were yet to come were shouted from the rooftops. Words such as "liberty" and "democratization" became magic talismans that converted current findings into rumours about the future. All the same, in this context, while many hopes have coexisted and continue to do so, there are two that fuel all others: the idea of control and its transference to the reader under the sign of interactivity. Alongside the hopes, there has been one aspect—in my view—that has received far more emphasis than it deserves: I am referring to the much-trumpeted "novelty". There are people who brandish this as the distinctive feature of what they produce. They forget, however, that, as part of its evolution, words, poetry and literature have established links with space and form, with a physicality that goes beyond the written word and becomes image. We often feel that we are immersed in an all-encompassing modernity, as if nothing had been invented and that certain novelties have only been able to flourish with the arrival of our epoch and our knowledge. However, these are considerations that are simply a sign of our arrogance or ignorance. We know that Rimbaud gave colour to the vowels: *"A noir, E blanc, I rouge, O bleu, U vert"*, and the aesthetic practice of relating poetry to spatial coordinates has a long and venerable history, despite often being received with incomprehension. We have to go back to the very birth of writing to find the first instances of tension between the word and artistic creation. Since then, and right up to the hyperfiction and electronic poetry of the present day—including avant-garde movements as well as figural, visual and phonetic poetry—we find that the whole history of poetry illustrates how we human beings have sought new literary expressions in order to feed our imagination and our souls: a history of experiment and exploration.[1] Down the centuries,

---

[1] We can date the first visual poems to around 1700 BC. The first known calligrams are the three by the Greek poet Simmias of Rhodes from about 300BC: "The Hatchet", "The Wings" and "The Egg". We should remember that the word calligraphy comes from the Greek words *kallos*, meaning beauty, and *graphos*, meaning writing, so that a calligram is concerned with the visual art that

creativity has undoubtedly led many authors to seek an escape from the limits of the word, to the point where they have been forced to struggle with the synergic artistic tension that attempts to fuse different artistic languages, almost like a game that takes shape between voice, word and image and all their multiple interrelations. We can thus say that poetry today—and by extension literature—has passed through many cultures and many movements contesting its very nature. One of these movements is the one that has to do with the dual dimension—iconic and verbal—of the poem, because visual poetry draws on the relations that arise between all types of languages, such as spoken language, sounds, phonetics, music and mathematics. If we are dealing with *visual poetry* in its multiple and varied aspects (the persistence of a practice in poetry and writing where word and image fuse, leading to the construction of a complex and heightened meaning)—visual poetry in the shape of a figure, poetry for the eyes, a poetic discourse, where reading and looking form part of a unique identical instant, a space where the word that seeks its own labyrinthine universe reflects internally the image of itself, a search for the beauty, the dream and the infinity that lies behind every word of poetry, in a word, a poetry that manifests itself as a means to visualize concepts—then I fail to see why, in such cases, we cannot consider all these desires to have now been transferred, or transported, to the digital environment.

In general, this type of literature, that allows the convergence of verbal and iconic elements, whatever name we give them, creates a balance between the plastic and the discursive character of literature. We therefore find ourselves in a new situation, but only in part and only from a certain perspective: in part, because it is true that the medium has changed and this has strategic consequences for literary production in that the computer as a space for creation is new. However, as regards perspective, we feel that the encyclopaedists, to mention just one example, conceived of a supposedly horizontal order that did not allow vertical hierarchies. Thus, for example, in the alphabetical ordering of the *Encyclopédie*, "God" was just one term among so many others, the same as "hell". But after all, they in no way renounced paradise. Utopias have continued to succeed each other: from a social utopia we have moved on to a technological utopia, and now we are probably in a biological utopia, even though it is the technological one that is instrumental in allowing any changes. The sequences are obviously very distant and even apparently in opposition.

---

emphasizes the beauty of the written sign. For a more detailed consideration of these issues, see my article "Digital literature and theoretical approaches" in the journal *Dichtung Digital* (http://www.dichtung-digital.org/2004/3-Castanyer.htm).

However, the chimera is always the same, extending chapter after chapter into every stage of human existence, because this illusion is probably nothing more than the wish to overcome time and death; its main testimony down the millennia has been this terrain, so plural and protean, but so unique, which—or want of a more exact term—we call art, of which literature, logically, is a part.

Digital Textuality: *Lector in Machina*

> You can't have art without resistance in the materials.
> —William Morris

Although it might seem paradoxical, the advent of digital technology may lead us to rethink the most basic questions related to the nature of texts and documents. Thus, while etymologically the word "text" derives from the Latin noun *textum* and its verb *textere*, i.e. "weave", alluding not only to the marks on the page, but also to the physical feeling of a textured material, the word "document" comes from the Latin *documentum*, which derives from the verb *docere*, meaning "to teach". In fact, a document is a text that serves to justify or authorize something, but at the same time refers to the instruction and teaching of a certain subject matter. From this dual perspective, I will use the term "electronic or digital text"[2] for the set of words we find suspended in the liquescence of the screen, which, although merely the emergence of another language and another set of processes that remain hidden, are documents because they use writing in order to "teach"[3] and do not leave marks. I am thus referring to the emergent literary reality, born from digital procedures in a digital environment, that can only be consumed in this environment.

In order to consider briefly some of its characteristics, I will mention four of its inherent aspects:[4] physical complexity, authorial complexity,

---

[2] Both adjectives derive from the "*electronic digital computer*" designed by Atanasoff and Berry at Iowa State University in the 1940s; they consequently represent a single computational, procedural and informatic reality in spite of the dual use in American and European contexts (with the exception of the francophone area, probably due to its older literary tradition of experimentation with informatics). We have in mind groups like Oulipo or Alamo, who have tended to use the concepts "numérique", "computational", "algorithmic", or simply "informatic".

[3] In the dual sense of "show" and (why not?) "instruct".

[4] See Laura Borràs Castanyer, "Textualitats electròniques: cap a una eròtica de la

typological complexity and perceptual complexity. I should say at the outset that all of these are intimately related in that one must analyse the relations between the algorithmic nature of the code and the pragmatics of the text, or reflect on the reader's responsibility and the author's intentions through the "observable ephemera" that appear on the screen while the work lasts.

1. Physical Complexity

Here we have to include all the contingencies of the materials involved. For one thing, we have to consider the material that makes up the work, in other words, not only the system, the platform, the software or the programming language that has been used to make it, but also the means of storage and dissemination—diskettes, CDs, Internet and installations, etc. It is important to bear in mind that programming (and not necessarily that of the program) is crucial. We must remember that programming is seen by many authors as a new type of material, like the raw material artists use for sculpture and modelling. But here we also have to consider the structural characteristics of this kind of writing, like the space-time relation (which is decisive, given that these are innovative coordinates in digital literature: for example, we think of the spatial layout, of the idea of control over what is read, of the mobility implied by temporality, a text that disappears, that moves or explodes—in short, a text that is alive.

Examples

Screen by Noah Wardrip-Fruin can only be seen inside a 3D device, *The Cave*, in specially-prepared installations such as those at Brown University in the United States. This is a text controlled by the touch of the reader, which literally triggers the linguistic flow of a virtual text that is all around him or her, and which swoops down almost physically, in form and sound, onto the reader.

---

lectura". In *L'escriptura i el llibre en l'era digital*. Barcelona: Generalitat de Catalunya, 2006, 195-212.

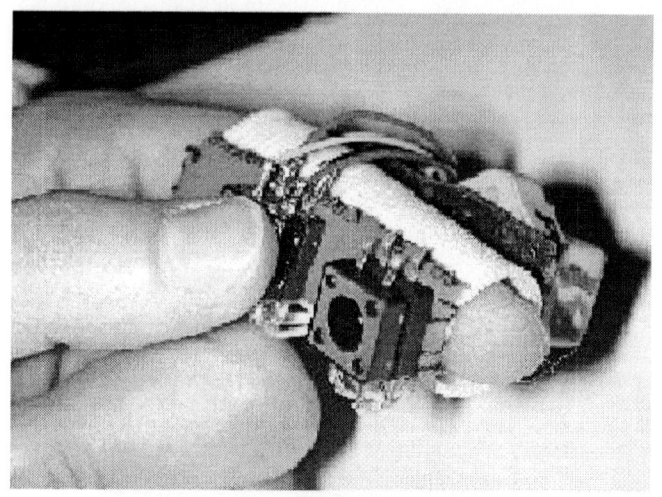

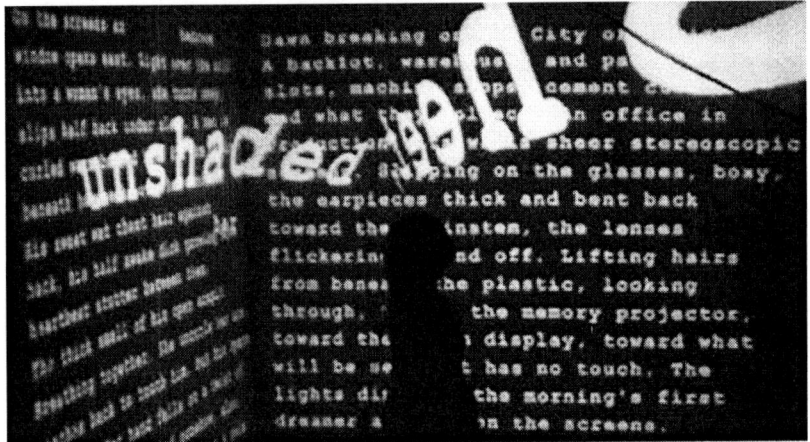

Susanne Berckenheger: *Bubblebath*. Narrative Prize, First "Ciutat de Vinaròs" Digital Literature Awards, 2005.

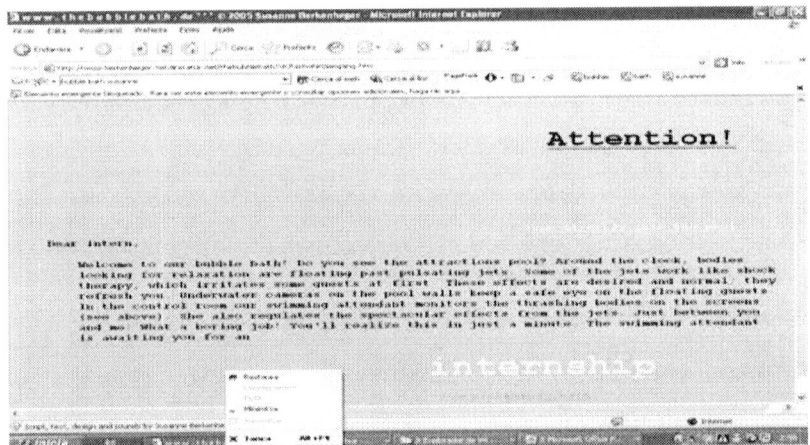

2. Authorial or Creative Complexity

Here, we will consider the human factor, that is to say the authorial possibilities manifested in some of these works, which on the one hand are either human or artificial, and on the other are individual or collective. In generative poems with a one-off reading, for example, when it is the machine that creates the text according to programmed parameters that realize the grammatical rules that have been introduced, who is the author?—the person or the machine? Similarly, how should we assign the authorship of written texts that result from a collaboration between engineers, musicians, poets and designers? The very concept of "author" becomes problematic as soon as authorship is multiple. On the one hand we have the result on the screen, and on the other we have the writer of the code, who manipulates the computer language so that the literary language becomes visible. Authorship thus comprises this dual language, and consequently the concept of creation appears perhaps more hybrid than ever. Who is the author?—the creative artist or the technician who implements the creation? Do we return to a distinction between author and artisan? There has even been talk of the "wreader". When the reader goes beyond the physico-cognitive activity of textual cooperation (for example, in certain open texts where the collaboration of the reader has a significant textual presence in the work in that he or she becomes involved in it, or in interactive stories), what is the role of the reader in the authorship?

Examples

Multiple authorship: Originator and project leader: Chico Marinho[5]

---

[5] Originator and project leader: Chico Marinho
3D environment
Idea and design: Alckmar Luiz dos Santos, Cristiano Bickel and Tânia Fraga
Animation and modelling: Carlos Augusto Pinheiro de Sousa and Chico Marinho
Procedural animation and poem bots: Gustavo Morais
Image handling: Carlos Augusto Pinheiro de Sousa and Walisson Costa
Poems
Graphic poems: Fernando Aguiar
Poebots: Álvaro Andrade Garcia and Chico Marinho
Poem "Palavra Viva" (audio): Álvaro Andrade Garcia
Poem "Globo da Morte" (audio): Alckmar Luiz dos Santos
Audio
Main track and environment audio: Jalver Bethônico
Poem sound track "O Buda da Palavra": Álvaro Andrade Garcia
Videos
Poem "Palavrador": Chico Marinho
"Esquadrão Atari" (parts): Daniel Poeira
Images
Photos: Marcelo Kraiser
Software
AI - Collision: Rafael Rodrigues Cacique
AI - swarm behaviour: Gustavo Morais
Webcam recognition and interface integration: Leonardo Souza and Lucas Junqueira

Lector in Machina: Towards an Erotic of Reading 131

From the work *Palavrador*. Poetry Prize, Second "Ciutat de Vinaròs" Digital Literature Awards, 2006.

3. Typological Complexity

Under this heading we will focus on the different types of examples found: the varying degrees of openness or closure, the possibilities for changing a text and for "textual transition" that is part guided and part free, the types of links chosen, the characteristics of both screen and surfing interfaces, the degree of linearity involved, the extent to which works are complete (work in progress), opportunities for integration, i.e. the combination of different artistic and technological forms resulting in a hybrid expression, and originality—not in the sense of aesthetic judgement but in the capacity to incorporate elements derived from different sources. The problem of genre is also found at this typological level: Are we dealing with fiction or non-fiction? One speaks of the classical genres—mystery, science fiction, essays, poetry, etc.—in the digital environment, but there are certain others unique to this for which we will need to create new terms.

Examples

i) Antón Ferret: *Retorn a la Comallega.* Vicent Ferrer Special Mention at the Second"Ciutat de Vinaròs" Digital Literature Awards, 2006.

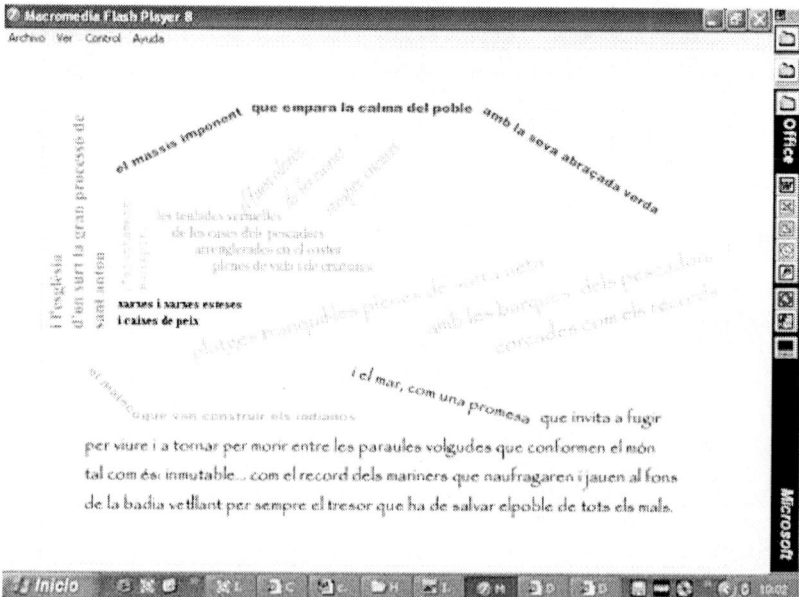

Lector in Machina: Towards an Erotic of Reading   133

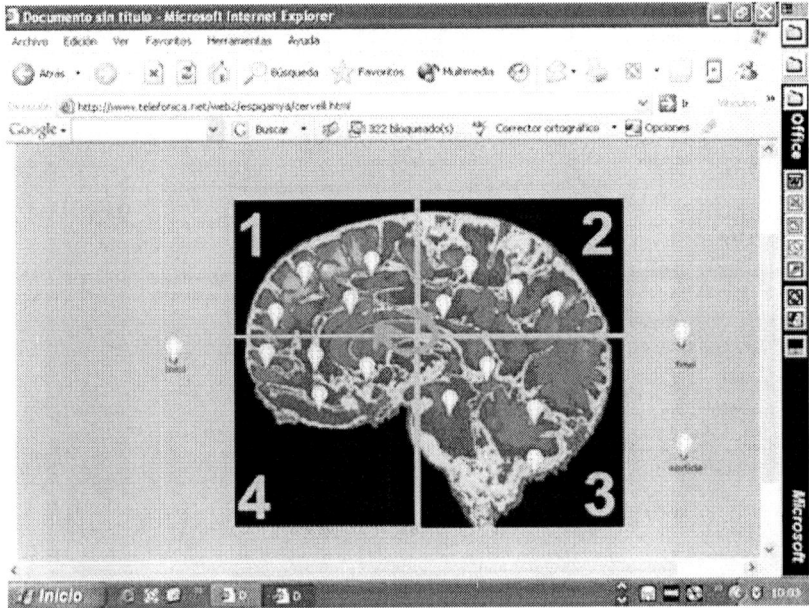

ii) Marc Lloan: *Ja tornaré*. Vicent Ferrer Special Mention, Second "Ciutat de Vinaròs" Digital Literature Awards, 2006, in PowerPoint.

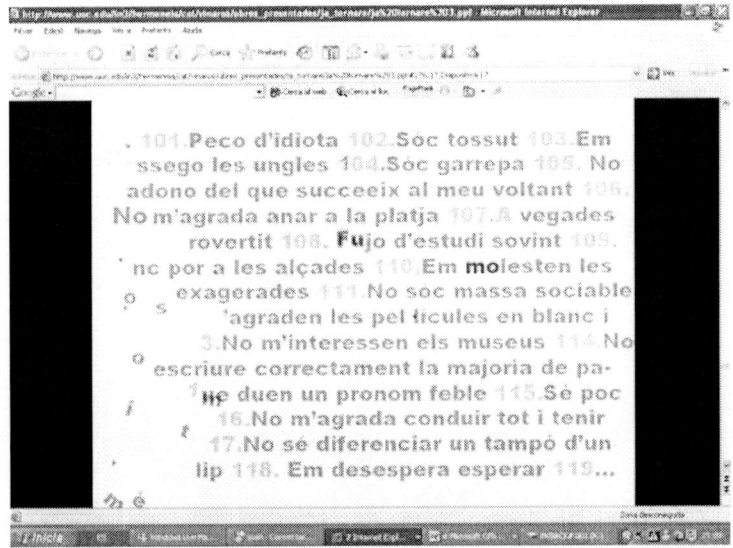

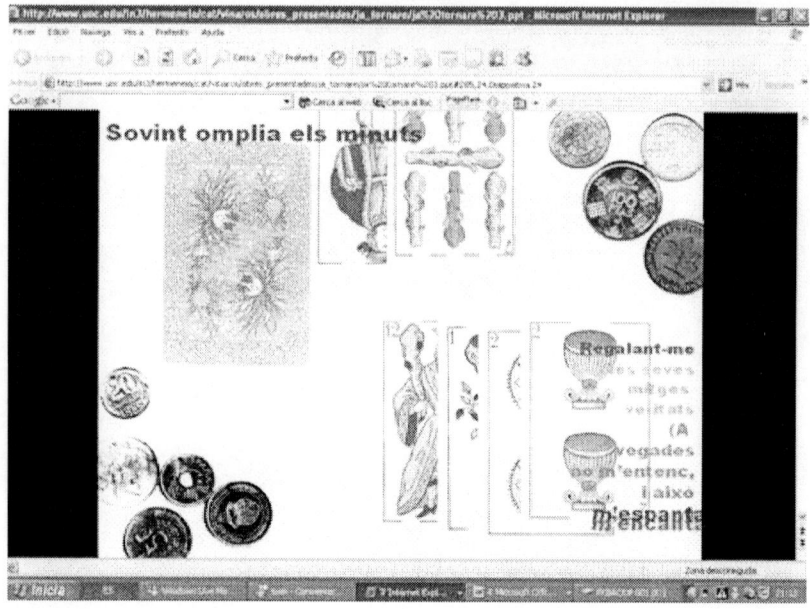

4. Perceptual Complexity

How is the act of reading realized? If we reflect for a moment on the way these creations are received, we realize that there is a variety of norms of use. Sometimes when we access a digital work, we do not know how to react: Do we have to click or not? Do things happen when I provoke them or do the words, does the text, start to do things without me being able to stop it? How should I act when faced with these unknowns in order to come to grips with the content of the work? A hypertext narrative, for example, requires the reader to start making decisions on the text, to be interactive—an active spectator who considers his or her interests and follows those paths through the text that might best satisfy them. In these circumstances, readers might be forced to play a strange and undoubtedly discomfiting version of Mastermind, where they are forced to reconstruct the author's intention for the material in order to understand the logic of the links and the structure of the hypertext. In this way, instead of striving to reduce the author's sovereignty over the text and guarantee a greater autonomy for the reader, the hypertext might oblige readers into the awkward position of having to guess the intentions hidden behind the configuration of the text before dealing with the matter of the narrative itself, when what the reader perhaps wants is just to be carried along. In the same way, the choice of a certain reading itinerary takes us into the labyrinth, a labyrinth where we grope our way, without knowing where we are heading because it is structured so as not to allow us to see what other paths we might follow. They are paths that arise out of immediacy, out of the here and now. Without temporo-spatial dimensions, we do not know as readers where we came into the spatial text or where we should start to read: Is this the beginning? Is it the end? Warning: it might be that a certain text has neither a beginning nor an end, and this—culturally speaking—puts us in a very awkward situation. Finally, which of the body's organs are involved in the act of reading?

Examples

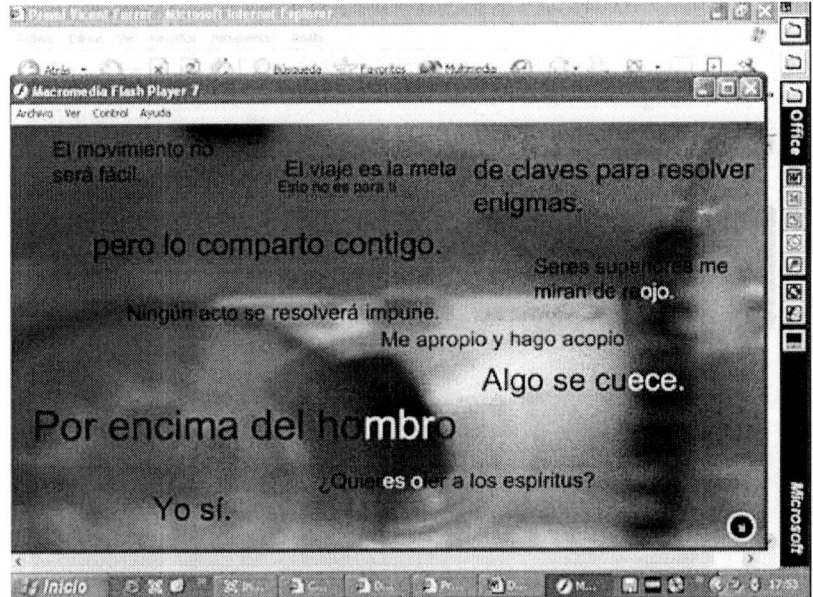

i) Isaías Herrero: *21 días*. Narrative Prize, Second "Ciutat de Vinaròs" Digital Literature Awards, 2006

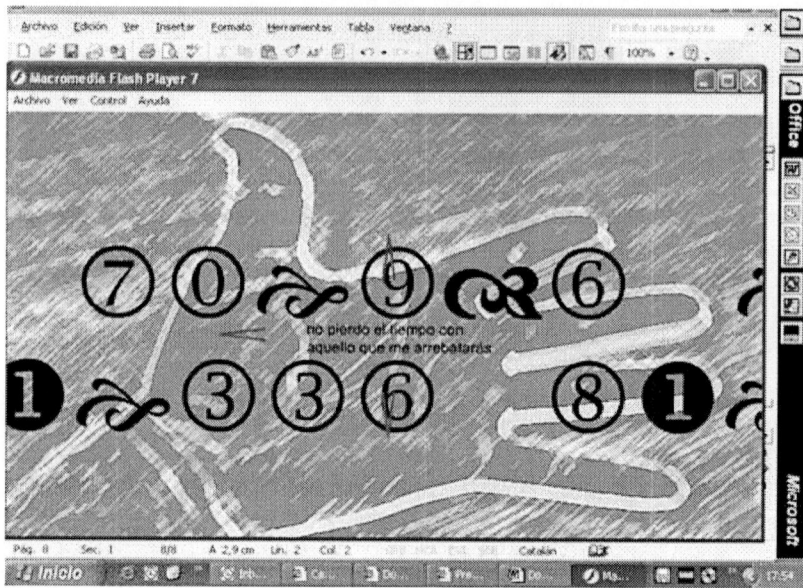

ii) Jason Nelson: *Another Emotion.* Poetry Prize, First "Ciutat de Vinaròs" Digital Literature Awards, 2005, http://www.heliozoa.com/resume/color.html

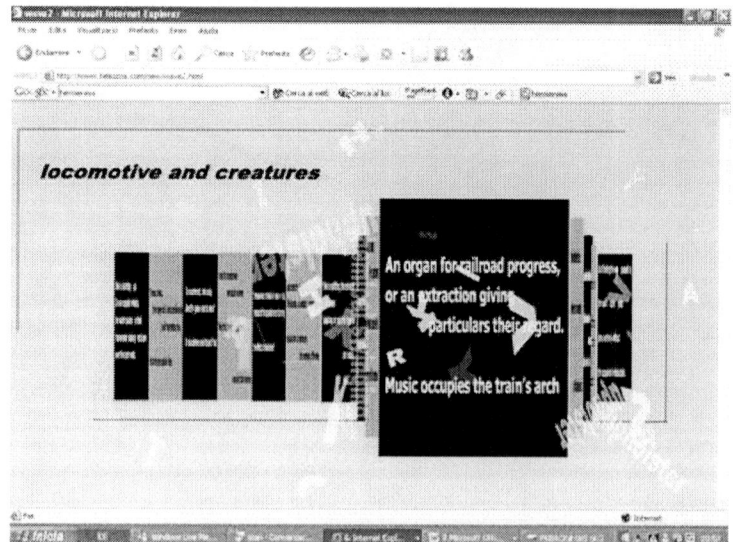

Lector in Machina: Towards an Erotic of Reading 137

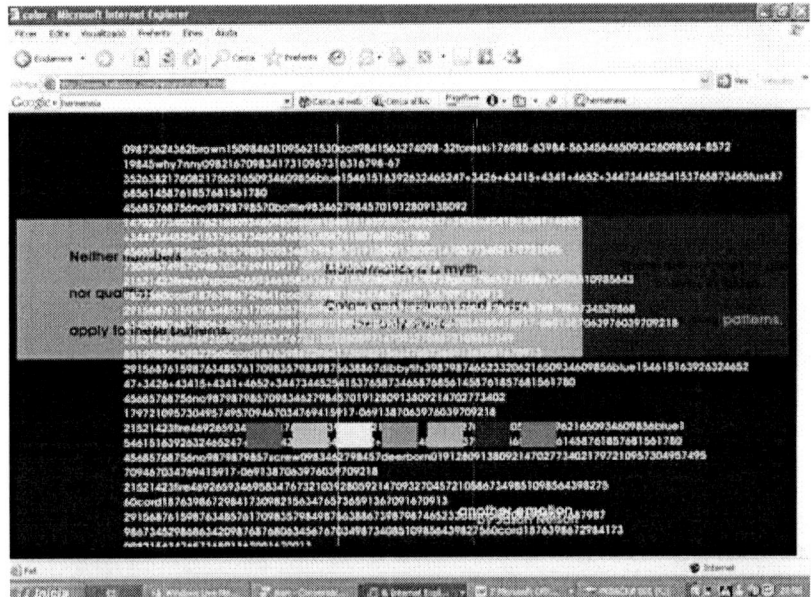

At times, for decoding to be really effective, different senses are involved that are beyond the clicks and movements made with the mouse. I have already spoken of the "erotic" in digital reading, but this is not really new. At all events, we can either consider these new forms of reading and writing as heretical and be horrified by the world we live in and what it is coming to, or we can try to avoid a schism in the arts by revising the canonical laws in order to make room for realities which, beyond their experimental nature (or perhaps precisely because of it), allow us to establish lines of creative continuity with earlier epochs in our cultural history. We shall see.

Our Textual Heritage

The study and application of digital codes leads us to new investigations into our textual heritage. For me, perhaps because my training in philology reached its apogee in medieval studies, it is often useful to look to the past in order to discover clues to the future. This explains that what has been enlightening for me is the importance of sensation for understanding the experience of reading the "iconic pages" of medieval manuscripts with regard to the predominance of the integration of languages (computer, visual, sound, etc.) in the literature under consideration. Consequently, I ask myself: Is it possible to regain this importance of the senses in digital space? We have various similar starting points whose strongest common factor is the elevation of "seeing" above the other senses, both nowadays and in the medieval world.

We say that manuscripts are "miniated" because extensive use was made of red lead—or "minium", i.e. lead oxide used as a pigment—both for colouring and to set off the contents on the page (titles, initial letters and the most important sections were almost always in this vermilion). What was written in this way was called a *rubrica*, and the special copyist whose task was precisely to do the parts written in red was the *rubricator miniator*. This rapidly gave rise to the verb *miniare* and to the "miniature", in which red was not necessarily the only colour used.[6] A "miniated"

---

[6] This activity of *rubricare* served as a metaphor for the blood spilt by martyrs and, long before the classic "spare the rod and spoil the child", there was a frequent association of books, blood and religion. For example, Prudentius (5th century C.E.) in his poems about martyrs, the *Peristephanon*, compares Saint Eulalia, and

illuminated manuscript is, by its very nature, an object that is typologically, physically and perceptually complex: a special type of book that exists thanks to a delicate balance—as a work of art and, at the same time, as a book, i.e. an everyday object. We have here, then, an article composed at different times and in different ways that can be summarized at two levels: that of composition, writing and painting, and that of reception, reading and contemplation. This requires multiple authorship and manufacture (a "division of labour" corresponding to the duality of a message expressed in a single medium), and a composition process in different genres and at different times: the writer or copyist for the literature at one time, and the painter or illuminator for the graphic art at other times. (Because they never coincided and normally worked separately, the instructions that the copyist left for the illuminator often appear in the text itself; even if they were later covered or erased, they still left a trace.)

I have mentioned the "division of labour" that corresponds to the duality of the message expressed in one medium. In fact, the decoration of medieval codices can present a dual relationship to the text: either there is a physical nexus that links the two, or there is a relation of sense and significance between them. In the first case, the illustrator contributes directly to the written code, while in the second case, he uses his imagination and accompanies the text by illustrating it. The former is represented by the "miniated" illuminated initials—the *incipit*—those large letters, and occasionally longer portions of writing, at the beginning of the text.

---

the wounds she received at the hand of her tormentors, to a purple script where one could read the name of Christ.

We are dealing with examples where, thanks to the chromatic range and painterly beauty, the emphasis is normally on the art, but the illustration also forms a direct part of the script, which is an element integrated into the text. From the receiver's point of view, what happens is that the perceptual emphasis rests on the individualized letter as being worthy of special attention. This is a decorative effect, both in terms of the material involved and what the letter represents; in the beginning, letters depicted plants and animals but this slowly gave way to all sorts of anthropomorphic creations and even monsters. It is nevertheless an aesthetic element, even though it is divided between writing and image. However, this gradually led to an "iconic translation" of the passage (either in the space devoted to the initial letter, in the margins of the manuscript, or integrated into the text) which allowed the reader to see in figures what the text described in words. To put it another way, the images here acted as an element of hermeneutic support for the written text in that they provided a visualization of written meaning, with the aim of making it clearer.

Lector in Machina: Towards an Erotic of Reading

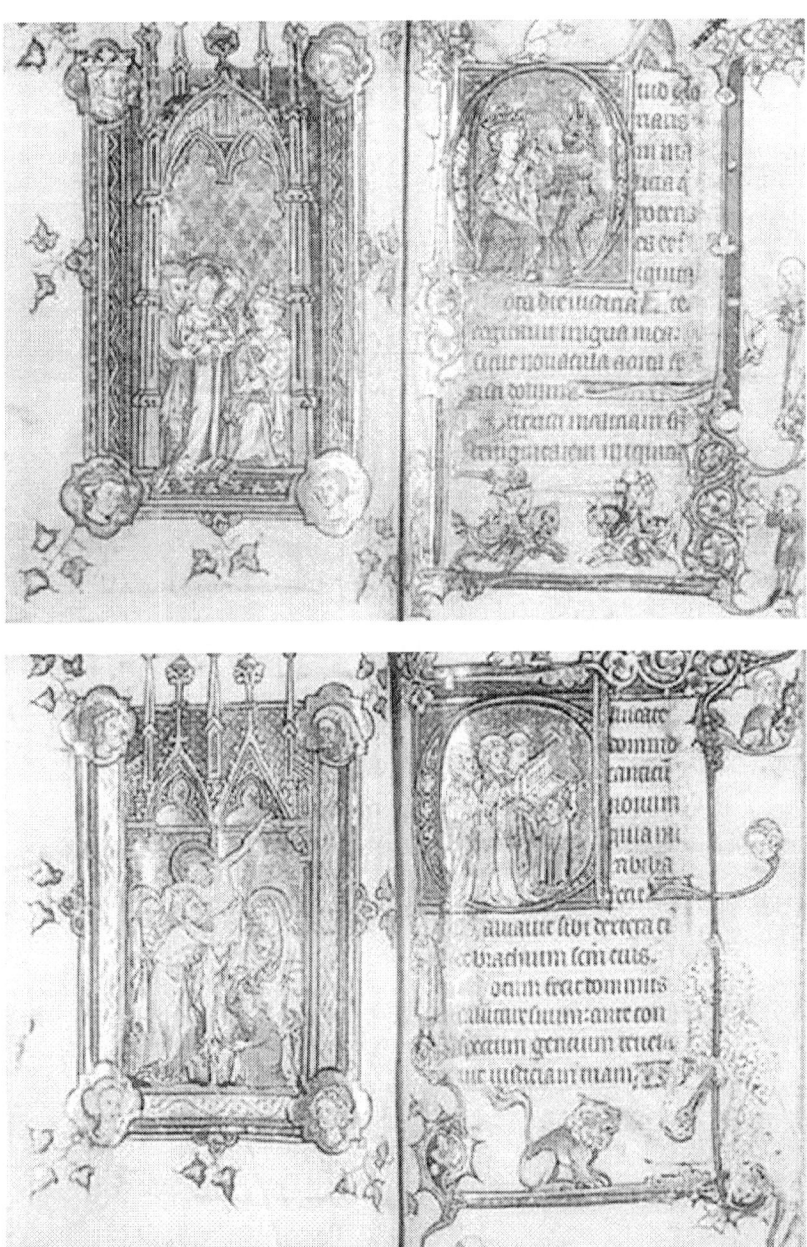

At all events, in neither case should we underrate these elements in a "miniated" codex read as a book whose sequential nature is a fundamental perceptual aspect. The relationship between text and image is effective as a composition in that it allows the establishment of hierarchies of values (above and below, inside and outside, central or peripheral, etc.) that anticipate or delay units of meaning, which can prepare the reader, create expectations, clarify the sense of what has been read, and so on. In short, this provides different possibilities of aesthetic communication resulting in a visual script that is metapoetic, since there is an interaction of two types of script; rather than one being imposed on the other, they create a composition that offers the receiver a space for the consideration of the multiple uses of writing.

The reading of any page of an illustrated manuscript allows a different approach to the object. For one thing there is the eye that follows the flow of the text—letter by letter, word by word, page by page—necessarily moving from left to right and from top to bottom in our Western culture. But there is also the access of the eye that is free to approach the whole of the page or the frame of the double page as if it were a painting; the eye can pause to choose any element in order to enter, slowly, and after careful observation, the different levels of meaning. This panoramic view, which is the normal way we look at these texts from the past, escapes from the linear route and finds new ways of achieving meaning that are doubtless complementary to those that derive from the linear approach. The same thing happens here as in a lot of experimental poetry: the order of meaning is inverted, facilitating direct perception and aesthetic feeling rather than a cerebral discovery of the sense.

The Erotic in Reading

Let us now concentrate on a medieval miniature from *De sensu et sensato* by Aristotle, (Geneva University Public Library, ms. 175, folio 327,) which represents each of the five senses as an individual cognitive act effected by a masculine human subject. The senses of sight and touch are "superior" and are therefore placed in the upper part of the capital, since the medieval world was so given to a visual representation of hierarchies, using very clear spatial coordinates. At top left is a man looking in a mirror, representing the sense of sight, which, according to Aristotle's text, is the pre-eminent sense. Then there is a figure playing a harp with delicate finger movements. The French verb *toucher* is what is important in this iconographic rendering (rather than the sense of hearing, for instance, shown in the middle of the lower part of the letter), because it is used for touching as well as for playing an instrument. There is a traditional association between touch and the sensitive parts of the body par excellence: the hands. What is surprising is that the iconography gives precedence to the sense of touch over that of hearing, which for Aristotle is, after sight, the most important sense for the mind and for wisdom. In any case, the fact that in *De anima* Aristotle himself described touch as the most elemental faculty perhaps explains this graphic layout acting as the inter-textuality to be seen in the iconography.[7] Then comes the figure of hearing, represented upright and playing small bells with one hand and a flute with the other; this is in the lower middle, flanked by the sense of taste (a man eating) to the left, and the sense of smell (a man smelling a flower) to the right. It is worth emphasizing that the reason for bringing out this difference derives in part from the fact that the other two senses are found in the French verb *sentir*, which can mean both "smell" and, more generally, "feel", thus implying the other senses.

Continuing in this sensorial vein, we should bear in mind that during this period texts made frequent use of metaphors concerning eating and drinking, for example, the monastic *ruminatio*, which literally means to "chew" the words in order to digest their meaning. However, this apart, powerful images of bibliophagy, like that of St. John of the Apocalypse eating a scroll proffered by the angel in Revelations 10 (a gesture present in many other examples, such as Michel Jeanneret's *A Feast of Words*), are interpreted in 13th century notes as a metaphor of reading. The omnivorous reader, then, savours the sound and the sense of the words in a way parallel to the savouring of food; in this way the parallelism with eating tends to make the text more concrete and natural, while connecting at the same time with the biblical tradition of articulating knowledge as a realm of sensorial delight (we are reminded of Paradise and the fruit of the tree of Good and Evil). Consequently, the miniated manuscripts are profusely decorated with floral and vegetal motifs that contribute to the stimulation of this sensorial aspect, which reaches us as much through sight as through touch or smell. This is no exaggeration if we consider that the manuscripts are made of animal materials (treated animal skins) or vegetal ones (sheets of parchment) which have a special porous texture, a silkiness evident to the touch that gives off a smell intensified by the passage of time and all the organic remains that have accumulated there. When I speak of the passage of time, I am referring to the dirt, to the

---

[7] Other miniatures incorporate variations that are probably due to the influence of Arabic medical theory (e.g. Reims, BMun, Ms. 864).

ageing and hardening of the sheets, and to traces of "interaction" (some of which are clearly radical or destructive). These are found in many manuscripts and they are not always recent (I have in mind readers who have left a trace by marking, noting, crossing out or tearing what they were reading if they didn't agree with it, etc.) And when I mention organic remains, I mean both the "stains" left by early readers—tears, sweat, saliva[8] or blood—and the work of different insects and bacteria that have fed on and lived in the paper for centuries, either becoming a physical part of the work or severely damaging it, even to the point of total destruction.

Manuscript codices and computer screens constitute epochal *loci* of textuality. Perhaps through this somewhat forced analogy we will be able to appreciate the cultural history of the hidden corporeality that links textuality with the five senses.

Computers with the Five Senses

Up to now the interaction between people and machines has been restricted to sight and sound. Indeed, twenty-five centuries after Aristotle first classified human perception into the five senses, computer engineers are attempting to go beyond the basic two by developing machines with screens that provide flavours as well as giving off smells.

The Open University of Catalonia invited Dan Maynes, Professor at Stanford University and expert on the interaction of people and computers, to visit Barcelona. Maynes has worked with such important companies in the computer field as Google, Walt Disney and Microsoft, and during his visit to Barcelona, he demonstrated some prototypes of his that include tangible experiences, such as Beancounter and Tastescreen, both designed to allow users to appreciate taste via the PC screen.

---

[8] In certain manuscripts intended for liturgical use, the priest celebrating mass had to kiss the crucifix painted inside the initial letter of the *Te igitur*.

In the first prototype, a mechanical system releases small sweets with different flavours in line with what the user is seeing on the screen. In the second, a gadget installed in the upper part of the screen gives off combinable edible essences following instructions it receives from the computer. When the essence cartridges receive an instruction, they allow liquids to slide down the screen for the user to lick. "It's designed for individual use, not for a cybercafé," jokes Maynes. The aim of his research is that "computers should be capable of representing other interfaces beyond those of sight and sound in order to make computers more expressive": in other words, "to expand the reality of the virtual world".

Maynes is aware that this line of research will not lead to important results in the short term. "We will have to wait twenty years for this to be an everyday thing," he reflects, "until the machines can capture the brain's signals." What is more, he believes that these technologies could be useful for promoting food and drink on the Internet. We can even imagine smelling the sea when we look at a photograph of a beach. Sitting in front of a computer will thus become a much more complex experience than it is now.

In any case, opening a medieval manuscript is very different from opening a printed book because when we have a manuscript in front of us, we become conscious in a very immediate fashion of the manual labour in the materials used in its production, its script and its illumination. At the same time, we are conscious of the way the manuscript has been received on a physical level, in other words we notice its state of preservation straight away (whether it is in a good or bad state, whether it is damaged, stained, perforated, erased or protected) from all the traces left by different bodies (animal, vegetable and human). In a way, therefore, a manuscript is a relic that involves pain, desire and death.

In contrast, the dislocation, the immateriality of everything to do with computers—including both the linguistic aspect of programming and the virtual nature of the marks on the screen—acts at times as a blindfold and a barrier. This is because, when faced with a screen, we are incapable of imagining the linguistic and metalinguistic processes that take place behind it, which occasionally we may not even be aware of since, just as if it were a secret formula, we cannot access the code. However, I have had the privilege and pleasure of living alongside some of the most marvellous manuscripts of the European Middle Ages, and I realize that it is in this electronic textuality that we can regain the essence of the work as a whole and as an object (without the physical dimension, of course, but with a significant increase in sensorial activity compared to reading a book off the press). I see it as drawing us towards medieval manuscripts and their nature as "performative texts" (text as process, like a screen, as a surface where things happen[9]), rather than "perceived texts" (text as object, as the end product). Thus, just as images play a crucial performative role in activating the text, I believe that one of the great potentialities of our current technological exploration lies in this interface between the verbal and the visual. Sight and a certain sense of touch (which in virtual reality is much more developed than we have seen in the example of *The Cave*) have been joined by the sense of hearing because sound has now been included. Who knows whether in the future smells will also appear in the digital environment (with the sense of smell this will experience a digital blooming), so that the five senses will once again be present in the act of reading!

What is beyond doubt is that writing as a form of production and configuration corresponds to the importance of reading as a form of reception and study. We thus find texts that aspire to the condition of music, pieces that strive to collapse the distinction between the physicality of their language and the immateriality of the ideas contained in them, committed works that have what Shelley called "intellectual beauty". This is why I claim a certain erotic in reading or, if preferred, an interpretation via the *performance* of language; since writing is a space that disperses desire, and since it is words, of all artistic materials, that are most often "tamed", the performative aspect, the interpretation, the "running" is vital for ergodic textuality, which is the opposite side of the functional aspect.

And this *mise-en-scène,* which can be generated by the author, by the text as program (that is to say, the machine), by a participating reader—or by any combination of these—focuses on both the content of the text and

---

[9] Even at the level of the senses: sight—images = words, touch—smooth and rough side of the paper felt at each turn of the page, hearing—words pronounced or simply formed with the lips during a silent reading.

the way the text is expressed or inscribed. This empirical development must pave the way for a methodological step consisting of an increase in the philological focus to enable the opening of the anthropological one. The object of study here is more a process (the changing text) than a product (a static text) because digital texts, at their level of textual inscription, are certainly complex in that they include a visible text and an invisible, opaque text: the programming language. From this point of view, the work is even more a texture, a true textual tangle that has to be unravelled in order to discover all its nuances and possibilities.

To finish with, I would like to contrast two "manuscript" texts but this time from "modern" poetry, in order to highlight this commitment to investigation and research and the evocation of pleasure in a text. The first is the principle expressed by Seamus Heaney in the poem from the *Electric Light* collection, significantly entitled "The Fragment", the last lines of which are:

"Since when", he asked,
"Are the first and the last line of any poem
Where the poem begins and ends?"

The second is prose fragment number 30 by Emily Dickinson:

"Did you ever read one of her Poems backward, because the plunge from the front overturned you? I sometimes (often have, many times) have—A something overtakes the Mind"

The force of this assertion, handwritten in a notebook, lies in the idea that Dickinson has of the poem itself. For her, as her letters and poetic writings show, language is an interactive medium. If we go backwards through a poem, we reveal in a surprising way its reciprocal inertias at the level of interpretation. In our search for digital discovery, we might draw on Dickinson's proposal to read poems "differently" as a talisman for the reconsideration of our interpretative resources. Reading backwards is a critical move that invades the unvisited places of imaginative works. It is a paradigmatic model of any operation of critical deformation. A model like this draws our attention to areas of poetic and creative media that normally escape our consideration. Reading backwards is an extremely controlled method for disordering the meanings of a text. Interpretation is the effort to elucidate one discursive form in the terms of another, an application of *scientia* to *poieseis*.

For a book culture like ours, the digital media have brought a rude awakening. All in all, at the present time, more than forty years after the first samples of creation using a computer, we can be certain that we are not faced with the extinction of a species; rather we are involved in the historic convergence of two great machines for the production of symbols and therefore of human consciousness. This is a critical process that throws light on differences and contrasts. And we need to constantly remind ourselves that "critical" means to "cause a crisis". However, it must always be preceded by evaluation, since it is impossible to generate a crisis without prior evaluation. Let us remember what Leonardo said: that one can neither hate nor love anything if one has not previously got to know it. This is the greatest struggle that remains for us: the struggle to know.

Let us return once more to Emily Dickinson:

Much Madness is divinest Sense -
To a discerning Eye -
Much Sense—the starkest Madness -
'Tis the Majority
In this as All prevail -"

But the majority is not everything. And some of us want to experience more things generated by these "creative minorities", which is why our research group, Hermeneia,[10] has tried to encourage creativity through the establishment of the international 'Ciutat de Vinaròs' awards (the source of some of the images in this text). These accept creations in languages that already have a tradition of electronic or digital literature, such as English, French and Portuguese, but they also serve to stimulate creative work in languages like Spanish, Italian and Catalan. Such works are subsequently studied by the research group and at the same time on undergraduate and postgraduate courses, thus promoting interchange between the areas of creation, teaching and research.

---

[10] http://www.uoc.edu/in3/hermeneia

Chapter Eight

Reading Guidelines for Electronic Literature

Alexandra Saemmer

The word "dog" does not move its tail, notes Baruch Spinoza; a succession of letters does not form a physical "unit" with its referent. Drawings or photographs of a dog seem to have more resemblance to the "real" animal. On a paper medium, however, the image remains fixed in an eternal stasis. On an electronic support, the word "dog" can run across the screen. When the reader clicks on the letters, he can make the dog bark. Since words on-screen are hyperlinked and animated, certain authors have started to dream about a new semantic proximity and even the possibility of a faithful translation between words and images. Indeed, they seem to share the same data-processing "origin". On the surface of the screen, they also share the same qualities. On the one hand, images become animated, transgress their secular fixity and approach the fluidity of reading. Animated images are thus permanently changing; they seem to be able to communicate feelings of movement. On the other hand, words rediscover their "materiality", they become coloured and are transformed into new graphic forms; being freely laid out in space, they suggest a simultaneity which was formerly characteristic of images; in becoming animated, they acquire a new plastic dimension; by being hyperlinked, they are now palpable, touchable.

One of the main objectives of this article is to analyse the consequences of hypertext and animation on the meaning of texts. On electronic supports, texts become signal while conserving their meaning, they are read like images *and* as supports of meaning—they acquire a new "materiality" and nevertheless remain words. In order to understand these complex evolutions, it is necessary to establish precise categories. Critics have already made some proposals, but they often do not take into account the *meaning* of the hyperlinked and animated word. I have therefore developed categories to help understand the exact function of hyperlinks in the logical and temporal organization of texts, and to determine the influence of animations on their meaning. I will show their relevance by exploring some extracts from the website *dreamingmethods.com*: the *10 Poèmes en Quatre Dimensions* by Xavier Malbreil, *In the White Darkness* by Reiner Strasser, and *The Revolution Took Place in New York* by Gregory Chatonsky.[1]

Narrative functions of the hyperlink

A hyperlink can fulfil very different purposes according to the style of writing and the graphic layout of the text, its "content" and its "container", depending on its context of publication, its meaning, and the exact place of a hyperlinked fragment in the global matrix of a website. This statement can easily be verified in what we call "hyperfictions"—narrative texts based on hyperlinked fragments.

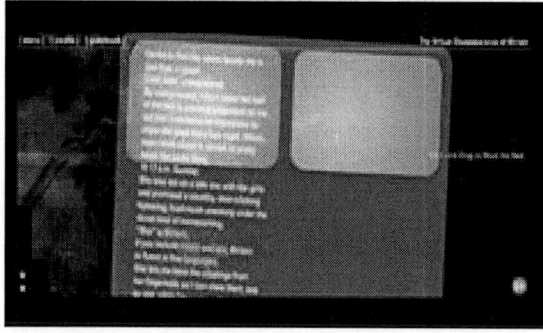

Let us explore *The Virtual Disappearance of Miriam* by M.Bedford (*dreamingmethods.com*). Miriam has dis-appeared; her place in the narrator's bed is empty. He tries to understand what has happened. By activating certain hyperlinks announced by green highlighting, the reader can discover details about the narrator's life with the disappeared girl, about their friends and the recent past. When he clicks on the link "Miriam" in the first fragment, a pop-up window appears and gives access to a portrait and a short description. Admittedly, the photo does not really represent Miriam. A veiled reference is thus addressed to all these curious netsurfers who frantically click in order to "know" and finally arrive on an advertising page. Concerning the narrative organization of this story, the link on "Miriam" can be called a *lien-incise* (Clement, 2004: 7)—

---

[1] For further interpretations and for a detailed description of all the categories presented here, I would like to announce my book *Matières textuelles sur support numérique*, which will shortly be published by Presses Universitaires de Saint-Etienne.

interpolated link—because the activated fragment could be omitted from the matrix without disturbing the logical and temporal organization of the current text. In hyperfictions, interpolated links often give access to *descriptions* that determine the story's atmosphere without any progress being made in the "principal" action. In order to categorize the semantic function of interpolated links more exactly, I propose to call all hypertexts that fill the space between two narrative clauses *catalytic links*; *informing links* confer a time and a place to the plot, while *clue links* imply an activity of deciphering or reconstruction. The link on "Miriam" falls in this last category. In the third fragment of the second part entitled "House of Sam", for example, the interpolated link "Here is a plan of Sam's basement flat" fulfils the purpose of an informing link by allowing a look to be taken at the plan of Sam's house. It is necessary to insist on the fact that the activation of all these interpolated links in *The Virtual Disappearance of Miriam* slows down the exploration of the "principal" action. They nevertheless play an important part in the comprehension of the cultural and geographical context, the social framework and the general atmosphere of this story.

The omission of other links in *The Virtual Disappearance of Miriam* would have disastrous consequences on the comprehension of the story's logical and temporal organization. By activating green arrows below each textual fragment, the reader can advance to the next episode. Whereas in the first fragment the reader stays in bed, in the second fragment he gets up, goes to the toilet, washes himself and starts investigating: he calls Miriam's cell phone; later, he phones her workplace. The reader can activate a link on the word "office". The narrator, however, does not know Miriam's role in this office. Thus, the link appears analeptic: instead of exploring a map, we learn more details about the lives of the narrator and Miriam before her disappearance. These kinds of "liens-bifurcation" (Clement, 2004: 7)—*branching links*—build the narrative plots in hyperfictions. Unlike interpolated links, branching links govern the chronological order of events and actions in a story. Activation of the green arrows in *The Virtual Disappearance of Miriam* allows the story to be followed by what I would call *chronological links*, that is, according to the temporal development of the plot. *Analeptic links* call up fragments that tell about events and actions that occurred before the principal action. *Proleptic links* project the reader towards the future.

It should be pointed out, however, that the inscription of branching links on the temporal axis of a hyperfiction is often conditioned by the reader's decision for or against the activation of a link. In a traditional novel on a paper medium, the different plot developments on the story's temporal axis are determined by the order of the pages and chapters. In a hyperfiction, the position of each link varies, because the reader can explore them at different moments during the reading process. In spite of what is often advanced by critics, these "protean" functions of branching links do not *systematically* endanger the traditional organization of a story, the order of present, past and future episodes. As long as the fragments are equipped with markers to determine their position on the temporal axis and their place in the causal structures of the story, the reader can easily reconstitute its chronological order.

But some specific kinds of hyperfiction have the designated objective of *destroying* the logical and temporal order of the traditional novel. In this case, the hyperlinked fragments are managed without any temporal or causal clue. Conjunctions of opposition and concession, which traditionally coordinate the logical structure of novels, are omitted: instead of constituting branchings, the hyperlinks are reduced to their interpolated function. One may understandably wonder whether such a hypertextual matrix, based exclusively on interpolated links, definitively transgresses the limits of the novel. Perhaps such a text ought rather to be called a poem, a poem that makes characters, places or objects rhyme. I would also like to discuss whether these textual forms are as revolutionary as some critics and authors contend. The poetizing potential of the novel was already tried out with the *Nouveau Roman*. Does the contemporary reader really want to engage in stories of fragmented tracks? Does he like wandering again in narrative "geographies"? Does he want to lose himself in complex settings—even if those narrative structures find an ideal technical support on an electronic medium?The danger of remaining in an epigonal situation compared to the literary avant-gardes of the twentieth century was especially perceptible in the early days of textual experiments on electronic support. A number of years before hypertext tools started structuring knowledge in a new way, poets and novelists had already dreamed of texts which could be "open" to reader intervention: *A Hundred and Thousand Billion of Poems* by Raymond Queneau constitutes one of the most striking realizations on paper, allowing readers to manipulate texts in a very palpable way. We are therefore not surprised by George P. Landow when he considers these new experiments in reading as the starting point of hypertextual adventures. Before the arrival of the World Wide Web and its multiple technological innovations suggesting new relations between author and reader, Roland Barthes in *S/Z* had already considered the reader as a "producer of texts". However, this textual production is strictly mental; it does not leave traces in the written material. "What is unnatural in print becomes natural in the electronic medium and will soon no longer need saying at all, because it can be shown", affirms David Bolter in *Writing Space* (1990: 143). Certain members of the French OuLiPo had explored the limits of paper by combinative tools, just prior to discovering the electronic support. But in OuLiPo's *electronic* creations, instead of generating really innovative text practices, the computer is often reduced to the role of an "amplifier of complexity" (Abraham Moles). A new generation of authors and creators today are liberated from the prerogatives of the New Novel and OuLiPo. I would like to present three of the main new tendencies: the renarrativization of the text, the rediscovery of the text as a material, and, last but not least, programmed literature.

The renarrativization of electronic literature

Certain hyperfictions form part of a tendency that Bruno Blanckeman (2000: 15) qualifies as "renarrativization of the text": the story produces fiction and underlines this production, expresses a novelistic approach and denounces its devices. The use of fictional parameters is ambivalent; the limit between fiction, the work that produces it, and the act of reading is erased. In this context, "post-avant-gardist" hyperfictions play freely with interpolated *and* branching links, and also try out new "stylistic devices" which emerge on the visible surface of the screen.

In *The Virtual Disappearance of Miriam*, it frequently happens that the narrator intervenes in the plot, or that the reader is invited to participate. In the last fragment of the first chapter, for example, the narrator receives an e-mail. If the reader wants to look at its content, he is invited to click at the same time as the narrator and decide whether he wants to download a file. His decision opens the way towards the next episode of the story. This intrusion of the narrator or reader in the story can be called an *interactive metalepsis*, because the reader opens "material" doors on an electronic support and paves the way by activating a part of his body. He moves elements; he gropes on the surface of the screen—the requested gestures are multiple: they can be *deictic, constructive* or *catastrophic* and are no longer limited to a simple click. More than on paper, these interactive effects underline "the importance of the limit they contrive to transgress regardless of any plausibility, and which are precisely those of narration (or representation) itself; this moving but sacral limit between two worlds: that where one tells, that which one tells." (Genette, 1972: 245).

Where animated and/or hyperlinked letters seem to draw the hand of the reader, to imitate the motor activity suggested by the narration, I propose to talk in terms of an *animated hypotyposis*. Hypotyposis is defined as a description, which tries to evoke an object not only by the meanings of words, but also by imitative or associative stratagems. It forms part of the processes that circumvent the dogma of arbitrary sign by stimulating the plastic and mimetic potential of language. Between the last fragments of the second chapter in *The Virtual Disappearance of Miriam* onomatopoeias imitating bursting noises appear and disappear. We also find these processes in comics: "Hu-up Bam", "Whumpf", "Kra-ack".

The rediscovery of the text as a material

Traditionally, "we show by resemblance, we speak through difference" (Foucault, 1973: 39). But when text on an electronic support rediscovers its "materiality", it acquires graphic qualities that during centuries had been reserved for images: colour, form, space, and animation. No longer are written signs condemned to transport only meanings; they can now show what they indicate; they reign in the non-representable *and* in the representable world. In the notes on his creation *La Révolution à New York a eu Lieu*, (The Revolution Took Place in New York), Gregory Chatonsky evokes his fascination for the common technical origin of texts and images on electronic supports. On the visible surface of the screen, they also seem to share the same qualities. Thus, in Reiner Strasser's *In the White Darkness*, words appear between photographs and disappear in a jumble symbolizing the fragmented memory of patients suffering from Alzheimer's disease. Words and images do not only belong to the same graphical space; they melt into one another and become indistinct. In Reiner Strasser's creation, words are perceived, handled and "remembered" as images would be. The textual material appears and disappears on the interactive page—it behaves both as "container" and "content".

The rediscovery of the plastic and graphic potential of texts has seen a rapid emergence of the utopia of words and things being able to find a common ground on electronic supports. This utopia can be experienced in the mimetic rhetorical devices previously discussed, particularly in the "animated calligram".

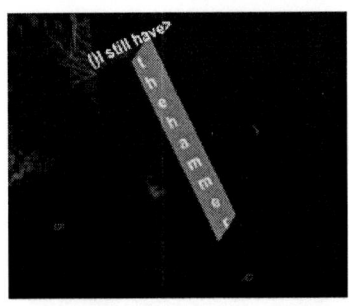
In theory, a drawing of a hammer appears to maintain a more direct relationship with its referent than the word "hammer". In one fragment of *The Virtual Disappearance of Miriam*, the word "hammer" takes on the contours and colours of the indicated tool: it forms a calligram. On an electronic support, this calligram can even move like a hammer on the surface of the screen. The "animated calligram" thus solves the problem of the fixity of drawings and words; it inscribes them within a temporal development. Seduced by the graphic and plastic "materiality" of texts on electronic supports, certain authors dream about the third, or even fourth, dimension. Hypertext would insert the textual material in space; the passage of time in animated spaces would be closely attached to this material by gradually transforming it into the fourth dimension.

Xavier Malbreil named one of his hyperlinked and animated creations *10 Poèmes en Quatre Dimensions*. In the introduction to *10 Poèmes*, the author indicates one of his inspirations for that work: Plato's *Cratylus*. In the passage cited by Xavier Malbreil, Socrates is discussing the origin of words with Cratylus and Hermogen: Are they formed by the essence of things, as Cratylus advances? Or are they pure invention, as Hermogen believes them to be? "*Quand les mots ne faisaient qu'un avec les choses*" ("when words and things were one") is written on the first page of *10 Poèmes en Quatre Dimensions*. The dream of a mythical era is outlined, a time when a stable and *essential* contract, a magical correspondence between words and things was supposed to exist—the childhood of humanity, a reassuring belief that Michel Foucault describes in his book *Les Mots et les Choses*. Both words and images constituted mirrors on the world, in the sense of a doubling of their presence; they drew a reality that already existed. If words and things were one, and if language was the mirror on the world, the visibility of the world was considered to be obvious: ancient myth—modern myth...

While the text introducing *10 Poèmes* yearns for a *stable* link between words, images and things, the centre of the page sets words and images into motion and points out the flaws of that myth. The word *nuage* (cloud), written in the shape of a cloud, passes through the mist in which the triangular schema of human communication lies. Next to that word, one can see the word that describes the activity of the *nuage* icon: *nage* (swim). "*Nage nuage*" sounds like a children's rhyme. It is likely to reassure us on the coherence between the "swimming" activity of the cloud, its "cloudy" aspect and the cloud "thing". The magic of a new correspondence between words and things, between images and things, between three elements which for centuries were "running after one another" without ever coming together—this magic seems to be operable in the animated space of the web page. The word *nuage* has taken the shape of a cloud.

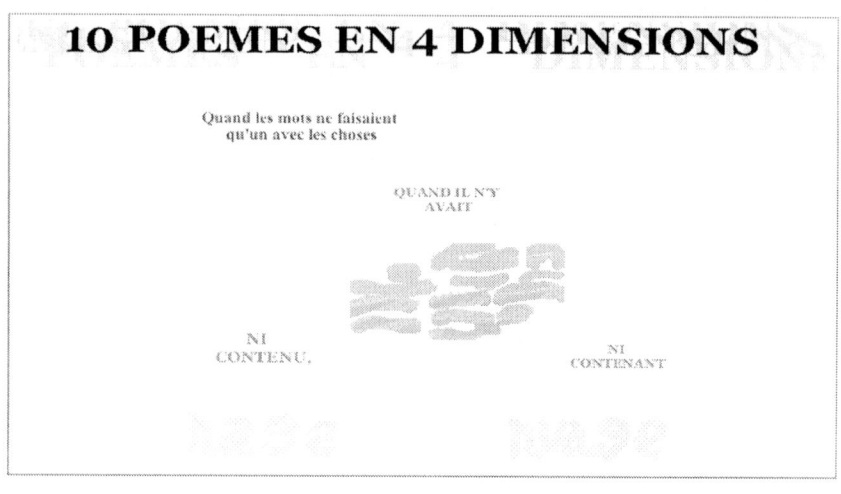

The word *nage* has started to swim. The cloud image has taken ton he shape of the word. The animated word has embodied the swimming activity. Each mode of representation rubs off on another one, giving up some of its qualities to the other. Walter Benjamin uses the term "cloudy place" (*wolkige Stelle*) for that point in a text where the incomprehensible springs up, at least in the sudden suspension of meaning and the disorientation produced by the apparent non insertion of a fragment in the whole text. Do we get access to another reality through that "cloudy place"? Is it through the contamination between words, images and movements, drawn and triggered by interaction, that "cloudy" places are formed in electronic literature between the different systems of signs—*wolkige Stellen*—that would give us access to a new "dimension"? "*Nage nuage*"—a sweet rhyme, sung in a childhood dream... Actually, the drawing proves to be one done by an adult. The unity between the word and the "cloud" thing is not as fixed as the introductory text suggests it is; the word "cloud", although imitating its colour and texture, does not melt into the shape of the indicated object—the word that points out the activity of the object is separated from its "container". The whole system is in perpetual motion: "container" and "content" follow one another closely, but they never meet. The "cloud" thing never takes the shape of the word "cloud", even if the word "cloud" imitates the colour of a cloud, thus suggesting an immersion in the material world. A word never draws cloudy letters in the sky, and a rain of words will never fall on earth... Calligrams and onomatopoeias are usually used to give "substance" to words. Onomatopoeias strive to imitate "things" with sound effects. The hissing of the snake coiled round the Tree of Knowledge in poem 5 is translated by Malbreil with the following letters: "b-z-z-z-z". But when we pronounce them, we only *imitate* the sounds given by a snake. When we read them, that hissing remains imaginary. Let us click on the textual block on page 2 in *10 Poèmes en Quatre Dimensions*: while a written cloud had gone through the communicational mist on the previous page, it is now a wind made out of letters, a "w-i-n-d", that sweeps away the textual zones in the middle of the screen. *Quand les mots contenaient l'action* (when words contained action) can be read in the textual field. But once again, the animation shows only a part of this intention. Although the words *choux...choux*[2], passing through the page in the same way as the coming and going of the "w-i-n-d", actually imitate the whistling of the wind, they also get a double meaning when they are displayed: the reader inevitably associates the onomatopoeic "*choux*" with the vegetable of the same name. The onomatopoeia reveals itself to be polysemous, with "improper" relations to the thing it tries to imitate.

The picture of a cloud seems to have a more direct link to its meteorological referent than the word "cloud" itself. When the word "cloud" puts on "cloudy" shapes and colours and when the drawing of a cloud takes the shape of a word, they form calligrams. As in *The Virtual Disappearance of Miriam*, the calligram in Malbreil's poems is equipped with a new quality: animation. Malbreil's "animated" calligrams break the "simultaneity" of drawings and inscribe them into the logico-temporal process of reading. The word "cloud" that passes across the screen in the same way as a "real" cloud, or the "w-i-n-d" that messes up the organization of the page, must nevertheless be *read* to be understood, and it is at this precise moment that the two modes of signs come into conflict. Despite its cloudy contours and colours, "cloud" remains a word. The

---

[2] This is a play on words that cannot be translated: *chou* (pl. *choux*) means "cabbage"; when pronounced (approximately like the word "shoe" in English), it imitates the whistling of the wind.

word that describes the movement of the cloud is floating behind the animated calligram without ever joining it. The word and the image are in permanent tension with the "thing" they describe without ever coming together. On an electronic support, the process of recognition provoked by the animated calligram cannot find a successful conclusion. Its two written forms constitute a "trap in meaning". Moreover, the movement of the words turns in an eternal loop: the animated material changes in time, but in non-programmed literature, time will never transform the material. The fourth dimension in traditional animation must remain u-topos—a non-existing place.

By analysing recent electronic creations, we have noticed, however, that textual animation and hypertextuality are not *inevitably* limited to the exploration of mimetic devices. Neither are they condemned to vain realizations of all the utopias that impregnated critical speeches in the early days of the Internet: the fourth dimension, the rhizome... Animated and interactive letters, forms, words and sentences can acquire a *metonymic,* or even *metaphorical,* radiation that opens up their semantic field to new meanings.

As pointed out by Gérard Genette, the term "metaphor" tends more and more to cover the whole analogical field (1972: 28). The metonymic "worth for" and the metaphorical "being for" are mixed up. This confusion can also be noticed in critical discourses about electronic literature. Some critics have been quick to suggest the resurgence of new rhetoric figures in electronic literature, and have resorted to the traditional concepts of "metaphor" and "metonymy" to characterize them—without indicating what exactly they mean by these terms which, throughout the centuries, have been defined in many different ways. Jean Clément affirms that applied to hypertext, the concept of metaphor signifies that a fragment is subjected to several readings depending on the process it is part of—according to Clément, the metaphorical radiation of a hyperlinked word would be conditioned by its ever-changing contexts in a hypertextualized system. One should nevertheless wonder whether the term "metaphor" is really appropriate to qualify what is happening on the semantic level during the activation of a hyperlink. The metaphor provokes "a fusion as well as a transport", as formulated by Paul Ricœur. Therefore, by making texts and contexts merge in multiple configurations, the hyperlink seems to carry the meaning of the hyperlinked word to new semantic fields. Nevertheless, the main characteristic of the metaphor remains its "being like", abandoning the *fusion* and the transport on a purely "imaginary" level. The power of a traditional metaphor, such as "sleep is a petrifying fountain", therefore lies in the merging of the nouns "sleep" and "fountain" with the adjective "petrifying" in a single syntactic context. A hyperlink between "sleep" and "fountain" would reveal the first half of the sentence, and then discover the second one: it would thus belong to the category of *metonymy*. That is why, in a more recent article, Jean Clément gives a metonymic value to the hyperlinked word: "It represents the text to come" (1994). Whereas on paper the reader must accept that the "whole" in a metonymy will only be suggested, on electronic supports he can go towards the "whole" by activating a hyperlink. I therefore propose to use the term *interactive metonymy* to refer to the transport of meaning that takes place when a hyperlink connects a word to the textual fragment it "represents". For example, at the beginning of *The Virtual Disappearance of Miriam*, the hyperlinked word "music" gives access to a complete piece of music.

Whereas metonymy characterizes the transposition of meaning that is effectuated when a hypertext link connects a word to the textual fragment it is supposed to "represent", in the digital medium, metaphor has found a new area of application in the field of *animation*.

Textual animation can produce an opening of semantic fields that evokes a metaphorical process. While becoming animated, the textual material acquires a plastic dimension: it is read and contemplated; it signifies while being drawn. The *animated metaphor* is not the same as the calligram, where the plastic resources of textual material are exploited in a purely mimetic aim. But a belief in the forces of *evocation* of the language is also conserved in the animated metaphor. From the tension between the semantic and graphic dimensions of language, an inexpressible and non-representable "essence" of reality can emerge.

On the background image of *Spawn*, we can see a transparent jar that has been turned upside down on a grey surface. A plant has been pushed into the jar, and small black circles turn around it—insects, atoms or pollen? It is up to the reader to associate a particular meaning to these forms. While clicking on the black circles, the reader cannot only influence the movement of the circles. After each activation lines of text emerge. Many of these texts appear, disappear, and fall off the screen to reappear and turn again. Often they do not transport meanings in the traditional sense of the word. Certain combinations of letters are reduced to their onomatopoetic function. Others still form words, but these words do not describe the movements suggested by the animations. After the activation of one of the circles, a crowd of short words, strewn with indents and brackets, populates the screen: (br)e a(k)-();)(only)(; (do)-- (wn); ()-(as); (i). Because of the punctuation marks, these words already say more than their semantic contents. The wings of the butterfly seem to have pushed against the word "only"; the butterfly moves in the jar as if moving around a fatal source of light. Or do the brackets replace missing letters? When the word)(only)(is reversed on itself and continues its insane race on the screen, we easily could read "lonely" instead of "only". The word (i), taken between brackets, seems more isolated than ever. However, by tracing a series of dance steps around the plant, it joins the other words. The word (do)--(wn) falls downwards, but it always rises again and continues "to do" something. Perhaps the transmitted message is positive. Indents and the empty place in the word (do)--(wn) could be supplemented as follows: "i do only a break". Perhaps the message is pessimistic: "lonely i break down". Sense and meaning permanently change, like all these words that turn and are turned over. The graphic realization, animation and signification of words form part of a complex metaphorical system.

The aim of metaphorical animation of the text material (sometimes called kinetic) is to suggest. Its scenographic tools recall those used in theatres: sets of shades, lights, graphic slides and animations metamorphose the screen into an oneiric space of immersion. The author is not only a writer; he is a stage director and an art technician. Poetry seems particularly adapted to this electronic art of the metaphor and the sublime. Rather than in hyperfiction, it is in interactive and animated poetry that the new qualities of text on electronic supports are today being explored in a truly convincing way.

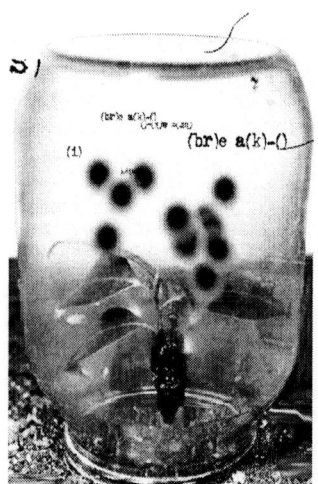

Programmed literature: towards new "objects of pleasure"

But what can we observe in these kinetic creations concerning the new freedom of the reader, this freedom that was so often recommended and discussed in critical speeches? Jean-Pierre Balpe thinks that freedom is extremely reduced: "a video text [...] dictates by its development the rhythm of reading." The exchange of roles between author and reader is only an illusion in kinetic art: The author tries to remain the absolute master of his text (Balpe, 2006: 61). We are far from the utopia of a "scriptible" hypertext and far from the utopia of the Internet as a place without hierarchy and borders. But we should wonder whether we have lost something essential in this evolution. Should the success of electronic art really be sought after as an exchange of roles between author and reader?

And if today the reader wants to *read* again... if he wants to get pleasure from what he reads?

In a research programme undertaken in 2006 at the Université Lyon 2 with 596 students[3], we noticed that many of them do not really appreciate the freedom given by hyperlinks. Readers today know that each link forces them to make a choice, and that this choice can be fatal. Rather than recommending the "miracle" of hypertext and interactivity, a certain number of participants seemed to be seduced by the graphic and plastic aspects of the text on screen. In the opinion of one of them, reading this way on electronic supports corresponded to "interpreting images": "We *look* at a text on the web". Another student noted: "We do not only read a text". In our investigation, we distinguished two main types of reading on electronic supports: reading based on a fast race towards information and the practice of "frantic" navigation, often regarded as unpleasant by the participants, and an immersive, intuitive activity, where the reader is sensitive to the graphic and plastic dimensions of texts. Through this second practice of reading, an important evolution in textual creation on electronic supports can be noted: a return to the text-result.

A second evolution seemingly goes in the opposite direction, towards the abandonment of the text-result to the benefit of the text algorithm. Continuing his critical remarks on the reader's role in hypertextual and kinetic creation, Jean-Pierre Balpe (2006: 62) makes a plea for programmed literature in which "the algorithm of the text *constitutes* literature". Jean-Pierre Balpe was among the first artists to try out electronic text generators. He explicitly affirms that texts produced by a generator do not have a literary value by themselves (Balpe, 2006: 62). Indeed, as Jean Clément also points out, when the reader activates a traditional generator, "the pleasure comes less from the reading of the texts than from the discovery of a process that delivers its secrets only in reiteration" (Clement, 2006: 71).

However, after being present at performances during which Jean-Pierre Balpe and Jacopo Baboni Schilingi *read* the text produced by generators, I wonder if this text really does not have any literary value. The better a generator is designed, the more the produced texts are readable—surprising, even—even literary! Besides, why wouldn't they be literary? Because the combinations were effected by a machine? It is precisely

---

[3] Project based on questionnaires directed by Claire Bélisle, LIRE (Université Lyon 2- CNRS).

OuLiPo that has shown us that literary creation is also based on combination.

In more recent programmed creations, the text produced has increased value. The author does not seek complete domination of the textual material: he ensures the programming of creations whose actualizations are not entirely foreseeable. These creations are thus characterized by a "technological sublime", which indicates what escapes from the field of possibilities, and is defined by the "ideal" qualities of virtuality. Programmed art must be clearly dissociated from hypertextual and animated creation, where the author tries as much as possible to control the visible "surface" of his work, and where the computer only plays a supporting role. Whereas for Jean-Pierre Balpe, "reading is the blind part abandoned to the reader, who does whatever he wants because on the one hand, he is never sure to read the same text again, and on the other hand, he is never sure that anyone else will read the same text" (Balpe, 2006: 62), authors like Philippe Bootz install "adaptive generators" to ensure the conformity of the produced result with their aesthetic project. Unlike Queneau, they do not seem interested in the possibility of manufacturing a hundred thousand billion texts; they want one *Text* to be manufactured (an "object of pleasure"). The energy that transforms a discourse in writing can perhaps be drawn from the changing context of a partially open system. This open system then constitutes the virtual part of electronic art. In traditional combinative literature, time neither arranges nor disturbs the potentialities of the textual material. New generators change with time; perhaps they indeed project animated textual material towards the fourth dimension.

This evolution of programmed literature also has its risks, however. In certain works, for example *The Revolution Took Place in New York* by Gregory Chatonsky, the textual and iconographic components, automatically generated in relation to Google, seem to clash in disconcerting metaphorical relationships. These relationships sometimes create "incidents of meaning", which could also result from "human" creation. We are shocked by such incidents; they disturb the myth of inspiration to which we still adhere, which defends territories that have been explored exclusively by humans for millions of years. Perhaps Jean-Pierre Balpe is right to suggest that "the aim of automatic generation of literature is to show the activity of literature" (1997). The animated poems by Philippe Bootz are inspired by neurology, psycholinguistics and semiotic. Combinative actualization is adaptive, taking into account the precise electronic environment. Michel Bret creates artificial beings whose behaviours are conditioned by the interaction with an artificial or real environment. In the future, users will not only be like autonomous and auto-adaptative systems in front of a data-processing tool; they will face a partner. However, I for one wonder whether such literature still needs readers.

Bibliography

Balpe, J.-P. *Trois mythologies et un poète aveugle.* 1997. http://cv.uoc.edu/~04_999_01_u07/balpe3.html

—. "Règles, contraines, programmes". *La Littérature numérique et caetera, Formules 10*, S. Bouchardon, E. Kac et J.-P. Balpe (eds.). Paris: Noësis, 2006.

Bedford, M. *The Virtual Disappearance of Miriam.* http://www.dreamingmethods.com/miriam/

Blanckeman, B. *Les Récits Indécidables : Jean Echenoz, Hervé Guibert, Pascal Quignard.* Villeneuve d'Ascq: Presses Universitaires du Septentrion, 2000.

Bouchardon, S. *Hypertexte et Art de l'Ellipse* , http://archivesic.ccsd.cnrs.fr/documents/archives0/00/00/03/58/sic_0 0000358_02/sic_00000358.html

Bolter, J. D.. *Writing Space: The Computer in the History of Literacy*, Hillsdale, N.J.: Lawrence Erlbaum, 1990.

Chatonsky G. *The Revolution Took Place in New York.* http://www.incident.net/works/revolution_new_york/

Clément, J. *Fiction Interactive et Modernité* 1994. http://hypermedia.univ-paris8.fr/jean/articles/litterature.html

—. *Hypertexte et fiction : une affaire de liens,* 2004. http//hypermedia.univ-paris8.fr/jean/articles/Lien.pdf

—. *Jeux et Enjeux de la Littérature Numérique. La Littérature Numérique et caetera, Formules 10*, S. Bouchardon, E. Kac et J.-P. Balpe (eds.), Paris: Noësis, 2006.

Foucault, M. *Ceci n'est pas une Pipe.* Paris: Fata Morgana, 1973.

Genette, G. *Figures III.* Paris: Seuil, 1972.

Malbreil, X. *10 Poèmes en Cuatre Dimensions.* http://www.0m1.com/10_poemes_en_4_dimensions/index.htm

Ricoeur P. (1976). *La Métaphore Vive*, Paris, Seuil, 1976.

Strasser, R. *In the White Darkness*, http://www.nonfinito.de

Spawn, http://www.dreamingmethods.com/spawn/

PART III

HYPER-EDITING

MARÍA GOICOECHEA

The first article in this section, "Aspects of Scholarship and Publishing in the Age of New Media Technology", introduces us to the real-life vicissitudes of an online publisher, Steven Tötösy de Zepetnek, the writer of the article himself. Tötösy draws a picture of the situation in which the publication of online scholarly journals in the humanities finds itself. According to him, there is reluctance in the field of the humanities to embrace and defend online publishing at the same level as traditional printed journals.Through an exposition of his own experience as editor of the *Canadian Review of Comparative Literature* and later of the CLCWeb, Tötösy tells us how he made the definitive jump to the digital medium, as he defends his struggle to keep scholarship in the humanities in an open-access mode and provides pragmatic ideas to make it work. Tötösy's article helps to underscore the political, economical, and cultural decisions that shape the world of editing. This section will focus on the irruption of digital technologies in the field of editing and the changes introduced in the way knowledge is processed and distributed .

The following two articles trace the philosophical imprint of postmodernity in the practices of hyper-editing. The intrinsic characteristics of electronic textuality—non-linearity, inconclusiveness and spatiality—shape the type of editing philosophy generated within electronic space. As Jola Skulj argues in "A Dynamic Authenticity of Texts in E-Archives: On Digitized Cultural Resources in Comparative Literary Studies", the digital medium fosters a shift towards a different presentation of literary phenomena that is open to participation and collaboration among scholars, a multi-linear, complex, networked and inconclusive shift that is always a work in progress.

Along similar lines, Marko Juvan's article, "Postmodernity and Critical Editions of Literary Texts: Towards the Virtual Presence of the Past", charts the evolution of editing philosophies until the advent of electronic media. Juvan discusses how editing is both a physical act that affects and transforms the material presence of literary works, and a critical, philosophical act that replicates the underlying philosophies and theories of literature that inform it. The medium in this case is also the message. But what is the message with regard to the concept of literature transmitted by electronic editions or "hyper-editing"?

Juvan's insight comes across the apparent paradox "that it is computer-generated *virtual* cyberspace that meets postmodern efforts to restore the *concreteness* of historical presence." By creating a medium with an immense capacity for storage and easy retrieval, digital technologies facilitate the accumulation of documents in e-archives, which can be organized, compared, and perused at leisure by the reader. Electronic editions may contain a constellation of various pre-texts, editions, book covers and critical commentaries of literary works, which, given their new position among the editorial apparatus, no longer appear as stable, closed, tangible entities, with a clear authorship or well-defined boundaries. Juvan remarks, however, that all computer markup languages are also pre-defined and constrained by rules; therefore, they also impose their own order on the primary documents. This means that there is a textual dimension that escapes electronic assimilation, essentially the unpredictable, organic, dynamic nature of textuality.

The following two articles in this section deal with the uses and frontiers of "hyper-editing" in practice: how hypertextual structure can be used to yield accurate representations of writing processes (Van Hulle), and how electronic editions confront the limits of their own digital nature with respect to their diffusion and reception (Paixão de Sousa).

Dirk Van Hulle's article "The Hypertextual Structure of Writing Processes" exposes different hypertextual representations of the writing processes of Proust, Joyce and Beckett, showing how a hypertextual architecture can be a useful tool for visualizing and analysing the *avant-texte* (which is indeed a hypertextual structure), and to compare the writing methods of different authors. As Juvan has noticed, this use of the digital medium seems to foster a weakening of the author's subject. By offering the reader glimpses into the mess in his or her workshop, which is full of imperfect scraps of writing, the image of the author as a creative genius in control of his or her subject matter is undermined. As we come to share some of his or her creative meanders, hesitations, sketches, influences, etc. in the virtual sense, we may also come closer to the reality of literary composition.

The last contribution to this section, María Clara Paixão de Sousa's article, "Digital Texts: Conceptual and Methodological Frontiers", examines digital texts from a "strictly *material* perspective". This apparently simple move yields potent conclusions as it exposes the intrinsic revolutionary quality as well as the limitations of digital media.

What do we actually have in mind when discussing digital text? Are we referring to its dimension as a product, such as texts whose final form is digital, or to its dimension as a process, such as texts that have been processed in an electronic device? Where do we place partial and global digital processing? How do we come to terms with their virtual nature, with the interferences provoked by codification and decodification along the diffusion chain? De Sousa brings to the forefront the complex material nature of digital text by providing examples of the different stages involved in text codification and reception, showing how digital programming systems are also susceptible to causing loss of information. Moreover, as programs evolve to become more "intuitive" and straightforward for the average person, the complexity and sophistication of their programming increases, making it progressively more difficult for text producers and receivers to have any control over intermediation processes.

It is therefore of crucial importance for literary text editors to become hyper-editors. In de Sousa's words: "This is not to say that specialized text editors who make use of electronic media will suddenly turn into computer scientists; it simply means that artificial intelligence has to be included as a related area in textual studies, in the same way that paleography or codicology have traditionally been included".

Chapter Nine

Aspects of Scholarship and Publishing in the Age of New Media Technology

Steven Tötösy de Zepetnek

In this paper, I discuss several aspects of new media, the digital turn and the humanities by focusing on the pragmatic side of knowledge transfer and knowledge management such as they pertain to the field of publishing. Generally speaking, scholars in the humanities are cautious about new media technology in general and online scholarship in particular. Among the debates and many examples of this caution and reluctance, perhaps the most basic criticism is with regard to reading in its varied contexts, and how new media technology, from the now "traditional" medium of television to new media such as the World Wide Web, impacts negatively on reading. What tends to be left out in the logic of the argumentation about reading is that "reading today, unlike in the past, is no longer the principal available instrument for acculturation" (Petrucci, 361). What is more important for the debate on reading is that there is no evidence that reading in whatever mode—traditional or new media—might be in peril. On the contrary, the vast majority of surveys on reading in the industrialized world and virtually all publishers' statistics show that there is more reading today, proportionally speaking, than ever before, and that this situation includes all segments of society (see Ghesquiere, Ibsch and Tötösy [1992 and 1998] for examples of the many sources on this). This is obviously not the case when it comes to scholarship; one of the many problems with criticism of reading impacted by new media technology is that in many an influential text there is no differentiation made between the two types of reading: that of primary texts and that of scholarship. This lack of differentiation—resulting in the use of the argument against new media in scholarship—is, of course, important in a wider context than the one I intend to discuss here. At the same time, with regard to the specific context of scholarship and reading, the observation remains that "scholars still doubt that electronic text has much of a role in the humanities, particularly in literary scholarship" (Warwick, 49). This general view of scholarship online in the humanities is at odds with both the pragmatics of publishing and the epistemological contexts of new media, where, for instance, the perspectives of online reading and the functionalities of hypertext—a basic function of new media and online publishing—make the application and use of scholarship online relevant a priori (see, for example: Van Looy and Baetens's *Close Reading New Media* and Landow's *Hypertext 3.0: Critical Theory and New Media in an Era of Globalization*). On the pragmatic side—which is what I am concerned with here—the opinion expressed at the beginning of the *The Draft Report of the American Council of Learned Societies' Commission on Cyberinfrastructure for the Humanities and Social Sciences* (November 5, 2005) <http://www.acls.org/cyberinfrastructure/cyber.htm> is that:

> Libraries, archives, and museums are cultural infrastructures. So are schools for that matter. So are university presses. In the humanities, textual editing (which cuts across disciplines and communities of practice) contributes to the growth of cultural infrastructure, since it creates critical editions for scholarship in a number of disciplines, and these critical editions in digital form are another form of cultural infrastructure (11).

It concludes:

> We believe that a major, concerted, and structured investment in the capacities of the humanities and social science scholarship to operate in the digital world will help transform these fields of knowledge and the digital world itself (58).

Following the release of the *Draft Report*, *The Chronicle of Higher Education* published a paper confirming the importance of new media and digital publishing:

> John M. Unsworth, dean of the Graduate School of Library Science at the University of Illinois at Urbana-Champaign, was chair of the 11-member commission that wrote the report. He said in an interview that development of cyberinfrastructure for the humanities should coincide with digital efforts in the sciences. "What we're hoping to insert into development of cyberinfrastructure here is an awareness of both the needs and the contributions of the humanities and the social sciences," he said. "We can't afford to have a separate but equal cyberinfrastructure for the humanities and social sciences..." In drafting the report, Mr. Unsworth said, the commission debated how to take a "reasonable" position on open access. "That's a complicated issue," he said. "Publishers and libraries are

both critical parts of the infrastructure here, and they have different perspectives on that." The Open Content Alliance, a group of libraries and corporations that are working on an open access digital archive, is hailed in the report as a model. The alliance "has shown that commercial, non-profit, and university content creators can cooperate in powerful ways to increase open access to cultural resources," Mr. Unsworth said, adding that the more closed and commercial digitization efforts of Google also have value. After reading an advance copy of the report, he said in an interview that the nature of scholarly culture in the humanities and social sciences might hinder the adoption of some of the recommendations of the report. He was especially struck by the call for collaboration in the humanities. "The humanities are very much the culture of the solitary scholar," Mr. Wells said. "And yet it is very clear that the future is collaborative, and technology is not only an enabling factor in that collaboration, but it's also driving the users and consumers of information to a more collaborative understanding" (Carlson, "Humanities" <http://chronicle.com/temp/reprint.php?id=c9hf16kk7b59tt72zw6yc7f1h2zd6rfl>

Indeed, what Wells suggests in the *Chronicle* paper is evident in scholarly discussions and publications in the humanities generally, namely that the overwhelming majority opinion is that publishing scholarship online is not something the humanities should embrace, and that positive moves towards the World Wide Web viewed as a depository and medium for knowledge are supported by opinions published outside the scholarly world (see, for example, Cader). Taking the situation of literary journals as an example, Lynda Williams and Lorne Flagel correctly state that such journals "never have enough money to publish as much, or as frequently, as they would like, for distribution to as many readers as they desire...one might predict that literary journals will abandon their print form and appear solely on the Web" (115). While the situation of literary journals discussed by Williams and Flegel is somewhat different from the situation of scholarly journals in the humanities, what they are describing is representative of the publishing of scholarship online. There are numerous examples—published as empirical as well as anecdotal evidence—with regard to the problematics of the publishing of humanities scholarship online, whether subscription-based or open access. This state of affairs is evident from my own experience as an editor and publisher of scholarship in the humanities. As editor of an online scholarly journal in the humanities that I publish with Purdue University Press—*CLCWeb: Comparative Literature and Culture* at http://clcwebjournal.lib.purdue.edu-, I have encountered a great deal of aversion to the publishing of scholarship online. For example, in 2003 I had three mid-career scholars withdraw their submissions because they were advised, either by colleagues, the head of the department or the dean, against publishing online because such a publication would not be accepted as bona fide for the purposes of tenure and promotion (even if, as in this case, the publication were peer-refereed). Also, the lack of interest in online journals for the humanities is apparent on the web page of the US Library of Congress, where there are numerous links to web publishers in the sciences while for the humanities not a single publisher is listed (instead, the scholarly community in the US is organizing digital libraries, either at universities or independent, funded with both). The reluctance to embrace online scholarship in the humanities is also evident in such important scholarly associations as the US-based CELJ: Council of Editors of Learned Journals. Although the association recognized the importance of online publishing, at the same time it was reluctant until recently to reward such efforts, thus indicating in no uncertain terms that in its current perception online publishing is not something they embrace. The official web site of CELJ states:

> As we all know, electronic publishing is here and spreading; CELJ needs to keep up with this. But, as must be the case, contests such as this recognize what is currently happening among a specific constituency. We need to see what the extent of electronic publishing actually is among the CELJ member journals (see *CELJ: Council of Editors of Learned Journals* <http://www.celj.org/>).

In June 2003, the CELJ executive decided to accept nominations of online journals for its prestigious awards; more recently, in August 2006, the CELJ set up a committee in order to evaluate online journals for its awards. Another example is the situation regarding citation indexes. I have been trying since 1999 to get material published in the journal I edit to be indexed by the ISI: Institute for Scientific Information Arts and Humanities Citation Index, and although we are almost at the stage where *CLCWeb* would be accepted for indexing, the process has taken over four years and is not yet over; meanwhile, ISI states on its web site that provided its conditions are met, material from a journal will be indexed within six months (see <http://www.isinet.com/isi/>). Many more examples can be cited to illustrate this "ludditism" prevalent in the humanities (I should note that in my discussion I am dealing with the situation in countries where the availability of computers and access to the Internet for e-mail and the World Wide Web is not at issue, that is, industrially and technologically advanced countries). This objection can take on comical dimensions at times: in 2000 a tenured professor of English published an article in *The Chronicle of Higher Education* describing how she "held off on using e-mail because it didn't seem necessary." She then tried it—and discovered, *to her dismay*, just how "potent a tool it could be" (Perillo A64; my italics). Apart from the comical—namely, the discovery of e-mail by a tenured professor of English in 2000—there is the issue of accountability; in my opinion, an academic who is not in tune with the demands of pedagogical performance, in this case based on technological advances, is not earning his or her salary. And this is the case both in Europe, where education is financed with taxpayers' money and accountability should thus be to the taxpayers through the delivery of good teaching, and in the USA, where the student should be entitled to receive a product (the teaching of the subject matter at hand) commensurate with the money paid for it. It is yet another matter that *The Chronicle*—the main journal of higher learning in the United States—publishes such an item; I doubt the article was meant to be published in an ironic context but to me that is certainly how it ends up. A more complicated issue is the World Wide Web, understood here as a medium of delivery and a tool for the presentation of scholarship and the transfer of knowledge. This new tool is also underrated among a good percentage of scholars in the humanities and all too often I encounter colleagues who have no idea about the World Wide Web, or, if they do have some idea, they do not use it themselves; even those who do use it (for the presentation of course syllabi, for instance) do not perceive it as a medium worthy of attention when it comes to scholarship. To me, this lack of interest and attention is no trivial matter for scholarship and the publishing of scholarship, nor is it trivial in the pedagogy of the humanities (for more on this, see Tötösy 2001). Undoubtedly, much of the caution and reservation comes not only from the a priori mistrust of new technology residing in the humanities, but also because new media does not support or facilitate the traditions of scholarship in the humanities, that is, reflection and reflective reading. Reading scholarship on the screen is not the same as reading a tactile form such as a hard-copy book. I concede that it will take a few more years for technology to develop the use of hand-held devices that are able to make reading enjoyable. And I also concede that texts longer than 6000-8000 words online are difficult to absorb, that is, to read in the reflexive mode on the computer screen. But up to 8000 words the reading and absorption of a scholarly paper is possible and this is one of the reasons why current reluctance is misguided. The question of online journals in particular is one area where this reluctance is especially misguided from several points of view, including the question of the ability of libraries to pay for hard-copy journals. For a number of years now, some prominent scholars have argued for the realization of full-text, peer-reviewed and open access online journals, in other words, for the existence of journals which only differ from traditional journals in their mode of delivery: online. For example, cognitive scientist Stevan Harnad (Southampton University) argued as early as 1995—when the web was just emerging—for the implementation of online scholarship. More recently, another scientist, Harold Varmus, 1989 Nobel Prizewinner in Medicine, has stated in an interview that:

> Heute birgt das Internet das Potential, die wissenschaftliche Literatur viel breiter zugänglich zu machen—für die Wissenschaftler und für die Öffentlichkeit—, indem man digitale Bibliotheken errichtet. Der grösste Teil der Wissenschaft wird durch Steuern finanziert. Deshalb sind wir der festen Überzeugung, dass die Publikationen allen zugänglich sein sollten. ("Today the Internet affords us the potential to make scholarship accessible in a much wider way—for scholars and for the public—with the establishing of digital libraries. Most scholarship is financed with funding from taxes [in the European Union]. And this is the reason why I believe that all scholarly publications should be available to all in open access"; my translation) (Varmus, 29).

As proposed in the *Draft Report* of the American Council of Learned Societies and Varmus, full-text and open access online journals and libraries would make it possible to perform online research. This proposal regarding the inter-relationship of work in the humanities, the study of literature and new media scholarship and technology is even more controversial than the basic proposal to embrace online journals, and the discussion on this obviously extends to all sorts of matters, such as the contentious issue of distance education in all its facets.

Basic sources that reflect on aspects of online research in the humanities include:

- The Internet Public Library: "Skills for Online Searching". <http://www.ipl.org/teen/aplus/skills.htm>
- "Glossary of Library and Internet Terms". <http://www.bedfordstmartins.com/hacker/resdoc/glossary.htm>
- Johnson's "The World Wide Web, Computers, and Teaching Literature". <http://www.dsu.edu/~johnsone/webprof.html>
- Miles's *RMIT HyperText Project*: <http://hypertext.rmit.edu.au/>
- Ryan's *Literary Theory and Narrative as Virtual Reality*, the *Sociological and Ethnographic Research of Cyberspace* site. <http://www.socio.demon.co.uk/home.html>

Aspects of Scholarship and Publishing in the Age of New Media Technology   177

- Landow's *The Cyberspace, Hypertext, and Critical Theory Web: An Introduction*.
  <http://landow.stg.brown.edu/cpace/cspaceov.html>
- Thumlert's "Hypertextuality and Sociocultural Contexts of Education". <http://home1.gte.net/grnjeans/htext.htm>

As things stand today, peer-reviewed and open access scholarly journals online in the humanities in full-text number no more than dozen or so worldwide. While I am sure this will change in the future, the present situation is at best dismal. I present here the example of the full-text, open access, peer-reviewed online quarterly, *CLCWeb: Comparative Literature and Culture*: <http://clcwebjournal.lib.purdue.edu> as a parallel alternative to the traditional hard-cover mode of publishing scholarship in the humanities; there are many aspects of the journal's foundation and its life since that show the benefits and advantages of online publishing. After editing and publishing the *Canadian Review of Comparative Literature / Revue Canadienne de Littérature Comparée* in the traditional mode from 1989 to 1997 (at the time an innovation in itself, as it was the first desktop-published humanities journal with camera-ready copy in Canada that I edited and desktop-published between 1989-97), I realized the advantages of a peer-refereed, public access, full-text journal published online from the observation that, with the rapid development of new media technology, the humanities had to follow suit and capitalize on the advantages offered by this new media technology. The use of new technology—in this case the Internet and the World Wide Web—is advantageous and must be exploited in all its aspects for the advancement of scholarship in the humanities. I argue that the World Wide Web is a viable avenue for the dissemination and transfer of knowledge for the benefit of scholarship and the individual scholar and also for the general public. While this may be obvious in fields such as the natural sciences, medicine, or engineering—and, indeed, in a general context, in all fields— these advantages are not as yet accepted in the humanities, much to the detriment of the image, function and social relevance of the field, and to the detriment of scholarship and the study of the humanities, including by the current generation of students. (On the use of new media by students, see, for example, Carlson: "Students").

After giving up the editorship of the *Canadian Review*, I decided to found an online journal in the humanities. After consultation with colleagues in a number of countries across the globe, it became obvious that the launching of an online journal would indeed make sense and that such a journal would fill a gap on the landscape of scholarship of the humanities in literature and culture. In consequence, an advisory board and associate editors' group was set up, an ISSN number was applied for and obtained from the National Library of Canada (1481-4374), the listing, archiving, and mirroring of the new online journal with the National Library of Canada (as of 2005 renamed Library and Archives Canada) was arranged, and so on. (The journal is also mirrored and archived in two additional locations: in the UK with the BCLA (British Comparative Literature Association), and in the Stanford University LOCKSS [Lots of Copies Keep Stuff Safe] system: <http://www.lockss.org/lockss/Home>) The first issue of *CLCWeb* was placed online in March 1999 on the server of the Faculty of Arts at the University of Alberta where I was teaching at the time. The URL of the journal was provided by the Alberta Faculty of Arts on its server, together with the necessary disk space for the material of the journal (I had previously created and maintained a web site, since 1995, for the Department of Comparative Literature and the Research Institute for Comparative Literature; I discontinued the operation of these sites once the Department created its own official site in 1998 and carried the material such as bibliographies over to *CLCWeb*). The university's Help Desk and the University of Alberta Faculty of Arts Technologies for Learning Centre (TLC) provided occasional technical help for the journal and its functions, such as the *CLCWeb* moderated listserv (for news and calls for papers in the humanities). During its inception in Canada, the set-up and start-up of *CLCWeb*, including all technical aspects such as the design of its index page, took place without funding. The University of Alberta and the Department of Comparative Literature did not provide financial help either for the establishing or the operation of the journal and moral support was of a limited nature as it was felt that to support two journals in the same department, one published in traditional hard-copy mode and the other online, would create tension. I have attempted to obtain funding from the SSHRC: Social Sciences and Humanities Research Council of Canada (new technology and learned journals programme) but without success. Unfortunately, the programme administrators insisted that *CLCWeb* must have 200 paid subscribers, similar to the requirements for traditional hard-copy journals, and the argument that the journal was online in the mode of free access did not carry any weight. Moreover, the argument drawing attention to the already high web traffic of the journal with only two issues online, or the argument for accepting "hits" on the journal and "session use" of its material in lieu of paid subscriptions as a demonstration of its use in the scholarly community did not persuade the SSHRC to consider funding.

By January 2000, following the consideration of plans for the development of the *CLCWeb* and its legitimization on the landscape of humanities scholarship, in cooperation with the journal's advisory board and associate editors, I began exploring the possibilities of relocating the journal from the Faculty of Arts at the University of Alberta to a university press. After several months of contacts, e-mail exchanges, and discussions with up to a dozen university presses and virtual libraries across North America (US and Canada) and Europe, the editorial board of Purdue University Press approved its relocation to Purdue for publication. In my opinion, Purdue's decision is remarkable and far-sighted for several reasons. All the other presses, and even those who expressed an avid interest in hosting and publishing the journal, ceased to be interested upon my insistence that the journal should remain in public access mode (presses interested initially always suggested that the journal would have to be published in the paid subscription mode). Purdue, on the other hand, accepted my argument that *CLCWeb* should remain in free access mode because of principles such as social responsibility towards the relevance of scholarship in the humanities, and the notion of the Internet and the Web as a democratic venue for the globalization of knowledge, scholarly communication, and knowledge transfer. Of course, the question of where the money would come from if all online journals were in public access mode is valid (more on this below). However, the argument for public access mode for online journals in the humanities and social sciences—despite the fact that such scholarly journals online are very few to date—includes the proposition that by offering *CLCWeb* in the public access mode income for the press is generated by recognition of its name based on the high web traffic of *CLCWeb*. Thus, since issue 2.3 (September 2000), *CLCWeb* has been published by Purdue University Press. The journal and all its functions, including its *Library* (the international directory of comparatists, bibliographies, etc.) and its moderated listserv for news and announcements in comparative literature and culture. That the journal has touched a nerve in the humanities is obvious when one takes a look at its web traffic (link to the statistics from the journal's index page), which now has thousands of hits per day with the correspondingly high level of reading in other categories of use. Of course, this may in some cases be due to scholarship published in *CLCWeb*, such as Mabel Lee's paper about the work of the 2000 Nobel Laureate in Literature, Gao Xingjian, published in *CLCWeb*'s 2.3 (2000). Another reason for the high use of the journal's material is that *CLCWeb* maintains, in addition to the publishing of articles, a Library with bibliographies, diverse research material, an international directory of scholars in the field (with links to scholars' curricula where available) and a moderated listserv—all functions that are possible online which would be prohibitively expensive and circumstantial in hard-copy traditional print. In the case of online publishing in general and online publishing in the humanities in particular, the question of funding, that is, the financial operation of an online journal, is a matter of debate. In all fields, most journals published online opt for paid subscription similar to traditional hard-copy journals and there are several companies and institutions performing such services for profit (for example, the Muse Project of Johns Hopkins University). Put briefly and concisely, in my opinion, regarding the spirit of knowledge transfer and access to knowledge (knowledge management) in public access mode, made possible through the World Wide Web, it is institutions of higher learning which ought to bear the costs from internal as well as external funding, such as government funding or private sponsorship. There is yet another aspect of the new functions and possibilities of new media technology for knowledge management in the humanities and social sciences: I propose that the availability of scholarly material online (including public access peer-reviewed journals online) is a vital necessity. At the same time, new media technology for knowledge management can make an impact on another areas of scholarly publishing. I take Purdue University, the publisher of *CLCWeb* as an example: in addition to their foresight in taking on the journal and publishing it in public access, Purdue is also developing a "print-on-demand program" (called Digital-I at Purdue). This is particularly advantageous for the humanities and social sciences where even in the US, with its large population and many universities, a scholarly book rarely sells more than 400-500 copies. With the print-on-demand mode of publishing a press prints a book (in four colours; the product looks and feels in all aspects just like a regular book) on direct order to the press from the customer (by e-mail, phone, fax or order form).

    The book is advertised in the traditional way, through brochures and leaflets distributed to universities, academics, university libraries and book stores, etc. In other words, copy-by-copy printing of the book is not only financially feasible, but is beneficial to humanities publishing. As in traditional publishing, the book has an ISBN number and two copies are deposited with the Library of Congress. In my opinion, as with the publishing of *CLCWeb*, the print-on-demand program of Purdue University Press is at the forefront of current developments in knowledge management in publishing in general and in the humanities in particular. Considering that most university presses struggle to survive, to me it is a mystery indeed that there is not more interest in this solution to the problem of publishing in the humanities. As a peer-reviewed forum of scholarship and in a form that combines traditional scholarship and practices with new media scholarship and technology, the journal offers the possibility for training and involvement in the study of the humanities in general and comparative literature and culture in particular. Owing to the nature of new media scholarship and publishing, editorial assistants can be located physically, no matter where. For these reasons, as well as for assisting in the work needed on the journal, *CLCWeb* appoints graduate student editorial assistants for periods of one academic year (renewable). The tasks of these assistants include editing, file transfers and formatting, HTML, bibliography work and maintenance of the journal's *Library*, including the checking of active/non-active web links, technical, administrative and market dimensions, and aspects of new media scholarship and publishing, etc. In the two months following the posting of an advertisement on the *CLCWeb* listserv in May 2000, thirty positive responses were received from seven countries and since then a number of graduate students have assisted and still assist the journal. Since the 2002-2003 academic year, the Purdue Program of Comparative Literature has funded. The above description of some of the aspects of the creation and maintenance of a scholarly journal in the humanities would, I believe, serve as a good example of the hows and whys of publishing scholarship online today. Without any doubt, my enthusiasm for and aggressive promotion of open access publishing of humanities scholarship would necessarily have to take blind spots and handicaps into consideration. At the same time, while I do not anticipate much change soon with regard to online scholarship in the humanities, despite the obvious advantages of this, as expressed in the *Draft Report of the American Council of Learned Societies* referred to previously, I can perhaps at least outline some good arguments as to why the humanities ought to embrace online scholarship and online journals, where all the advantages of the new media, including hypertext, can and should be capitalized on. There is no doubt in my mind that the younger generation of scholars do recognize and appreciate the value and importance of scholarship online; as always, the paradigm shift takes time. Finally, I believe there is one further aspect that needs to be mentioned: the question of language and the World Wide Web, and therefore the question of language with regard to the publishing of humanities scholarship online. While it is widely accepted that the lingua franca of the World Wide Web and, in many ways, of scholarship itself, happens to be English, this acknowledgement begs the question of the contentious issue of US-American cultural hegemony (I discuss this problem in more detail in my 1989 book *Comparative Literature: Theory,*

Method, Application). Here, suffice to say that the World Wide Web and new media offer uncharted possibilities for the advancement of knowledge precisely because scholarship in languages other than English can be published online and accessed anywhere that has an Internet connection. This situation would allow for the creation of online journals in humanities scholarship in the widest possible range of languages, in addition to English. It goes without saying that under such circumstances, and with such possibilities, the perception of US-American cultural hegemony affecting scholarship becomes immaterial and without real significance. For its own advancement, humanities scholarship, wherever it takes place and in whichever language, should take advantage of new media and the possibilities of digitality and hypertext. I believe this is a real task as well as a possibility to act on.

Bibliography

Cader, M. "Never Mind the Friggin' E-Book. It's All About the Web." *Inside: The Business of Entertainment, Media & Technology* (2000): 37-38.

Carlson, Scott. "Students and Faculty Members Turn to Online Library Materials Before Printed Ones, Study Finds." *The Chronicle of Higher Education* (3 October 2002):
http://chronicle.com/free/2002/10/2002100301t.htm

—. "Humanities, Social Sciences Should Focus on Improving Digital Resources, Report Says." *The Chronicle of Higher Education* (27 July 2006):
http://chronicle.com/temp/reprint.php?id=c9hfl6kk7b59tt72zw6yc7fl h2zd6rfl

Ghesquiere, Rita. "The Reading Behaviour of Moroccan, Turkish, and Italian Children in Flanders." *The Systemic and Empirical Approach to Literature and Culture as Theory and Application*. Ed. Steven Tötösy de Zepetnek and Irene Sywenky. Edmonton: Research Institute for Comparative Literature, University of Alberta and Siegen: Institute for Empirical Literature and Media Research, Siegen University, 1997: 393-405.

Glossary of Library and Internet Terms. (2003):
http://www.bedfordstmartins.com/hacker/resdoc/glossary.htm

Greco, Albert N. "The General Reader Market for University Press Books in the United States, 1990-9, with Projections for the Years 2000 through 2004." *Journal of Scholarly Publishing*, 32.2 (2001): 62-86.

Harnad, Stevan. "Electronic Scholarly Publication: Quo Vadis?" *Serials Review* 21.1(1995):

http://www.cogsci.soton.ac.uk/harnad/Papers/Harnad/harnad95.quo.vadis.html

Ibsch, Elrud. "How Different is the Other? A Case Study of Literary Reading in a Multicultural Society." *The Systemic and Empirical Approach to Literature: Theory and Application.* Ed. Steven Tötösy de Zepetnek. *Literatura Comparada: Os Novos Paradigmas.* Ed. Margarida Losa, Isménia de Sousa, and Gonçalo Vilas-Boas. Porto: Afrontamento, 1996, 362-67.

Johnson, Eric. "The World Wide Web, Computers, and Teaching Literature." (2003): http://www.dsu.edu/~johnsone/webprof.html

Landow, George P. *The Cyberspace, Hypertext, and Critical Theory Web: An Introduction* (2003) http://landow.stg.brown.edu/cpace/cspaceov.html

—. *Hypertext 3.0: Critical Theory and New Media in an Era of Globalization.* Baltimore: Johns Hopkins University Press, 2006.

Miles, Adrian. *RMIT HyperText Project* (2003): http://hypertext.rmit.edu.au/

Perillo, L. "Instant Mortification." *The Chronicle of Higher Education* (3 March 2000): A64.

Petrucci, Armando. "Reading to Read: A Future for Reading." *A History of Reading in the West.* Ed. Guglielmo Cavallo and Roger Chartier. Trans. Lydia G. Cochrane. Amherst: University of Massachusetts Press, 1999: 345-67.

Ryan, Marie-Laure. *Narrative as Virtual Reality: Immersion and Interactivity in Literature and Electronic Media.* Baltimore: Johns Hopkins University Press, 2001

Sociological and Ethnographic Research of Cyberspace (2003): http://www.socio.demon.co.uk/home.html

The Draft Report of the American Council of Learned Societies' Commission on Cyberinfrastructure for the Humanities and Social Sciences (November 5, 2005) http://www.acls.org/cyberinfrastructure/cyber.htm

The Internet Public Library. "Skills for Online Searching" (2003): http://www.ipl.org/teen/aplus/skills.htm

Thumlert, Kurt. "Hypertextuality and Sociocultural Contexts of Education": http://home1.gte.net/grnjeans/htext.htm

Tötösy de Zepetnek, Steven. "Literature and Cultural Participation." *Comparative Literature: Theory, Method, Application.* Amsterdam: Rodopi, 1998: 43-78.

—. "The New Knowledge Management: Online Research and Publishing in the Humanities." *CLCWeb: Comparative Literature and Culture* 3.1 (2001): http://clcwebjournal.lib.purdue.edu/clcweb01-1/totosy01.html

—. *Comparative Literature: Theory, Method, Application.* Amsterdam: Rodopi, 1998.

Tötösy de Zepetnek, Steven, and Philip Kreisel. "Urban English-Speaking Canadian Literary Readership: the Results of a Pilot Study." *Poetics: Journal of Empirical Research on Literature, the Media and the Arts,* 21.3 (1992): 211-38.

Van Looy, Jan, and Jan Baetens, eds. *Close Reading New Media: Analyzing Electronic Literature.* Leuven: Leuven UP, 2003.

Varmus, Harold. "'Werdet Teil der Revolution!' Digitale Bibliotheken und elektronische Zeitschriften sollen das wissenschaftliche Publizieren ändern. Ein Gespräch mit dem Nobelpreisträger Harold Varmus." *Die Zeit* 26 (2003): 29.

Warwick, C. "'Reports of My Death Have Been Greatly Exaggerated': Scholarly Editing in the Digital Age." *New Media and the Humanities: Research and Applications.* Ed. Domenico Fiormonte and Jonathan Usher. Oxford: Humanities Computing Unit, Oxford University, 2001: 49-56.

Williams, Lynda, and Lorne Flagel. "Online Production." *Literary Journals in Canada: The Next Generation.* Ed. Dee Horne, 2005, 115-48. Lit Can: http://litcan.unbc.ca

CHAPTER TEN

A DYNAMIC AUTHENTICITY OF TEXTS IN E-ARCHIVES: ON DIGITIZED CULTURAL RESOURCES IN COMPARATIVE LITERARY STUDIES

JOLA SKULJ

Against the word and world fully mapped as logos, Deleuze and Guattari propose that we write ourselves in the gap of nomos, the nomadic. They pose wondering against the word, being-for space against being-in space. We are in the water, inscribing and inscribed by the flow in our sailing. We write ourselves in oscillation between the smooth space of being for-time (what happens to us as we go as well as what happens to the space in which we do so) and the striated space of in-time (what happens outside the space and us). Interactive electronic art seems to offer a paradigm for just such an oscillation, a constant becomingness as a way out of what we are in, a way in where we are put out. Interactive art gives way to giving ways: Things could have been different. (Joyce, 1995: 207)

The critical archiving of texts using electronic media is an implementation of the underlying philological model of a systematized collection of literary documents and related data—to preserve the text as a semiotically transmitted *reality*, placing it at the disposal of literary studies and other interests of the humanities for further use, and also as an available source of information for the interests of other less exclusive publics. However, because texts[1] as semiotically presented reality assimilate within

---

[1] According to Lotman's definition "the text is not only the generator of new meanings, but also a condenser of cultural memory"; it "has the capacity to preserve the memory of its previous contexts" (1990: 18). Texts "preserve their cultural activity" and "reveal a capacity to accumulate information, i.e. a capacity for memory" (id). Lotman asserts that the text's memory, the "meaning space created by the text around itself enters into relationship with the cultural memory

themselves a specific network of historical residues, they are not only bearers of cultural memory and part of what forms and expresses the identity of a nation, but are above all an available texture containing the meanings of historical traces of the existence of a given cultural space and the language reality behind it. In this case, the importance of archiving[2] literary texts goes beyond the interests of literary studies, since such a collection preserves semiotic material that is a thesaurus of historical memory and its various manifested forms, which are interpreted anew each time. The documents of literature, critically edited and stored in digital form, facilitate electronic accessibility to literary texts and enable textual segments to be linked with other data series by means of hypertext. In a hypertextual environment, critical editions of literature allow further study of texts (as historical facts of semiotic reality) using various methods to scrutinize the endless contexts of a literary work and reconsider it interpretatively from many angles. The basic quality of the alternative to using e-archives in literary studies is above all the option for research work done to remain as an open process. This means that it is possible to continually add new results and fresh data to the collection and connect them further to relevant network links which, with advances in knowledge, are constantly being established.

Through thematization of issues relating to the critical editing (in accordance with text encoding initiative standards) and storing of literature and related data in electronic form, we should take into consideration the

---

(tradition) already formed in the consciousness of the audience" (id.). This means that texts should be seen as "important factors in the *stimulus* of cultural dynamics" (id.) and we should recognize that they are themselves "a *reservoir of dynamism* when influenced by contacts with new contexts" (id., my italics). Characterized by "the inner and as yet unfinalized determinacy of its structure" text "acquires semiotic life" (id.). A text is involved in a semiotic space and it results in "the complex semiotic mechanism which is in constant motion" (Lotman, 1990: 203). A text has its life in the reality of semiosis and *a* reality becomes "the single-channel structure" (Lotman, 1990: 124) for decoding (or extracting meaning from) its encrypted message. When *a* reality happens to be the text's communicating channel—and we must bear in mind that natural language is constantly renewing codes and that (as Lotman also reminds us) "living culture has a 'built-in' mechanism for multiplying its languages" (id.)—then this "single-channel" is realized in a plurality of options. Both factors, the ongoing event of *cultural tradition* and *the individual mode* of entering into the text, are involved in an ever changing platform of circumstances of the text as a linguistically shaped reality.

[2] The point of archiving is to make material available to the public. (Lat. *archivum*, Gr. *archeîon* public office, repository of official records, Gr. *archein* to rule).

vital changes in literary studies which result in new comprehension, and the functions of information collection or literature databases, and assess how these new alternatives can be pertinent to research. In studying literary texts as specific semiotic repositories for cultural memory, the move of new technology towards collecting, linking, and generating knowledge of literature, and the process by which, with our daily interest, we map out and think about its role, has introduced a range of encouraging options which will likely also prove to herald a new threshold for the future recognition of the significance of the humanities. The records of the cultural legacy of the territory of Slovenia, by being linked to worldwide networks in the shared presence of the traditions of other cultures, can thus draw attention to the essential nature of their present as well as their past historical existence, as documented in the materials of manuscripts and literature. It can also reveal itself in an open, comparative perspective (given the presence of a multitude of different viewpoints of other national traditions) by means of a less distorted mirror, providing a more realistic basis for judging its own status; at the same time it enables many a stereotypical observation to be overcome, as indicated by a number of signs, including the one that regards Slovenian culture as having been blocked in its past development and "lagging behind" others.

Historically, the event of text in digital form represents a similar sort of far-reaching shift as the transition from orality to the written word. The experience of electronic text immediately challenged theoretical discourse on the space of culture and, by embracing some concepts from literary theory, subjected even an everyday exchange of views to inventive critical thought. The reasons for this can certainly be seen in the fact that electronic textuality, with its inherent principles and potential choices, involves—and above all radically re-examines—our understanding of ourselves in a new perspective, including what we comprehend as "body" or physical being; issues regarding our identity and differences and our changed views on totality continually extend the boundaries of reality, and so on. With the flourishing of computer technology, the World Wide Web, multimedia communication, the digitization of texts and virtual reality, not only are the humanities challenged, but also the human condition, which may truly be considered to be on the verge of a new renaissance, one that, with its interests and open discursive reasoning, extends new articulations of its own grasp of values. It presents an altogether different opportunity to test the cultural memory of a given linguistic space, which preserves the history of past interests in an open (inconclusive) world. Literary studies can turn the "creative chaos of electronic technologies" (Ryan, 1999: 1) positively to their own advantage: the significant development of *cybertext criticism* more than a decade ago manifests how actively theoretical thought was capable of inventing critical concepts to grasp new information technology realities. Faced with cybertext scenarios, literary criticism is no doubt challenged to address literary historical (or cultural) facts from earlier periods and from current literary inventions in its own way, and to draw attention to the meanings and roles of issues which have already been analysed and disseminated in studies on literature to date, but which were previously within reach in a much more reclusive form.

In the past decade, the features of cybertext structure have advanced initiatives that have caused a reconsideration of the rhetorical repertory of literary studies in a renewed context, and the founding of cybertext studies (cf. Delany and Landow, 1991, Landow, 1992, Delany and Landow, 1993, Landow, 1994a, Aarseth, 1997a, Ryan 1999, 2001). Faced with new information technologies, instances of e-textuality, and the alternative of hypertextually-linked fields of information for retrieving data non-sequentially, literary criticism has re-conceptualized some of the ideas launched through methodological shifts in this area of knowledge.[3] The discipline was already faced with such new aspirations in earlier literary inventions,[4] long before the rapid spread of texts in digital form. Several concepts put forward in the discourse on post-structuralism find relevance, though not automatic applicability, in the framework of computer-driven or electronic textuality. Computer-based textuality demonstrates specific entities of its own, and the field of literary studies finds itself faced with the task of reflecting on the facts of the texture denoted by cyberspace, virtuality and hypertext links, as well as that of implementing the advantages this new textual potential brings. At least in the case of digital archives of texts, it is possible to avoid the pitfalls of editing practices common to many critical publications of the classics in book form. Thus, humanities resources and databases of classic works stored in cyberspace

---

[3] Some concepts which imply connectivity or interrelatedness—Landow refers to the English words *link, node, web, network* or *interwoven* (French *liaisons, toile, réseau, s'y tissent*)—can already be found in Barthes, Foucault, Bakhtin and Derrida. The concept of intertextuality, as introduced by Kristeva, and the idea of rhizomes (Greek *rhizoma* root, stem) or nomadic in Deleuze and Guattari also indicate intricate, multilinear, web-like relations.

[4] The textual logic in modernist arts—with its features of incongruity in the represented "reality" and the suggestive juxtapositions of dissociated ideas, by means of the collage, or so-called *assemblage* in dadaist and surrealist art—with its "open form" and specific approaches to intertextual allusion has already implicated the properties of hypertextuality in non-electronic form. Landow draws particular attention to the characteristics of narrativity in Joyce's *Ulysses*. Modernist texts as well as hypertexts epitomize the *logic of the transfinite*.

can provide researchers and students as virtual-reality users with reliable and promising tools. Digitized texts of critical editions, digital images of first print versions of books, together with writers' manuscripts and archives of texts of the earliest critical responses are certainly of great benefit to the study of literature. Online access to historical sources is the finest instance of involving the use of computers to approach literary texts on a daily basis. The electronic form of the scholarly editing of texts as a research tool allows the non-revised appearance of the authentic first print edition (in JPG and text format) and takes into consideration the traditional ecdotics approach. The primary text is available simultaneously with a range of textual variants, original revisions by the author, reprints and similar. The electronic mode of critical editions represents the realization of the old philological aspiration of mediating text reality. Philology as *the study of literary texts and of written records, as the establishment of their authenticity and their original form, and the determination of their meaning*—the eternal dream of literary historical scholarship—appears to be more attainable than ever before due to the nature of cyberspace textuality and the potential hypertext environment.

The distinctive features of e-textuality imply attributes that traditional forms of critical editions and archiving of cultural memory in (linear) book form did not anticipate. In one of his earlier essays (1994), Espen J. Aarseth[5], who has addressed the theoretical re-examination of informatics in the humanities,[6] elaborated the idea of *non-linearity*[7] as a specific

---

[5] His earlier research work took place in the framework of the Department of Culture, Language and Information Technology at the University of Bergen in Norway, and since 2003 at the Department of Digital Aesthetics and Communication in Copenhagen.

[6] Aarseth in his article "The Field of Humanistic Informatics and its Relation to the Humanities", published in the fourth volume of the journal *Human IT*, which was launched in 1997 by the Swedish Centre for the Information Technological Study of the Humanities, in cooperation with the University of Göteborg, spoke of the emergence of humanistic informatics or *humanities computing* as an autonomous field, as something which has "a unique research profile" and is *not* just *a supporting discipline in the service of traditional humanistic scholarship*. In the abstract, he wrote: "This is important if the field is to go on expanding and its practitioners gain both self respect and the respect of others, something which today often is lacking, especially in the subfield of literary computing. [...] The field must be able to focus on something which is not already dealt with by other fields, and which is not an obvious object for other fields. The answer lies in focusing on aesthetic and media issues of information technology (computer games, Internet culture, and hyper/cyber/media). This direction opens up a fresh territory of huge potential and importance for humanistic research." He addressed

characteristic of cybertextuality.[8] With this concept it is possible to summarize the characteristics of so-called *inconclusive writing space* and *spatiality*. The logic of inconclusiveness and of spatiality is also inherent into the polylogue, and is also implied in the Deleuze and Guattari concept of smooth—nomad—space (*espace lisse*). As well as Deleuze and Guattari's conceptual context, the Bakhtinian idea of dialogue was frequently used in discussions of cybertextuality and cyberfiction. It is worth recalling certain discussions that have taken place on the Internet,[9] and, specifically, at two important meetings of experts organized by the Bakhtin Centre.[10] With the use of such binary terms as *striated* space/*smooth* space (*espace strié/espace lisse*), it is impossible, of course,

---

the question of how he understands the research profile of humanistic informatics in the conclusion of his paper, touching on "the problems of digital document representation, the rhetoric of pedagogical software, the uses of hypertext and multimedia, the limits of formal representation of aesthetic objects, the cognitive and political aspects of dynamic models, [...] the potential and limits of exploratory data analysis", and similar (http://www.hb.se/bhs/ith/4-97/ea.htm). He understands humanistic informatics as a relevant extension of the tradition of the humanities and its long-standing efforts to open up new strategies of reading and writing, and especially as a challenge whose technological options bring an integrative function of presenting newly examined roles which the humanities have for other fields of knowledge and self-understanding of human development. New discursive modes of locally unbounded communication of humanistic data intensify the meaning of this specific field of knowledge. It represents a subtle shift which commits humanistic informatics to give confidence to its vision and activity and draw attention to its greater significance.

[7] According to Aarseth's earlier formulation a *non-linear* text is defined as "an object of verbal communication that is *not simply one fixed sequence* of letters, words, and statements but one in which the words or sequence of words may differ from reading to reading because of the shape, conventions, or mechanisms of the text. Non-linear texts can be very different from each other, at least as different as they are from the linear texts." (1994: 51; my italics).

[8] Hypertext implies connections which do not take place in a sequential manner. Jerome McGann (2001) uses the concept of *dispersed* or *radiant* textuality.

[9] On the Deleuze and Guattari discussion list on the Internet in June, 1995, there was a debate over whether the World Wide Web, due to its particular qualities, is a striated space (*espace strié*) or a smooth space (*espace lisse*).

[10] "Reading Between the Lines: Materiality in the Age of Hypertext". *Crossing Boundaries: An International Interdisciplinary Conference*, University of Sheffield, 17-19 April, 1998; Colin Gardner, *Seeming Seamlessness: Ambiguous Pronominal References and Other (Con)textual Ambiguities in Hypertext Fiction*, The Bakhtin Centre Seminar, 13 February, 1997.

to resolve the issue adequately without objections, similar to Jakobson's use of the dichotomy of the metaphorical and metonymical principle.

What is *cybertext*? According to Aarseth, cybertext[11] is open, dynamic text in which the reader must *perform specific acts* in order to generate a semiotic sequence that can be changed with each reading. It is this effectuation of specific acts that (from units of available paradigms) can generate a sequence. Aarseth calls this phenomenon *ergodic*,[12] using a term appropriated from physics that derives from the Greek words *ergon* and *hodos*, meaning "work" and "path". The structure of cybertext textuality thus inscribes in itself the potential for making choices which allow access to selected segments of the text whilst others, according to reader's choice, are left behind unobserved and taken into account in other interpretations. A cybertext is thus, according to Aarseth,[13] an intricate operating system, "a machine for the production of variety of expression", involving "something more, and it is this added paraverbal dimension that is so hard to see" (1997a: 3). Cybertext is "a broad textual media category" or, as he claims, "a perspective [...] to describe and explore the communicational strategies of dynamic texts. [...] Even if cybertexts are not narrative texts but other forms of literature governed by a different set of rules, they retain, to a greater or lesser extent, some aspects of narrative. Most display some forms of narrative behaviour, just as can be found in other non-narrative literary genres." (1997a: 5) "The study of cybertexts reveals the misprision of the spacio-dynamic metaphors of narrative theory, because ergodic literature incarnates these models in a way linear text narratives do not. This may be hard to understand for the traditional literary critic who cannot perceive the difference between metaphorical structure and logical structure, but it is essential. The cybertext reader *is* a player, a gambler; the cybertext *is* a game-world or world-game; it *is* possible to explore, get lost, and discover secret paths in these texts, not

---

[11] The expression is a neologism derived from Norbert Wiener's use of the concept in the title of his book *Cybernetics. Control and Communication in the Animal and the Machine* (1948); Wiener's understanding of *system* is crucial: it can be organic or inorganic, but what is key is that it contains an *information feedback loop*.

[12] The term is taken from physics, modern dynamics and atomic theory. In the sense in which we know it in mathematics and statistics, the meaning of ergodic is explained in the Random House Webster dictionary: *ergodic*, of or pertaining to *the condition that, in an interval of sufficient duration, a system will return to states that are closely similar to previous ones*: the basis of statistical methods used in modern dynamics and atomic theory.

[13] Cf. also "Sample Chapter from Cybertext: Perspectives on Ergodic Literature" (http://www.hf.uib.no/cybertext/Ergodic.html).

metaphorically, but through the topological structures of the textual machinery. This is not a difference between games and literature but rather between games and narratives. To claim that there is no difference between games and narratives is to ignore essential qualities of both categories. And yet, as this study tries to show, the difference is not clear-cut, and there is significant overlap between the two" (1997a: 4-5).

Cybertextuality, as analysed by Aarseth, relates to the aesthetics and textual *dynamics* of digital literature and its many different types, such as hypertext fiction (cf. Michael Joyce: *Afternoon, a story*, 1990, and *Afternoon, Twilight*, 1996, and Stuart Moulthrop: *Hegirascope*, 1995 and *Victory Garden*, 1992), computer games, computer-generated poetry and prose and collaborative Internet texts such as MUD (*multi-user dungeons*). However, as Aarseth explicitly points out, cybertextuality should not be understood only as "specific computer-mediated phenomena" (1994: 51), but as similar to Wiener's idea of a cybernetic system that can be attributed not only to machines, but also to the organic world. If the concept of cybertext were to be limited only to the study of computer-driven or electronic textuality, "that would be an arbitrary and unhistorical limitation, perhaps comparable to a study of literature that would only acknowledge texts in paper-printed form" (Aarseth, 1997a: 1), and would exclude everything written before Gutenberg's invention. Thus, Aarseth does not insist on the uniqueness and novelty of "electronic writing" or on the concept of interactivity as an outcome exclusively of computer technology (e.g. interactive fiction in the case of cyberfiction), but situates new literary forms and forms of cybertextuality within a broader and substantially older field of ergodic literature, extending from the ancient Chinese book *I Ching* to the literary experiments of the well-known French avant-garde group OuLiPo.[14] But he does focus the concept of

---

[14] The exemplary text of OuLiPo literature is the one signed by G.[eorges] P.[erec]:

Pli ou Loi?
Oulipo
Lu ou Poli?
Oulipo
Li Po ou Lulli?
Oulipo
Oïl ou Oui?
Oulipo
Io ou Lou?
Oulipo
Ô

cybertext on "the mechanical organization of the text" (as a *constructed composition*[15]), "by positing the intricacies of the medium as an integral part of the literary exchange" (1997a: 1). It is precisely this delineation that allows him to note that the semantic ambiguities of linear texts (for example, the ambiguity as an instance of *literariness*) cannot be compared with the ergodicity of the non-sequential construction of cybertexts. The inaccessible import or message in a given reading of a non-linear cybertext "does not imply ambiguity but, rather, an absence of possibility—an aporia" (1997a: 3). By scrutinizing the ideas of ergodic and non-linearity, Aarseth formulated a theoretical model of cybertextuality and critically discriminated categories[16] which enable the classification of textual (including literary) forms[17], and above all revealed that from a strictly analytical viewpoint the widely-assumed distinction between texts on paper and electronic texts is not really essential. With his theoretical

---

Oulipo

The co-founders of the OuLiPo group, or *Ouvroir de Littérature Potentielle*, a workshop of potential literature, are considered to be Raymond Queneau and François Le Lionnais. We can also find some better known artists among the group: Jacques Bens, Claude Berge, Jacques Duchateau, Jean Queval, Marcel Duchamp, Georges Pérec, Italo Calvino, François Caradec.

[15] Aarseth, whose explanation of cybertextuality analytically addresses textuality, in which he is aware, of course, that there is no universal definition of text, claims that if we understand *text* as *an object with the primary function of conveying verbal information*, it is possible to distinguish between *scriptons*, i.e. "strings as they appear to readers", and *textons*, "strings as they exist in the text" (1997a: 62). As a complex, highly structured body of writing, a text is an endless series of verbal negotiations or *traversal functions*, "conventions and mechanisms that combine and project textons as scriptons to the *user* (or reader) of the text" (Aarseth, 1994: 61).

[16] For Aarseth, these categorical points of departure (describing *mode of traversal*) are merely pragmatic and experimental, and are at variance in different publications: topology, dynamics, determinability, transiency, manoeuvrability, user-functionality (cf. 1994: 61-62); dynamics, determinability, transiency, perspective, access, linking, user-functions (cf. 1997a: 62-64).

[17] Four models of non-linear textuality can be distinguished: "(1) the simple non-linear text, whose textons are totally static, open and explorable by the user [cf. the unreadable texts *I Ching* and Queneau, *Cent mille milliards de poèmes*, 1961], (2) the discontinuous non-linear text, or *hypertext*, which may be traversed by 'jumps' (explicit links) between textons, (3) the determined 'cybertext' in which the behaviour of textons is predictable but conditional and with the element of role-playing, and (4) the undetermined cybertext in which the textons are dynamic and unpredictable." (Cf. Aarseth, 1994: 63).

model of understanding cybertext forms (which are heirs to a longer tradition), Aarseth (1997a) discussed a new experience in the field of ergodic textology. He confronted it with the literary theoretical aspects of narrative, semiotics and rhetoric, and, what is most significant, by re-examining the details of this textuality, he rejected their applicability to the problem.

In conclusion, we should address the situation of literary studies in view of the experience of cyberspace, the advent of cyber-literature and the setting-up of hypertext information. In 1991, after a lecture on non-linearity by Aarseth at Brown University, Robert Coover pointed to the far-reaching initiatives of *participatory* literary criticism, which is pertinent to hypertext but much less likely with textual situations in the printed form. In the debate Aarseth identifies the future interests of literary studies in "the model from anthropology of the *participant-observer* who admits that he or she influences the narrative and thus inevitably colours all results" (Landow, 1994b: 36, my italics). That the future of literary studies in the hypertext environment—Ulmer employs the term *postcriticism*—is by its very nature essentially organized in a plurivocal, inconclusive, multi-linear way, and that there is "greater inclusion of non-textual information and fundamental reconfigurations of authorship, including the ideas of authorial property and of status relations in the text," has already been noticed by Landow (id.) in his discussions on hypertext and the role of the critical enterprise of literary research. In his work on *heuretics* as a branch of logic, which examines the "art" of discovery and invention, Ulmer also highlights the "border-violating collage-writing" of academic discourse[18] "capable of emphasizing imagination, discovery, and unexpected crossovers" (Landow, 1994b: 39), that is, the attributes of transgressive thought and a distinction of any true scientific pursuit. Literary studies as a theoretical and critical discipline, according to the views of Landow, Moulthrop, Ulmer[19] and others who pass on knowledge of new technological possibilities to future generations, thus anticipate

---

[18] Once again with these issues we come up against the idea of *spaces of transgressiveness*, which was raised by the discussion of the international comparatist colloquium in Vilenica 2003. Cf. *Literature and Space: Spaces of Transgressiveness. Primerjalna knjizevnost 27.* Jola Skulj and Darja Pavlic (eds.) Ljubljana: 2004. Special Issue. (153 pages). Ulmer in *Teletheory* (1989) introduces the term *mystory* as a novel form of academic discourse.

[19] Ulmer, whose books (*Applied Grammatology*, 1985; *Teletheory*, 1989; *Heuretics*, 1994) focus on the issues of literary studies discourse and electronic media, approaches the problem through the horizontal matrix initiated by French post-structuralists and the movements of the modernist avant-garde.

A Dynamic Authenticity of Texts in E-Archives: On Digitized Cultural   195
Resources in Comparative Literary Studies

new forms of electronic discourse. As promising implements of digitized literary resources to do research in comparative literary studies, e-archives set an efficient tool. With the advent of informatics as the science of the study, collection, and management of information, using computer storage and retrieval, electronic stores of literary data authorize new profiles for collecting, organizing, evaluating and disseminating facts about literatures. Could we say that success stories for comparatist studies—in view of improved access to knowledge regarding less known literatures—are coming to light? In the *hypertext explosion* (to employ Miller's phrase) future efforts in e-textual preservation and open access to the electronic storage of printed materials, with the potential for moving through texts by way of a series of hyperlinks, definitely constitute a textual gain for comparatistics. The field of humanistic informatics, which, according to Aarseth's comments, some might regard as an oxymoron, remains necessarily eclectic—part library, part encyclopaedia, part pile of discarded texts—but is in reality an extremely useful mass of material resulting from the successful advance of informatics.

Cyberspace and the fluid, contingent and multivocal nature of hypertext certainly create new circumstances for literary studies, and support critical thought to reveal new options for knowledge of literature. Not only does hypertext enhance a reader's ability to traverse texts; with its arrival, literary data can be observed in an unusually dynamic interplay. The cyberspace event should surely be considered a privileged provider, inscribing readers in ever-changing plot lines or text trajectories and other literary data. Literary facts and information communicated through electronic linking involve us in idiosyncrasies—in the very hermeneutic game of restatement and ever-rendered (newly-construed) comprehension. E-texts, given their virtual presentation, can only be negotiated through their dynamic authenticity. Thus, for the user of e-text, any fact (for example, to do with literature) is given to us through *narrativization* (H. White's concept).

At this point we can draw attention to the idea of hypertextuality and the scheme of modernist poetics, which are both characterized by their logic of the transfinite. At the beginning of the last century, the works of modernist painters at the *Salon d'automne* in Paris were found to be surprisingly shocking, and even frivolous by some critics and consumers; however, the matter was simply the very dynamic authenticity that the art of modernism, with its artistic inventions, had intervened as a theme. The negative response of some critics neglected the very idea of *narrativization* that the modernist approach manifestly initiated. The culture of modernism actualized a turning point in the representational

practices of the individual arts. It basically opened up a new relation to
reality; behind its shifts in narrativity was the awareness that actuality can
be understood from a number of different aspects, and that any true
existence is elusive, shifting, fluid, tentative, multi-focal and inconclusive.
In identifying inconclusiveness as a defining principle of modernist artistic
phenomena and forms (cf. Skulj, 1997), we ought to recognize that this is
the result of a shift in focus to the direct comprehension of the *present in
its immediateness*, which is also elusive, fluid and, as a rule, never
completed, and hence to the open fact of existence, to actuality in specific
time, to an instant of time or momentariness in the Baudelairian sense of
modernity. Barthes[20] finds modernist literature a kind of *intransitive*
writing in the style of *middle-voicedness*, while Fredric Jameson identifies
literary modernism as the product of a double crisis—on the one hand, a
"social crisis of narratable experiences" and on the other, a "semiotic crisis
of narrative paradigms" (1984: 211). Modernists were well aware that
giving an account of an experience or an event always implies focalization
or a certain point of view which, in the presence of a time interval,
inevitably renounces being a fixed point. Modernism was already well
aware that any representation, any narrated account of events, is arbitrary,
since it authorizes only a particular point of view, a singular aspect of the
factual or of a phenomenon, and that as such it is "impossible to tell any
single authoritative story about what really happened—which meant that
one could tell any number of possible stories about it" (White, 1999: 73).
Modernist techniques of representation (e.g. the imagist depiction of an
event as a *spatial* presentation of moments or different aspects of the
comprehension of the immediate present and instants of time) testify to an
awareness of the facts or events given in narrativization. Thus, the mode
of conveying the spirit or meaning of the multifaceted image of the factual
is reconsidered and represented by a tropological account; this means that
the *spectral* scope of the representation is a precondition for the mediation
of "meaning, which has been rendered spectral, seeming to consist solely
in the spatial dispersion of the phenomena" (White, 1999: 76). Modernism
in its unique comprehension of reality and events (and therefore also
literary history) has recognized how the point of view or *focalization*, (i.e.

---

[20] The specifics of modernist writing have been defined by Barthes along with
other concepts. In *Degré zéro* (1953) he wrote in reference to Camus of colourless
writing, of an *ambiguous self* in the novel of Proust, referring to Queneau of the
plural oral text as the negation of writing, referring to modern poetry of *vertical,
unworldly words*. After 1960 he launched the idea of writing as action; the idea of
neutral writing was revaluated into *plural writing* (Cf. the essay *Écrivains et
écrivants*, 1960).

the very act of linking or the state of being linked with reality and events) is insubstantial and fragile. *Modernist art, with its formal inventions, actually thematized this insubstantiality.* Because the evolution of modern art addresses the changing representation of reality and event, its praxes are driven by the necessity of inventing new strategies of *"scopic* vision" (Spivak, 2003:108) or stereoscopy.[21] Auerbach calls this modernist approach the "many-voiced treatment of image" [22] (1946: 481).

Beyond modernism, literary studies find that to keep on examining the historical records of literary facts as a simple, univocal story is indeed an illusion. A thorough shift in methodological frames to grasp literature historically was advanced after the experience of modernism. Literatures were no longer analysed and exhausted through a single insight, or as a semiotically self-sufficient, autonomous event. Unmasking the naïve view on identity, the postmodern approach to literary history overcomes the generally accepted idea of historiography in the 19th century: the shift towards the complex, networked presentation of the history of literary phenomena, i.e. not as a text with a fixed, linear structure, but using a kind of *spatial* (hypertext) system, and towards various analyses at the interconnection points of these networked presentations, be they strictly insights in literary writings or more extensive culturological aspects, is therefore a promising option for the adequate historical survey of facts, events, movements and trends in literature.

Bibliography

Aarseth, E. J. "Nonlinearity and Literary Theory". In Landow, 1994a: 51-86.
—. *Cybertext. Perspectives on Ergodic Literature.* Baltimore and London: Johns Hopkins University Press, 1997a.
—. "The Field of Humanistic Informatics and its Relation to the Humanities". In *Human IT*, 4/97, 1997b: 7-13.
Auerbach, E. *Mimesis. Dargestellte Wirklichkeit in der Abendländische Literatur.* Bern, A. Francke AG. Verlag, 1946.

---

[21] Cf. Shattuck's study (*Proust's Binoculars*, 1963) on Proust's prose writing as a stereoscopic technique and his remarks about Proust's special understanding of the spatial concept of time in this type of novel.
[22] In German *"die vielstimmige Behandlung"* (Auerbach 1946: 481). Auerbach also made use of two other phrases: "multipersonal representation of consciousness" (in German *"vielpersonige Bewusstseinsdarstellung"*, 1946: 477) and "synthesis of living relationships" (in German *"eine Synthese der Lebensbeziehungen"*, 1946: 478-9).

Barthes, R. "To write: an intransitive verb?" *The Rustle of Language.* Trans. Richard Howard. Berkeley: University of California Press, 1989.

Bolter, J.D. *Writing Space: The Computer, Hypertext, and the History of Writing.* Hillsdale, N.J.: Erlbaum, 1991.

Delany, P., and G. P. Landow (eds.). *Hypermedia and Literary Studies.* Cambridge: MIT Press, 1991.

Delany, P., and G. P. Landow. "Managing the Digital Word: The Text in an Age of Electronic Reproduction". In Landow, G. P., and P. Delany, 1993: 3-28.

Hayles, K. N. *How We Became Posthuman. Virtual Bodies in Cybernetics, Literature, and Informatics.* Chicago: University of Chicago Press, 1999.

Joyce, M. *Of Two Minds: Hypertext Pedagogy and Poetics.* Ann Arbor: University of Michigan Press, 1995.

Landow, G. P. *Hypertext: The Convergence of Contemporary Literary Theory and Technology.* Baltimore: Johns Hopkins University Press, 1992. (Of particular relevance are the chapters "Hypertext and Multivocality" and "Hypertext and De-Centring", 36-7.)

—. *Hyper/Text/Theory.* Baltimore: Johns Hopkins University Press, 1994a.

— "What's a Critic to Do?: Critical Theory in the Age of Hypertext". In Landow, 1994b: 1-48.

Landow, G. P., and P. Delany (eds.). *The Digital Word: Text-Based Computing in the Humanities.* Cambridge, Mass., London: MIT Press, 1993.

Lotman, Y. M. *Universe of the Mind: A Semiotic Theory of a Culture.* London/New York: I.B. Tauris & Co Ltd Publishers, 1990.

McGann, J. *Radiant Textuality: Literature after the World Wide Web.* New York: Palgrave Macmillan, 2001.

Ryan, M.-L. (ed.) *Cyberspace Textuality. Computer Technology and Literary Theory.* Bloomington and Indianapolis: Indiana University Press, 1999.

—. *Narrative as Virtual Reality. Immersion and Interactivity in Literature and Electronic Media.* Baltimore: Johns Hopkins University Press, 2001.

Schreibman, S., R. Siemens, and J. Unsworth (ed.) *A Companion to Digital Humanities.* Oxford: Blackwell Publishing, 2004.

Skulj, J. "Dialogism as a non-finalized concept of truth: Twentieth century literature and its logic of inconclusiveness". Javornik, M., Juvan, M.

Skaza, A. Skulj, J. and Verc, I. (eds.). *Bakhtin and the Humanities*. Ljubljana: Znanstveni inštitut Filozofske fakultete, 1997: 139-150.

Ulmer, G. L. *Heuretics. The Logic of Invention*. Baltimore and London: Johns Hopkins University Press, 1994.

Wiener, N. *Cybernetics. Control and Communication in the Animal and the Machine*. New York: Technology Press, 1948.

CHAPTER ELEVEN

POSTMODERNITY AND CRITICAL EDITIONS OF LITERARY TEXTS: TOWARDS THE VIRTUAL PRESENCE OF THE PAST

MARKO JUVAN

Although textual criticism or textology within literary studies is usually considered to be *ancilla philologiae* and thus little more than an auxiliary discipline or a cluster of technical skills (whose main goal is supposed to be the production of scholarly accurate and reliable editions of literary artworks), it is in actual fact deeply involved with and intricately related to the theory, interpretation and history of literature. I cannot but agree with Martha Nell Smith's claim that "editing is a physical as well as a philosophical act, and [that] the medium in which an edition is produced [...] is both part of and contains the message of the editorial philosophies at work" (Smith, 2004: 306). In the following sections I will attempt to demonstrate how, throughout their recent history, textological practices have been rooted in different aesthetic notions and text theories.

However, apart from their implicit "editorial philosophies", the tools of textual criticism have many other, more pragmatic powers, since "editing translates raw creative work into an authoritative [...] form" (Smith, 2004: 309). With hidden strategies of musealization, scholarly editing manipulates the historical profile and relevance of past literary works, secures their permanent presence in ever changing reading repertoires, enhances their significance and aesthetic impacts upon audiences, and, last but not least, transposes them from the artistic field to the discourses of scholarship and education, thus featuring scholarly editions as enduring points of reference for an auto-poietic textual processing in schools and academia. All of this presents textology as a key factor in the canonization process and, consequently, as one of the doorkeepers of cultural memory.

1.

From early times, textual critics and editors have striven to purge the bodies of preserved texts of the traces of secondary interventions—which they considered to be corruptions and violations—made either by copyists, typographers, editors, proofreaders, or censors. The purifying critical therapy of the textologists was meant to restore the spiritual authenticity of "the author's text", to cure it of all subsequent damage, thus helping the author to speak unhindered and convey an aesthetic message beyond the limits of his or her historical world (cf. Flanders, 1997: 128-132). It is now clear that these notions, which used to be legitimate textological work, were deeply rooted in metaphysical dualism (essence versus accidence; spirit versus matter; inside versus outside; will versus necessity).

1.1.

On this metaphysical basis, the "editorial philosophy" of historicism of the nineteenth and early twentieth centuries attempted, in the case of the older manuscriptal legacy, to reconstruct the textual image that was supposedly closest to the original archetype. When dealing with modern literary works, however, the "old" historicism exposed one single and binding textual version in its editions: that which was held to comply with the authentic will of the author—be it the author's manuscript, the text's first publication, or the last edition still authorized by the writer (cf. Thomasberger, 1992: 460; Vašák et al., 1993: 33-40).[1] Paradoxically, with their very efforts and procedures for recovering the purity of the authentic text, historicist editors in fact produced just one additional textual variant and gave it the stamp of normative finality.

---

[1] The notion of the author's final edition was actually produced in the late 18th century, in a legal conflict between two publishers who each believed they were entitled to print Wieland's early works, either following their first publication or the author's latest redaction, *Ausgabe von der letzten Hand* (Kittler, 1992: 50-51). The inclination towards the search for primordial originality is, for example, apparent in the 1916 statement of the Czech critic Arne Novák, who claimed that the main goal of "the philological criticism [...] is to discover the uncorrupted, original text that has come directly from the authors' hands" (quoted. in Vašák at al., 1993: 19). The opposite tendency, which is teleologic and believes that the author's *Kunstwollen* leads towards progressive perfection (o. c.: 35-36), may be exemplified by Beissner's formula "das *ideale* Wachstum des Gedichts" (Thomasberger, 1992: 457).

1.2.

Broadly speaking, twentieth century literary studies that considered the literary work primarily as an aesthetic, linguistic, or "spiritual" structure were less obsessed by the epistemology of sources. In their modern aestheticism, they largely neglected the text's genesis and the history of its publications, convinced that the material substance of literature (i.e., its medium, channel) was aesthetically and semantically irrelevant. Editors nurtured in modernist schools of literary criticism did not hesitate to construct and put forward textual images that literary works historically never had—neither in manuscripts, transcripts, or re-writings, nor in journal or book publications. What seemed important to these editors was to ensure that the readers' aesthetic experience would not be hindered by historical strangeness. For this reason they allowed themselves to filter the literary text's historicity.

1.2.1

Let me mention a telling example taken from the series of scholarly editions of Slovene "classics" titled *Collected Works of Slovene Poets and Writers*. In his 1965 edition of France Prešeren's (1800–49) collected works, the editor Janko Kos also published two text variants of Prešeren's early poem *To the Maids*. However, neither of these versions fully matches the documented historical appearances of the text, that is, Prešeren's original manuscript and his own transcript submitted to censorship, as well as the first imprint in the journal *Illyrisches Blatt* (1827), where the poem appeared along with Prešeren's self-translation, or the rewritten version published in the poet's volume of poetry of 1847 (*Poezije*). The scholarly/critical edition thus does not present accurate (i.e., diplomatic) transcripts of any of the poem's historical appearances, which in fact existed and were circulated in public. The editor's goal of drawing the reader's attention to Prešeren's personal style and aesthetic merits, as well as making the poem conform to the linguistic tastes of Kos's contemporary readership, lead to erasures of several symptoms of the text's historical otherness, e.g., its meticulous accentuation or capitalizing of verses. It is indicative that Kos thought that Prešeren's work might otherwise look "bizarre"; the bombastic poems of Jovan Koseski, Prešeren's rival contemporary, have been perceived as "bizarre" or "odd" since the 1870s, whereas Prešeren's reputation has grown and made him the first among the national classics. From this example it may be inferred that editorial emendations also serve to protect the author's canonicity and to portray his work as superior and incomparable to the *poetea minori* of his time, even though the latter were in fact much more similar to him than aestheticist literary historians would like to make out. What is even more symptomatic, is the move on the part of Kos's edition in which Prešeren's bilingualism and biliterarity, typical of Central European literary cultures of the nineteenth century, is put in the background. The poet himself, notwithstanding his pronounced national self-awareness, did not hesitate to make his first public appearance by printing his *To the Maids* in Slovene and his own German translation and continued publishing his German poems. However, the series of Slovenian classics foregrounds the author's Slovene text, thus paying tribute to the prevailing linguistic principle for organizing national literary histories.

2.

In conditioning the historical consciousness of the humanities, postmodernity demonstrates a paradoxical "post-" stance towards the past, through which the *rational* deconstruction of the historical presence is further undone by its *volitive* restitution. In the postmodern age, the critical impetus so characteristic of modernity becomes self-reflectively directed towards the discourse of modernity itself. As a result, the postmodern humanities disclose that—to rephrase Aristotle's famous wording— history is not that which has really happened, nor that which might have happened, but that which—by the scholarly procedures of acquiring and presenting knowledge, and with sufficient persuasiveness— is currently claimed to have happened. However, postmodernity recovers from the loss of historical presence by remaking the past aesthetically: "Material fragments of cultural artefacts from the past can trigger a real desire for possession and for real presence, a desire close to the level of physical appetite" and similar to the "aesthetic experience" (Gumbrecht, 2003: 6-7). This is to say, the past returns as something present only through structures of representation that are comparable to how we gain an image of our contemporary life-world: every slice of the past should be grasped in its modernity, its contingency, its incomprehensible contradictions, its polyphony of details, openness, and becoming. Any attempt to frame past fragments within the master-narratives of old historicisms has thus become obsolete.

2.1.

In the intellectual atmosphere sketched above, post-structuralism, discourse theory, and various historicizing currents in the humanities (among them New Historicism in literary studies) have shaped a radically new understanding of textuality: they conceive of the text as an open-ended process of writing and reading in which meanings and subjects are articulated dialogically and through ceaseless differing from otherness. Consequently, causality linking authorial intentions and textual meanings has proved to be problematic. Instead of positing the author as the privileged discourse controller, post-structuralism introduced notions of more complex intertextual and social relations, established through textuality and signifying acts within concrete historical discursive constellations (cf. Juvan, forthcoming). In this perspective, the text turned out to be a unique, historically concrete utterance, a fragment from the flow of discourse, which constantly builds and rebuilds social dependencies of the speaking and addressed subjects. This is why the social and ideological, or perhaps anthropological, structures of literary works became more interesting than their aesthetic or artistic properties.

The postmodern shift in notions about literary texts had a certain impact upon the practices and concepts of textual criticism in the last decades of the twentieth century, for instance in the French *critique génétique* or in the Anglo-American "new philology" and "bibliography."[2]

2.1.1.

The first change made by "manuscriptology" and the "new philology" is a certain weakening of both the author's and editor's subjects (cf. Gumbrecht, 2003: 28, 31, 38). Through our insight into the mess of his or her workshop, full of imperfect scraps of writings, the author loses the authority of a genius who masters the artistic subject-matter and controls it

---

[2] "Genetic criticism" or, as it is also called "manuscriptology" undercut the notion of a literary work of art as completed. It was supplanted by a minute hermeneutic interpretation of the dynamics of the textual meaning production, as can be traced through drafts, sketches, plans, variants, re-writings, first and revised editions (at the levels of *pre-text* and *post-text*). Genetic criticism helps the hidden biography of the writing process to come into sight from beneath the surface of a published text, together with fragmentary or potential artworks that have never been worked out and published (Contat & Ferrer, 1998: 7-9; Ferrer, 1998: 12-13; Biasi, 1998: 32-33, 55, 59-60; Grésillon, 1998: 91, 93; Zelenka, 2006). On the "new philology" see Nichols, ed., 1990; Tevooren & Wenzel, eds., 1997.

with his or her *Kunstwollen* until the work is completed and presented to the public as a finished, perfect product. Sketches, variants, corrections, and re-writing testify to the fact that, at least by indirect influence, many agencies, communities, or even institutions from the literary field are implied in the author's work on the text, forcing him or her to take, try, and eventually change uttering positions vis-à-vis the Other. The privileged role of the authorial subject is further debased by a twist in the research focus of new textologies; that is, their attempts to assess the ways in which the authorial text is appropriated by various media and modified to meet the expectations of different audiences. Nevertheless, editors are hardly in a better position than authors; they also become a sort of Vattimo's "weak subject", as they withdraw from the authority to adapt and emend the historical otherness of classics. Instead, editors now let the text speak for itself.

2.1.2.

The second change, originating from the post-structuralist idea of the open text, has already been mentioned. The textologist's gaze, especially in genetic criticism, penetrates behind the scenes of a work of art (which had normally been seen as a static, perfect monument, and the result of a consistent artistic intention) and focuses on *poiesis*, that is, on the dynamic process of textual genesis, in which the author is concurrently his or her own first reader (cf. Contat & Ferrer, 1998; Ferrer, 1998; Biasi, 1998; Grésillon, 1998).[3] Flaubert, for instance, used no less than 4,300 pages of working material to accomplish his *Madame Bovary* (Biasi, 1998: 32). Such pre-texts (*avant-textes*) should be interpreted as traces of the writers' efforts to articulate meaning and follow their artistic goals, as well as testimonies to their constant revisions of prior intentions and dilemmas that emerge on the threshold between the private and public spheres. Dostoevsky, to take another example, hesitated between the forms of a confession and a diary as he wrote his novel *Crime and Punishment*; Kafka, in the pre-text of his *Castle*, crossed out all of the first-person pronouns from the first version of the novel and replaced them with the acronym K. (cf. Ferrer, 1998: 26-27; Vašák et al., 1993: 40). Since pre-textual variants from writers' manuscripts may be considered matrices of virtual literary works, they deserve interpretive efforts in themselves; they are at least relatively autonomous instances that have been actualized in a

---

[3] In a different context, McGann also stresses that "the composition of a poem is the work's first reading" (2004: 204).

complex network in which authors continuously explore the structural possibilities of signifying systems.

An even greater degree of autonomy may be credited to "post-text" (*après-texte*), that is, the rewriting and revisions of the text that authors, editors, and others have produced since its first publication. In the process of creating post-text, versions of the literary artwork often follow communicative and aesthetic agendas different from the strategies that used to inform the genesis of the pre-text. Post-texts, rewritten by writers themselves (as they grow older) or edited by their friends, relatives, or professionals, target new socio-historically changed audiences, or else they are included in newly-conceived supra-textual compositions, such as cycles or posthumous books of poems. All these material and apparently superficial changes may modify textual meanings and, consequently, substantially alter the work's reception history.

To sum up, postmodern textology presents literary texts not as static, self-enclosed monads, but as dynamic phenomena (Thomasberger, 1992: 458) or "fuzzy sets" (Vašák et al., 1993: 46-47), in which the temporality of difference plays the crucial role.

2.2.

The changes in textological theory and practice described so far are generally in concord with post-structuralism and deconstruction (cf. Zelenka, 2006). Another important accent characteristic of postmodern textual criticism is its interest in the non-linguistic, material properties of manuscripts, codices, typewriting or prints. Similar to New Historicism and cultural studies, postmodern textology resists reducing literary texts to their linguistic structures, claiming that the circumstances of publication, the status and expressive means of the medium, contribute to the meaning of the text by placing it in societal relations (cf. Chartier, 2002: 111; 2002a: 113; McGann, 2002: 4-5, 77, 89-90, 206, 233). For example, Byron's poem *Fare Thee Well*, which appeared to be written as an intimate address to Lady Byron, had its meaning converted as soon as it began to be circulated in some fifty exemplars in London's high society (McGann, 2002: 77-92, 226): Byron's wife read it as an artful and cunning attempt by her husband to arouse public sympathy in order to improve his position during their divorce proceedings; readers of Byron's 1816 collection *Poems* in fact understood this poem as the emotional outburst of a wounded man, whereas in one of the satirical columns it was presented with the intention of unmasking Byron's hypocrisy. From cases like this, it follows that a literary work of art should be published in a scholarly edition in which non-linguistic semiotics (McGann's "bibliographic code") can tell us something important about the textual meaning. Such an edition should reproduce or describe the typography, print format, book design, and illustrations, as well as take into account the number of copies printed, their circulation, the publisher's reputation, and so on. After all, historical criticism attempts to represent meanings "in 'minute particulars', in forms that recover (as it were) their *physique* in as complete detail as possible" (McGann, 2002: 211-212, 226).

3.

It might seem paradoxical that it is computer-generated *virtual* cyberspace that meets postmodern efforts to restore the *concreteness* of historical presence. Kathryn Sutherland is convinced, along with J. Hillis Miller, that the computer "stores and gives access to particulars" and that "it works in the service of postmodern detailism and the micro-contexts of knowledge, and against the great meta-narratives of science [...] In their place it puts the closely bit-mapped context, a data-rich saturation so minute [...] that the illusion of proximity is achieved" (Sutherland, 1997a: 13)

However, as a scene of such proximity and historical concreteness, cyberspace is, of course, a digitally-generated, -simulated, and unstable space. For a computer user, cyberspace, with the help of prosthetic sensorial devices, merely creates an illusion of unlimited possibilities of cognitive and sensual immersion, nomadic and free identities, interactive participation, and de-territorialized exchange with other users of the World Wide Web (cf. Aarseth, 1999: 32-33; Poster, 1999: 43-47; Nunes, 1999: 62-70; Ryan, 1999b). Yet virtuality, characteristic of cyberspace, does not have only negative connotations ("appearance", "illusion", "deception"), but also positive ones ("potentiality", "productive capacity", "openness"; cf. Ryan 1999b: 89-93). Virtualization is a general feature that constitutes language as a system of recurrent elements from a multitude of singular utterances (ibid.: 93-94). It is an important characteristic of all structures and textuality because it allows texts to tear themselves away from the circumstances of their production and to refer to the ever-changing state of affairs. The evolution of media from oral traditions to electronic communication shows a progression of such virtualization. On-screen texts have lost tangible substance, well-defined authorship, and clear-cut boundaries. As such, they essentially differ from printed texts, which are normally perceived as discrete, singular, and self-enclosed units (Ryan, 1999b: 88, 95-99).[4]

3.1.

The advent of electronic media, and of the hypertext in the role of its central genre, has cast new light on the meaning-constituting role of already-existing media, primarily books (Ryan, 1999a: 10; Chartier, 2002b, 2002c). In the light of digital textuality, we have become conscious of the fact that the c-book is not merely a vehicle of linguistic signs but is an important factor that, through its physical and content properties, also structures systems of knowledge, co-determines generic identities, and shapes writing and reading practices, etc. For instance, the "revolution of reading" in the Enlightenment supplanted the type of "intensive" reader, who had been occupied with and almost devoted to a limited text corpus, with the modern "extensive" reader who consumed a variety of printed genres (Chartier, 2002b: 125-126). New media have also influenced the evolution of philology; something that happened long before the invention of computers. Since the mid-nineteenth century, the inventions of photography and facsimile have made it possible for classical philologists and medievalists to compare *in praesentia* various manuscripts and versions that are located at a distance from each other or are difficult to access (Kittler, 1992).

3.2.

Electronic hypertext is thus an ideal medium for the critical presentation of versions of the text produced from its genesis to the final authorized edition and beyond (see *The Literary Text in the Digital Age*; Finneran, ed., 1999). It is, then, no surprise that it was electronic scholarly editions and e-textual archives that were among the earliest and, especially in the

---

[4] E-texts are being re-generated by computers all the time, and displayed on screens only fragmentarily; they do not exist permanently nor have any single location (Sutherland, 1997a: 10-12). E-texts are, so to say, free from their bodies (Flanders, 1997: 127) and emerge out of electronic codes, whereas on-screen signs are nothing but simulacra of printed letters and pages (Landow, 1994a: 6). Digital technology thus undermines the traditional identifications of books by their physical objectivity, topic, and author (Chartier, 2002b: 128-129).

1990s, most prolific areas of the "digital humanities",[5] that is, the discipline in its own right, which attempts to unite the humanities culture with the exact sciences (cf. Schreibman et al., 2004a; Hockey, 2004: 9, 14; Willett, 2004: 241, 243). E-editions have also been more widely accepted by "mainstream" literary scholars, who were otherwise far more skeptical about the relevance of other major fields of the digital humanities, such as computer-assisted stylistics and authorship studies—regardless of the computer's ability to recognize, in very broad textual corpora, potentially significant structural patterns that are beyond grasp of human perception and memory (Rommel, 2004: 88-89, 92-93; Craig, 2004).

3.2.1.

In e-texts, it becomes clearer than ever that the text's identity is mobile, differential, embedded in situations, actions, and transactions of various agencies; it is steered by the psycho-dynamics of writing and the socio-dynamics of publishing. In short, hypertext is able to reveal documents about the writing subject's positioning in the literary discourse. Through an electronic archive and its paratactic presentation of textual versions from pre- and post-text (they appear as equals), textology gains a new perspective on literature, surpassing the teleological linearity of older criticism, which was largely dependent on the linearity of the c-book medium. The latter imposed the need to construct one single representative presentation of a text (cf. Ross, 1999: 226) and to place it at the centre of the edition, while all other preserved variants had to be expelled to the small type of the critical "apparatus". E-editions in hypertext do not demand such a focalization on a single, "definitive", or central text, because their structure is in principle not hierarchic; they acknowledge "the fluidity of texts instead of insisting upon single-minded, singularly-oriented texts" (Smith, 2004: 320). Smith's own work on Emily Dickinson's electronic archive confirms her conceptual differentiation between *hieratic* c-book editions, which impose order also "on that which is otherwise unruly" (e.g., Dickinson's chaotic literary manuscripts), and *demotic* e-editions, in which ordering decisions are for the most part left to the reader (2004: 316).

---

[5] However, according to Hockey, after some sample projects, the vivid interest "in the area of electronic scholarly editions [...] waned somewhat" in the second half of the 1990s (2004: 14).

3.2.2.

The notion that hypertext embodies and puts into practice post-structuralist theories of the text is advocated by many proponents of digital media. George P. Landow, probably the most influential among them, stresses several analogies between hypertext—as produced by information technologies—and (text) theories by Barthes, Derrida, Kristeva, Foucault, Bakhtin, and Deleuze (e.g., text as intertext, decentered writing, the death of the author, networks of power, polyphony, nomadic thought), which, according to him, stem from similar discontent with hierarchical thinking and traditional closures of books and literature (Landow, 1994a: 1). Espen Aarseth (1999: 31-33), however, shows an ironic stance towards the handy formula "the theoretical perspective of <fill in your favourite theory/theoretician here> is clearly really a prediction/description of <fill in your favourite digital medium here>", because he thinks that post-structuralist theories were based on essentially different, older media. But Aarseth himself also invented the term "ergodic discourse", by which he reinterpreted his older notion of "non-linear textuality". He introduced the latter to describe precisely the kind of combinatory textuality that predicts hypertexts—printed communication with no regular sign sequences (of letters, words, "textons"), in which textual syntagmatics, thanks to the medium's immanent technologies, vary with each and every use/reading. He had traced forms of non-linear textuality back to the French group OULIPO (e.g., Queneau's *Cent mille milliards de poèmes*) and the old Chinese *Book of Changes* (Aarseth, 1994). This reminds us that the newer media draw on and emulate, so to speak, the older ones. We are thus entitled to transpose post-structuralist concepts, although derived from printed texts, on digital texts, e-archives, and e-editions. On the other hand, Barthes and Kristeva themselves already used theoretical metaphors that can now, in the context of hypertexts, be read almost literally, for example, the text as *réseau*.

3.3.

Scholarly editions of literature in c-books always faced the problem of the location and extent of critical notes; the e-archive is much more flexible in this respect, as it can adapt the depth and extent of critical commentaries to the different needs of users (cf. Lamont, 1997: 48-56). A very extensive corpus of literary historical materials can be used in order to contextualize the edited text. E-editions of literary classics are thus becoming archives that can always be updated; see, for example, *The William Blake Archive* or *The Complete Writings and Pictures of Dante Gabriel Rossetti*. The question arises as to where to set limits for the inclusion of historical data. Some literary historians sharply accuse the presumed "cacophony of data" in e-archives of overshadowing that which is supposed to be of real importance—the text's literary structures. However, Flanders is right in claiming that this "cacophony" is "no creation of the archive, but the true realm of textuality from which, through the traditional edition, we seek to protect ourselves" (Flanders, 1997: 136-137). In other words: the cacophony is precisely the effect of the text's historical presence, which is deeply interlaced with the context—the latter, as we know from Derrida and Culler, has no limits.

3.4.

Electronic critical editions or literary archives have, in the light of postmodern textology, one further quality. In a similar way as the invention of the facsimile, which made largely faithful reproduction and accessibility of rare manuscripts possible, they "provide artifacts for direct examination" of scholarly community; even more readers can now handle documentary evidence, instead of relying on potentially manipulative print editions (cf. Smith, 2004: 310-311). E-editions are, in the words of McGann, "a marriage of facsimile and critical editing" (1999: 145). They not only transcribe—diplomatically or critically—the texts' linguistic structures, but also reproduce "the conditions of the writing scene in which they were produced" (Smith, 2004: 306). Users of e-editions are free to check scholarly transcriptions and descriptions of documents against their digitalized images, which provide surplus value: in this way, every user is able to see how, and to what extent, the text's physical body affects its linguistically-constituted meaning. Electronic text-encoding via SGML, XML, and, specifically TEI, enables analyses of both the semantic and visual "bibliographic" properties of the edited work. This is all taken into account,for example, in the current project of electronic scholarly editions conducted by the research centre of the Slovene Academy of Sciences and Arts (cf. Ogrin, ed. 2005).[6]

Yet McGann is cautious, reminding us that all computer markup, however flexible, is pre-defined metalanguage that both imposes order on and interprets and disambiguates primary documents, not only in order to store them in ever evolving software and hardware environments, but also to make from them objects of quantitative, computer-assisted study (e.g.,

---

[6] See the Appendix.

of style); as "allopoetic systems", the existing markup languages are still unable to represent and deal with "the autopoetic character of textual fields", that is, with unpredictable, dynamic, multi-relational, self-engendering, and inter-subjective nature of textuality, especially poetic literature (McGann, 2004: 200-207).

4.

In conclusion, with the help of scholarly editions in electronic media, literary historians can better treat texts in terms of postmodern "contextual detailism" and devote more attention to the role of difference in text production and distribution. Cyberspace, with its simulacra, also brings into their view the "materiality" of media and "the expressive function of non-verbal elements," as well as "a wider world of objects and practices of literacy," which until recently had always been abstracted from literary works of art (cf. Chartier, 2002, 2002a).

Bibliography

Aarseth, E. J. "Nonlinearity and Literary Theory". In Landow (ed.), 1994: 51-86.
—. "Aporia and Epiphany in *Doom* and *The Speaking Clock*: The Temporality of Ergodic Art". In Ryan (ed.), 1999: 31-41.
Bennewitz, I. "Alte 'neue' Philologie? Zur Tradition eines Diskurses". In Tevooren & Wenzel (eds.), 1997: 46-61.
Biasi, P.-M. de. "Qu'est-ce qu'un brouillon? Le cas Flaubert: essai de typologie fonctionelle des documents de genèse". In Contat & Ferrer (eds.), 1998 : 31-60.
Chartier, R. "Kratek uvod v problematiko" (A Short Introduction). Trans. D. B. Rotar. *Monitor ISH* 4, no. 1-4, 2002: 111-112.
—. "Tekstna kritika in kulturna zgodovina. Tekst in glas, XVI. – XVIII. stoletje" (Textual Criticism and Cultural History). Trans. D. B. Rotar. *Monitor ISH* 4, no. 1-4, 2002a: 112-123.
—. "Preteklost in prihodnost knjige" (The Past and the Future of a Book). Trans. D. B. Rotar. *Monitor ISH* 4, no. 1-4, 2002b: 123-130.
—. "Bralci in branja v dobi elektronske tekstualnosti" (Readers and Reading in the Age of Electronic Textuality). Trans. D. B. Rotar. *Monitor ISH* 4, no. 1-4, 2002c: 131-141.
Contat, M. & D. Ferrer, eds. *Pourquoi la critique génétique? Méthodes, théories*. Paris: CNRS Editions (Textes et Manuscrits), 1998.

Contat, M. & D. Ferrer . "Introduction". In Contat & Ferrer (eds.), 1998a: 7-10.
Craig, H. "Stylistic Analysis and Authorship Studies". In Schreibman et al. (eds.), 2004: 275-288.
Ferrer, D. "Le matériel et le virtuel: du paradigme indiciaire à la logique des mondes possibles". In Contat & Ferrer (eds.), 1998: 11-30.
Finneran, R. (ed). *The Literary Text in the Digital Age*. Ann Arbor: The University of Michigan Press, 1999.
Flanders, J. "The Body Encoded: Questions of Gender and the Electronic Text". In Sutherland (ed.), 1997 : 127-143.
Grésillon, A. "La critique génétique à l'oeuvre. Étude d'un dossier génétique: 'Vivre encore' de Jules Supervielle". In Contat & Ferrer (eds.), 1998: 61-93.
Gumbrecht, H.-U. *The Powers of Philology: Dynamics of Textual Scholarship*. Urbana & Chicago: University of Illinois Press, 2003.
Hockey, S. "The History of Humanities Computing". In Schreibman et al.(eds.), 2004: 9-29.
Juvan, M. *History and Poetics of Intertextuality*. West Lafayette: Purdue UP (forthcoming).
Kittler, W. "Literatura, izdaja in reprografija" (Literature, Edition, and Reprography). Trans. I. Kramberger. *Dialogi* 28, nos. 3-5. 47-59, 60-69, 1992: 14-22.
Kos, J. "Pripombe k izdaji" (Editorial Notes). InPrešeren, F., *Zbrano delo* 1 (Collected Works), J. Kos (ed.). Ljubljana: DZS, 1965: 201-217.
Lamont, C. "Annotating a Text: Literary Theory and Electronic Hypertext". In Sutherland (ed.), 1997: 47-66.
Landow, G. P. (ed.). *Hyper/Text/Theory*. Baltimore & London: The Johns Hopkins University Press, 1994.
—. "What's a Critic to Do? Critical Theory in the Age of Hypertext". In Landow (ed.), 1994: 1-48.
McGann, J. J."The Rationale of Hypertext". In Sutherland (ed.), 1997: 19-46.
—. "The Rossetti Archive and Image-Based Electronic Editing". In Finneran (ed.), 1999:145-183.
—. *Byron and Romanticism*. James Soderholm (ed.). Cambridge: Cambridge University Press, 2002.
—. "Marking Texts of Many Dimensions". In Schreibman et al. (eds.), 2004. 198-217.
Nichols, S. G., (ed.). *The New Philology = Speculum: A Journal of Medieval Studies* 65, no. 1, 1990.

Nunes, M. "Virtual Topographies: Smooth and Striated Cyberspace". In Ryan (ed.), 1999: 61-77.
Ogrin, M., (ed.). *Znanstvene izdaje in elektronski medij* (Scholarly Editions and the Digital Medium). Ljubljana: ZRC, 2005.
Poster, M. "Theorizing Virtual Reality: Baudrillard and Derrida". In Ryan (ed.), 1999: 42-60.
Rommel, T. "Literary Studies". In Schreibman et al. (eds.), 2004: 88-96.
Ross, C. L. "The Electronic Text and the Death of the Critical Edition". In Finneran (ed.), 1999: 225-231.
Ryan, M-L., (ed.) *Cyberspace Textuality: Computer Technology and Literary Theory.* Bloomington & Indianapolis: Indiana University Press, 1999.
—. "Introduction". In Ryan (ed.), 1999a: 1-28.
—. "Cyberspace, Virtuality, and the Text". In Ryan (ed.), 1999b: 78-107.
Schreibman, S. & R. Siemens & J. Unsworth (eds.). *A Companion to Digital Humanities.* Oxford: Blackwell Publishing, 2004.
—. "The Digital Humanities and Humanities Computing: An Introduction". In Schreibman et al. (eds.), 2004a: xxii-xxvii.
Smith, M. N. "Electronic Scholarly Editing". In Schreibman et al. (eds.), 2004: 306-322.
Sutherland, K., ed. *Electronic Text: Investigations in Method and Theory.* Oxford: Clarendon Press, 1997.
—. "Introduction". In Sutherland (ed.), 1997: 1-18.
Tevooren, H. & Horst Wenzel, (eds.). *Philologie als Textwissenschaft: Alte und neue Horizonte = Zeitschrift für deutsche Philologie* 116, Sonderheft, 1997.
Thomasberger, A. "Textsicherung und Textkritik". In *Literaturwissenschaft: Ein Grundkurs*, H. Brackert & J. Stückrath (eds.). Reinbek bei Hamburg: Rowohlts Enzyklopädie, 1992: 455-466.
Vašák, P. et al. *Textologie: Teorie a ediční praxe* [Textology: Theory and Editorial Practice]. Prague: Univerzita Karlova, 1993.
Willett, P. "Electronic Texts: Audiences and Purposes". In Schreibman et al. (eds.), 2004: 240-253.
Zelenka, M. "Manuscriptology and Its Significance for Literary History in the Context of Contemporary Methodology". In *Writing Literary History: Selected Perspectives from Central Europe*, M. Juvan & D. Dolinar (eds.). Frankfurt/M. etc.: Peter Lang, 2006: 153-168.

Electronic Sources

Scholarly Digital Editions of Slovenian Literature. Principal researcher: M. Ogrin, digital encoding: T. Erjavec. Ljubljana: Institute of Slovenian Literature and Literary Studies, SRC SASA. http://nl.ijs.si/e-zrc/index-en.html

The Complete Writings and Pictures of Dante Gabriel Rossetti: A Hypermedia Research Archive. Ed. J. McGann. http://jefferson.village.virginia.edu/rossetti/index.html

The William Blake Archive. (eds.) Morris Eaves, Robert Essick, Joseph Viscomi. http://www.blakearchive.org.uk/main.html

Appendix
Scholarly Digital Editions of Slovenian Literature

Introduction

The aim of the project *"Scholarly Digital Editions of Slovenian Literature"*[7] is to compile a collection of digital text-critical editions of Slovenian literary works and sources for literary studies. Our goal is to leverage the advantages offered by the electronic medium and, using advanced IT methods as well as applying principles of traditional textual criticism or ecdotics, show the communicative potential, historical complexity and linguistic idiosyncrasies of these texts.

What kind of editions?

A scholarly digital edition aims to capture the complex nature of a text with a view to enabling the most diverse types of research. Ideally, the structure of such an edition should not prevent any conceivable research perspective. In order to achieve this goal, it is necessary that a scholarly edition includes all forms or appearances of the text.

- A *digitized facsimile* of a manuscript makes possible the establishment and verification of the authenticity of the text and enables graphological and paleographic studies. A manuscript that contains corrections, particularly the manuscript of a literary work, is useful in analysing textual aspects and text genesis. A digitized facsimile of a rhetorical text enables the study of the relation between the original and the spoken version. Finally, a digitized facsimile makes possible direct contact with the text, an experience that the wider public has been deprived of until now.

---

[7] Principal researcher: Matija Ogrin, Institute of Slovenian Literature and Literary Science SRC SASA; Digital encoding: Tomaž Erjavec, Department of Knowledge Technologies JSI.

- A *diplomatic transcription* of the text preserves the authentic orthography, syntactical and lexical images of the original, including the mistakes and omissions, in authentic typography. It is particularly indispensable for historical philological studies of older literature.
- A *critical transcription* is a critical reconstruction of the original based on clearly defined editorial standards. As a rule, it involves the harmonization of certain orthographic elements, especially punctuation, and the observance of some other elements, appearing on other linguistic levels, with respect to the linguistic standards applied at the time of text creation. The critical copy resolves doubtful or difficult to read points in the original, and documents the unintelligible or destroyed parts of the manuscript. It represents one form or meaning of the text as resulting from the editor's selection of variant parts, if such exist; traditionally, the editor will aim to determine the author's final intention or "final touch of hand."
- A digital critical copy incorporates a scientific apparatus which includes critical and author annotations, editor's comments, and hypertext links to the external bibliographic or information sources. Furthermore, important components of the e-edition apparatus are a search tool, a cross-referencing tool (used for comparing different copies or variant parts), hypertext links between the index and the critical copy, a computer generated dictionary and concordances. In scientific studies, the e-edition represents an important advantage over the printed version. What makes a digital edition especially valuable is the possibility of including a virtually unlimited number of digitized facsimiles of manuscripts, rare prints, versions of the texts and transcriptions, as well as a comprehensive apparatus, which would not be possible with the printed version of the book because of financial obstacles.

The various forms of the appearance of the text in a digital edition enable the widest possible array of research approaches.

A specific purpose of this project is to empirically establish how the literary genre and the time in which the text originated—the two key factors in every critical edition—influence the choice of the material and editing procedures.

What Texts?

Our digital editions will comprise various types of literary texts and sources, from the oldest to the contemporary, including various literary and semi-literary genres. At present, two editions are available: one comprises three rhetorical texts by Bishop Anton Martin Slomšek (written between 1825 and 1841), and the other the selected correspondence of Žiga Zois (1812-1813). Work on the digital edition of the first Slovenian dramatic text, Romuald's spiritual Baroque play *Škofjeloški pasijon* (*The Passion of Škofja Loka*), written in 1721, is currently in progress. Also underway is work on two editions of modern poetry: a collection by Anton Podbevšek, *Človek z bombami* (*A Man with Bombs*), from 1925, and poems by Srečko Kosovel, not included in *Zbrana dela* (*Collected Works*). Modern prose will be represented by the digital edition of the novel *S poti* (*Notes From The Journey*) by Izidor Cankar (1913). Our plan is to concentrate primarily on literary works and older Slovenian literature, since with these works the potential of digital editions, which lies in exposing the multiple layers of such texts, may be put to full use. The juxtaposition of facsimiles, diplomatic and critical copies enables the reconstruction of the text, seen as embodying the interplay of the individual and the temporal, and the cultural and historical contexts. Such editions resurrect the communicative power of older literary works, bringing to light their many intriguing layers and, last but not least, conveying their cultural value to a wider circle of readers. With these editions we continue the tradition of the publication of scholarly editions that are particularly complex in terms of editorial work, which is one of the main activities of the Institute for Slovenian Literature and Literary Studies.

Technology

All our digital editions are based on the XML standard and follow the Text Encoding Initiative Guidelines. The advantages of digital editions, especially scholarly editions, lie in the option of text encoding, whereby the latent and passive text structure is transformed into a computer-manageable and readable structure. A good encoding standard uses unambiguous markers and offers the greatest possible independence from computer hardware and software. This is the objective pursued by XML, the leading technology for text encoding and data exchange. Its crucial advantage is a clear description of the text structure based on a definable set of markers that are used to explicate the text structure and relations between various elements of the text and their connections. The presentation of a structure described in this way is a matter of choice and it is selected in the process of transforming an XML encoded text into, say, HTML format. In contrast to XML, HTML is concerned with the presentation of hypertext and uses a fixed number of pre-defined tags not suitable for the description of a complex text structure.

Inside XML we still need to define the particular elements that are used in the digital edition. For our vocabulary we chose the most elaborated standard for text encoding, the TEI Consortium's Guidelines for Electronic Text Encoding and Interchange P4.

CHAPTER TWELVE

THE HYPERTEXTUAL STRUCTURE OF WRITING PROCESSES

DIRK VAN HULLE

One of the research areas in which digital media prove to be useful is the analysis of writing processes and literary geneses, or comparative genetic criticism. Since Time is an essential element in the reconstruction of a writing process, the three case studies in the following analysis are three twentieth-century works focusing on time: Marcel Proust's *A la recherche du temps perdu*, one of the *Tales Told of Shem and Shaun* (part of *Finnegans Wake*) by James Joyce, and the short work *Lessness* by Samuel Beckett.

1. Marcel Proust

The hypertextual structure of Marcel Proust's writing method becomes evident in the development of three musical scenes in *La Prisonnière*, the fifth part of *A la recherche du temps perdu*: the Tristan scene (*RTP* III 664-5), the Septet (*RTP* III 753-68), and the Pianola scene (*RTP* III 873-8). In the genesis of *La Prisonnière*, the musical reflections were originally not divided in this way. They were developed on the basis of several textual nodes or units. Most of these units can be retraced to a series of notes in the so-called *carnets* 3 and 4. A distinction is made in studies of Proust between *carnets* or notebooks (containing notes and jottings) and *cahiers* (containing more extensive blocks of text).

The notes in *carnets* 3 and 4 were subsequently elaborated in Cahiers 57, 73 and 55. During this process they were shuffled and reshuffled. Blocks of text wander around in the *cahiers*, so that Almuth Grésillon speaks of Proust's writing as "*écriture vagabonde*". To reconstruct the process of this "*écriture vagabonde*" the notes in *carnets* 3 and 4 can be divided into textual units, numbered according to the sequence in which they appear in the *carnets*, and labelled with a keyword in order to follow their evolution and continuously altered sequence. These textual units could be treated as what Roland Barthes (in *S/Z*) called "lexias":

(1) lexia "langue":
Carnet 3: 4v-5r: "Pour Vinteuil dans le second volume
Les notes ces belles étrangères dont nous ne savons pas la // *langue* et que nous comprenons si bien.

(2) lexia "extérioriser":
Carnet 3, f. 5v-6r: pour Vinteuil
Comme les couleurs du spectre *extériorisent* pour nous la composition intime des astres que nous // ne verrons jamais, ainsi la couleur du peintre, les harmonies du musicien, nous permettent de connaître cette différence qualitative des sensations qui est la plus g[ran]de jouissance et la plus g[ran]de souffrance de la vie de chacun de nous et qui reste toujours ignoré[e] car elle est indépendante de ce que nous pouvons raconter (les faits, les choses) qui sont les mêmes pour tous.

(3) lexia "étoiles":
Carnet 3, f. 6r-6v: Mais grâce à l'harmonie de Franck, de Wagner, de Chopin, à la couleur de Ver Meer, de Rembrandt, de Delacroix, nous allons vraiment dans les cieux les plus ignorés volant d'*étoiles* en étoiles. Bien plus que si des ailes nous étaient données ; car ce qui fait pour // nous l'uniformité des choses, c'est la permanence de nos sens, et si nous allions dans Mars ou dans Vénus, les choses ne nous paraîtraient jamais très différentes puisque ce seraient toujours des visions de nos mêmes yeux.

(4) lexia "jouvence":
Carnet 3, f. 6v: Le vrai bain de *jouvence*, le vrai paysage nouveau, ce n'est pas d'aller dans un pays que nous ne connaissons pas, c'est de laisser venir à nous une nouvelle musique.

(5) lexia "cloches":
Carnet 3, f. 6v-7r: Pour Vinteuil encore fin de la symphonie de Franck. Il semblait dans sa joie tirer les *cloches* à toutes volées par un dimanche de soleil où on s'écrase sur la place de Combray. La phrase était boiteuse et pas belle mais elle enivrait de joie et de soleil.

(6) lexia "monotonie":
Carnet 3, f. 7r: Vinteuil encore.
La *monotonie* des harmonies quel que soit le sujet, est une preuve de fixité des éléments composants de l'âme.

(7) lexia "moelleux":
Carnet 3, f. 7r: Chez S[c]humann un certain fond familial—met du *moelleux* dans les intervalles, même pendant que le poète parle on entend toujours l'enfant qui dort. (...) Puis trop souvent c'est un Beethoven étriqué. (...) grandeur soudaine sincère et pathétique d'une phrase de S[c]hubert.

(8) lexia "familier":
Carnet 4, f. 2v-3r: pour musique (...) // phrases habituelles
harmonies habituelles à Franck demi déesses de moindre grandeur qui lui sont *familières*, ses nymphes et ses sylvains qu'on reconnaît.

(9) lexia "variété / différence":
Carnet 4, f. 4r: Musique /—La *variété*, la *différence*, que nous cherchons en vain dans l'amour, dans le voyage, la musique nous l'offre.

(10) lexia "brumes":
Carnet 4, f. 4r: Les oeuvres de cette dernière période de la vie de Vinteuil se ressemblaient. Dans presque toutes flotter ne tardait pas à s'élever une certaine atmosphère mélodique comme (...) des *brumes* particulières à certaines contrées.

(11) lexia "visage":
Carnet 4, f. 4v-5v: La phrase de S[c]humann dans le Carnaval de Vienne (intermezzo je crois) douce inconnue que tant de soirs je vis passer et repasser sans jamais voir son *visage* (...) j'en ai encore maintenant les yeux pleins de larmes comme devant l'offre du seul parfum qu'il aurait valu la peine de posséder.

The character of the fictitious composer Vinteuil in *A la recherche du temps perdu* was not present in the drafts from the beginning. As Karuyoschi Yoshikawa has demonstrated, it is the result of a fusion of two different characters: on the one hand, a scientist called Vington, and on the other, a composer called Berget. Around May 1913, Vington became a piano teacher; Berget got another name and became 'Vindeuil' and in a third movement both became the same "Vinteuil". By turning the scientist into a fictitious composer, Proust gave himself the difficult task of creating an equally fictitious set of compositions. Originally he had planned to use the third act of Wagner's *Parsifal* as the composition that triggers a revelation, causing the narrator to suddenly realize the common essence of memory, and to see that such a revelation could be made possible through art.

A palpable trace of the decision to create a fictitious *oeuvre* for Vinteuil appears in a note in Cahier 57, mentioning "*un concert où on jouait des choses de Vinteuil*" with this explicit addition between brackets: "(*car il vaut mieux que ce soit Vinteuil*)" (Cahier 57. 4r). Originally, Proust was thinking of a cantata, but eventually he decided to create a fictitious quartet. The performance of this quartet is drafted in Cahier 57, for which he used his notes or lexias in *carnets* 3 and 4. He did not use all of them. Some of them, such as the *"variété"*, *"brumes"*, *"cloches"* and the *"extérioriser"* lexias, were elaborated separately. For instance, the lexia *"cloches"* was developed in Cahier 57 and marked to be inserted at another place (*"à intercaler dans la page suivante au verso"*), which indicates the degree of textual movability that characterizes Proust's writing method:

> (5) lexia "cloches":Cahier 57, f. 2v: La phrase pouvait être parfois titubante de tristesse elle sonnait à toute volée comme des *cloches* une joie qui ruisselait de soleil plus que tous les pays que j'avais vus, et déjà dès la sonate le déferlement de certains accords ne déployait-il pas plus de soleil que les vagues de Balbec à midi.

But some of the original lexias were clustered into one single paragraph. Thus the *"familier"*, the *"langue"* and the *"visage"* lexias became one single passage.

> (8 + 1 + 11): "familier"—"langue"— "visage":
> Vinteuil avait ainsi certaines phrases qui de quoi qu'il parlât, quelque sujet qu'il traitât habitaient son oeuvre dont elles étaient comme le peuple *familier*, les dryades et les nymphes, divines étrangères dont nous ne savons pas la *langue* et que nous comprenons si bien !, si caressantes et si belles que quand je les sens passer et repasser sous le masque nocturne des sons qui me dérobe à jamais leur *visage* (...) mes yeux se remplissent de pleurs.

Although Proust used his *carnets* to draft these passages, there is a difference between the notes in the *carnets* and the passages in the *cahiers*. The notes in the *carnets* mention the names of several existing composers (such as César Franck, Robert Schumann, Richard Wagner, Franz Schubert, Frédéric Chopin and Ludwig van Beethoven). But in Cahier 57 Proust carefully omits these names, and combines his impressions of all of these different composers' works to create one work by one fictitious composer; at this stage in the writing process Proust calls it *"le quatuor de Vinteuil"*. The performance of this quartet was meant to take place after the series of involuntary memories in the final part, *Le Temps retrouvé*. The performance is then elaborated and described in more detail in Cahier 73.

In his *cahiers*, Proust often makes notes to himself. One of these notes in Cahier 73 indicates the extent to which he conceived of his texts as combinations of mobile units:

Se rappeler que je n'ai mis ni les fées familières, ni la composition astrale (...), ni bien d'autres choses toutes dans les petits *cahiers de bonhommes* et que peut-être je mettrai là, peut-être au pianola, peut-être à la soirée finale (Cahier 73, f. 43v ; emphasis added)

What Proust calls "*cahiers de bonhommes*" are the *carnets*. In Cahier 55 Proust incorporated most of these lexias in the Septet. For example, the "*jouvence*" lexia

(4) lexia "jouvence":
Carnet 3, f. 6v: Le vrai bain de *jouvence*, le vrai paysage nouveau, ce n'est pas d'aller dans un pays que nous ne connaissons pas, c'est de laisser venir à nous une nouvelle musique.

was developed as follows in Cahier 55:

(4) lexia "jouvence":
Cahier 55, f. 34r: Le vrai bain de *jouvence*, dans le seul paysage nouveau, ce serait d'avoir d'autres yeux, de voir tout d'un coup l'univers d'un autre, c'est ce prodige que l'art accomplit.

In the published text, this lexia eventually ended up in the performance of the septet:

(4) lexia "jouvence":
RTP III 762: le seul bain de Jouvence, ce ne serait pas d'aller vers de nouveaux paysages, mais d'avoir d'autres yeux, de voir l'univers avec les yeux d'un autre.

Eventually all the lexias were shuffled around and distributed over the three musical scenes in the published version of *La Prisonnière*.

Carnets 3&4. 3: 4v-7r; 4: 2v-5v	Cahier 57. 3r-3v	Cahier 73. 15v-16; 42r-43r	Cahier 55. 31r-34r	Ed. Pléiade. III 665; III 755-64; III 875-7
1. Langue	9. Variété	9. Variété	7. Moelleux	9. Variété
2. Exterior	8. Familier	2. Exterior	10. Brumes	2. Exterior
3. Etoiles	1. Langue	10. Brumes	8. Familier	5. Cloches
4. Jouvance	11. Visage	5. Cloches	1. Langue	7. Moelleux
5. Cloches	10. Brumes	8. Familier	11. Visage	6. Monotonie
6. Monotonie	5. Cloches		2. Exterior	2. Exterior
7. Moelleux	2. Exterior		3. Etoiles	4. Jouvance
8. Familier			4. Jouvance	3. Etoiles
9. Variété			6. Monotonie	8. Familier
10. Brumes				10. Brumes
11. Visage				11. Visage
				1. Langue
				8. Familier
				5. Cloches
				6. Monotonie

This distribution of blocks of text is referred to in Proust criticism as *"éclatement"*. In the *avant-texte* of the *Recherche* there are two types of *"éclatement"*: shuffling, or the "cut and paste" method, and bifurcation, or the "copy and paste" method. According to the first method, a particular description is first written as a whole and subsequently cut into pieces and distributed over different parts of the novel, to create, for instance, the effect of a *Leitmotiv*. According to the second method, a particular description is more or less duplicated and used twice. A good example is the *"névralgie"* lexia in *carnet 2*: *"Pour Franck / Ce n'est pas un motif qui reprend, c'est une névralgie qui recommence."* This was used both in the Tristan scene and in the Septet: (a) in the first scene the narrator is reminded of certain themes in Wagner's music, which are *"si internes, si organiques, si viscéraux qu'on dirait la reprise moins d'un motif que d'une névralgie"* (*RTP* III 665); (b) in the Septet, the narrator is fascinated by a musical phrase, *"presque si organique et viscérale qu'on ne savait pas, à chaque de ses reprises, si c'était d'un thème ou d'une névralgie"* (*RTP* III 764). It is not clear whether this repetition was done on purpose or was simply a mistake, an involuntary result of the intricate web of shuffled and reshuffled lexias. Contemporary authors have computers at their disposal to create hypertextual structures; Proust only had the space of his bed to shuffle his papers around.

George Landow referred to Barthes notion of "lexias" to define the concept of hypertext: "Hypertext (...) denotes text composed of blocks of text—what Barthes terms a lexia—and the electronic links that join them" (Landow, *Hypertext 2.0*, 3). With reference to the genesis of literary works, hypertext is not merely a metaphor to describe the kind of processes that take place during the composition history. As Daniel Ferrer has argued, it proves to be a suitable concept for visualizing the writing process in an electronic environment (Ferrer 1995), so that it becomes clear that the *avant-texte* is indeed a hypertextual structure, a text composed of lexias and the electronic links that join them. These electronic links thus enable the user to follow the author's mental process, which brought about this constant reshuffling of lexias.

2. James Joyce

This hypertextual structure is not just typical of one particular author's writing method, but characterizes other composition histories as well. Hypertext facilitates the visualisation of a work's genesis and proves to be instrumental in reading texts "through time". A good example is the fable of "The Ondt and the Gracehoper" in James Joyce's last book, *Finnegans Wake*. While he was writing this "Work in Progress" he was quite sensitive to criticism in the review of his previous book, *Ulysses*. In *The Art of Being Ruled* (1926), for instance, Wyndham Lewis lashes out at the majority of modernist writers who—according to him—put too much emphasis on Time at the expense of Space. Marcel Proust is, of course, one of them. He calls them "proustites". Joyce is another author who belongs to this group of what Lewis calls worshippers of "the Great God Flux" (Lewis, 1989: 335). In reaction to this criticism and to Lewis' "Analysis of the Mind of James Joyce" in his book *Time and Western Man*, Joyce started writing—among other things—two fables. The second of these fables is called "The Ondt and the Gracehoper," based on Aesop's fable of the ant and the grasshopper. The Ondt is the representative of Space, the Gracehoper represents Time. The fable roughly follows the same narrative as Aesop's: the Ondt works hard during the summer, building a house and collecting supplies for the winter. Meanwhile the Gracehoper laughs and dances, and by the time summer is over he has no choice but to beg for the Ondt's humiliating charity. Joyce makes his Gracehoper sing a song at the end of the fable; he praises the Ondt, telling him that his "genus is worldwide" and "his space is sublime," but the last line is the crucial question: "Why can't you beat time?" (Joyce, 1992: 419).

(1) In the first draft, Joyce does not immediately seem to conceive this final speech as a song or a poem. He continues writing the running text, as if it were a continuation of his prose text:

> The veripatetic figure of the Gracehoper, actually and presumptuably sinctifying chronic's despair, was too great for // his chorous of gravitates. He larved & he larved & he merd such a nause that the Gracehoper feared he would swallow his jaws. (British Library 47483-87r/88r)

The words "nause" and "jaws" form the first rhyme, which indicates the start of the song. The draft already closes with the punch line:

> ...Your spaces sublime, But / Holy Saltmartin, why / can't you beat time?" (British Library 47483-89r)

(2) To this 12-line poem Joyce added *six more lines* on the facing verso page [88v]. This 18-line text remained rather stable, and it appeared (with 18 lines) in the magazine *transition* (number 12) in March 1928.

(3) Joyce subsequently prepared a new version for incorporation in a separate publication of three stories from his work in progress, collected under the title: *Tales Told of Shem and Shaun*, published by the Black Sun Press in 1929. In the setting typescript *four extra lines* are added, as well as the closing formula: "In the name of the former and of the latter and of their holocaust. Allmen."

(4) To the proofs for *Tales Told* he added another *six lines*, so that by now the poem consisted of 28 lines in total. The biographer Richard Ellmann mentions an anecdote about the printing of the fable at the Black Sun Press. Because the last page contained only two lines, the printer suggested to the publisher, Mrs. Crosby, that she ask Joyce if he would be willing to write eight extra lines, whereupon the publisher "indignantly refused this preposterous idea" (Ellmann 1983: 614-5). But the printer secretly told Joyce what the problem was, and Joyce immediately added a few lines. Since some sets of proofs are missing or incomplete, it is difficult to reconstruct this remarkable story.

(5) However, to the third set of proofs for *Tales Told*, Joyce added a few sentences in the running text and *six extra lines* to the Gracehoper's song, resulting in a 34 line poem, composed of five temporal lexias (in the following presentation of the genesis the letters are replaced by the number of the corresponding lexia):

11 1111111 111 11 1111111 111 11 1111 1111 1 111111
111 111111111 111111 11 11111 11111111 111 111111.
1 1111111 111, 111111 1111, 1111 111 111111111, 1111111,
111 11111 11111 11 111 11111 111 111 1111 11 11111 1111111.
11111 1111 111 1111 111111, 1111 111111 11111'1 11111
111 11 1111 111111111 11111 111 1111 11 1111.
11 1 1111 111111 111 11111 1 1111 111 111 111 11111
11 11111 11 111111111 111 1111111 11 1111 11111!
444 444 44444 4444 44444 44 4444 44444 44 4 4444'44;
4 44444 444 4444 4444444444 44 4444 444 4444444444.
2 2222 22 2222 2222222, 222 222222222 22 2 222222,
222 222 22222 22 2222 2222 22 222 22222 22 22 22222.
333 3333333333 3333333333333 33 3333333333 3333333 '33
33 333333 3333 33333 33 33333 333'3 3333 333?
3 33333 33 3333, 3 3333 33 3'333333333,
33333 33333 333 333 33333 3333 3333 3333 33333333
444 444444444 4444 444444 44 44 444
 44444 444 444444 44 4444 44 444 4444444 44444444
444 4444 44444444 444 444 44444444 44444 444 44444
4444
44444 444444444444 44444 444444 4444444444 444   44444 4444444?
11 111 11111111 1111 1111, 111111111111, 111 111 1111,
1111 111111 11 111111 111 11111111 1111 1111.
555 55555 555555555 555 5555555 555 5555 5555
55555 555 55 555555
55 5555555 5555 555555, 55 555555 5555 555555.
55 55 5555555 555555555, 55555555, 555 555'5 5555
55 5 5555 55 5555 5555555 5555 55555555 55 55 5555.
5555555555 55 555555555 555555 55 55555 555555   55555555 55
5555 55555'5 55555555555 5555 5555'5 55555555555 55555 55.
22 22 2222222 22222222 222222 2222 2222
22222 222222222222222 2222 22222 222222?
2222 22222 222 22222222, 2222 2222222 2222222
(222 222 222222 2 22222 222 2222 2222 22222222 2222 22222!)
1111 11111 111 111111111, 1111 1111111 1111111!
111, 1111 111111111, 111 111'1 111 1111 1111?

In qualitative terms, the notion of "Work in Progress" may suggest that the final version is an "improvement." The first 12-line version already contains all the key elements and the basic structure of the Gracehoper's song, notably the last line: "Why can't you beat time?" One could easily argue that this compact version is more powerful and intense. But then again, this poem is part of a larger work, which Joyce originally conceived as a history of the world. His notion of history is comparable to the proliferation of rumours, such as the rumours concerning the protagonist

HCE's alleged crime in Phoenix Park, Dublin. The more elements from hearsay that are added to the first rumours, the harder it becomes to separate fact from fiction. To a certain extent Joyce allowed the writing to generate itself, but he incorporated degeneration into the composition process as well, which also implied "writing its own wrunes forever" (Joyce, 1992: 19), i.e. both its own "runes" and its own "ruins."

In quantitative terms, the poem was almost tripled in size in the space of one year, between publication in the magazine *transition* and publication in *Tales Told of Shem and Shaun*. This is the complete opposite of what Edgar Allan Poe proclaimed in his *Philosophy of Composition*. The first thing a writer has to decide, according to Poe, is the length of the text he is going to write—which is what he did (he retrospectively claimed) when he started writing *The Raven*: "The initial consideration was that of extent (...) for it is clear that brevity must be in direct ratio of the intensity of the intended effect" (Poe 1986: 483). The French genetic critic Louis Hay would probably categorize Joyce's approach as "*écriture à processus*" (a writing process that proceeds without much preparatory planning), as opposed to "*écriture à programme*". An example of the latter approach is a remarkable text by Samuel Beckett.

3. Samuel Beckett

In 1969, the year he received the Nobel Prize for literature, Beckett wrote a short text called *Sans*. Originally written in French, it was subsequently translated by the author himself under the title *Lessness*. This is the opening paragraph:

> Ruins true refuge long last towards which so many false time out of mind. All sides endlessness earth sky as one no sound no stir. Grey face two pale blue little body heart beating only upright. Blacked out fallen open four walls over backwards true refuge issueless. (Beckett 1995: 197)

Rosemary Pountney has analyzed the composition of this remarkable piece of writing, the synchronic structure of which is inextricably linked up with the diachronic structure of its writing history. Beckett created a rigid framework within which he allowed chance to be a major structuring principle. As Ruby Cohn (2001: 305) and Rosemary Pountney (1987) show, the text's 120 sentences are in fact 2 times the same 60 sentences, repeated in a different order. Beckett wrote each sentence on a piece of paper, mixed them in a container, and picked them out twice in random order. Beckett's own "key" to this text, preserved in the Yale University Library, explains that *Lessness* is "composed of 6 statement groups each containing 10 sentences, i.e. 60 sentences in all. These 60 are first given in a certain order and paragraph structure, then repeated in a different order with a different paragraph structure. The whole consists therefore of 2 x 60 = 120 sentences arranged and rearranged in 2 x 12 = 24 paragraphs." (Beckett in Pountney 1987: 69). The highest number of sentences in a paragraph is seven. With this information it is possible to reconstruct the underlying grid of 6 x 10 statement groups:

(A1) In four split asunder over backwards true refuge issueless scattered ruins. [34]
(A2) Blacked out fallen open four walls over backwards true refuge issueless. [4]
(A3) Ruins true refuge long last towards which so many false time out of mind. [1]
(A4) Slow black with ruin true refuge four walls over backwards no sound. [27]
(A5) Four square true refuge long last four walls over backwards no sound. [17]
(A6) True refuge long last issueless scattered down four walls over backwards no sound. [36]
(A7) True refuge long last scattered ruins same grey as the sand. [54]
(A8) Scattered ruins ash grey all sides true refuge long last issueless. [39]
(A9) Scattered ruins same grey as the sand ash grey true refuge. [5]
(A10) Blacked out fallen open true refuge issueless towards which so many false time out of mind. [47]
(B1) Ash grey all sides earth sky as one all sides endlessness. [20]
(B2) All sides endlessness earth sky as one no stir not a breath. [37]
(B3) Flatness endless little body only upright same grey all sides earth sky body ruins. [44]
(B4) Grey sky no cloud no sound no stir earth ash grey sand. [18]
(B5) Earth sand same grey as the air sky ruins body fine ash grey sand. [42]
(B6) No sound not a breath same grey all sides earth sky body ruins. [26]
(B7) Earth sky as one all sides endlessness little body only upright. [24]
(B8) No sound no stir ash grey sky mirrored earth mirrored sky. [8]
(B9) All sides endlessness earth sky as one no sound no stir. [2]
(B10) Grey air timelessness earth sky as one same grey as the ruins flatness endless. [52]

(...)
(C9) Grey face two pale blue little body heart beating only upright. [3]
(...)

The opening paragraph, quoted above, thus appears to be a combination of sentences (A3), (B9), (C9) and (A2):

[1] Ruins true refuge long last towards which so many false time out of mind. (A3)
[2] All sides endlessness earth sky as one no sound no stir. (B9)
[3] Grey face two pale blue little body heart beating only upright. (C9)
[4] Blacked out fallen open four walls over backwards true refuge issueless. (A2)

Each sentence is conceived as a mobile textual unit or lexia. With a colour code, the underlying proto-hypertextual structure can be visualized. In an electronic environment the clickable colour-coded lexia can thus be recomposed and decomposed according to a system that resembles the system applied in the Hypertext edition of William Faulkner's *The Sound and the Fury* (eds. R. P. Stoicheff, et al.) to facilitate the analysis and reassembly of the scrambled flashbacks in the first two chapters of the novel, and thus reconstruct the chronology of the different temporal lexias.

In the case of *Lessness* this "reading through time" has a direct relevance to the text's content. Beckett's structuring tools correspond with the conventions to systematize time: 12 months in a year, 12 hours in a day, 7 days in a week, 60 minutes in an hour. But he infuses this rigid grid of human systematization with chance, arbitrariness, and randomness. The rigidity of this grid, which human beings tend to impose upon reality, is a comment in itself. It also expresses a fundamental paradox of art in general. The attempt to grasp the fleetingness of time is doomed to fail; as soon as it is fixed it loses, or has already lost, its most essential quality: its volatility. Beckett was of course well aware that this also applied to the very text in which he expressed this idea. The seemingly fixed nature of the printed text is confronted with the fluidity of the writing process—which may have been one of the reasons why Beckett donated most of his manuscripts to university libraries for his work to be studied as part of a poetics of process.

With the support of the Beckett Estate, a first electronic genetic edition of Samuel Beckett's last bilingual texts was completed during the Beckett centenary year, containing both linear and topographic transcriptions (Beckett 2007). The digital approach, using XML, makes it possible for the reader to compare all versions of the same unit of text (in three sizes: Large [the section], Medium [the paragraph] and Small [the sentence]), and to view the textual material from different perspectives (according to language, according to the order of the documents, in the order of the writing sequence, and with a focus on abandoned sections or dead ends in the *avant-texte*). The XML encoding makes the *avant-texte* flexible enough to allow readers to follow the mental process underlying the shuffling and reshuffling of textual units. Genetic criticism can benefit from the employment of electronic media in order to reconstruct the mental dynamics, of which the manuscripts are merely the material traces. With reference to comparative genetic criticism, every literary genesis seems to suggest its own hypertextual visualization. In an ideal situation, the chronology of the writing process would coincide with the order of, for example, the chapters of a novel, but usually this is not the case. In the genesis of a literary work, shuffling text blocks or lexias around seems to be the rule rather than the exception, even though in this respect not every writing process is as extreme as Marcel Proust's "*écriture vagabonde*". The tension between the chronological course of the writing process and the final narrative structure is often enhanced and complicated by different factors. A hypertextual architecture proves to be an adequate way of visualizing and analysing these complex structures, and comparing the writing methods of different authors.

Bibliography

Barthes, Roland. *S/Z*. Paris: Seuil, 1970.
Beckett, Samuel. *The Complete Short Prose 1929-1989*. Ed. S. E. Gontarski. New York: Grove Press, 1995.
—. *Stirrings Still/Soubresauts & Comment dire/What Is the Word: A Genetic Edition*. Ed. Dirk Van Hulle, with Vincent Neyt. Turnhout: Brepols, 2007.
Cohn, Ruby. *A Beckett Canon*. Ann Arbor: University of Michigan Press, 2001.
Ellmann, Richard. *James Joyce*. New and Revised Edition. Oxford: Oxford University Press, 1983.
Faulkner, William. *The Sound and the Fury: A Hypertext Edition*. Eds. R. P. Stoicheff, Muri, Deshaye, et al. Updated Mar. 2003. University of Saskatchewan . http://www.usask.ca/english/faulkner
Ferrer, Daniel. "Hypertextual Representation of Literary Working Papers." *Literary and Linguistic Computing* 10.2, 1995: 143-5.
Grésillon, Almuth. "Proust ou l'écriture vagabonde: à propos de la genèse de la 'matinée' dans *La Prisonnière*." *Marcel Proust: Ecrire sans fin*. Eds. Rainer Warning and Jean Milly. Paris: CNRS Editions, 1996: 99-124.
Hulle, Dirk van. *Textual Awareness: A Genetic Study of Late Manuscripts by Joyce, Proust, and Mann*. Ann Arbor: University of Michigan Press, 2004.
The James Joyce Archive. Eds. Michael Groden, Hans Walter Gabler, David Hayman, A. Walton Litz, and Danis Rose. New York: Garland Publishing, 1978.
Joyce, James. *Finnegans Wake*. London: Penguin Books, 1992.
Landow, George P. *Hypertext 2.0: The Convergence of Contemporary Critical Theory and Technology*. Baltimore: Johns Hopkins University Press, 1997.
—. *Hypertext 3.0: Critical Theory and New Media in an Era of Globalization*. Baltimore: Johns Hopkins University Press, 2006.
Lewis, Wyndham. *The Art of Being Ruled*. London: Chatto and Windus, 1926.

Nattiez, Jean-Jacques. *Proust musicien.* Paris: Bourgeois, 1984.
Poe, Edgar Allan. *The Fall of the House of Usher and Other Writings.* London: Penguin Classics, 1986.
Pountney, Rosemary. "The Structuring of Lessness." *The Review of Contemporary Fiction* VII: Samuel Beckett Number (Summer 1987): 55-75.
—. *Theatre of Shadows: Samuel Beckett's Drama 1956-76.* Gerrards Cross/Totowa, New Jersey: Colin Smythe/Barnes and Noble Books, 1988.
Proust, Marcel. *À la recherche du temps perdu.* 4 vols. Gen. (ed.). Jean-Yves Tadié. Paris: Gallimard Pléiade, 1989.
Ryan, Marie-Laure, ed. *Cyberspace Textuality: Computer Technology and Literary Theory.* Bloomington: Indiana University Press, 1999.
—. *Narrative as Virtual Reality: Immersion and Interactivity in Literature and Electronic Media.* Baltimore and London: Johns Hopkins University Press, 2001.
Shillingsburg, Peter L. *From Gutenberg to Google: Electronic Representations of Literary Texts.* Cambridge: Cambridge University Press, 2006.

CHAPTER THIRTEEN

DIGITAL TEXT: CONCEPTUAL AND METHODOLOGICAL FRONTIERS

MARIA CLARA PAIXÃO DE SOUSA

Introduction

The upsurge of text circulation in the electronic environment has been attracting the attention of various fields of investigation in recent years. Historians have observed the role of digital texts in transforming the cultural practices of reading and writing; the cognitive sciences have investigated digital formats as knowledge representation models; literary studies have interrogated digital writing as a genre.[1] A less populated debate on the "digital revolution" is their place in the history of the technology of language processing in written form, a sphere of investigation traditionally covered by philology, linguistics, and textual studies. It could be said that in this regard "digital text" is an object-in-waiting for conceptual and methodological exploration. This paper investigates some routes in this direction.

We shall examine digital texts from a strictly *material* perspective, exploring their characteristics as *artefacts* and the functionings of their *diffusion* (that is, of the chain of transmission from their production to reception), and endeavour to understand their significance in the material transformation of written language production. We shall argue that digital text, rather than an incremental point in the evolution of text-production techniques, is a watershed in the history of text diffusion. In digital text production, an unprecedented stage is introduced into the chain of information processing: the mediation of codification by mathematical programming. This singles out digital text as an entirely novel form of written language. As such, it claims a central place as an object of study, and at the same time, constitutes a breakthrough instrument for the varied

---

[1] See Chartier, 2001; Lesk, 1997, among others.

fields in which the written word, in any form, is an object of investigation—an instrument which can only be fully explored if the material singularities of digital texts in terms of information codification are taken into account.

1. "Digital text" as a Concept

1.1. Material Singularity of "Digital Texts"

Texts, in a very strict, material sense, are spatial-temporal "bridges"—language registers produced at one point in space-time which may be received at a different point in space-time. In order to build these bridges, human cultures have invented means of both representing information and materially holding this representation, producing different artefacts that enable it to be carried around.

The history of the techniques for "writing" in this material sense[2] is the history of the transformations in the technology of carrying linguistic units around through space/time by means of a symbolic system. The fundamental means of representing (or codifying) information invented by human cultures consists of a system of correspondences between graphic symbols and linguistic information (concepts or sounds)—in other words, writing. This symbolic correspondence is achieved visually; the traditional means of materially "holding" the representation are strictly linked to its visual essence—quite simply, the graphic symbols somehow have to be made apparent.

For this purpose, different cultures have invented different techniques, generally techniques whereby an instrument traces the symbols into or onto some form of support. For example, an instrument such as the chisel can trace symbols onto hard supports such as stones, as can an instrument such as chalk. With time, aided by the inclusion of other materials, techniques were perfected so that the instruments could deposit apparent matter onto soft supports (for example, a pen depositing pigments onto animal skins, and later paper, or a stamp pressing the pigments onto paper with a mechanical press). Some technical transformations are considered to be crucial stages in the development of this technology—the substitution of soft supports (skin and paper) for hard supports (stone), the invention of mechanical instruments (the press).[3]

---

[2] Or the perspective of the "*history of the forms or techniques*", as contrasted to the "*history of the cultural practices*" and "*the history of reading*" (Chartier, 2001).

[3] This historical development provides room for complex debates, such as the relation between such technical transformations and the history of the cultural

Techniques for "holding" symbolic information have therefore undergone considerable changes; on the other hand, methods for codifying language have not varied much in spirit. They have all consisted of a system of immediate correspondences between graphic symbols and linguistic information (concepts or sounds). It is true that the systems can take different forms and symbols but that is not our point here; it is rather that their functioning is always based purely on *immediate visual correspondence*.

Where, then, does the place of digital texts lie in this history? Are they a new technique for holding the symbolic system, following the same line of development that took us from clay tablets to printed books? We shall argue that there is more to it; in our perspective, digital texts are not an "evolved" format of the same technology historically involved in producing texts—they are artefacts produced by an altogether different technology, in which the linguistic correspondence in the symbolic system is established by means of mathematical representation.

What makes a digital text *digital*, therefore, does not lie simply in the technique for *holding the symbolic system*, but also in the technology for *building the correspondences between the symbols and the linguistic information*. This is unprecedented in the history of text production; in previous transformations in text production, new techniques were mainly involved in perfecting ways of *carrying around* codified information. With traditional texts, whether engravings on a piece of clay or stone, or paintings on a piece of paper, i.e. whatever the technique for holding the symbols, the command of a particular writing system (and a particular language, of course) sufficed for writers to write and for readers to read the text, in other words, for the information contained within to be processed. With digital texts, something else is needed beyond the producers' and receivers' command of a writing system for processing of the information. Human writers and readers do not process (codify and de-codify) the information immediately; an artificial logic programming is needed to mediate in this task.

Let us illustrate this at the level of character strings. In writing a text by hand, the producer ultimately traces characters from a writing system onto the support (e.g. paper) with an instrument (e.g. pen) and apparent matter (e.g. ink); these immediately codify the character and the character

---

practices of reading and writing. As Chartier, 2001, points out, the transformation of cultural practices in particular cannot be simply derived from formal or technical transformations; material and cultural transformations are two distinct lines in the history of reading—here we are strictly focusing on some aspects of material transformations.

is immediately de-codified into conceptual information by the reader through visual contact:

> {traced graphic symbol A = viewed graphic symbol A}.

This process can be aided by more sophisticated instruments, such as typewriters. In this case, instead of being *traced* by the hand of the producer, the characters are *stamped* on the paper by a series of arms (typebars) in a mechanical apparatus (the typewriter). Notice, however, that *information* is still codified directly by the producer, and de-codified directly by the receiver, just as with hand-drawn characters. So here we would have the sequence:

> {stamped graphic symbol A = viewed graphic symbol A}.

How does this compare to "writing" a text on a computer? At first sight, the process appears to be similar to that of writing texts with a typewriter: the producer presses keys with characters on them, and the characters then appear on a screen. But the similarity is, of course, illusory. With typewriters, between the action of pressing the key and the appearance of the corresponding character on paper, there is a *mechanical process* (i.e. the key activates the arm that raises the stamp; the stamp prints the character on the page using ink stored in a ribbon). With computers, what takes place between our pressing of the key and the appearance of the character on the screen is not a mechanical process but *a mathematical process, in which information is codified and de-codified*, so that mathematical relations stored in the form of electronic pulses are transformed and re-transformed into graphic (humanly readable) symbols. So in this case, instead of {**traced/stamped graphic symbol A = viewed graphic symbol A**}, we would have a sequence that resembles:

> {command x activated by keys [shift +'A'] > code &#0065 > viewed graphic symbol A}.

Notice that now, between the ultimate action on the part of the producer (*pressing a key*) and the "final product" to be processed by the reader (*viewed graphic symbol*), there is an intermediate stage (*code &#0065*), in which commands activated by the computer keyboard are dealt with by mathematical programming which needs to follow conventions for character codification.

This brief comparison of computers and typewriters as "writing instruments" reveals that the difference between hand-writing and typewriting is incremental: the basic technology is the same, that is, *graphic symbols are being deposited onto a support*; in typewriting, the technique of tracing is essentially substituted by the technique of stamping. So the evolution between hand-writing and typewriting may be termed as an incremental stage in a gradual evolution of one technology, that of imprinting graphic symbols onto some sort of material. In contrast, the difference between this technology and digital text processing cannot be termed as an incremental stage in a technical evolution. It is not simply a case of being aided by a new instrument that improves existing technology for imprinting graphic symbols, but rather a new technology for text production and diffusion. The technology of text production is the technology of rendering a system of symbols readable. In the case of non-digital texts, this has meant simply making the symbols *visible*; the different techniques for "carrying" information in a non-digital text (engraving, painting, or pressing symbols onto some material) are derived from the visual essence of the codification system. In the case of digital texts, the means of codifying the information is not simply visual (and conducted inside human minds) but includes digital representation (conducted artificially, in electronic media). The technology here consists of making such artificial representations humanly readable. It is not a technical difference: it is another technology, i.e. another combination of codifying and carrying the code about.

It is therefore in the combination of information codification and the means of diffusion that we may observe the material singularity of digital versus other forms of text.

1.2. The Artefact and the Processes

At this point we have to face the somewhat staggering task of defining what, in the end, digital texts actually *are*. We could start by vaguely determining that they are texts in which the use of digital technologies (mathematical representation) is involved at some level. At the process level, we have seen a little of what mathematical representation does: it intermediates in the correspondence between symbols produced and received by humans via visual contact.

But a text is not only a process; it is also an artefact: What kind of an artefact is a digital text? As artefacts, digital texts are nothing but *mathematically encoded information.* This encoded information is presented in the form of humanly readable "writing". But it is not actually *writing,* only sets of codes programmed to *appear* as writing.

This can be illustrated by comparing the figures below. *Figure 1* shows a sample text produced digitally, as it would be read by a browser with a Western (ISO-8859-1) encoding system, *Figure 2* shows the "same text" as it would be viewed with a browser programmed for a different encoding system, Unicode (UTF-16) and *Figure 3* shows the source code that corresponds to both Figures 1 and 2.

Figure 1

> This is a sample of text in Times New Roman font, size 12, bold, justified paragraph, as rendered by a regular web browser programmed for the Western (ISO-8859-1) encoding system. Below is a chunk of the "same text" as viewed in a browser programmed for a different encoding system, Unicode (UTF-16). Further below is the html source code for both presentations.

Figure 2

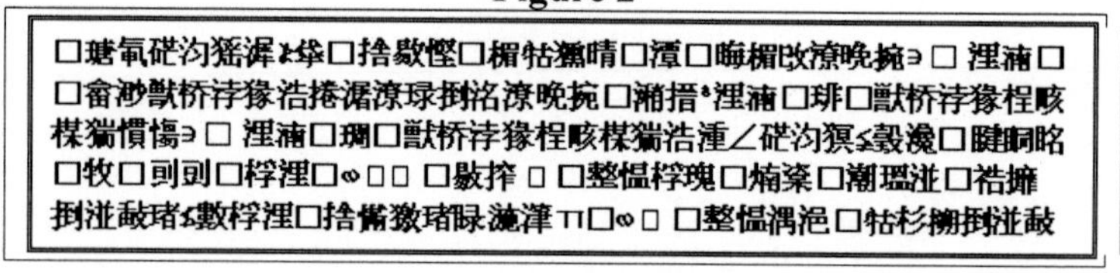

> □蝫氧砼沟猺渥∠埤□拾敫硜□榍牯灪晴□潭□晦榍收潒晚挽϶□ 浬浦□
> □畲沙獣桥浒豫浩捲湨潒琮拥铭潒晚挽□瀦摺*浬浦□珄□獣桥浒豫桯咳
> 楳猶慴惕϶□ 浬浦□珊□獣桥浒豫桯咳楳猶浩渾∠砼沟猌≤毄漫□鍵峒略
> □牧□剆剆□桴浬□ω□□ □敤搾 □ 整慍桙湮□焗桨□潮琚泩□浩摊
> 捌沍鼓琂≤数桴浬□拾嘴欼琂跾滝漼 ∏□ω□ □整慍渇氾□牯杉柵拥沍鼓

Figure 3

```
<html xmlns="http://www.w3.org/TR/REC-html40">
<head>
<meta http-equiv=Content-Type content="text/html; charset=windows-1252">
    <title> sample chunk of digital text</title>
</head>
<body>
<p align="justify">
<font face="Times New Roman" size="12pt" weight="bold">
This is a sample of text in Times New Roman font, size 12, bold, justified
paragraph, as rendered by a regular web browser programmed for the Western
(ISO-8859-1) encoding system. Below is a chunk of the "same text" as viewed in
a browser programmed for a different encoding system, Unicode (UTF-16). Further
below is the html source code for both presentations.</font>
</p>
</body>
</html>
```

If we regard the source code as the core material defining *text*, then Figures 1 and 2 have to be called *the same text*; yet how could they be *the same text* if the same reader with a command of the western alphabet might be able to read the writing represented in Figure 1 perfectly, but not the writing represented in Figure 2? If we consider that the text is the presentation (i.e. the humanly readable form rendered by a program working on the source code), then clearly Figures 1 and 2 are two *different texts*; yet how could they be *different texts* if they have been rendered materially by the same source code? From the material point of view, which should be conceived as the artefact *text*—the source code (Figure 3) or the potential presentations rendered by a browser (Figures 1 and 2)?

Because the source code is what materially constitutes the text, it cannot be dissociated from the concept *text*, and because the presentation is what we as humans can process, the source code cannot be dissociated from this either. Actually, then, in their final form (i.e. as a product), digital texts are *a layered combination* of mathematically encoded information and humanly readable presentation; it is this combination that we perceive as *the text*.

The definition of digital text, therefore, includes the double dimension of process and product; this is important for trying to define a typology of digital texts. If we limit the definition to the dimension "product", *digital texts* would be texts whose *final form* is digital, i.e. actuated in an electronic environment (which relies on numerical representations). In this sense, a text which is not received in the electronic environment would not be considered a "digital" text, even in those cases where it might have been produced within the electronic environment (such as the printed form of a text that has been processed in a computer).[4] Conversely, in this case, the term could ultimately be used to refer to a text that is received in the electronic environment, even though it has not been originally produced in the electronic environment (such as a digital photograph of hand-written text). If we extend this to include the dimension "process", however, the term *digital* would be applied to texts that have been *processed* in an electronic device. This includes partial processing, such as texts that have been produced digitally but received in other forms, and global processing, such as texts for which the whole transmission chain—from production (writing) to reception (reading)—is actualized in an electronic environment.[5] For our present purposes, this seems to be a more adequate

---

[4] There is a parallel duplicity of terms in other forms of text production: for example, *printed text* is used either to describe the object's final form, or its production process. Evidently, many texts that we call "printed" have been produced by the handwriting process and subsequently printed.
[5] Less clearly so in the reverse case—a digital copy of a text produced in another medium. In a processual sense, digital copies produced by transcribing the original text would be classified as "digital text" (because the transcription is the

approach; we shall therefore consider as *digital* those texts in whose construction language has been *processed* in the electronic environment (whether or not the final form of the text is received electronically).

It is important to realize, then, that even texts whose "final form" is not digital, but that have been processed digitally, may be included in our description of "mathematically encoded information presented in the form of humanly readable writing". Take a printed issue of a digitally produced document; it is presented in printed form, but it has been processed digitally up to the moment at which a printer (via logical programming) was able to deposit the ink onto the paper. It is now a "printed text" artefact, but, when analysed, some of the aspects pertaining to digital text diffusion will apply to it as well.

We have therefore tentatively defined digital texts as artificially encoded linguistic material rendered humanly readable with the intermediation of logical programming. This allows us to briefly explore the functionings of digital text diffusion, which essentially consists of the multi-layered copying of a source code.

1.3. Digital Text Diffusion

In the process of reaching out in time and space, texts may be altered and transformed—a factor that is central to textual studies, textual criticism and the art and science of retrieving alterations and understanding how the elements of written culture are transmitted. Different factors are involved in this transformation: factors pertaining to material deterioration, and the process of transmission itself. Traditionally, factors that may potentially impair text integrity are classified into endogenous (internal, i.e. material decay of the support and apparent matter) and exogenous (external, i.e. caused by interferences in the chain of transmission). Potential factors in the endogenous modification of digital texts might be found in hardware or software decay,[6] while in studies of manuscripts or printed text diffusion, paper and ink decay are the main endogenous factors impairing

---

processing); however, digital copies produced as images would not (because there is no processing of text in the electronic medium, only the production of an image of a text).

[6] We consider informatic decay as an endogenous (i.e. internal, non-human) factor because it may take effect independently of any external action—it is not necessarily a transmission failure; bugs in text-processing softwares, software obsolescence, etc. may affect a text that has been quietly stored in a machine without anyone ever handling it.

text integrity. This rather obvious difference already indicates that digital texts deserve a singular approach on studies of diffusion.

However, it is when we consider factors pertaining to the transmission process (i.e. exogenous) that the singularity of digital texts in such studies becomes more interesting. For traditional textual studies, *copy errors* are the major source of exogenous interference along the diffusion chain (cf. Blecua, 1983 among others). For digital texts, the process of "copy" acquires an expanded significance; digital texts are always diffused as copies, but not copies produced by humans; rather, they are copies produced by programmed machines.

Take the "texts" that we read on the web; for each sample hypertext we access, there is naturally a corresponding source code. In a regular situation of remote digital text diffusion, what the writer *writes* is ultimately the source code (even if they are not aware of this fact, as we shall comment further on). But what the reader *reads* is the presentation—the code as translated by the programming. Consider, further, that a text which is received in the electronic environment, such as the worldwide computer web, may be "read" by several people at the same time. However, what is stored in the source computer is a document containing the encoded information (the source code), and what is received by each of the simultaneous readers are multiple renderings of this source code by multiple browsers (i.e. processors)—actually, multiple *copies* of this rendering. What the receiver receives is a presentation of the source code as rendered by a translating machine; this is also the case in local access, be it on a screen or via a printing program.

In any case, remote or local, digital text diffusion functions by means of the copying of multiple layers of source code and its presentation. This brings us back to the previous statement that for digital texts, the process of *copy* acquires an expanded significance for the study of text diffusion.

Traditionally, interference in the transmission chain is studied mainly with regard to manuscript cultures—reproduced by means of human copy, rather than mechanical duplication. In copying, humans may alter the text (among other things) by logical influence—copying is an active process in which mobility is inherent. In the diffusion of digital texts, copy is also a stage which involves logical processes. It is important to point this out, as one could argue that printed texts are also diffused as copies—as in multiple reproductions of an original document. But this is an entirely different process: a mechanical press will mechanically reproduce a source document with no logical process involved; a computer will reproduce a source document by means of logical processing. Text reproduction in the digital environment differs from human copying in that the logical processes involved are artificial, but they differ from mechanical reproduction in that there is a logical process involved at all.

This makes digital diffusion more akin to human copying than to mechanical reproduction—an interesting state of affairs for the study of copy errors and *mobility*, a term traditionally used to describe the tendency towards transformation by copying in manuscript writing cultures. *Copy errors* in the logical stage of digital text processing are a major source of problems for the integrity of digital texts. Such "errors" may be better defined as interferences in the logical programming at some point in the transmission chain: problems pertaining to encoding, or to the rendering of the presentations by subsequent programming.

This could again be exemplified with character processing: at the producer's end a typical diffusion problem would be a situation in which the producer cannot find the proper key combination for diacritics (such as ´, ^, ~, ç etc.) on a given computer keyboard, and, at the receiver's end, the difficulty of reading web documents with character encoding problems, in which a sequence such as *diacrítico* reads *diacr tico*. Mediation of artificial processing occurs at other levels of digital text processing, such as spatial organization. One rather ironic example is the separation of digital texts into "pages". A "page" is, naturally, a spatial unit closely connected to paper as a support material—there are obviously no such things as "pages" on a computer screen. Nevertheless, most available text processing applications make up a visually recognizable space similar to a "page" so that we can write comfortably and preview the results of printing a document. Obviously, though, the "page" that appears on the screen is nothing but a visual representation fabricated by codes, to which the text producers and receivers are usually oblivious—unless, thanks to some programming inadequacy, this representation fails to work, and at the receiving end, the copy of a digital document appears with the wrong "page-breaking" (a situation only too familiar to anyone who has tried to share the edition of a document with different machines or softwares). This goes to show that the intermediate stage of information codification via digital programming represents fertile ground for the potential loss of information by diffusion.

In order for textual studies to be able to bring digital texts into their horizon as objects, the stage of mathematical codification and decodification must be included as an area of investigation. At the same time, this expanding of horizons towards the inclusion of logical programming has a bearing on those disciplines in which texts and their diffusion are an instrument of investigation; digital processing constitutes breakthrough tools in the form of scholarly editions that take full advantage of controlled encoding.

2. Digital Text as a Method

2.1. Transparency and Control in Information Codification

We have argued that the mediation of artificial language in the codification of information singles out digital texts as a watershed in the history of text diffusion. Interestingly, this intermediate stage—the mediation of artificial processing—is one to which producers and readers are usually oblivious. It is mostly when the transmission chain is truncated that the average producer/receiver may become aware of the intermediation process. For instance, the brute fact of character encoding is normally only perceived by receivers and producers when a link in the transmission chain presents a malfunction (i.e. inadequacies in encoding or presentation); the same is true for other information codified in digital documents, such as spatial organization.

Intermediation in the codification of information, a fundamental stage in the production chain of any kind of digital text, is not always evident—or "transparent", as we shall term it; rather, current forms of digital text processing can vary considerably with respect to how "transparent" the intermediation of information codification is. We shall now see that the level up to which human writers and readers can understand and control the processes of text codification makes all the difference for the potentialities of digital text as an object of study and as a methodological instrument.

The least transparent processes seem to be associated with *partially digitally processed formats* (documents that are *produced* in digital environments, but not necessarily meant to be *received* in digital environments, typically, those to be stored in a computer and eventually printed). These include most of today's text formats that can be produced in text processing applications.[7] Such formats are typically processor-bound, that is, they depend on the text processing application used to write or read them.[8] They also share the contingency of proximity to paper

---

[7] For example: DOC files (*Document*, texts processed by Microsoft Word), ODT files (*Open Document Text*, processed by Sun Open Office), PDF files (*Portable Document Files*, processed by Adobe Writer/Reader).

[8] The code used in such formats can be open (Sun .ODT) or closed (Microsoft .DOC, Adobe .PDF); open codes mean that the code can be studied and manipulated by programmers. However, our main point remains: even in open

formats, as most current text processors go a long way towards adapting digital processing to non-digital processing for convenience in production and reception.

The wealth of sophisticated encoding possibilities embedded in such programs makes digital processing quite intuitive and straightforward for any literate person, which is certainly a convenient state of affairs. But as an accessory consequence, this sophistication of programming embedded in "intuitive" applications results in increasingly complex intermediation processes, over which text producers and receivers have little or no control. This impact on studies of text diffusion and mobility, and on other fields for which text processing and text edition is a crucial scientific tool.

Take, for example, linguistic studies in which the exact form of text structure can be a crucial factor in the investigation, such as historical linguistics studies based on texts. It is quite unusual nowadays for such studies to have paper databases; rather, they make use of digitally-processed editions. Moreover, they need texts edited in a specialized format: philological editions, in which, for example, the original orthography and text organization is kept faithfully close to the originals. When such editions are produced in regular text processors, the editors are not in a position to have full control over the codification of crucial information such as correct graphic symbols for characters, faithful reproduction of spatial organization, etc.; as mentioned already, in regular text processors, these elements are codified by increasingly complex and opaque intermediation processes. Specialized editions cannot afford to allow formatting and elements of information organization to be modified by programming stages in the course of diffusion; in order to ensure some control over the encoding of these elements, they need to turn to more transparent text processing.

Relatively more transparent processes of information codification are associated with *globally* digitally-processed formats (i.e. produced in digital environments and intended to be received in digital environments). This group is formed mainly by the hypertext family, which includes formats such as HTML (*HyperText Markup Language*), XML (*eXtensible Markup Language*) and XHTML (*eXtensible HyperText Markup Language*). Notice, crucially, that in this case the formats are not processor-bound. The classification of the formats and the differences between them refer to the *language* used for marking up the texts for

---

code cases, in such formats the codification is not meant to be manipulated by regular users.

subsequent processing; these languages are not processor-dependent;[9] rather, they are regulated by an international consortium, the W3C (W3C 1997a) for the regulation of HTML, and (W3C 1997b) for the regulation of XML. It makes sense for hypertext to be a processor-independent format. It has been conceived for global digital processing, that is, to be produced and received in the electronic environment of the World Wide Web; it must be remotely readable by (any) machines via a browser (the de-codifier).

For our present purposes this essentially means that codification in hypertext can be made transparent to the producer and to the receiver. What is more, in hypertext construction the codification of information can be manipulated by the producer within a scheme that is controlled and normatively regulated. This is, in fact, the very spirit of hypertext markup language: it permits a human text constructor to control the levels of information to be handled by the intermediate stage of mathematical programming. Text markup languages in the spirit of hypertext can also be quite flexible; this is especially so with extensible languages such as *Extensible Markup Language* or XML (W3C, 1997a), which predict a properly structured syntax but an open semantics. This means that in preparing a text to be processed, the editor can significantly mark up any level of information that he or she regards as relevant. As we shall see below, this possibility has been turned to the advantage of several initiatives in specialized text editing.

2.2. Digital Text in Scholarly Editions

The instrumentation of text encoding for the production of scholarly editions has turned out to be one of the most interesting frontiers of digital text production in recent years. Digital processing and automatic controlled codification has been turned to the advantage of specialized edition processes with various aims; for general textual and literary studies, the wealth of electronic editions available nowadays is, in itself, evidence of the role of digital texts as instances of the preservation of the written tradition.[10] In the specific field of linguistic analysis, digital

---

[9] There are, of course, a number of available applications, commercial or otherwise, that can handle hypertext formats; the important point here is that hypertext can be processed independently of a particular process or application.
[10] We have in mind initiatives such as:
The Oxford Text Archive (http://ota.ahds.ac.uk/),
The Oxford Digital Library (www.odl.ox.ac.uk),

annotation has been applied to encode different levels into the texts, from graphic organization to morphology and syntax, providing research with large databases of unprecedented volumes of linguistic information in the form of annotated corpora,[11] most of which follow standards regulated by consortia such as the XML Corpus Encoding Standard (http://www.xml-ces.org/).

A substantial part of the current annotation standards applies to marking up elements, such as cataloguing information or 'metadata', text organization (paragraphs, sections) and linguistic levels (morpheme, word, sintagm); however, information regarding stages in previous text diffusion and editorial interference can also be marked into texts, with potentially interesting results for electronic scholarly editions. We have recently conducted an experiment on the annotation of diffusion layers within the Tycho Brahe Annotated Corpus of Historical Portuguese (TBACHP, 2006). The corpus is formed by 15th-19th century Portuguese texts which have been marked up with XML for regular text-organization information and for annotation of the modernization of orthography;[12] the basic idea in this *Controlled Edition Technique* (Trippel and Paixão de Sousa, 2006) is to allow our own interferences as editors to be marked up and recovered in a text. Editorial interference is annotated in layers in one document so that each layer may be produced separately on demand as different presentations (for human readers and subsequent automatic tools);[13] in the

---

Biblioteca Virtual Miguel de Cervantes (http://www.cervantesvirtual.com/index.jsp),
Biblioteca Nacional de Lisboa Digital (http://bnd.bn.pt/),
Projeto Vercial (http://alfarrabio.di.uminho.pt/vercial/index.html),
The Victorian Web (http://www.victorianweb.org), to cite only a few of the most influential current text archives.
[11] The several text markup projects in this spirit have produced annotated corpora such as:
The Corpus Diacrónico del Español, (http://www.rae.es),
The British National Corpus, (http://www.natcorp.ox.ac.uk/),
The American National Corpus, (http://www.americannationalcorpus.org/),
The Lácio-Web, (http://www.nilc.icmc.usp.br/lacioweb/)
and the several corpora united under web-based resource centres such as the Open Language Archive Community (http://www.language-archives.org/).
[12] Modernization of orthography is a necessary edition stage for those texts, as the final aim is for them to be processed by automatic programming which annotates morphology, and which cannot satisfactorily handle the variation in orthography found in Classical Portuguese writing.
[13] Via XSLT (Extended Stylesheet Transformation Language, cf. www.w3.org/TR/xslt) transformations.

presentation documents produced in this way, each item that has been interfered with can be linked to its counterpart in the equivalent version; a glossary of editors' interferences can also be produced.[14]

More recently, we have been exploring the annotation of some other specific text particularities, such as deterioration in the original support material of transcribed documents due to ink blotting, corrosion, bugholes, etc. In cases where other editions are available for a transcribed text, the interferences of previous editors are also annotated in overlapping layers onto the interferences of the current editor.[15] The same technique can be applied to compare multiple previous editions of one text by annotating each subsequent stage,[16] and it could ultimately be applied for the comparison of subsequent stages of text elaboration by one author, making it an interesting tool for genetic critique. The fundamental spirit of the *Critical Hyper-editions* elaborated in this recent project (Paixão de Sousa, 2006) is to capture, by digital annotation, the signs of *text mobility* in subsequent edition processes.

This brief account of some recent experiments in text annotation has attempted to illustrate the potential role of digital processing as a tool for textual studies. Electronic editions with scholarly purposes—linguistic analysis, literary studies, textual studies—are "specialized" in two senses: they involve specialized knowledge of text editing and specialized knowledge of the electronic processing of language.

This is not to say that specialized text editors who make use of electronic media will suddenly turn into computer scientists; it simply means that artificial intelligence has to be included as a related area in textual studies, in the same way that palaeography or codicology have traditionally been included. Scholars have generally relied on their knowledge of texts as cultural objects *and as material artefacts* to produce specialized editions—a conjunction of horizons which includes cultural, literary, linguistic *and material* dimensions (such as the typology of support materials, the typology of alphabets and the typology of transmission failures). The same conjunction between cultural and material knowledge is needed for editions carried out digitally, only here the material dimension must include digital programming.

---

[14] For an example of the encoding of a text with one edition layer in this system: http://www.ime.usp.br/~tycho/participants/psousa/memorias/sample_1.html.
[15] For an example of the encoding of a text with two edition layers in this system: http://www.ime.usp.br/~tycho/participants/psousa/memorias/sample_2.html.
[16] For an example of the encoding of two different editions on text in this system: http://www.ime.usp.br/~tycho/participants/psousa/memorias/sample_3.html.

3. Final Remarks

Digital text is yet to reveal its full potential in our historical times, both as an artefact to be technically developed and an object to be conceptually explored. The conceptual exploration of digital texts requires taking on some important challenges in some of the fields that have traditionally been dedicated to the study of text diffusion and its correlated issues. Theoretical approaches to digital texts in the material perspective must take into account mathematical programming as a stage in the chain of production; it is more than evident that the study of "mobility" in the diffusion process cannot be carried out without taking this fact into consideration. The challenge is thus posed for philology and textual studies: their scope of action must expand to include this cycle of procedures. Quite simply, these fields must begin to regard artificial intelligence as one of their related areas.

With regard to technical developments, it could be said that digital texts as artefacts are still constructed in a general way with too much dependency on typically "paper-bound" concepts. We are witnessing today a transition stage, maybe similar to the one that took place with the advent of the mechanical press. As Chartier (2001) and Eisenstein (1998) have pointed out, the first books off the first presses were simply printed transpositions of texts as they would appear in manuscripts; it took some time for the technical paradigm of manuscript production to give way and for the full technical potentials of printing to be explored. With time, digital text production may become relatively more independent as well, and the full technical potentials of digital text production may be explored in different directions.

One area in which this exploration is already in motion is the use of digital processing for scholarly editions, in experiments that explore the digital environment as an instrument for text studies in general in ways that could never be achieved with other text processing technologies. Controlled text annotation, in which any number of layers of information can be merged into one document, allows the several different aspects in a text to be captured and analysed—graphic organization, content, linguistic structure (lexical, morphological, syntactic and semantic) and marks of the stages of diffusion—both vertically and horizontally, in parallel with other texts. This is very much what textual studies have been pursuing over the centuries in their task of notating slight differences of terms in the margins of manuscripts, tracing the footprints of previous editors, and drawing intricate interpretation signs for editors to come: the weaving of delicate tangled webs of correspondences between different versions of different documents. This interweaving of different dimensions or layers of information acquires enhanced technical possibilities as we start to work with digital processing, in the intersections between code and presentation. We can push the frontiers of *text* as "a system of roots that can be excavated into itself" (Carvalho, 2003)[17]—and from this spiralled continuum of information layers, renewed perspectives may come to flourish.

Bibliography

BACHP (2006) "Tycho Brahe Annotated Corpus of Historical Portuguese". http://www.ime.usp.br/~tycho/corpus

Blecua, Alberto. *Manual de crítica textual*. Madrid: Castalia, 1983 (1987).

Carvalho, Rosa Borges Santos. "A Filologia e seu Objeto: Diferentes perspectivas de estudo". *Philologus - Revista do Círculo Fluminense de Estudos Filológicos e Lingüísticos*, ano 9, n. 26, Rio de Janeiro, 2003. http://www.filologia.org.br/revista/artigo/9(26)03.htm

Chartier, R. *Cultura Escrita, Literatura e História*. Porto Alegre: Artmed, 2001.

Eisenstein, Elizabeth. *A Revolução da cultura impressa*. São Paulo: Ática, 1998.

Ide, Nancy, and Laurent Romary. "XML Support for Annotated Language Resources". *Linguistic Exploration: Workshop on Web-Based Language Documentation and Description,* Dec 12 - 15, 2000, University of Pennsylvania.

Lesk, Michael. *"Hypertext"*. *Practical Digital Libraries*. New York: Morgan Kaufmann, 1997.

Paixão de Sousa, Maria Clara."Edições Críticas Eletrônicas: Fundamentos e Diretrizes", 2006 http://.www.ime.usp.br/~tycho/participants/psousa/memorias/critical_h yper/ece.html

Trippel, Thorsten, and Maria Clara Paixão de Sousa. "Building a Historical Corpus for Classical Portuguese: Some Technological Aspects". *Papers from the V International Conference on Language Resources and Evaluation,* Genoa: LREC, 2006.

W3C (1997a). "Extensible Markup Language". http://www.w3.org/XML

---

[17] In the original: *"Todas essas disciplinas [...] têm tomado o texto como um sistema de raízes que pode ser escavado nele próprio, ou seja, constrói-se teoria a partir da análise de seus componentes, daí afloram as diversas abordagens conforme os modelos teóricos e métodos adotados"* (Carvalho, 2003).

W3C (1997b). "HyperText Markup Language".
http://www.w3.org/MarkUp

PART IV

HYPER-PRAXIS

MARÍA GOICOECHEA, COMPLUTENSE UNIVERSITY

Under the rubric of hyper-praxis, we have collected a series of essays dealing with the practice of literary criticism from a perspective informed by the hyper-paradigm. This new paradigm applies not only to the new generic formations that have appeared in the wake of digital technology, but to traditional literary modes and genres, which are scrutinized through a different lens. The hyper-paradigm gathers momentum as it is materialized in concrete literary praxis, becoming a particular way of experiencing literary and artistic phenomena. As a second-generation wave of criticism, the contributions to this section also assess the state of previous hypotheses regarding hypermedia and point to new trends inside the digital medium.

A hyper-bridge between past and present modes of writing

The contribution of Marie-Therese Abdel-Messih, "The Hyper in Calligraphy and Text", is one of these retrospective analyses of traditional art forms that have acquired new meaning in the digital era. Abdel-Messih's essay draws attention to the hyper quality of Arabic calligraphy and makes a claim for a reconsideration of "the premodern and postmodern divide". She develops an analogy between Arabic calligraphy and computer hypertext as two kinds of legible/visible text, both being self-contained systems that require non-linear and interactive reading to disclose their meaning. Abdel-Messih's perspective helps us widen our sense of the *hyper* experience to include the literary and graphic legacies of other cultures, which in turn facilitate the unmasking of certain theoretical vices and naturalized conceptualizations regarding hypertextual criticism.

Along similar lines, Anastasia Natsina's article, "Hypertext: An Alternative Route to Short Stories Theorizing", sheds new light both on the study of short story collections and cycles, and on literary hypertext. An advantage of hyper-praxis is, according to Natsina, that this relatively new field of literary criticism is "unburdened by the automatisms imposed on other genres by long critical practice". Issues regarding the tension between components and whole, narrative closure, immersion, cohesion, and interpretation, are explored in both short story cycles and hyper textual fictions, bringing to the forefront the literary experiments of the past and using their reading conventions to understand better the demands of new digital genres.

Trends in hyper-praxis

The following contributions to this section offer a revision of three of the tenets of first-wave hypertextual criticism: interactivity, the death of the author and narrative fragmentation.

The term "interactive", for example, has been used both as a publicity stunt to promote all sorts of products (from toothpaste to children's carpets), and as a generic category for works of digital fiction demanding an unusually "active" participation from readers. Interactivity has become the trademark of most literary products of the digital canon, promising the reader new and exhilarating experiences, which in too many cases have failed to reach the expectations raised.

As befits the legitimate son of a second-wave of hyper-criticism, Lee Scrivner deconstructs this myth of digital interactivity in his article "The Echo of Narcissism in Interactive Arts". Scrivner discusses several examples of interactive art across different media, revealing the assumptions underlying their supposed interactive nature. The new scenario drawn by Scrivner manifests a reversal of the traditional roles between text and reader, art and audience. Using the myth of Narcissus and Echo as a metaphor representing the drives behind artistic production and reception, Scrivner reaches the conclusion that Echo (symbolizing poly-vocality, appropriation, repetition, replication...) has been hailed as the patron of interactive art. But if this is truly the case, then it follows that "an art of which Echo is the trope must have an audience or interactor that is troped by Narcissus and inscribed by narcissism". Interactive art is not more interactive than other art forms, since all art is interactive. What is characteristic of this type of art, however, is the way in which it has exploited and integrated the narcissism of its audience in its process, and in so doing, it has become Echo.

Florian Hartling revises the role of the author in "Hypertext and Collective Authors. The Influence of the Internet on the Formation of New Concepts of Authorship". His conclusions contradict those who heralded the death of the author as inevitably precipitated by electronic textuality and artificial intelligences. Even electronic text that appear to be authorless, as in "codeworks" (a term coined by Alan Sondheim to describe works which poetically combine elements of programming languages with natural ones), are thus only on the surface. In Hartling's words: "The Internet (...) does not stand for the 'death' of the author. Instead, it actually appears to be a fountain of youth for literary authorship".

Regarding narrative fragmentation, Ana Pano, in her essay "Hypermedia Narratives: Paratactic Structures and Multiple Readings", contends that, even when the reader of hypermedia fiction is diverted from following a conventional sequential reading related to causality and temporality, this does not do away with all linearity and logic connection of facts. Hypermedia fiction uses other techniques to reinforce linearity and logic, such as the creation of paratactic structures or variations of a single theme.

New hyper-genres and software supports

As Susana Pajares comments in her contribution to this volume, the theoretical bias of the first generation of hypertext critics made them ignore a significant portion of what was happening on the Internet, because it was not *really* hypertextual. Nowadays, it is hardly possible to ignore phenomena such as blogs if one wants to offer a representative overview of the literary trends that are becoming popular in cyberspace. Fictional blogs, like Casciari's *Blogonovela*, have emerged as the digital reincarnation of the traditional diary.

The last two articles deal with this new writing mode. It is interesting to note that both highlight the hybridity of digital genres, approaching their analysis from a cross-mediatic perspective that traces the evolution and reconfiguration of the media ecology as it adapts to integrate new modes of literary communication.

Priscilla Ringrose's contribution, "Salaam Baghdad: Warblogs in the Textual and Social Economies of the Internet", discusses the two different critical approaches that have been used to analyse blogs: as a transformation of the traditional diary and as a form of social action evolved from the social trend of mediated voyeurism. Within this context, she proposes a third view for analysing a particular type of blog, the warblog. Ringrose argues for a third perspective that takes into account their function as spaces of political and personal resistance, and as a means of communication across political and cultural boundaries. She finds it more appropriate to examine them as bridge blogs within what Yochai Benkler has termed the *sharing economy*.[1] The last essay of this volume explores the evolution of Latin American hyperfiction as it adjusts to advances in technology and new trends in reader-writer interaction. "From Hypertexts to Blogs: *El primer vuelo de los Hermanos Wright* and '*Más respeto que soy tu madre*" is the title of Perla Sassón-Henry's contribution, dedicated to the analysis of Juan B. Gutiérrez' and Hernán Casciari's pioneering work. Gutiérrez, author of the first Latin American hypernovel, *El primer vuelo de los Hermanos Wright*, in 1995, adapted his first version to a new writing environment called Literatronic in 2005. This new authoring system can be described as adaptive hypertext, since it is an artificial intelligence designed to model a fiction specifically for each reader on the basis of his or her interaction with the system. Casciari's style and use of the digital medium also provides a unique contribution to Latin American electronic literature. *Weblog de una mujer gorda* was the first blog in Spanish to appear in a print version. The book was titled *Más respeto que soy tu madre: Una novela sobre la mujer que nos parió,* and was published in 2005 in Spain by the well-known publishers, Plaza & Janés.

---

[1] See Benkler's article, "Sharing Nicely", in *The Yale Law Journal* 114 (2004): 273-358. Also found at http://benkler.org/SharingNicely.html.

CHAPTER FOURTEEN

THE *HYPER* IN CALLIGRAPHY AND TEXT

MARIE-THÉRÈSE ABDEL-MESSIH

The prefix *hyper* linked to the term *text* is a neologism that not only insinuates its digital nature and rhizomatic[1] irreducibility, but also implies its open-endedness, its admission of the pictorial and the aural along with the written. The holistic view of *hyper* may also be perceived in Arabic calligraphy as a writing system that includes pictographic elements, avoids linearity and turns reading into an interactive process exploiting endless options by re-processing a pre-written text in a new space. Calligraphy and hypertext merge technology and art, mathematics and text; as writing media, both evoke a three-dimensional space.

In *Of Grammatology,* Jacques Derrida already considered ideogrammatic, pictographic, phonetic or alphabetic marks, as well as the digital image, as effects of "arche-writing" (1976: 9-10). This gives scope for exploring how far hypertext and calligraphy articulate a double experience of the present. This paper proposes ways of reading that help debunk the *naturalized* aspect of hypertext, and the *mystified* attributes of Arabic calligraphy. Such reading will ultimately reconsider the pre-modern and post-modern divide; hypertext and calligraphy reflect the post-modern symptom of assembly and dispersion. Hypertext appropriates texts from the past in a context in the present. Calligraphy belongs to the past and the present; it resists reactionary/revolutionary classifications, whose outdatedness is confirmed by this past/present exchange, or what Bruno Latour designates as "the diffusion of temporalities", and both writing systems may be classified under what he considers as practices by "translation", which merge different sources (1993: 74; 11); calligraphy combines the material and immaterial, whereas hypertext is a hybrid of the human and non-human.

---

[1] For a discussion of hypertext as rhizome, see G. Landow, 2006: 58.

No previous readings have ever been explicit about the relations between these two practices. The reading of such convergences anticipates possibilities for mutual interchange between both technologies, an interchange implying that they are both inscribed within signifying practices that need to establish dialogical relations with each other. Such reading heralds new perspectives for interrelating texts belonging to different cultures, which is the threshold to an international society Landow models as one in which "no one conversation, no one discipline or ideology, dominates or founds the others." (2006: 123).

1. Calligraphy: Legible/Visible Text

The phrase or sentence stylized in calligraphy is a well-known fragment of a more expansive text, whose origin is at times uncertain. Landow makes an analogy between pre-print texts and hypertext, on account of the scribe's re-writing of the text being urged by the uncertainty that others had read it the same way (1994: 35). This uncertainty arouses another proposition by Khatibi who postulates: "[...]if modern thought repeats, the origin is nowhere [...] if the imagined dawn of writing can be realized only in sacred song, calligraphy too has its place in this voyage of discovery[...]" (2001: 42). What is sought is a language that frees writing from the linguistic barrier to communicate through the visual medium. The art lies in bringing out the infinite variety of what is already there: "calligraphy of the absolute" (Khatibi, 2001: 169). The alternation between the formal geometric design and the script requires a non-linear reading that deviates from the antecedent text. The legibility of a text relies on its visual design, its adherence to the law of proportion and the variations effected. For the Arab calligrapher, the *alif,* or first letter of the alphabet, which is an alphanumeric symbol (marked as a straight line, similar in writing to the figure "one"), and the dot (a square or round impression, akin in shape to the Arabic "zero") are the universal units of proportion.[2] In a 10th century study, Ikhwan al-Safa[3] propounded that geometry was generated from the dot "which forms the head of the line, and in geometry it is as important as figure 'one' in composing numbers"

---

[2] The dimensions of the dot depended on the pen cut made and the pressure of the calligrapher's fingers; each native had his individual pen cut fashioned by the local culture. It was also determined by the quality of the text transcribed.
[3] Ikhwan al-Safa (Brethren of Purity, 10th to 11th CE) a group of scholars combining Quranic, Aristotelian and Neoplatonic philosophy; they owe their numerology to Pythagoras.

(1957, Vol. I: 79).[4] The zero, in turn, recapitulates original knowledge, that which is in eternity, eternity being the Invisible (Dagher, 2006: 9). The *alif* and dot, or 1 and 0 may be metaphorically linked to Bolean algebra, where everything can be expressed in the binary terms 0 or 1.

Consequently, it may be postulated that the calligrapher is conscious of the functional use of writing to transmit meaning, its autonomy being a visual object in itself. The visual has deliberately distanced the referential value of writing, without the intention of being self-referential. As a practice, calligraphy operates visual transformations that create a self relation with the beyond or an *other* space. The classic calligraphic text is not the product of authorial genius as it is most often anonymous. Anonymity in a textual system is a sign of social accord, an invisible equilibrium between self and other that cannot be translated into writing and acquires a transcultural value liberated from historical contingencies. The expressible is expressed by the inexpressible since direct expression necessitates the creation of a reality that claims permanence. (Grabar, 1996: 120-22). The calligrapher aspires to a design that communicates the *material* objects of his environment within a transcultural conceptualization of the *immaterial*.

Throughout different generations, Arabic calligraphy has mediated interactive communication in diverse cultures, constantly adapting to transformations; it is therefore not a closed system, but an interactive system of signs. The notion of interactivity is instigated by the same impulse for communal solidarity that is behind the call for group integration within a secular or religious institution. The practice of calligraphy in secular or religious texts blurs the boundaries between them. This scriptural interchange of differently oriented texts releases the tension their actual confrontation evokes, eventually unsettling the finality of the word.

Such interchanges are represented in the calligraphic configurations of Mouneer Al Shaarani[5] (b. 1952), who also creates an interchange between Arabic calligraphy and his institutional training in the basics of contemporary graphic design (Ghazoul, 2001: 247-64). In *Contrariety*

---

[4] My translation.
[5] Syrian calligrapher, book designer & critic of Islamic art, based in Cairo. He has participated in several public exhibitions, and has held one-man shows all over the world: http://www.elshaarani.com.

Reveals Verity (1998)[6] he makes use of colour contrast and alternations in linear relationships, modifying the traditional *kufi* script. The line extending from the middle characters breaks the regularity of the unidirectional inclinations by swerving in an opposite direction. The parallel placement of the three words forming the statement and the balanced dynamism of the diagonals give the eye the sense of an upward and downward movement, an alternating rhythm transcribing the possibility of reading the statement both ways: "contrariety reveals verity"/"verity reveals contrariety". There is no fixed point at which the legible/visiblebegins or ends, as every part is compatible with the overall ornamental character of the figures.

In another design, *Speech is a Pitfall* (1997),[7] the relationship between the rectilinear and the curvilinear impresses on the mind the snare involved in speech. The movement conveyed by the circular form suggests the impossibility of escape from the labyrinth. Again, the placement of the characters as entwined units makes them legibly and visibly interchangeable. In this design, the calligrapher does not make use of the ornamental, as in the previous one; rather, he moves from repetition, inversion and alternation of elements to a simplification of the square *kufi* script, which is far from simple. 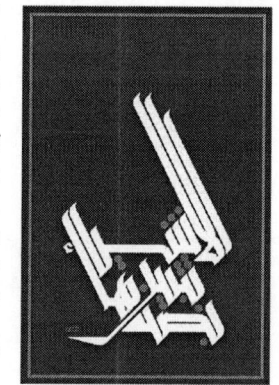 This legible/visible system used at the beginning of urbanization in the multilingual Arab region to bridge the gap between orality and literacy is now used to create immediacy, and ensure the durability of the text by suggesting possibilities for modifications.[8] In a graphics program, elements of design may form "a closed and articulated code" (Bolter, 1991: 54). But in calligraphy there is a more comprehensive repertoire of codes, enabling the construction of new elements from traditional ones.

---

[6] Well-known fragment from one of Mutanabi's (915-965 CE) panegyrics. Gouache on coloured cardboard. 100X66cm. Ms. Mariam Fakhru, Bahrain. Photo Emad Abdel-Hamid.
[7] Fragment from Palestinian poet Walid Khazendar (b. 1950). Gouache on coloured cardboard. 100 X 70 cm. Private Collection Oman. Photo Emad Abdel-Hamid.
[8] Landow points out affinities between hypertext and orality (2006: 152).

Issues of self-relation to experience emerge, and may be related to the conflict between creativity and mathematical formalisms. Joseph Tabbi refers to such conflict thus: "'Programmatic fixed rules' are always in tension with the 'procedural' that acts in the present designing self set rules." (2003: 5). This conflict may be traced in the above calligraphic configurations; the actual results transgress fixed rules generating their autonomy. Calligraphy as a process does not sacrifice text for technology, and its reading does not entirely depend on cognition. The reader reads what may already be known to him or her, but is distanced by the innovative processing of the line, as a result of the conflict

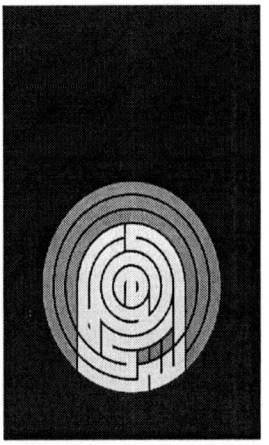

between reading the characters considered as signs representing units of language and as drawings bearing their independent signification (Lapacherie, 1994: 65). There is a movement away from the linguistic content to an unlimited spectrum of signs evoked by visual variations. The act of reading becomes a decoding through selection rather than following the linear arrangement of characters; the legible and the visible become an integral process.

2. Reading the past: Writing the present

Computer hypertext is another legible/visible system processed by electronic language that sustains the growth of global communications. It has had an impact on the structure, syntax and lexicon of language, allowing people with different languages to communicate in cyber-English.[9] Unlike print text, hypertext, being interactional, is subject to constant transformability, and is as liquid as a flowing conversation, orality being inscribed in it. (Landow, 2006: 116-17). The significance of

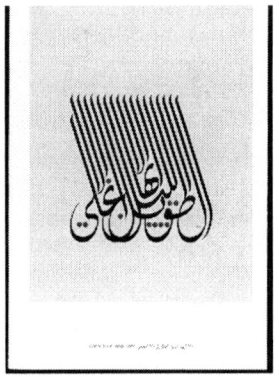

---

[9] Joe Lockard is among those who called for resistance against the primacy of English in Internet communication "Resisting Cyber-English" *Bad Subjects*. Issue #24, February 1996, *Political Education for Everyday Life*. http://eserver.org/bs/24/lockard.html.

such writing is that it involves legibility and visibility, memory and action, perception and emotion, the computational process thus becoming a transformation of the original idea into a visualized image, not a mere record of it. Hypertext devises different ways of retrieval in the present to make up for the limited capacities of the human mind; it also diverts the rational concatenation of thought into a series of optional considerations; pleasure is derived from discontinuity and disorientation rather than order. (Landow, 2006: 146).

Hypertext may be technically superior in its storage space; however, the act of reading calligraphy is a process of focus and selectivity, the two major creative forces, retrieving from the past what enhances experiencing the presentness of the present. What counts is not how much has been stored or recorded, but the process of transformation, and the fluid passage from past to present. As such, a single textual fragment may be configured in two or more distinct styles. In *Come Clear Long Night* (2005),[10] the self experience of the text becomes a problematization of calligraphic rules and their modulation in self-devised technics. In the first work, the classical *diwani* characters are retained with variations.

The second configuration (2005)[11] in square *Kufi* combines traditional Islamic architectural design with contemporary graphic design. The positioning of line against line represents a rhythm of shifting light and darkness, which in turn reproduces alternations between vowel qualities and consonantal elements of the visual configuration.[12] Although moves are made following the rules, there is no fixed rule for transformation, which releases diverse configurations of the same text depending on itsrelation to the experience of the present.

---

[10] Fragment from Umru' al-Qais (d. 540 CE) pre-Islamic Arab poet known for his *Mualakat*. Gouache on coloured cardboard. 80 X 110 cm. Museum of Islamic Art, Malaysia. Photo Emad Abdel-Hadi.
[11] Gouache on coloured cardboard. 80 X 110 cm. Private Collection, Syria. Computer processed by Mouneer al-Shaararani.
[12] More on this visual technique in Sowers (1990: 52-4).

In Al-Shaarani's calligraphy, citations from static sources belonging to a distant or near past become active elements within a current composition. Hypertext or calligraphy that depend on too much citing or emulating past styles become inflated corpses drenched by information. Whenever summoned, the past should be in the service of the present; it is the writer's responsibility to go beyond the preservation of information and devise a technology that promotes inter-subjectivity, or what Jay David Bolter calls "a network culture" (1991: 232). With the breakdown of cultural hierarchies and social affiliations, a global community should inevitably participate in the experience of presentness through diverse writing systems.

3. The *Hyper* Experience of the Present

Calligraphy and hypertext are different technologies that have related philosophy to the sciences, enabling us to see relations between the human and technics,[13] formerly considered in opposition (Ali, 2006: 186-90; Stiegler, 1998: 134-79). However, the fact that calligraphy and hypertext refer to sciences of organization should not obliterate their cultural differences. The specificity of hypertext resides in its foundation in modern technics, characterized by speed of innovation, an acceleration that for Stiegler has raised the "question of time" (1998: 9). Nonetheless, changes brought about by acceleration should not be envisioned as evolution or progress, but as a process of concretization that depends on interchanges with diverse signifying systems enabling communication between them. Therein lies the complexity of any technics, as their globalization is, in a sense, their de-territorialization, leading either to cultural interchange or global consumerism. It is commonly believed that its relation to modern technology makes hypertext susceptible to consumerism and alienation.

To address such a problem, one has to be aware of the different sets of relations between "communicative action" and "purposive rational action". In the former, Stiegler propounds, "communicative action forms the basis of social authority... whereas in the latter, legitimation is dominated by technical and scientific rationality", thus denying the communicative (1998: 11). However, the susceptibility to technical rationality and consumerism should not be attributed to hypertext alone.

---

[13] According to Stiegler, technics *(tekhne)* designates all the domains of productive skill (1998: 94). Milet also refers to it as the constitutive domain of practice and thought (1995: 19).

Although the different use of technics means a change in intelligibility, all forms of communication technology—including calligraphy—are subject to power politics.

As power politics cannot be ascribed to a single technology, technological genius cannot be restricted to one people. Leroi-Gourhan postulates that the emergence of technical objects is beyond ethnic characteristics, which accounts for universal technical tendencies. Technological diversity is the product of contacts with ethnic particularities (1943; Stiegler, 1998: 49). Steigler elaborates on Leroi-Gourhan's premise, adding that history continues as assigned by new laws brought about by inter-ethnic relations that stimulate technical tendencies to expand universally (1998: 50). Thus, the technical phenomenon emerges as the relation of the human to its milieu, a process by which the human both organizes and is organized, producing a particularity whose subsistence calls for a dialogical relation between one and the other. Calligraphy and hypertext are self-contained text systems; however, both generate a holistic view, linking texts, temporalities and people. This fact justifies Latour's proposition that "time is not a general framework but a provisional result of the connection among entities" (1993: 74). The present ongoing digitalization of texts should not be a pretext to eliminate other writing systems belonging to other temporalities, since hypertext involves a reshuffling of the near and remote. If the digitalization of memory is effectuated at high speed, it is at risk of commercialization, which raises a need for rethinking other memory storage technics. On the other hand, if it pleases some to shelve calligraphy as *traditional* technics, it is worthwhile remembering that the choice of the traditional involves repetition and rupture. It engages in a process of selectivity whose ultimate objective is to experience the present, an experience that may be activated by multiple technics.

Conclusion

Although legible/visible systems are self-contained, it is worthwhile tracing their interrelations to intensify our awareness of their links, particularly now that art and literature have exchanged the aesthetic of the monumental for the portable in a de-territorialized space. Such links may also help us trace the transformability of visual forms across cultures through design inversions, whereby each organizational system assumes some of the characteristics of the other.

The *hyper* experience of the present is not processed solely through electronic communication systems but by connecting with other communities through different text systems. This calls for an urgent revision of previous conceptualizations *naturalizing* hypertext to be able to gain access to other writing systems, such as calligraphy, by transcending the concepts *mystifying* it. Both systems have created a space hosting new collective identities whose inter-communication anticipates a new form of cultural order.

The *hyper* is not a prefix added to *text* to gain access to the present in the mode of information technology; it is not a pretext for generating new forms and repressing others. The *hyper* is a new entrance to the present through writing, which, as Jay David Bolter notes, is a way of "constructing our cultural world [which] is the sum of the texts that we write" (1991: 240).

Bibliography

Books

Ali, Nabil. *Contemporary Issues: An Informational Perspective.* Cairo: Al-Ein Publishing House, 2006.
Bolter, Jay David. *Writing Space: The Computer, Hypertext, and the History of Writing.* New Jersey: Lawrence Erlbaum Associates, 1991.
Derrida, Jacques. *Of Grammatology.* Gayatri Chakravorty Spivak (trans.). Baltimore: Johns Hopkins University Press, 1976.
Grabar, Oleg. *Penser l'art Islamique.* Abdul-Galil Nazim and Said Alkensali (trans.). Tunis: Dar Topqal, 1996.
Ikwan Al-Safa Wa Khilan Al-Wafa. *Rasa'el* (Epistles). Vol. 1. Beirut: Beirut Publishing Co., 1957.
Khatabi, Abdel Kebir, and Mohammed Sijelmassi. *The Splendour of Islamic Calligraphy.* London: Phaidon, 2001.
Landow, George. *Hypertext 2.0: The Convergence of Contemporary Literary Theory and Technology.* Baltimore: Johns Hopkins University Press, 1997.
—. *Hypertext 3.0: Critical Theory & New Media in an Era of Globalization.* Baltimore: Johns Hopkins University Press, 2006.
Latour, Bruno. *We Have Never Been Modern.* Catherine Porter (trans). Boston: Harvard University Press, 1993.
Sowers, Robert. *Rethinking the Forms of Visual Expression.* Berkeley: The University of California Press, 1990.
Stiegler, Bernard. *Technics and Time 1: The Fault of Epimetheus,* Richard Beardsworth & Georges Collins (trans.). California: Stanford University Press, 1998.

Articles

Dagher, Charbel. "Language: An Alternative to Existence; Calligraphy as Drawing". Unpublished paper delivered in Tunis: Bayt al-Hikma, May 2006.
Ghazoul, Ferial. "The Poetics of Calligraphy: An Interview with Mouneer El-Shaa'rani". *Alif: Journal of Comparative Poetics* 21, 2001: 247–65,
Lapacherie, Jean-Gérard Lapacherie. "Typographic Characters: Tension between Text and Drawing," *Yale French Studies* 84 *Boundaries: Writing & Drawing,* M. Reid (ed.), 1994: 65.
Tabbi, Joseph. "The Processual Page: Materiality and Consciousness in Print and Hypertext". *NMediac: The Journal of New Media Culture.* 12 (Summer), 2003: 1-2.
http://biblio.org/nmediac/fall2003/processual.html

CHAPTER FIFTEEN

HYPERTEXT: AN ALTERNATIVE ROUTE TO SHORT STORY THEORIZING[1]

ANASTASIA NATSINA

The increasing popularity of the new literary genres developing under the general heading of "hypertext" offers a potentially innovative prism for the theorizing of short story collections. The scarcity of systematic theoretical studies on the short story as a genre—which are far from exhausting the subject[2]—together with the strong theoretical tradition of authors who

---

[1] A first form of this paper was presented in Greek at the Conference of the *Greek Society of General and Comparative Literature*, "The short story in Greek and other literatures: Theory, writing, reception" (Athens, 8-11/12/05).

[2] A major theory of the short story, such as Bakhtin's theory of the novel, remains among the *desiderata* of literary studies. Systematic monographs or essay collections are equally rare. Amongst the most important of these, listed in chronological order, are Frank O'Connor. *Lonely Voice: A Study of the Short story*. London: Macmillan, 1963; Sean O'Faolain. *The Short Story*. London: Collins, 1948; Ian Reid. *The Short Story*. London: Methuen, 1977; Charles E. May (ed.). *Short Story Theories*. Athens OH: Ohio University Press, 1976; Valerie Shaw. *The Short Story: A Critical Introduction*. London: Longman, 1983; John Bayley. *The Short Story: Henry James to Elizabeth Bowen*. Brighton: Harvester, 1988; Susan Lohafer and Jo Ellyn Clarey (Eds.). *Short Story Theory at a Crossroads, Study in Theory and Practice*. Cambridge: Cambridge University Press, 1992; Charles May (ed.). *The New Short Story Theories*. Athens OH: Ohio University Press, 1994; and Charles May, *The Short Story: The Reality of Artifice*". New York: McMillan, 1995, where more related references can be found. There was a trend during the 80s towards a cognitive approach to short fiction (see, for instance, Susan Hunter Brown: "Discourse Analysis and the Short Story" in Lohafer & Clarey, ibid.: 217-248; Charles May. "On the Nature of Knowledge in Short Fiction" in *Studies in Short Fiction* 21 (1984): 327-338; Susan Lohafer. *Coming to Terms with the Short Story*. Baton Rouge: Louisiana State University Press, 1983, and, from the same author, "Preclosure and Story Proceeding" in Lohafer & Clarey ibid.: 149-275 and "A Cognitive Approach to Storyness" in May (ed.). *The New Short Story Theories*:

defined their art in formalistic terms, have turned the attention of specialists to individual short stories, irrespective of their context. However, while these approaches assume that a short story is read in "one sitting" (as in the famous definition by E. A. Poe), it is in fact quite rare for a reader to read only one story per sitting. Short stories, rarely published individually, flourish in newspapers and all kinds of magazines and are mostly issued in collections and anthologies. They are thus characterized by a conditional tension between individual text and overall context, at both synchronic and diachronic levels. This fact, perhaps because it is the very reason short stories are largely overlooked in the literary world, is rarely taken into consideration in specialist discussions or studies on specific texts. Scholars generally prefer to see the publication of short stories in collections with other stories or texts, as well as their conditional mobility, as a necessary evil, an external factor unrelated to their "essence". Literary hypertexts share notable structural elements with short story collections, at the same time as they present a relatively new field to literary criticism, unburdened by the automatisms imposed on other genres by long critical practice. In this sense, they offer an auspicious area for comparison that may help some frequently ignored aspects of short story reception to be recognized and the latter genre's potential in our current literary horizon to be explored.

The digital text, assembled into a whole through active links, or similarly branching out to the infinite realm of Internet textuality, is the most common form of text in the new reality of reading by technological means. Although literary exploitation of the options offered by active electronic links is quite recent, it has already presented a noteworthy assortment of hypertext types, ranging from the linear sequence of chapters linking the end of one chapter to the beginning of the next or the more frequent option of opening every narrative section with more links to various parts of the whole work, to the multimedia-based development of a story that seeks the active participation of the reader/user and the opening up of the work to the boundless labyrinth of the World Wide Web. The corpus of literary hypertexts is already substantial and is growing rapidly; these are either sold in the form of CR-ROMs or freely distributed via the Internet, attracting ever-widening academic attention.

However, hypertext is not something entirely novel. Electronic means have allowed for the explosive development of literary potentials already recognized since Chinese antiquity and the famous *I Ching* or *Book Of*

301-311, which presented substantial proposals but failed to overcome important methodological restrictions.

Changes, which much later became the subject of extensive experimentation by OuLiPo, Vladimir Nabokov (*Pale Fire*), Italo Calvino (*Se una notte d'inverno un viaggiatore*), Jorge Louis Borges, Julio Cortázar (*Hopscotch*) and many others. In discussions of these experimental "proto-hypertexts" and the recent production of hypertext literature, Espen Aarseth proposes (based on combinations of various parameters of interactivity) no less than 576 types of "cybertexts", a name given to the widest possible category of hypertext and proto-hypertext literature.[3] From a different viewpoint, Katherine Hayles refers specifically to a series of artists' books that challenge the conventional book form with results similar to those of hypertext literature.[4]

One could argue that, despite the growing volume and importance of literary hypertexts, it is the essentially hypertextual structure of the World Wide Web, with its increasing penetration into our everyday lives, that has made these eccentric experiments of the past central. This fact may make it even easier to recognize some of the inherent characteristics of short story reception, which on the one hand are more befitting of older experimental literature, and on the other reveal it as a form that has been ready for quite some time to participate in the new literary reality of hypertext. In order to develop the comparison between hypertexts and short story collections, I have considered hypertexts with relatively limited interactive features, excluding from the present discussion those that are more akin to adventure games.

Let us move on to look at some of the characteristics common to short story collections and hypertext fiction. The first of such characteristics is the tension between the completion of component texts and the work in its entirety.

Fictional hypertexts presented to readers as complete works, not as collections of individual pieces, are composed of different parts interlinked to each other in various ways. As a kind of measure, let us take the example of what is possibly the best-known hypertext fiction: *Afternoon, a Story* (1987) by Michael Joyce. It is made up of five hundred and thirty-nine sections and almost twice that number of links connecting them to each other. Except for rare instances, such as Stuart Moulthrop's *Victory Garden* (1991), which includes a text map, readers remain clueless about the work as a whole and discover it only gradually as they explore its different nodes.

---

[3] Espen J. Aarseth. *Cybertext: Perspectives of Ergodic Literature*. London: Johns Hopkins University Press, 1997: 60-67.
[4] Katherine Hayles. *Writing Machines*. Cambridge: MIT Press, 2002: 65-75.

Although the story sections, or different screens, comprising such works are comparatively smaller than conventional book chapters, we could consider them as structural elements corresponding to these. However, the screen has an inherent deficiency, making it hard for the reader to return to it as a fixed and integral part of the total. Going sequentially through two links, it is often impossible for the reader to return—via text links—to the original screen. It should also be noted that the web browser's "back" button is often deactivated in these hypertexts, preventing readers from finding out a posteriori the position of the screen in the reading sequence. Furthermore, the randomness of hypertext sequences as readers are led blindly by links, and the inability to preview the content of these screens, make it harder for the reader to recollect the content of each screen as part of a continuous work. This situation predisposes some kind of narrative closure for each section, which places additional demands on both the work of the author and, more importantly, on the interpretational approach of the readers. The latter are therefore called upon to perceive screens as individual units, while at the same time they need to mentally attach them to the overall picture of the work as it unfolds while being read.

In a similar manner, short stories comprising a collection are presented as whole pieces, the sum of which, to a varying degree and depending on subcategories, is greater than the aggregate of their parts. The greatest tension between part and whole can be seen in the short story cycle. This subcategory, which has also been termed as the "composite novel"[5] and includes works such as James Joyce's *Dubliners* (1914) and Sherwood Anderson's *Winesburg, Ohio* (1919), develops around a community, a piece of land or a segment in time, with each story contributing new meanings to it. Nonetheless, the classic definition of the short story cycle by Forrest L. Ingram as "a book of short stories so linked to each other by their author that the reader's successive experience on various levels of the pattern of the whole significantly modifies his experience of each of its component parts"[6] shows that despite the placement of the cycle in an area between novel and collection (as proposed by Jason Nagel),[7] the short story cycle is not very different from collections with a seemingly looser structure.

---

[5] See Maggie Dunn & Ann Morris. *The Composite Novel: The Short Story Cycle in Transition*. Twayne: Boston, 1995.

[6] Forrest Ingram. *Representative Short Story Cycles of the Twentieth Century: Studies in a Literary Genre*. The Hague: Mouton, 1971: 18-19.

[7] Jason Nagel. *The Contemporary American Short Story Cycle: The Ethnic Resonance of Genre*. Baton Rouge: Louisiana State University Press, 2001: 17.

In this kind of collection, the title, either taken from one of the stories or completely independent, marks a common frame of reference, guiding the expectations of the careful reader and raising relative interpretation demands for individual stories and the compilation as a whole. There are cases where individual stories lose much of their effect if read outside the confines of a collection. Such is the case of Oscar Wilde's *The Happy Prince* (1888) which contains a number of wonderful stories that tread a line between the conventions of myth and tale to arrive at a moral conclusion. What one would miss out when reading the stories independently of each other is that the morals are frequently contradictory and actually appear to undermine both the genre of the moral tale as well as the idea of moral systems in general.

It may seem that the tension between components and the whole is reduced in cases of looser bound collections, where the title is taken from one of the stories (usually the longest, or the most effective either in the opinion of the author or, not infrequently, of the editor/publisher) followed by a subtitle in the form of "and other stories", thus making the collection seem like an anthology. However, even in cases where these titles are not a playful challenge to an old literary convention, both the reading experience and the testimonies of short story writers indicate that the stories are bound together by a range of concerns characterizing the period of writing up to the point of publication of the book, a fact that offers plenty to the interpretational manner of those who care to consider it.

Another issue related to the tension between components and the whole is the reader's option to choose what sequence of stories to read. In hypertext fiction, links and other interactive features allow readers a substantial amount of freedom in navigating through the texts. Of course, the author exercises a varying degree of control, specifying screen content and link points on each screen and thus either allows readers to navigate some courses or prevents them from going along others. It may also be possible that the author sets some screens or courses as prerequisites before the reader is allowed to move on to another point. Still, in the end the reading experience is only culminated by the will and wish of the reader as to how to tread through the texts, a kind of responsibility that J. Hillis Miller refers to as "the ethics of hypertext".[8] By the same token, the reader is responsible for the final construction of the narrative produced by his or her active (as well as random) combination of the various sections.

Short story collections present a similar reading convention. Given both the publishing mobility of short stories and their frequent

---

[8] J. Hillis Miller. "The Ethics of Hypertext", *Diacritics* 25:3 (Fall 1995): 38.

appearances as parts of anthologies, short story collections are offered to each reader as an array of possibilities, allowing him or her the freedom to set the reading sequence. This does not mean that the author is without control; structuring the collection is always a strong instrument for guiding the reading, regardless of the fact that many authors leave this option unexploited, allowing editors to do it for them, which, of course, speaks volumes for the reading convention mentioned here. In any case, just as in hypertexts, it is clear that in order for readers to fully appreciate the work they are perusing, a linear/sequential reading is not enough; they are required to follow the text on different levels, none of which is usually placed at the forefront of their attention by the work itself.

The structure of short story collections and hypertext literature described here, as well as the reading behaviours it triggers, seriously impedes the creation and maintenance of fictional illusion. The need for readers to constantly decide in hypertext fiction both the course to follow and the handling of unexpected discontinuities in plot development hinders their visualizing of a unified fictional universe. Furthermore, the fact that some works require the active participation of the reader, such as answering simple questions, as happens, for instance, in Michael Joyce's *Afternoon*, further enhances the sense of construction and the realization on the reader's part that the work will not be completed without his or her own active involvement.

On the other hand, it is common knowledge that the lesser popularity of short story collections as compared to novels is not due to their supposed lower quality (assuming that quality is in any way related to popularity), but rather to the repeated frustration of the reader's expectations for the development of an illusionary world. Book form, defined once and for all—colonized, one might say—by the novel, predisposes reader expectations towards the establishment of a complete fictional universe created on their behalf by a professional writer. However, the multitude of fictional worlds provided by definition in short story collections drastically undermines the fictional illusion itself, and the comfortable role of the reader invited into it, by counteracting conventional reader expectations.

Similar to the frustration of reader expectations for immersion into a fictional world is the lack of a central point or climax, both in short story collections and hypertext fiction. Of course, the latter include episodes with more intense storylines and some sections that are more compact than others. However, the fact that readers may encounter them in a variety of narrative sequences takes away—to a large extent—the definitive, meaning-giving character they might have had in a more rigid narrative structure. On the other hand, the variety of conclusions available for the different subplots acts equally subversively for the final conclusion of the story. In a study undertaken to examine reading behaviour for Stuart Moulthrop's *Forking Paths* (1987) researchers found that, instead of processing the plot metonymically to arrive at a comprehensive metaphoric pattern for the story, as happens in linear narratives,[9] readers tried to grasp the entire arrangement of the work as a single metaphor and thus give meaning to its chain of metonymies.[10] In the end, the reader is forced to negotiate the meanings of various sections as if they were independent stories, and look for their relations at various contextual levels without the guidance of a single major storyline.

In short stories the climax (or some type of revelation point) continues to define the horizon of reading expectations. And thus, in defining reading with its presence or absence (let us remember what the effectiveness of Raymond Carver's stories owes to the successful handling of this expectation), it is inevitable that it weakens the ability to concentrate the threads of the various texts towards a single climax or overall meaningful conclusion for the collection. Even in short story cycles, known for their more cohesive structures, where one would expect greater levels of guided conclusions, Gerald Lynch notes that "inconclusive concluding stories seem to be the dominant characteristic of short story cycles".[11] Clearly, then, collections have multiple conclusions, and none of these has a distinct privilege over the others in the context of the whole work; the reader is again presented with the challenge of comprehending a pattern for the entire collection in order to fit each of the stories accordingly into its wider context.

It is clear that for both genres examined here, the works presented to readers either in the form of books, CD-ROMs or websites do not base their effectiveness on the cohesion of their plot and/or writer-controlled development of their various semantic levels. On the contrary, the common parameters establishing cohesion, both in hypertext and collections of short stories, are: the process of recurring subjects (or their rhizomatic development), manipulation of various viewing angles,

---

[9] See Peter Brooks. *Reading for the Plot: Design and Intention in Narrative.* New York: Vintage, 1985.
[10] Douglas J. Yellowlees. "Gaps, Maps, and Perception: What Hypertext Readers (Don't) Do". n.d. http://www.pd.org/topos/perforations/perf3/douglas_p3.html (19 Aug. 2006).
[11] Gerald Lynch. "The One and the Many: Canadian Short Story Cycles" in Barbara Lounsberry et al. (eds.). *The Tales We Tell: Perspectives on the Short Story.* Greenwood Press: London, 1988: 43.

alternative or different solutions to similar or identical situations (mostly seen in hypertexts) and different development of a recurring theme or character. Arriving at this point of convergence, we may be ready to discern the survival and transmutation of short story collections in the numerous hypertexts developed that exploit a common frame of reference, as in the cases of *Subway Story* (2000) by David Yun,[12] *Patchwork Girl* (1993) and *My Body:A Wunderkammer* (1997) by Shelley Jackson,[13] the *Museum* (2004) by Adam Kenney,[14] and *Fast City* (2002) by Don Bosco.[15]

Although we cannot consider texts like these as transfers of short story collections into the hypertext environment, we must admit that they function within a dialectic of part and whole which, if not directly derived from the short story tradition, certainly contains it in a familiar way. Hypertext fiction, in bringing to the fore the marginal experimental attempts of the past and supporting them with greater optimism as regards their representation potential, makes manifest the dynamics of the short story format while providing directions for the contextual reading of story collections as it establishes, even for the most traditional collections, a "precedent" from the future.

Bibliography

Aarseth, Espen. *Cybertext: Perspectives on Ergodic Literature*. London: Johns Hopkins University Press, 1997.
Bayley, John. *The Short Story: Henry James to Elizabeth Bowen*. Brighton: Harvester Press, 1988.
Bosco, Don. *Fast City*. 2002.
  http://www.cyberartsweb.org/cpace/fiction/bosco/index.html.
Brooks Peter. *Reading for the Plot: Design and Intention in Narrative*. New York: Vintage, 1985.
Douglas J. Yellowlees. "Gaps, Maps and Perception: What Hypertext Readers (Don't) Do". n.d.
  http://www.pd.org/topos/perforations/perf3/douglas_p3.html

---

[12] Available on line at
http://www.scholars.nus.edu.sg/cpace/ht/dmyunfinal/frames.html
(19 Aug. 2006).
[13] Available at http://www.altx.com/thebody/ (19 Aug. 2006).
[14] Available at http://www.cyberartsweb.org/cpace/fiction/museum/index.html
(19 Aug. 2006).
[15] Available at http://www.cyberartsweb.org/cpace/fiction/bosco/index.html (19 Aug. 2006).

Dunn, Maggie and Ann Morris. *The Composite Novel: The Short Story Cycle in Transition.* Boston: Twayne, 1995.
Hayles Katherine. *Writing Machines.* Cambridge, MA: MIT Press, 2002.
Head, Dominic. *The Modernist Short Story: A Study in Theory and Practice.* Cambridge: Cambridge University Press, 1992.
Hunter Brown, Susan. *Discourse Analysis and the Short Story* in Lohafer, Susan & Jo Ellyn Clarey (eds.). *Short Story Theory at a Crossroads,* Baton Rouge: Louisiana State University Press, 1989: 217-248.
Ingram, Forrest. *Representative Short Story Cycles of the Twentieth Century: Studies in a Literary Genre,* The Hague: Mouton, 1971.
Jackson, Shelley. *My Body. A Wunderkammer.* 1997.
http://www.altx.com/thebody/
—. *Patchwork Girl.* Electronic text. Watertown, MA: Eastgate Systems, 1993.
Joyce, James. *The Dubliners* (Introduction and Notes by Terence Brown). Penguin Books, London, 1992.
Joyce, Michael. *Afternoon, a Story.* Electronic text. Watertown, MA: Eastgate Systems, 1987.
Kenney, Adam. *Museum,* 2004.
http://www.cyberartsweb.org/cpace/fiction/museum/index.html
Lohafer, Susan. *A Cognitive Approach to Storyness.* In Charles May: *The New Short Story Theories.* Athens OH: Ohio University Press, 1994: 301-311.
—. *Preclosure and Story Processing.* In Lohafer Susan, and Jo Ellyn Clarey, (eds.). *Short Story Theory at a Crossroads.* Baton Rouge: Louisiana State University Press, 1989: 149-275.
—. *Coming to Terms with the Short Story.* Baton Rouge: Louisiana State University Press, 1983.
Lohafer, Susan, and Jo Ellyn Clarey (eds.). *Short Story Theory at a Crossroads.* Baton Rouge: Louisiana State University Press, 1989.
Lynch, Gerald. *"The One and the Many: Canadian Short Story Cycles".* In Barbara Lounsberry et al. (eds.). *The Tales We Tell: Perspectives on the Short Story,* London: Greenwood Press, 1998: 35-45.
May, Charles E. *The Short Story: The Reality of Artifice.* New York: Macmillan, 1995.
— (ed.). *The New Short Story Theories.* Athens OH: Ohio University Press, 1994.
—. *On the Nature of Knowledge in Short Fiction. Studies in Short Fiction* 21, 1984: 327-338.
—. (ed.). *Short Story Theories,* Athens. OH: Ohio University Press, 1976.

Miller, J. Hillis. The Ethics of Hypertext. Diacritics 25:3 (Fall 1995), 26-39.

Moulthrop Stuart. *Victory Garden.* Electronic text. Watertown, MA: Eastgate Systems, 1991.

—. *Forking Paths.* In Noah Wardrip-Fruin and Nick Monfort (eds.). *New Media Reader.* CD-ROM, Cambridge MA: MIT Press, 2003.

Nagel, Jason. *The Contemporary American Short Story Cycle: The Ethnic Resonance of Genre.* Baton Rouge: Louisiana State University Press, 2001.

O'Connor, Frank. *The Lonely Voice: A Study of the Short Story.* London: Macmillan, 1963.

O'Faolain, Sean. *The Short Story.* London: Collins, 1948.

Reid Ian. *The Short Story.* London: Methuen, 1977.

Shaw, Valerie. *The Short Story: A Critical Introduction.* London: Longman, 1983.

Yun, David. *Subway Story.* 2000.
   http://www.scholars.nus.edu.sg/cpace/ht/dmyunfinal/frames.html

Wilde, Oscar. *The Happy Prince.* Toronto: Stoddart Publishing, 2002.

CHAPTER SIXTEEN

THE ECHO OF NARCISSISM
IN INTERACTIVE ARTS

LEE SCRIVNER

Cultural theorists have long likened and linked artistic disciplines with Ovid's account of Narcissus. They establish such links either directly, or through a mediating semiotic or a psychoanalytic discourse, thereby retelling Ovid's myth, retooling accounts of the formation of the psyche, and reassessing the nature of artistic processes simultaneously. Examples of such trine claims are so numerous they can be grabbed in fistfuls: Gray Kochhar-Lindgren conflates Narcissus with the novelist, citing Linda Hutchins' claim that "the novel from its beginnings has always nurtured a self-love, a tendency towards self-obsession" and, with a nod to Freud and Lacan, he sees Narcissus, novelists and entities in general as sharing a subjectification by the "symbolic order of language and culture" (4). Film theorist Charles Altman claims that, like Narcissus-centred readings of Ovid, much of film theory and Lacanian psychoanalysis valorize masculine-visual experience over feminine-aural experience (270). Steven Levine notes that the process of painting turns an artist's canvas into Narcissus' mirror. He imagines Monet "bent over," with his "self-reflective presence" "implicitly mirrored" in his lily pond paintings:

> There we come face to face with the writing body of the aged artist. Bending over the scumbled surface of his art, we watch as he entrusts his inevitably vain efforts at self-possession to the allegories of Narcissus, or at least to their real counterparts in the weeping willows and passing reflections in a pond. (191)

Indeed, considering his own book on such artistic narcissism, and bending over the pages of his preface, Levine imagines himself exhibiting the same narcissistic tendency as Monet: "Suspended over an image in these pages, I am Narcissus," he says. But he goes on to say that "separated from the sources of these words, I am Echo as well" (xvii). Thus Levine, and many who have used the myth as metaphor, imagine a paradigm in which Narcissus represents the process of artistic production of the quintessential male subject reaching toward the symbolic, the unattainable phallus. On the other hand, Ovid's wood-nymph Echo, Narcissus' spurned lover, represents the environmental receptacle, the world's reception of and response to that art. In her review of Levine's book, Jennifer Shaw describes this Lacanian use of the Ovidian metaphor as "proceed[ing] according to a paradigm in which 'feminine' nature becomes a screen for male self-actualization" (1). Echo here is the spectator that stands in attentive awe at the Narcissistic artist's creation, and lacks the voice to impinge upon and critique that creation, save with re-contextualized, second-hand words and images provided by and originating from the original art or artist.

Spring-boarding from Kristeva and Salomé's interest in the creative instinct inherent in narcissism, and, indeed, Lacanian theories of the mirror-stage, cultural theorists attempting to explain artistic and semiotic/psychoanalytic processes thus tend to leave Echo in a subordinate, secondary or subaltern position, rather than depict her as a helpful counterpoise to Narcissus. Yet there is a growing wealth of critical work that re-situates or celebrates Echo somewhat in this paradigm. Music theorist David Schwartz claims that Steve Reich reflects what "happens to Echo in Ovid's Metamorphosis", saying the figure of Echo resembles a solo performer's relation to a taped performance, mimicking a Lacanian acoustic mirror, a pre-symbolic relation between a not-yet-perceived-as-such self and the mother's voice: "... each of these pieces presents the listener with a fantasy of sonorous oneness; as the soloist and tape diverge, we hear a clear acoustic mirror as one voice literally echoes another" (46). Feminist theorists especially, and perhaps understandably, have taken up Echo's neglected voice as their own. Amy Lawrence notes the Echo-like repression of women's voices under the dominant paradigm of the masculine, narcissistic image in 20th century film. And, in that it answers western, narcissistic views of the body, as Ovid's Echo "answers" Narcissus, Ava Gerber's "body art" is taken by feminist theorist Gayatri Spivak to exemplify an echoistic trope that advances beyond a "rotarian epistemology of *advancing* from the Imaginary to the Symbolic[...]" (35-38)

Altman, Lawrence and others have pointed out the mutual inclusiveness of the audio and visual image, that "even the Greeks [...] knew that the story of Narcissus is incomplete without that of Echo: the audio mirror completes the video mirror" (Altman, 1977: 270). Hollander notes that when Ovid's Narcissus says "Keep your arms from me! / Be off! I'll die before I yield to you", what is echoed back to him is determined by environmental factors. He shows that the ricochet of sound waves in an echo cannot come back to the ear of the speaker until the speech terminates, or else the primary and secondary sounds would collide in mid-air. Also, if Narcissus' original elocution ricochets off, say, distant mountainsides, the post-terminal echo will seem of longer duration to the speaker than if it bounced off a nearby cliff (19-20). That Echo cannot respond to Narcissus with "I'll die before I yield to you", but rather just "I yield to you", thus serves to embody and position her and him in space and time. Seeing the "newness" of an echo is not a new seeing on the part of Hollander. He is only echoing Thoreau's "Sounds" chapter from *Walden*, where, describing distant echoing bells, Thoreau writes:

> The echo is, to some extent, an original sound, and therein is the magic and charm of it. It is not merely a repetition of what was worth repeating in the bell, but partly the voice of the wood; the same trivial words and notes sung by a wood-nymph.
> (Hollander, 1984: 20)

Similarly for Anne-Emmanuelle Berger, Echo, by figuring this "alteration which insinuates itself in all repetition, thus call[s] into question, by the acoustic return of the utterance onto itself, its originary intention and identity" (629). Hollander notes that sound is made possible only in the bounce-back of forces off objects of resistance or tension: the larynx, the nasal cavity, molecules in the air, the diaphragm in a telephone receiver. That this law of acoustics and physics has semiological repercussions and parallels informs post-structuralists who maintain that "it is impossible for us to say exactly what we mean, for if we say anything at all we say more than one thing" (Humphries, 1983: 33). If Echo is thus vital in the formation of Narcissus' identity, her echo-locutions no longer seem post-lapsarian, corrupted, inferior, or even secondary. The two would-be lovers' relationship becomes non-hierarchical, though they remain inter-dependent, non-identical entities.

Such an Echo, no longer secondary and subaltern to an original Narcissus, seems ideal for this so-called post-modern age in which poly-vocality is valorized and authors and artists are relentlessly toppled from their pedestals of narcissistic subjectivity. Echo's rise is the rise of the DJ who feels as much an artist as the musicians he or she samples and loops. It is the rise of the collage artist appropriating and re-contextualizing the work of the photographer. And it is the rise of their opinion that their artistic echoings represent no falling away from a primal, perfect originality.

Echo's rise seems especially well-suited to interactive hypermedia in the digital realm. Online, on MySpace and YouTube, art, video and music endlessly multiply and permeate a non-hierarchical democratic framework of hyperlinks. Digital realms manifest an incorrupt Echo, for the copied ones and zeros of binary code do not deteriorate; there are no "originals." Accordingly, during the last few decades, "first-generation" hypermedia enthusiasts, J. David Bolter, George Landow, and Richard Lanham and others, have generally touted new interactive hypertext technologies, claiming they subvert tyrannies of linearity in old-school left-to-right print, fixed meanings and one-way flows of signs from subject-author to object-reader:

> The characteristic flexibility of this reader-centered information technology means, quite simply, that students have a much greater presence in the system, both as potential contributors and collaborative participants, but also as readers who choose their own paths through the materials (Delaney, Landow, 1991: 14).

Early hypertext enthusiasts have rallied postmodernist theorists behind them, arguing that "hypertext embodies many of the ideas and attitudes proposed by Barthes, Derrida, Foucault, and others" (Landow, quoted in Shakelford, 2005: 283). Stuart Moulthrop quotes Barthes to complain that Borges' stories "for all their allusiveness and formal instability," are "definitive, material productions restricted both by the immutability of their medium (the printed page) and by social practices (authoritative texts, the law of copyright) to a single set of discursive possibilities" (Delaney, Landow, 1991: 123). While authorial subjectivity and the printed word have been thus pooh-poohed, Echo has been hailed as "a patron deity of interactive art" (Rokeby, 1996: 8).

But in the midst of all this celebration of the echo, what happens to Narcissus? Has he drowned in his own image? Or has a happier ending to Ovid's tale been ushered in by interactive hypermedia? Are the two lovers now somehow closer or more compatible? To attempt an answer, to find what new scenario this new heightened interactivity gives us, let us consider some specific examples of interactive art—non-digital and digital, text and hypertext.

Obliquely placed in one of the British Library's many odd corners sits a bronze sculpture of a ball and chain tied to a half-opened book nearly the size and shape of a park bench. This is Bill Woodrow's *Sitting on History* (1990), the meeting point for many who take the library's guided tour. If you take the tour, the guide will probably end up telling you a little bit about the piece, adding that the work is not yet finished, and will only be finished when someone "comes and sits on it." According to this guide, the sculptor and the sculpture were inviting me to give up being a mere passive observer and to integrate myself into their master plan, thereby re-contextualizing it.

The artist and this tour guide were taking literally, and realizing physically, Marcel Duchamp's famous, now almost clichéd, declaration that "the spectator makes the picture". I didn't sit on the bench, but stood at mid-distance, observing, considering and re-interpreting it. To force this book into a bench shape, Woodrow had had its covers ostensibly thoroughly abused: bent and pulled back nearly to their binding. There was this rupturing spine, the humiliation of the ball and chain. I considered what must have been the artist's point: It was that books are, like a ball and chain, *incarcerating* objects, especially for British Library readers who have chosen a life of dusty cloistered study. To help us get our revenge on this effigy book, I figured, Woodward here has violently ripped back its covers so any passers-by could viscerally express disdain for the world of books by having a sit, a pantomimed shit or symbolic defecation on the pages of all books everywhere. One could, I thought, so easily rewrite the title: not *Sitting on History*, but *S(h)itting on History*.

The guide put an end to this rather quickly. She said she knew the ball and chain looked like a negative critique of books, but she was keen to "assure" us it referred to a bygone era when books were chained to desks to discourage thieves. Immediately, my echoing inner voice, reconfiguring and reinterpreting as a spectator of art, was shut down.

Of course, Duchamp's point need not be taken literally, or necessarily involve physically sitting on a work of art. It needn't have any more to do with interactive art than art in general. He was likely trying to make a point that all art is interactive, just as the repetitious echoings of interpretation occur in the mind of any viewer of art, and it is that same mind that makes the perception and conception of art possible by its ability to reproduce a concept of that art within itself. The separation of mind and art then can be understood to be:

...ungraspable in linguistic, poetic or phenomenological terms. Neither in the form nor the content of a statement could we assign an intrinsic difference between the statement I am pronouncing here, now, in my so-called speaking voice [...] and the same sentence retained in an inner instance, mine or yours (Derrida, 1982: 288).

This sense of the interdependence of art and audience is the interdependence of Narcissus and Echo. Every identity can thus be seen as locked in a continuous process of self-formulation by echolocation at the moment that its "sonorous source attempts to rejoin itself, dividing, differing, deferring without end" (Derrida, 288). In this way, Woodward's *Sitting on History* is not, in my view and relatively speaking, interactive art, other than in the sense that you can sit on it, because interactive art makes *physical as well as conceptually manifest* this proposed symbiosis between Narcissus and Echo. The physical manifestation of a bench on which I as an audience could physically integrate myself was apparently not backed up by an equivalent interpretive flexibility that every other piece of art in existence has (according to Duchamp). But if we do accept, as in our reading of Duchamp, that *all* art is in a way interpretively flexible (except Woodward's), and therefore interactive, then we must come up with other qualifiers for what makes proper "interactive" art. Should we agree with David Rokeby, an interactive artist, who claims that "some artists work to discourage subjective readings and others work to encourage them" (1)? To *measure* the extent to which subjective readings are encouraged or discouraged, if such measurings are even possible, we must consider more art.

Laurence Sterne's novel, *The Life and Opinions of Tristram Shandy*, is an early example from the 18th century of an art piece that is physically modified by the reader. The reader is asked to call for pen and ink in order to "paint" a picture of a hypothetical mistress to better illustrate the tempestuous charms of a "widow Wadman." Sterne then leaves a page blank in the middle of the tome, upon which one might ostensibly follow these instructions. Imagining the instructions to have been followed, Sterne then cries:

> Was ever any thing in Nature so sweet! - so exquisite! [...] Thrice happy book! thou wilt have one page, at least, within thy covers, which Malice will not blacken and which Ignorance cannot misrepresent (from Rokeby, 1996: 2).

This becomes a physical representation of a conceptual structure of interplay, troped by Narcissus and Echo, between art and audience. For here Sterne makes "literal and visible the implicit inscription of the reader's subjectivity into the body of the book" (Rokeby, 1996: 2). Such re-configurable literature emerged again in 1979, over two centuries after Sterne's book was written, when Random House published the first book in its *Choose Your Own Adventure* series. This short novel, *The Cave of Time*, was a novelty for me in that it used the second person "you" to address me, asked me to choose from a series of storyline options, and then directed me to the page that would show how my choice panned out.

Fine. But in a strict sense, there really isn't much interactivity going on in these examples. For Sterne's interactivity is simply spawned by an authorial injunction for the reader to "paint" X, and after a blank page, the authorial text picks up again under the assumption that the reader, like a good automaton, had done precisely as he or she was told. Similarly, *The Cave of Time* offers hardly anything more than the *illusion* of physical interactivity. Its choices are prescribed binaries, and the same author or authors who wrote the choices also wrote their consequences for the reader or the art's audience.

Interactive artist Steven Rokeby imagines the possibility of a far more malleable interactivity in art, a far greater creative role for its spectator. He imagines systems that are so interactive they become, as McLuhan terms them, "extensions of man", where:

> the flow of information goes both ways; the apparati become more like permeable membranes. If there is a balance of flow back and forth across this membrane, then the interactive technology is an intermingling of self and environment. If there is an imbalance, then the technology extends either outwards from the organic boundary of the interactor or inwards into the interactor (from Rokeby, 1996: 13)

For Rokeby, this notion of the permeable membrane becomes a guiding principle in his interactive pieces. In his interactive art piece *Very Nervous System*, a computer, through a video camera, sees and tracks the movements of an interactive spectator who physically permeates the art's membrane entirely. The computer instantly reconfigures impressions made by the interactor's motions into sounds. These sounds, then, simultaneously reflect and accompany the person's gesticulations, "thereby transforming the interactor's awareness of his or her body" (9). This transformation, this on-going metamorphosis, is the *raison d'être* of *Very Nervous System*. Interactive to the highest degree, without the movements of its audience, the art physically ceases to exist. Unlike *Sitting on History*, *The Life and Opinions of Tristram Shandy* or *The Cave of Time*, *Very Nervous System* is thus no longer a closed, predetermined, authorially-inscribed system. As its voice is in flux and configured by its audience, who are physically able to permeate it and act upon it, its inner structure becomes the echo-chamber. "Like Echo," Rokeby says, "the interactive artist transforms what is given by the interactor into an expression of something other" (8). Indeed, structurally speaking, interactive art *becomes* Echo.

But it cannot be Echo all alone. As we have seen, Echo and Narcissus are independently non-existent. Thus, an art of which Echo is the trope must have a spectator or interactor who is troped by Narcissus and inscribed by narcissism. Such a role reversal, which increasingly becomes the case as interactive art becomes increasingly interactive, fulfils the general paradigmatic dynamic in Spivak's "Narcissus-Echo *pair*," which she rightly describes as ever *spinning* in *flux*, in a "contentless, enclitic, monsterative vector" (35). Thus, the spectator in *Very Nervous System* become a multiple of Narcissus, creating extensions of themselves into the device that has become nothing more than the echoing servomechanism of their whims. All interactive art, then, all hypermedia, seems to do nothing to "free" their audience, as has been claimed by the proponents of such art and media. In fact, interactivity secretly privileges the eternal phallocentrism of Narcissus, as it turns its audience into him. As much as it gives us, it taketh away. It tends to ignore our desires to be acted upon as much as it fulfils our desires to be the narcissistic actor.

This inherent narcissism of the interactor in interactive systems has been underscored by George Felton, who claims that "interactivity's key premise is that, at long last, I get to direct the action... I'll soon be able to sit in my living room and press a button routing the movie/book/CD/experience-mechanism in the direction I want it to go" (1). But Felton soon sees the limits in hyper systems over which he has complete complete control: "When I'm finally free to direct where everything goes, I'll never go anywhere I don't intend. In fact, I'll never learn anything new, just keep recycling a few of my favourite things"(1). Turning into Narcissus, Felton soon becomes nostalgic for the non-interactive paradigm, in which he would be acted *upon* by art, and imagines the benefits of a non-hypertext version of *Walden:*

> Nor do I need to have a "conversation" with Thoreau in which I determine what's interesting and get appropriate text bytes in response. If it took him two years to live the book, nine years to write it, and six drafts to get it right, I can at least shut up and let him determine what's interesting. (1)

"First-generation" hypermedia enthusiasts seem to miss the clandestine phallo-centric desire inherent in interactive media whenever they tout hypertext as an escape from the linear tyrannies of print. As has been recognized by Amanda Griscom and others, the Internet puts words and information into the hands of "ordinary people", as did pamphleteering during the English Civil War. Griscom cites Robert Coover's claim that the "novel's alleged power is embedded in the line, that compulsory author-directed movement from the beginning of a sentence to its period, from the top of a page to its bottom" (4). But, other than shifting the roles, and making the audience Narcissus and the art Echo, interactive art does not seem to allow for any less tyranny nor any more conceptual freedom than does standard, non-interactive media, since art only ever exists in the conceptions that we hold of it in our heads.

Griscom seems mildly to taunt the so-called "Luddite" Sven Birkerts, when she asks him if "hypertext [is] capricious in that it supplies 'gaps' into which the reader fills his or her imagination?"(26). Is she implying that Birkerts shies from interactive hypermedia because he has questionable imaginative skills? If so, I must raise a flag in his defence, as suggested by the last 40 years of post-structuralist semiotics. For I would maintain that language in general, every word of it, is riddled with such "gaps", the very ones "into which the reader fills his or her imagination." We cannot have it both ways. We can either read language as having a phenomenological power over us, or as absolutely indeterminate, arbitrary and shifty. Some words cannot have relatively greater gaps, even though they might come couched in a hypertext link. Such links, and all interactive art, can physically trope that gap, for that is what interactive art does and is, but the gap it makes allows no greater room for interpretive manoeuvring.

Interpretations of art are neither accurate nor inaccurate. For representation of mental activity becomes altered the moment Sterne's reader translates it to ink and paper. And if his reader were to accidentally drip ink upon the page, and close Sterne's book, the resultant Rorschach inkblot would forever be a sign for him to interpret or mis-interpret as arbitrarily as he would had it been there in Sterne's hand. Reading Thoreau's *Walden* from cover to cover, the old-fashioned way, with a playful mind, will elicit, facilitate, or host just as many newnesses and revelatory inter-mental echoings as if the reader were in front of an online interactive network, because just as a non-active mind is told what to think and when to think it by linear tyranny, similarly he or she is told what to click, and where that click will take him or her, in an interactive network.

The tyranny of the link only incarcerates those who cannot (not click, but) think beyond its confines.

Bibliography

Altman, C. "Psychoanalysis and Cinema: The Imaginary Discourse." *Quarterly Review of Film Studies* 2. August (1977): 257-72.
Berger, A. "The Latest Word from Echo" *New Literary History*, 27. 4. (1996): 621-40.
Delaney, P., and G. Landow. "Hypertext, Hypermedia, and Literary Studies: The State of the Art" in *Hypermedia and Literary Studies*. Eds. MIT Press, 1991.
Derrida, J. *Margins of Philosophy*. Chicago: University of Chicago, 1982.
Felton, G. "A Read-Only Man in an Interactive Age". *Minutes of the Lead Pencil Club*. Pushcart Press, 1996.
http://marylaine.com/exlibris/xlib117.html
Griscom, A. "Trends of Anarchy and Hierarchy: Comparing the Cultural Repercussions of Print and Digital Media". 1996.
http://marylaine.com/exlibris/xlib117.html
Hollander, J. *The Figure of Echo: A Mode of Allusion in Milton and After*. University of California Press, 1984.
Humphries, J. "Haunted Words, or Deconstruction Echoed", *Diacritics*, Vol. 13, No. 2. Summer (1983): 29-38.
Kochlar-Lindgren, G. *Narcissus Transformed, The Textual Subject in Psychoanalysis and Literature* Pennsylvania: Pennsylvania State University Press, 1993.
Lawrence, A. *Echo and Narcissus: Women's Voices in Classical Hollywood Cinema.* University of California Press, 1991.
Levine, S. Z. *The Modernist Myth of the Self.* Chicago: University of Chicago Press, 1994.
Rokeby, D. "Transforming Mirrors: Subjectivity and Control in Interactive Media". *Critical Issues in Interactive Media*, Simon Penny (ed.). SUNY Press, 1996.
http://www.people.arch.usyd.edu.au/~petra/2004/DESC9068/David_Rokeby_TransformingMirrors.doc
Schwartz, D. "Listening Subjects: Semiotics, Psychoanalysis, and the Music of John Adams and Steve Reich". *Perspectives of New Music,* Vol. 31, No. 2 Summer, (1993): 24-56.
Shaw, J. L. "Monet, Narcissus, and Self-Reflection: The Modernist Myth of the Self". 1995. Reviewed in *Art Journal*.

http://findarticles.com/p/articles/mi_m0425/is_n3_v54/ai_17631637/pg_1

Spivak, G. C. "Echo". *New Literary History*, Vol. 24, No. 1, 1993: 17-43.

Shakelford, L. "Narrative Subjects Meet Their Limits: John Barth's "Click" and the Remediation of Hypertext". *Contemporary Literature*, 46.2., (2005): 275-310.

CHAPTER SEVENTEEN

HYPERTEXT AND COLLECTIVE AUTHORS: THE INFLUENCE OF THE INTERNET ON THE FORMATION OF NEW CONCEPTS OF AUTHORSHIP

FLORIAN HARTLING

1. Introduction: Phenomenon Authorship

The author and the literary text have always represented a suspenseful, somewhat contrasting pair in the field of literary-theoretical analysis. The post-structuralist dictum of "death of the author" has overshadowed the literary-scientific debate critical of the author for some time (cf. Barthes, 2001 [1968]; Foucault, 1997 [1969]). Nevertheless, the powerful "return of the author" (cf. Jannidis et al., 1999; Detering, 2002) has been evident in theoretical discourse since the 1990s.

Ironically, however, the past dictum of "death of the author" still seems to have validity in the most recent literary medium. The Internet, according to euphoric literature theoreticians, will finally bid farewell to the author. Such somewhat biased and naïve beliefs could certainly be attributed to the early stages of the Internet. More recent positions are more differentiated and have (re-)accepted the author online as well (cf. Simanowski, 2004; Landow, 2006: 125-143). Still, there is a tendency in Net Literature generally to marginalize the author.[1]

In the following, I will discuss more closely the thesis of the author's "disappearance" on the Internet. For this purpose, it should be understood

---

[1] I use the term "Net Literature" as a comprehensive term for Internet-typical literature. Net Literature is literature that structurally reflects the specific characteristics of the Internet. The use of the Internet medium can be viewed as self-referential within Net Literature. The Internet is not only used for the creation, propagation and reception of literature; it also enters literature and shapes it.

that the Internet is structured and analysed as a media *dispositif* (apparatus) (cf. Hartling / Wilke, 2003). In this respect, I follow Michel Foucault (cf. Foucault, 1978: 118-175) and the German media scholar Knut Hickethier (cf. Hickethier, 2003: 186-201). In my opinion, new forms of authorship are being created in the Internet *dispositif* which, furthermore, enables the creation of ultimately challenging collaborative models of writing literature. In this discussion, I will examine three different genres of German-speaking Net Literature, in which more and more the author seems to "die", or rather disappear.

2. Genealistic Authorship

The genres of "classic" Net Literature continue the experiments of modern printed literature: narrative hyperfiction based on the idea of non-linearity, as tested, for example, by E.T.A. Hoffmann in the classical book medium. In contrast, hypermedial-oriented works follow the experiments of concrete and visual poetry. This is certainly not old wine in new skins. While there is always the *possibility* of infringing on normal serial reading in the written medium, this breach of the norm has become a rule in the Internet *dispositif*. The reader's interactive involvement forms the basis of poetry. Detached from the word as the only feature of importance, and supplemented by new interactive elements, new literary qualities are formed. However, the classical characteristics of literature are also continued: such works represent a strong sense of authorship, which manifests itself, for example, in the author's production. Despite all the interactivity, the reader can still only take the paths provided by the author. The importance of the code and the machine-made barely experiences artistic reflection. Finally, works are still oriented primarily on examples from the offline world.

3. Collaborative Authorship

Net Literature also enables the carrying out of collaborative joint writing, in which the function of authorship is no longer fulfilled by one single author. Collaborative writing projects not only make use of the Internet *dispositif* for publication and distribution; they use its attributes primarily as a communicative and interactive medium for literary production. A characteristic of this type of literature is that it consistently appears to try and reverse the traditional relationship between author and reader and in the end even attempts to sever it: each reader is invited and encouraged to participate in the writing. The organizers of such writing projects see themselves as technicians and moderators; they remain in the background. The work itself is created through the collaboration of very different writers.

Conceptions of collaborative writing convert the already-discussed dictum of "death of the author" into "birth of the reader": new digital media allow for completely new literary text production. The Internet therefore seems to stand for the redemption of older utopical post-structural promises by Barthes and Foucault. In the meantime, the overly-simplified formulation of this idea has been refuted by research (cf. Simanowski, 2004; Landow, 2006: 125-143).

Two (strange) counter-tendencies take the place of this simplified formula of "death of the author". The first is that the author is formally reborn or rather continues to live in the Internet *dispositif*. This has partly brought about an even more pronounced personality cult compared with the traditional terms of linear texts: on the Internet, the usual selection mechanisms of the book market are done away with. Both traditional and Internet authors can therefore practise almost unlimited, exaggerated self-portrayal and self-production as authors. The famous collaborative project "NULL"[2] ('Zero') in 2000 is very convincing evidence for the thesis of the rebirth of the author on the Internet. It was designed as the collective project of a group of well-known German-speaking authors, whose contributions were consistently published under their respective names. The texts themselves are barely net-affine. It might even be suspected that clear affiliation with the contributions, and therefore fairly traditional "authorization" of the texts, was a condition of collaboration. It therefore comes as no surprise that the project was intended from the beginning to be published as a traditional book by DuMont, the well-known German publishing house; this surely was also a condition of participation by the traditional authors.

---

[2] This project is no longer accessible on the Internet. It was published in book form in 2000 (cf. Hettche/ Hensel 2000).

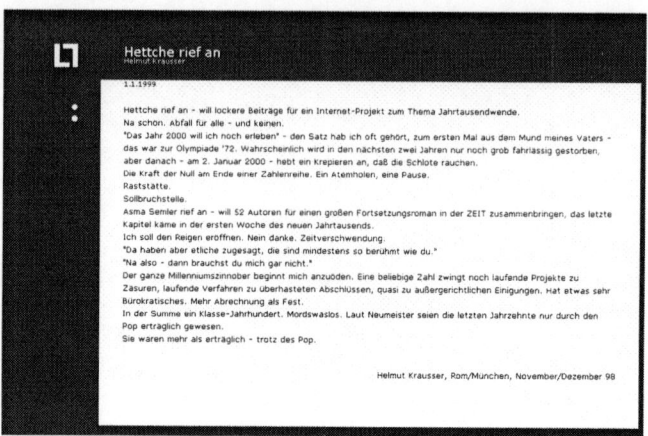

Illustration 1: "NULL" (2000): Entry by Helmut Krausser

Conversely, the aforementioned excessive "personality cult" also refers to authors who explicitly identify themselves as not being the author. In this way, initiators and moderators of collaborative projects are regularly identified as the authors. The fact that this affiliation is not completely off-base is made clear by the boundaries for writers set by moderators. Affiliation is further legitimized by how these collaborative projects are usually concluded by the moderators. The result of their technical power of control over the web server and programming of the texts is clearly visible authority, despite the apparent lack of authorship: for example, the power to announce that the text is finished, thereby denying access to others .

The second counter-tendency to the alleged "death of the author" is that collaborative literary works, as opposed to extensive collaborative journalistic text productions such as "Wikipedia" (<http://en.wikipedia.org/>) and "Slashdot" (<http://slashdot.org/>), are still relatively rare. There are apparently more literary-critical and academic texts *on* collaborative projects than projects themselves. This appears to be due in the first place to frustrating experiences in connection with collaborative projects: ambitious artistic expectations are often unfulfilled and participation frequently abates quickly. Secondly, it seems to be a consequence of how the systems of social, artistic and economic gratification are structured: these are still tied to the name of the author and, furthermore, to the traditional book *dispositif.* Thirdly, the meaning of authorship is fundamentally different in artistic and non-artistic texts. From these two counter-tendencies, I have come to two conclusions regarding the authorship of Net Literature.

Firstly, I have concluded that many tendencies in classical and traditional literature are continued in the Internet *dispositif,* such as the coexistence of multifaceted and rival models of authorship, which are activated depending on the artistic program. There are certain "fashions" regarding this, hence the temporary preference towards stronger individualistic or collaborative models. The second conclusion is that on the Internet there are completely new forms of collaborative models resulting from the *dispositif,* which is associated with a stronger preference for such collaborative conceptions. Due to its structure, a new quality of collaborative and cooperative authorship is being created on the fringes of the Internet *dispositif.* However, this new quality should not be reduced to the inappropriately simplified common denominator of "death of the author".

The fascinating potential of the *dispositif* for successful collaborative productions has already been shown in the non-artistic, journalistic sense. In the meantime, established systems and platforms for the cooperative creation of content have developed, which successfully compete with traditional media. These systems are based on the "open source" movement, as well as on methods and technologies of software production, which have always been structured collaboratively out of necessity.

The technologies of collaborative experimental "writing", tested and refined particularly in journalistic terms, have consequences for the artistic production: Collaborative Net Literature projects use writing platforms, which were initially designed solely as means of communication or information. Wikipedia and Slashdot are testing mechanisms for quality assurance of contents produced collaboratively and without hierarchy. These probably also lead to challenging collaborative literary works. It is expected that through this a new artistic quality of authorship will be created in the *dispositif.* The goal here—in turn—is to find a definition removed from the dichotomy of "death" or "return" of the author.

4. Marginalized Authorship

Up to now, I have examined digital literature, which still requires humans, not only for the conception of projects, but also for content creation. However, the meaning of software and its relevance for artistic work indicates another advance: software can self-produce, thanks to already existing databases and the codes contained in them. I have now reached the so-called Codeworks and, in a way, the temporarily last revolutionary upheaval in the *dispositif*. Both classic digital literary works and apparently authorless, collaborative writing projects move artistic perception towards the centre of attention. They are "interface works". The term *interface* describes the screen as a gateway between computer and user but also covers the meaning of the aesthetically-received design of Net Literature.

In contrast, Codeworks are literary projects which reflect and illustrate the fact that digital literature is always based on software. In this way, they move the conceptual "behind the scenes" of digital literature to centre stage. They explicitly refer to the digital and allow for conclusions on the relation between "code" and "interface." At the same time Codeworks provide a glimpse of future "versions" of "digital authorship." In Codeworks, elements of programming languages and network protocols are combined poetically with natural and artificial languages; this questions the meaning of code and the role the computer plays in artistic production. The multifaceted processes "in the computer" are made visible on the screen. Placed at the gateway between interface aesthetics and code aesthetics, they not only challenge the user's traditional understanding of art, but force him or her to reflect on things apparently taken for granted: Codeworks often appear to be system malfunctions, which confuses the user; they are films alienated beyond recognition, de-constructed computer games and even viruses.

```
|      |           |      |           |      |           |
|  365 |    <---   |  825 |    --->   |  693 |           |
|_____|           |_____|           |_____|           |

Catholic <-->         a <--> an <-->           and <--> awf
decamp <--> el        ude <--> epito          me <--> father
eneral <--> it        <--> of <-->            of <--> prude
senile <--> th        e <--> the <--          > to <--> udg
wrath
.I. --> .Next,        . --> .a. -->           .bath. --> .b
-> .but. -->          .convinced. -->         .everywhere.
her's. --> .fo        r. --> .in. --          > .look. -->
.my. --> .qui         te. --> .there          ,. --> .they.
k. --> .would.
I <--> Still,         <--> a <--> a           nd <--> bad <-
-> father's <-        -> greatest <-          -> having <-->
-> it <--> la         ughing, <--> l          evity <--> mig
my <--> not <-        -> not <--> n           ote <--> pocke
evolver <--> s        uch <--> the <          --> the <-->
--> to <--> w         ith <--> witho          ut <--> writte
```

Illustration 2: "plaintext.cc" (2005); detail

Florian Cramer's work "plaintext.cc", done in 2005, vividly shows what code-oriented "story-telling" can achieve with an attractive concept and aesthetically interesting graphics. In his online installation, new and exciting texts are generated from a heterogeneous pool of all sorts of texts. They remind the user of concrete and visual poetry, but represent "code art": an e-mail conversation with the artist Mez is intermingled with source code parts and pornographic quotes by George Bataille. These texts "contaminate" one another and also undergo transformations and typographic formatting. In this, Cramer plays with the ironic alienation of the concept "bachelor" by mixing software elements and programming with pornography.

But what do "code-based" and "code-reflecting" works mean for authorship? Apparently, this form of art is the bulkiest and least accessible of the forms presented: the programmer only takes background responsibility for a frequently invisible program algorithm. The computer seems to "let off steam on the screen". This is no longer aesthetically-received literature, but the breaking open of traditional opposites which until now were incompatible: machine versus man, software versus user, or interface versus code. The final product on the screen is no longer at the centre of this art form; the concept behind it—or "code"—is.

This much is obvious: if the conceptual is so clearly in the foreground in this genre, traditional author concepts barely play a role any more. The telling of an aesthetically-received story is also marginalized. Traditional story-telling is ironized with this production of association material; making sense of it is the task of the reader, who generates his or her own story from what he or she sees. But it is also clear that the programmer is no longer the sole author; the code and the reader take on a big part. Hence my third conclusion: the Internet *dispositif* and digital literature specifically have in common the demolishing of author function. This is made exceedingly clear with "Codeworks". This eccentric form of literature marks *one* end of the large bandwidth of possible realizations of the Internet author: superficially authorless texts. At the other end of the spectrum are those authors with an excessive personality cult—apparently also very typical of the Internet *dispositif*. My fourth conclusion is: The author cannot disappear into the network, because the *dispositif* will not allow this to happen. Therefore the Internet does not stand for the "death" of the author; it actually appears to be a fountain of youth for literary authorship instead.

Bibliography

Barthes, R. "The Death of the Author". In *Image, Music, Text*, S. Heath (ed.). 22. print. New York: Hill and Wang, 2001[1968]:142-148.
Cramer, F. "plaintext.cc", 2005. http://plaintext.cc

Detering, H. (ed.) *Autorschaft*. Stuttgart, Weimar: Metzler, 2002.
Foucault, M. *Dispositive der Macht*. Berlin: Merve, 1978.
—. "What Is An Author?" In *Language, Counter-memory, Practice*, D. F. Bouchard (ed.), 10. Paperback print. Ithaca, NY: Cornell University Press, 1997 [1969]:113-138.
Hartling F., and T. Wilke. "Das Dispositiv als Modell der Medienkulturanalyse". *Siegener Periodicum zur Internationalen Empirischen Literaturwissenschaft* 22.1, (2003) 1-37.
Hettche, T. and J. Hensel (eds.) *NULL*. Köln: DuMont, 2000.
Hickethier, K. *Einführung in die Medienwissenschaft*. Stuttgart, Weimar: Metzler, 2003.
Jannidis, F., G. Lauer, M. Martínez, and S. Winko (eds.). *Rückkehr des Autors*. Tübingen: Niemeyer, 1999.
Landow, G. P. *Hypertext 3.0*. 3rd edition. Baltimore: Johns Hopkins University Press, 2006.
Simanowski, R. "Tod des Autors? Tod des Lesers!" In *p0es1s. Ästhetik digitaler Poesie*, F. W. Block, C. Heibach and K. Wenz (eds.). Ostfildern. Hatje Cantz, (2004): 79-91.

CHAPTER EIGHTEEN

HYPERMEDIA NARRATIVES:
PARATACTIC STRUCTURES
AND MULTIPLE READINGS

ANA PANO ALAMÁN

Storytelling involves the recounting and shaping of events by portraying in words, images, and sounds what happens in realistic or fictional worlds. Whether in traditional formats like books or new media formats like CD-Rom and World Wide Web hypermedia, narratives combine a series of events, characters, and settings which may be understood by a reader, listener or viewer through complex structures. However, hypermedia narratives call into question the idea of plot associated with traditional narratives, which present a certain stability in their arrangement of parts as well as an unambiguous extent. In this paper, I argue that the "performing" dimension—links and interactive devices such as reader control-animated images—within hypermedia fiction splits narrative in that it conveys paratactic structures and variations on a single theme, that contribute to the volatility of meaning and the constant reconfiguration of the narrative sequence.

I intend to explore this phenomenon in four examples of digital works: *The Book of Waste* (2004), *Nada tiene sentido* (Ara; Lorenzo, 2002), *The Jew's Daughter*, (Morrissey, 2001), and *Serial Letters* (Malbreil, 2002). Approaching storytelling across media as a cognitive construct activated by various types of signs displayed through different supports, implies taking into account three fundamental levels of narrative: firstly, semantics or content, secondly, syntax, relating to the structure and the way these signs interact, and thirdly, pragmatics or narrative seen as performance.

Stories conveyed in what Marie-Laure Ryan calls "genuinely digital texts" (Ryan, 2000: 329) rely upon digital platforms to be constructed, displayed and performed, but, like hybrids, they combine the characteristics of several media. The format in which this genuinely digital fiction is displayed does not alter the essence of a story as an account of events or actions provoking global changes in a world populated by characters. These formats convey stories which, like those in certain print texts and films, imply similar non-conventional and complex interpretative strategies on the part of the reader.

Digital stories have traditionally been approached as non-linear texts, as a series of apparently disconnected events which, exacerbated by a plurality of pathways, favour non-sequential reading and confusion. While this is the case for many hypermedia narratives, most stories, either told, written in a book or projected on a screen, are complex and, like life, non-linear in the sense that at any moment they live in the past, the present and the future. This complexity is suggested, for instance, by stories conveyed in modernist and post-modernist print narratives and films, which symbolize the non-linearity of life not only through flashbacks and premonitions, but also by enabling different plot lines to develop at the same time. Events do not appear in a strict chronological order, and the whole narrative is usually fragmented by means of digressions, illustrations and other devices aimed at giving further information about a character or a setting. This technique distracts the reader from the conventional sequential reading related to causality and temporality, but removing a single probable or necessary sequence of events does not do away completely with linearity and the logic connection of facts.

It is my contention that the reader who follows a reading path in hypermedia fiction also notices linearity and logic by associating meaningful signs, even if the path curves back upon itself or heads off in strange directions. However, the lack of a definite ending and, more precisely, the reader's involvement in shaping the text, added to the very connective and dynamic nature of hypermedia fiction, enable multiple narrative dimensions that echo one another; this has an impact that affects the semantic and syntactic level and consequently the very perception of the content and structure of a given story.

Moreover, these narrative sequences develop within a double schema as some of them relate to associative and static textual elements which dwell on more or less extended nodes of text projected on a screen, while others correspond to connective and dynamic components which, like links and multimedia devices, allow the reader to enter, wander around and quit the story, more or less at random. The first level of this schema relies upon engagement and the second encourages immersion; thus, engagement and immersion alternate within narratives in which there is tension between the text as a story and the text as a structure of allusions (Bolter, 1991).

Hypermedia fiction like *Nada tiene sentido* requires a series of clicks that let the reader traverse the story through a myriad of links. The text seems to be controlled by the receiver whose action evokes a particular *momentum* to the story. This involves a certain degree of engagement in spite of total immersion and feeling for the thematic stream. The story is perceived through several nodes which convey a multidimensional overview of the whole. However, more recent hypermedia fiction, such as *The Book of Waste* stories, tends to reduce the number of links and automatically displays animated texts and images which require only the minimum input, or no input at all, on the reader's part to allow the story to progress.

Let me now focus on connectivity and the way it conveys paratactic structures and echoes narrative sequences in hypermedia fiction. It is generally accepted that digital stories dwell on linkage, which forces the reader to happen upon connections between and among the various elements of the text within a space that is basically layered. In this sense, the link is the electronic representation of a perceived relationship between two pieces of material, a relationship instantiated electronically that plays a role corresponding to that of sequence in conventional print text (Slatin, 1991: 877).

Yet, as Adrian Miles (2001) forcefully argues, although the link is regularly discussed in terms of what it enables (for example, multi-linear narrative), it is rarely explored ontologically. The traditional approach to hypermedia fiction and the way stories are told in this particular digital format loosely perceives anchors and links as agents that simply serve the reader with a choice. As meaningful signs, anchors and links provide our minds with representations of imagined worlds. At the same time, they serve as multipliers of meaning and as shifting and subverting devices which, at the instant of the click, make the story progress in several directions.

Like Peirce's *interpretant*, the link represents the sign as a possibility, a fact or a reason, three elementary sequences that in the context of narrative theory relate to what Claude Bremond (1970: 5-11) identifies as the three functions of any basic narrative sequence. The first function opens up the possibility of the process by promising an event, the second implements this *virtuality* in the form of the event taking place, and the third closes the process in the form of a result of the same event. From this perspective, the link is a mere bridge between a sign and what the sign represents in a self-contained system. Yet, in hypermedia fiction the bridge, or space in between, does not only associate signs but echoes similar signs. As Francisco José Ricardo (1998) claims, the fact that text and links argue separately and together a case for different possible thematic linearity and a universe of possible linearities is evidence that links play an important role in the construction of paratactic structures within narrative. In fact, these *paths to follow* are part of the process of signification; as such, they transpose, rearrange and dislodge the text, expanding meaning and multiplying the narrative, not in the sense of increasing points of view or facilitating different plot lines embedded in the text, but in the sense of mirroring content and structures which will then be perceived as altered.

Pantomime, a story included in *The Book of Waste*, introduces the reader to Lisa, who is obsessed with a friend who committed suicide. Nodes telling us she has an empty relationship with a boy, that she fears her parents, and that her life has no meaning at all suggest that she too will commit suicide. In fact, the last words are: *Lisa no breathing, Lisa no life, Lisa no meaning*. Words linking these nodes are *mind, position, forget it, breath, secure,* and *failed*. This is a double story in the sense that nodes and links on the one hand and the very linking dimension on the other convey two versions of the same story. The reader may read the whole text but by simply clicking on highlighted words and focusing on the visual development of the story, he or she may follow a second restrained plot and figure out what is going on through a narrow storytelling space. In fact, Lisa seems to meditate on her *position*; she does not feel *secure*, her life is a *failure* and so she *fails* to *breathe*.

In *Trap/Findings*, the narrator threatens a sleeping woman with a gun and attempts to kill her as he remembers certain stages of their relationship. Text appears automatically as we read so that when a first sentence is complete a second sentence appears, and so on. The gradual display of developments in the narrative contributes to the intensification of violence and suspense. In this sense, it seems to me that such automatic devices also convey meaning and somehow symbolize the tension unfolded by the narrative.

It is therefore important to stress the relationship between linkage and dynamic storytelling and interpretation in digital media by approaching links and multimedia connective elements both separately and together from the textual nodes they interconnect. Indeed, all these components have a descriptive power to the point where they become a reading by themselves. As Ricardo (1998: 148) puts it, if the semantic power of links can be established, it is possible to show that they can sustain communicative intentions of their own, hence the idea of an "alternative parallel text, or *paratext*", which sets up paratactic structures and multiple readings in digital stories.

In a given node, a particular event, a character description, even a setting, can not only be displayed through a series of sentences or paragraphs but it can also be told through a clickable word or syntagma, or a dynamic visual component. The reader adjusts his or her cognitive framework or schema on the basis of these juxtaposition or collage devices.

In contemporary print works it is also possible for words that are highlighted, or visual elements accompanying the text, to be understood separately from the whole work. Yet links and animated images in hypermedia are intrinsically connected to the main story to the point where they physically spread it out to make the story progress. The general narrative schema could not be understood without this second connective dimension, which seems to prevail in the text in the very act of reading at the pragmatic level of narrative. In works like *Serial Letters*, the story is narrated through long nodes of text, which coexist with key sentences, and even dialogues hidden *behind* images that only unfold if the mouse is passed over the image. Engagement and exploration of the whole storyspace is thus necessary for full immersion in the story, but these hidden elements in the text somehow impose a new and original perspective which compresses the long narrative sequences in previously read nodes. In this sense, in Joyce's words, links are "doubly illusory" as they expand the meaning of a given text and restrain it once the reader clicks on it and passes through it; not only do they provide important clues about the story, together with the actual node and the incoming one, they also add a second perspective on the same story. Events are somehow re-told through these collage devices which make possible multiple variations on a single theme.

The Jew's Daughter, for instance, is built upon a series of disordered thoughts concerning some of the events related to the life of the narrator, a wanderer who meditates about his past and his relationship with a woman who is gone. The story is conveyed through long nodes in which flashbacks and flash-forwards abound. The few clickable words (there is one per node) impel the reader to follow a story that is continually modified. Rolling over a highlighted word subtly changes the entire narrative on the page so if the reader clicks on *criminal* or *June* the text changes and adopts a new perspective. The story is continuously reshaped, so one is forced to review the whole node, which takes a new direction on the basis of this dynamic and connective narrative space.

In addition, storytelling relies here on two spaces. Whereas one dimension is dynamic, connective, eventful and actual, the other is static, associative, stable and generally relates to past and future events. While one space is made up of words, sentences, and images, the other dwells on paragraphs and long nodes of text. The latter would correspond to the episodes of a traditional story, while the former would be not only breaks, sequences or decision points, as Slatin and Bolter argue, but also storytelling agents which convey meaning too.

Early hypermedia fiction provided a series of menus and lists of clickable words in order to give a general overview of the story. However, more recent digital stories avoid a general index and merge such words into nodes in a more complex way. These connective words are embedded in the content and structure and thus make the story progress. At the same time, they not only provide enough clues for a story to be followed as a series of transformations and events but also create a mirroring, though somehow distorting, dimension.

As an example, see *Nada tiene sentido*, a journal which records the actions and thoughts of a man called Pedro who gradually comes to terms with his mental deterioration. At the beginning, the reader accesses several nodes containing long linear sentences and traditional paragraphs. By clicking a single word or an arrow in the text, one node is made to follow another. As the symptoms of insanity become evident, the storyspace changes; the text is suddenly populated with links which lead the reader from the text of the narrator's journal to a sort of chat or e-mail space where the narrator communicates with Ordep—the other Pedro, as his name spelt backwards suggests. While the visibly anguished narrator continues with his impressions, the reader is gradually asked to engage with a highly dynamic and connective narrative that mirrors the narrator's troubled impressions through short sentences, dynamic images and hidden links, so that the story tells itself in a more compressed, symbolic way.

The interpretation of the significance of a segment is tied up with the reader's perception of a word, an image or a dynamic sentence, which is not only a "central junction in the structure of the text" (Douglas, 1999: 105) but also a sign conveying meaning and telling something by itself. Thus, it is possible to state that hypermedia components are by themselves narrative sequences that tend to overcome the primary narrative sequence traditionally rooted in the text. In so doing, they enable paratactic structures or variations on a single theme possible and contribute, like subtly split images, towards the volatility of meaning.

Bibliography

Ara I., and I. Lorenzo. *Nada tiene sentido*, 2002. http://www.unav.es/digilab/proyectosenl/2002/nada_tiene_sentido/

Bolter, J.D. *Writing Space: The Computer, Hypertext, and the History of Writing*. Hillsdale, NJ: Erlbaum, 1991.

Bremond, C. "Combinaisons syntaxiques entre fonctions et séquences narratives", in *Sign. Language. Culture*, Greimas, A.J. et al. (ed). The Hague: Mouton, 1970.

Douglas, J.Y. *The End of Books – or Books Without End?* Ann Arbor: University of Michigan Press, 1999.

Lanham, R.A. *The Electronic Word: Democracy, Technology, and the Arts*. Chicago: University of Chicago Press, 1993.

Malbreil, X. *Serial Letters* (2002) http://www.livredesmorts.com/

Miles, A. *Hypertext Structure as the Event of Connection*. HT'01, 8/0, Aarhus: ACM, 2001. http://www.acm.org/sigs/pubs/proceed/template.html

Morrissey, J. *The Jew's Daughter* (2001). http://www.thejewsdaughter.com/

Ricardo, F.J. *Stalking the Paratext: Speculations on Hypertext Links as a Second Order Text*. HyperText 98, Pittsburgh: ACM, (1998): 142-151.

Ryan, M.-L. *Narrative across Media. The Languages of Storytelling*. Lincoln: University of Nebraska Press, 2004.

Slatin, J. "Reading Hypertext: Order and Coherence in a New Medium", in *Hypermedia and Literary Studies*, Landow, G.P., and P. Delany (ed.). Cambridge: MIT Press, 1991: 153-169.

The Book of Waste (2004). http://www.dreamingmethods.com/waste/

CHAPTER NINETEEN

SALAAM BAGHDAD:
WARBLOGS IN THE TEXTUAL AND SOCIAL
ECONOMIES OF THE INTERNET

PRISCILLA RINGROSE

1. Warblogs: Textual and Social Production

A recently started English-language weblog authored by a prominent English civil servant, with a defence portfolio and a learned interest in literature, music, the theatre and science, has gained notoriety, not least because it has chronicled his extra-marital liaisons with various women, including, in one case, one of his wife's companions, using a mixture of English, French and Portuguese when relating intimate details. The potential for exposure and ruin may appear excessive if I were not to explain that the blog is in fact a presentation of the diary of Samuel Pepys, the renowned 17th century diarist, in blog form. A new "post" from the original diary has been published each day since the first entry on 1st January 2003 (covering 1st January 1660), and will run over the course of several years. Even a cursory look at the website glaringly reveals the difference between the digital diary and its "equivalent" paper version, not least pointing to the way technology both limits and opens up readers' choices. On the one hand, the blog offers a search function enabling the reader to instantly access mentions of, say, the Second Dutch War, and boasts a "catch-up-on-the-story-so-far" facility. On the other hand, since it is being published as an "ongoing blog", its readership community cannot, unlike conventional diary readers, skim ahead to discover whether Pepys' hapless wife Elisabeth does, in fact, discover him in flagrant embrace...

This paper will address a particular sub-set of blog—warblogs—using the case study of two popular English-language warblogs, by two pseudonymous Iraqi bloggers, Salam Pax, an architect, and Riverbend, a computer programmer, both of whom began blogging from Baghdad in the period immediately preceding the onset of hostilities in Iraq.[1] I will discuss two approaches which have been employed in the analysis of blogs and assess the extent to which they provide an appropriate mechanism for analysing these warblogs. The first approach looks at blogs as a cultural genre which has "retooled" the traditional diary (van Dijck, 2004). The second assesses them as a form of social action which has evolved from the social trend of mediated voyeurism (Miller and Shepherd, 2004). I will show that these warblogs force a renegotiation of some of the assumptions made in both of these approaches, before arguing for a third perspective from which to examine them, namely as bridge blogs, within what Yochai Benkler terms the *Sharing Economy* (Benkler, 2004).

1.1. Diaries Retooled

According to Jose van Dijck, "cultural practices or forms never simply adapt to new technological conditions, but always inherently change along with the technologies and the potentialities of their use. In the case of lifelogs, the digital materiality of the Internet engenders a new type of reflection and communication. This shows traces of the former analogue genre but functions substantially differently" (van Dijck, 2004). The most common analyses of the blog as a genre, van Dijck claims, stubbornly perpetuate the same binary distinctions that dominate analyses of the traditional diary genre, which tend to focus either on directionality or on content. Such approaches set up oppositions between texts written for private reading and those intended for public use; or, alternately, between the diary as an exploration of personal life and the journal as a record of external events. These distinctions are misleading, van Dijck notes, since both the traditional diary and blog genres are particularly hybrid genres, and the blog has, if anything, amplified the ambiguities still further. We find a recent instance of this kind of binary differentiation in weblog analysis in a 2006 Pew report, which distinguishes between bloggers who regard their art as aimed at "the sharing of personal experiences" and those who view it as "form of journalism" (Lenhart, 2006: ii).

Although diary-writing is conventionally viewed as a private performance, an intrinsic property of all diaries is their addressee: "Whereas some authors directed their diaries to an imagined friend (like Anne Frank's 'Kitty', or André Gide's mysterious addressee), to God, or to the world at large, the notion of addressing is crucial to the recognition

---

[1] I will also refer to a military blog authored by Colby Buzzell, a former US Brigade gunner who started to blog in June 2004 when based in Mosul, Iraq.

of diary writing as an *act of communication*" (Marty, quoted in van Dijck, 2004). Samuel Pepys chose to write out his diary in fair copy from rough notes, had its loose pages bound into six volumes and catalogued them in his library with all his other books, all of which signals a tacit acknowledgement of its interest for posterity: "Writing, even as a form of self-expression, signals the need to connect, either to someone or something else, or to oneself later in life", or, one may add, in the case of Pepys, to future generations (Marty, quoted in van Dijck).

Both blogs and traditional diaries may have single or multiple implied or actual readers, but blogs are distinguished from diaries by the potentially limitless number of readers who are coterminous with the writing event, whereas print diaries may also reach a mass anonymous audience, but only after publication. The significance of this difference is that warblogs, unlike war diaries, have the potential to influence the perspective of their readership communities on the war *as it progresses*, and under some exceptional conditions, may have the potential to put pressure on public opinion and affect political outcomes.

But how, as political scientists Dreznell and Farell put it, "[g]iven the disparity in resources and organization vis-à-vis other actors, [can] a collection of decentralized, non-profit, contrarian, and discordant websites exercise any influence over politics and political outputs?" (Dreznell and Farell, 2004: 2). Addressing this question, they conclude that under certain conditions the blogosphere does have the capacity to influence political outcomes, and does so in a manner that mimics the workings of the mediasphere. The first condition is when a large number of blogs frame a single issue, elevating it to the political arena and thus "shap[ing] the boundaries and content of political discourse and public opinion" (17). The second is when a single blog with a very high number of links becomes a focal point, rising to the top of the blogosphere. As salient blogs, Salam and Riverbend's blogs constituted significant voices in the political debate around the legality of the war and occupation in Iraq. Kelly Dougherty, co-founder of *Iraq Veterans against the War*, explicitly credited Riverbend's blog with contributing to the mobilizing of public opinion against the occupation.[2]

I argue that in the case of warblogs, it is useful to look not only at categories of directionality and of content, but also at the way the technology of the medium impacts on the relation between the two categories. Salam and Riverbend were assailed by comments and emails from members of their readership communities curious to discover more

---

[2] Citation taken from inside cover of Riverbend's *Baghdad Burning*.

about their personal experiences, and intent on soliciting and questioning their interpretations of the conflict situation. Both bloggers regularly quote readers' responses and respond directly to them within their posts. The consequent instant intertextuality results in the warblog constituting an inherently more responsive and less self-directed form than that of its "paper" counterpart. Its narrative flow is continuously interrupted and the nature of its contents redirected by external intervention. Here, Salam explains how readers changed the course of *his* blog:

> It was going to be very personal, nothing to do with politics, just about what we're doing in Baghdad. Later on when more and more people started to come and read it and ask all these questions about Baghdad... when it took a more political turn... (Pax, 2004)

1.2. Blogging as Social Action

The connectivity, which literally *in-forms* the warblog's textuality, necessarily affects its function as a social action, but not, I argue, uniquely in the ways theorized by Miller and Shepherd. For Miller and Shepherd, blogging is also a responsive phenomenon, but one which responds to the general demands of a voyeuristic culture, rather than to the specific commentaries of a readership community: "As our expectations of privacy increase, our expectations for receiving more information—our expectations about what is public—increase" (Calvert, 2000: 78). Although the technology of the Internet "makes it easier than ever for anyone to be either a voyeur or an exhibitionist—or both" (Miller and Shepherd, 2004), the traditional paper diary is also reacting to the shifting demarcations of the boundaries between private and public. One such diary, published in April 2006, to wide media coverage, was *The Notebook Girls*, a collective diary written by four girlfriends who currently attend an elite public school in Manhattan (Baskin et al., 2006). Printed in their own handwriting, with photos and doodles included, and reviewed as "sometimes distressing, often vulgar, and always self-involved", the diary chronicles their private thoughts about society, religion, race and self-esteem but also gives intimate details of their some of their sexual adventures and misadventures (Bradshaw, 2006). Focusing on sensationalist elements, US TV channel ABC's website headlined its feature on the diary with "Diary Reveals the Racy Life of Teens" and "Even these Good Students Experimented with Sex and Drugs".[3]

---

[3] See ABC News Good Morning America Site feature on the diary at http://abcnews.go.com/GMA/story?id=1846097&page=1

The Notebook Girls themselves do not, however, share bloggers' self-consciousness about the size of their potential readership communities, since, by their own admission, they never anticipated that their diary would be published. Unlike most bloggers, they regarded the potential exposure of their writing as an inhibiting, rather than motivating, factor: "Once we found out we were going to publish it, we had to stop writing because there is no way to write a diary knowing someone will read it and still sound like yourself"[4]. Such sentiments contrast with the tenure of Riverbend's opening post, which points to the existence of an audience as instrinsic to her conception of the viability of her blog: "So this is the beginning for me, I guess. I never thought I'd start my own weblog. All I could think, every time I wanted to start one, was 'but who will read it?'" (Riverbend, 2005: 5).

Miller and Shepherd's analysis takes bloggers' desire for exposure as their starting point. They argue that the *kairos* of the blog must be understood as evolving from two cultural trends related to the increasing destabilization of the separation between the private and public realms—the democratization of celebrity and the rise of mediated voyeurism. According to Myra Stark, the age of "democratic celebrity" was ushered in by the attacks of September 11th 2001, which heralded the end of the celebrity culture of sports heroes and entertainers of the 1980's and 1990's (Stark, 2003). In their place, a new heroic prototype was born, the *ordinary celebrity*, typified by fire-fighters and policemen who emerged from the Twin Towers. Stark points to the blurring of the distinction between celebrities and ordinary people in many areas of life, both in the entertainment industry (reality TV shows, talk shows) and in politics (from awards to ordinary activists to the elevation of Monica Lewinsky to star status) and on the Internet, where blogs "mak[e] it possible for people to reach out of obscurity [...] and become known to millions" (Stark, 2003). This was the case for Salam Pax, whose blog became an international sensation within weeks of being linked to Glenn Reynold's top *Instapundit* blog, and who has gone on to become a media celebrity, as well as a media player, with a Guardian column and guest television presentation to his name.

In the case of warblogs, the authors' desire for exposure may converge with readers' desire for sensationalist material. According to Calvert, one of the factors which drives mediated voyeurism is "the chance to observe real people as they face their moments of reckoning" or "moment of truth

---

[4] Citation taken from Susan Lehman's interview with the four girls at http://www.moleskinerie.com/2006/04/the_notebook_gi.html

attraction", borne of a displaced sense of identification: "As we watch these people confront these 'pulse-pounding' moments [...] a sense of 'it could happen to me' amongst audience members leads, in turn, to speculation about 'what if it really did happen to me?'" (Calvert, 2000: 64). The inherent unpredictability and risks of extreme situations, such as war, augment the sense of suspense generated by "live" narratives of the real: "If the basis of storytelling is the surprise of what is going to happen next, reality can be better than fiction because no one, not even the protagonists themselves, can predict the outcome" (Gabler, 2000). US soldier Colby Buzzell's infamous *Men in Black* post staged such a "moment of truth" with his "riveting account of a bloody firefight between his unit and scores of black-clad [Iraqi] insurgents", which reverberated through the global blogosphere (Kline and Burnstein, 2005: 265):

> People were hooting and hollering, yelling their war cries and doing the Indian yell thing as they drove off and locked and loaded their weapons. Bullets were pinging off our armor and you could hear multiple RPGs [rocket propelled grenades] being fired and flying through the air and impacting all around us. I never felt fear like this. I was like, this is it, I'm going to die. (quoted in Kline and Burnstein, 2005: 264-65)

Warbloggers themselves may also derive gratification from the risks involved in politically subversive acts of self-disclosure. Salam describes his compulsive need to continue blogging in the highly charged pre-invasion period, despite the risks of being apprehended by the Iraqi security services: "My friend Raj in Jordan emailed me and said 'look, you are turning into warblogger, be careful'. But by that time, I was too hooked, too excited about it and having so much fun that I couldn't stop" (Pax, 2004). For Salam, however, the personal risks of anti-regime blogging from within Iraq before "regime change" were so high that his action had the unexpected benefit of defying belief:

> They thought it could never be an Iraqi from within Iraq because it's just so foolish, so stupid to write something bad about Iraq or Saddam from within Iraq because obviously you end up in a very uncomfortable place. (Pax, 2004)

1.3. More than Exhibitionism

Salam Pax's chosen anonymity, a necessary precaution given his "almost giddy irreverence about Saddam's regime", points to another function of self-disclosure common to webloggers writing in war zones, which goes beyond the gratification of self-promotion (Katz, 2003: ix). In contexts where the public sphere is closely monitored and regulated by state forces, blogs act as *spaces of political and personal resistance*. To the extent that this resistance is externally directed and that the blog functions as a conduit for commentary on external events, warblogs "resist" the narcissism associated with exhibitionism. For journalists and civilians living in war zones, the blogging form presents the obvious and perhaps sole mechanism for expressing opinions without censure. As the Reporters Without Borders' *Handbook for Bloggers and Cyber-dissidents* puts it: "Bloggers are often the only real journalists in countries where the mainstream media is censured or under pressure" (2005, 5). The handbook aims to help bloggers living under repressive regimes to acquire the technical expertise to blog anonymously and to circumvent state-directed Internet filtering and monitoring, while ensuring that their blog is picked up by the major search engines (64).

Warblogs may provide a displaced conduit for sensationalist experience but they also function as alternative sources of information. But do warblogs reach and preach only to the converted or do they function as means of communication across political as well as cultural boundaries? According to Cass Sunstein, "new technologies, emphatically including the Internet, are dramatically increasing people's ability to hear echoes of their own voices and to wall themselves off from others" (quoted in Drezner and Farrell, 2004: 21). Arguing against the thesis of cyberapartheid, Jack Balkin points out that the technological features intrinsic to blogging which facilitate intense inter-commenting and cross-linking work against this kind of segregation (Balkin, 2004). Evidence from a 2004 Pew report, which includes an assessment of the US public's view on the war in Iraq, substantiates Balkin's view, concluding that Internet users "have a wider awareness of political arguments" and also "hear more challenging arguments" (Horrigan et al., 2004: i-ii). The wide range of political views within Salam's readership community further corroborates this, as do the attendant conflicting conspiracy theories surrounding his political allegiance: "Wonderfully, the conviction of those that he [Salam Pax] was a Baathist agent was matched only by the suspicion of others that was a Mossad or CIA operative" (Katz, 2003: x).

The range of political views expressed by Salam's readers not only problematizes the thesis of political self-segregation, it also attests to what Katz identifies as "the most compelling attributes of Salam's diaries: he directs vitriol in all directions" (xiii). The Manichaeism of the cyberapartheid argument is thus not only undermined by the plurality of political views represented in Salam's readership community, but also by Salam's own refusal to be "cocooned" into any particular political camp.

On 15 November 2002, he voices his ambivalence about the impending hostilities:

> I know the war is inevitable [...] and I know Saddam is a nutcase with a finger on the trigger. But this is my country and I love its people. There is no way you can convince me that war is OK [...] On an emotional level I cannot and will not accept a war in Iraq. But on the other hand...Look, there is no way I am going to say it, mainly because I don't trust the intentions of the American government. (Pax, 2003: 38)

Salam Pax and Riverbend's blogs' capacity to engage creatively with multiple perspectives and to enter into dialogues with individuals outside their own culture qualify them as "bridge blogs", a term coined by Iranian-Canadian journalist and weblogger Hossein Derakhshan. Derakhshan proposes three models for the ways people can use weblogs to communicate between cultures— windows, cafés and bridges:

> Windows allow us to look into another culture, but not interact [...] Cafés are complex spaces where groups of people can meet to discuss [in a context that would be impossible] in the real world, due to geography, politics or language. [...] Bridges are more interactive than windows, but less complex than cafés. They are usually the project of a single blogger or a small group of authors. Bridge bloggers write for an audience outside their everyday reality.[5]

The concept of bridge bloggers has been adopted by Harvard Law School's Berkman Center for Internet and Society, as the basis for setting up the *Global Voices Wiki* project (part of *Global Voices Online*, a "non-profit global citizens" media project"), which contains a growing global index of bridge bloggers[6]. The rationale behind the compilation of bridge blogs worldwide was to counter the biases of the mediasphere: "It [mainstream media] ignores many international stories [...] and when it does tackle them it tends to reinforce stereotypes about foreign countries rather than shed new light on them" (Boyd, 2003). Surprisingly perhaps, the drive to remedy stereotypes brings us back to the discussion of exhibitionism. A survey of participants in the sensationalist US TV talk-show *Donahue* found that the most commonly-expressed motivation of participants, especially by those who represented marginalized groups, was a "desire to remedy stereotypes and to educate a national audience

---

[5] http://www.globalvoicesonline.org/wiki/index.php/BridgeBlog
[6] http://www.globalvoicesonline.org/wiki/index.php/Main_Page

about discrimination and alternative lifestyles" (quoted in Calvert, 2000: 85). Similarly, two of the driving forces of bridge bloggers writing during the Iraqi war is the desire to *educate global audiences* and to *combat Western stereotypes* of Iraqi culture:

> I am female and Muslim. Before the occupation, I more or less dressed the way I wanted to. I lived in jeans and cotton pants and comfortable shirts. Now, I don't dare leave the house in pants. A long skirt and loose shirt (preferably with loose sleeves) has become necessary. A girl wearing jeans risks being attacked, abducted, or insulted by fundamentalists who have been... liberated! (Riverbend, 2005: 17)

1.4. The Sharing Economy

Riverbend and Salam's blogs function within two conflicting economies. As blogs they are situated by default within what Miller and Shepherd refer to as the culture of exhibitionism or within what Andrew Kitzmann terms an "economy of recognition" bolstered by technological functions which both facilitate and stimulate its growth (Kitzmann, 2003: 58): "I checked my stats today" writes Salam "and found out that I had been linked by Pandavox [...] The goddess of linkylove has blessed me. Burning that modem and doing my sacred linkwhore dance around it worked" (Pax, 2003: 3). Rankings produced by weblog search engines or by RSS readers generate lists of Top 100 blogs which, along with reader polls, are used to assign an increasingly wide range of blog awards. So while blogging is widely regarded as providing alternatives to mainstream media, it is also, paradoxically, proliferating "digital seals of approval" which are mimicking the "tropes and discourses of mainstream media" (Kitzmann, 2003: 58).

Riverbend and Salam Pax have secured both digital and non-digital symbols of recognition. Their book deals illustrate the phenomenon of bloggers crossing back into traditional print media, while the theatre production of Riverbend's blog is a rare example of a blog crossing over into the performance arts. While they undoubtedly circulate within the economy of recognition, I suggest that they also circulate within a second, conflicting Internet-based economy, dubbed *the Sharing Economy* by Yale Law Professor Yochai Benkler. Benkler uses the term in the context of an emerging Internet-based model of economic production, based on common-type behaviours or peer-production. *The Sharing Economy* refers to large-scale Internet-based projects which are produced as the result of the participation of large numbers of individuals, such as open-source software Linux, the volunteer-written online encyclopaedia Wikipedia or music-file sharing (Benkler, 2004: 275-81):

> My claim is not, of course, that we live in a unique moment of humanistic sharing. It is, rather, that our own moment in history suggests a more general observation: that the technological state of a society, particularly the extent to which individual agents can engage in efficacious production activities with material resources under their individual control, affects the opportunities for, and hence the comparative prevalence and salience of, social, market [...] and state production modalities. (278)

Although Benkler claims that new technologies are increasing the *economic value* of social behaviour by turning peer-production into something economically valuable, he does not expect this form of production to pose a major challenge to the market system. Blogs, which are more often the independent works of individuals, rather than contributions to a large scale production, are not included in Benkler's elaboration of the *Sharing Economy*. Salam and Riverbend's blogs have, however, entered into the Global Voices Wiki, a project which aims to exploit the collective power of bridge blogs as an information resource for general Internet users, academics and media representatives; as such, they circulate within this sharing economy. Bridge blogging is turning into something economically valuable, even though, to extend Benkler's argument, it does not represent a *major* challenge to mainstream media.

1.5. From Sam to Salam: Bridges and Walls

> People in the West never saw the people of Iraq, never understood the people of Iraq or saw the individual. It was always Saddam. Wars, sanctions, occupations, invasion of Kuwait and the rallies Saddam would hold – 'Long live Saddam, we love you, we go to death with you.' But we're not so very different from you. We have to do certain things because we need to live. At some point I realized that this is what the weblog is good for, basically putting the bridge there. (Pax, 2004)

The information, knowledge and connectivity provided by Salam and Riverbend's blogs—features which, according to Benkler, represent some of the most important products of the information economy—are intrinsically linked to one of the most significant achievements of their social/textual actions. As bridge blogs, they function as an antidote to "the portrayal of Iraqis as poor, anti-Western, frequently hysterical and altogether very different from us" (Katz, 2003: ix). This deconstruction of difference is, for some, a frightening prospect:

For there are closer ties between apparently warring civilizations than most of us would like to believe; both Freud and Nietzsche showed how the traffic across carefully maintained, even policed boundaries moves with often terrifying ease [...] Hence the altogether more reassuring battle orders (a crusade, good versus evil, freedom against fear, etc.) drawn out of Huntington's alleged opposition between Islam and the West... (Said, 2001)

Acting as a counter-current to the kind of facile reassurance provided by Huntington-style rhetoric, the fast flow of Internet traffic associated with Riverbend and Salam's blog provides, I believe, a different kind of reassurance, a closer comfort, not the "comfort of strangers" but the knowledge that "you are very not so different from me".

1.6. From Sam to Salam: Bridges and Barricades

Ironically, the mechanics of military aggression afforded both our contemporary Iraqi bloggers and our historic British diarist what we could call peer-recognition, and in both cases, acclaim was expressed in analogies from the semantic field of construction. But while Salam and Riverbend are recognized for their ability to build bridges across supposedly warring civilizations, Pepys was celebrated for erecting barricades in the interest of military expansionism: "To your praises", the orator of Oxford University declared to Pepys, "the whole ocean bears witness; truly, sir, you have encompassed Britain with wooden walls"—a reference to Pepys' doubling of Britain's naval force during his reign as Secretary for the Admiralty (Encyclopedia Britannica Online). Pepys established the Royal Navy as the world's greatest armada, a legacy he would bequeath to Nelson and which would live on to World War I, at the end of which, to go full circle, Britain would use its military might to take control of Salam and Riverbend's native land, duly baptising it the "State of Iraq".

Bibliography

Balkin, J. "What I Learned about Blogging in a Year". *Balkinization.* 2004.
http://balkin.blogspot.com/2004_01_18_balkin_archive.html#107480769112109137
Baskin, J., L. Newman, S. Pollitt-Cohen and C. Toombs. *The Notebook Girls*. Clayton: Warner, 2006.

Benkler, Y. "Sharing Nicely". *The Yale Law Journal,* 114. (2004): 273-358.
http://benkler.org/SharingNicely.html
Boyd, C. "Global Voices Speak through Blogs". *BBC News/Technology.* 2005. http://news.bbc.co.uk/2/low/technology/4414247.stm
Bradshaw, M. *The Notebook Girls.* Review. 2006.
http://www.watermarkbooks.com/review0506-007.html
Buzzell, C. *My War: Killing Time in Iraq.* New York: Putnam, 2005.
Calvert, C. *Voyeur Nation.* Boulder: Westview, 2000.
Dreznel, D.W. and H. Farrell. *The Power and Politics of Blogs.* 2004.
http://www.danieldrezner.com/research/blogpaperfinal.pdf
Gabler, N. "Behind the Curtain of TV Voyeurism". *The Christian Science Monitor.* 2006. http://www.csmonitor.com/2000/0707/p1s4.html
Horrigan J., K. Garrett and P. Resnick. *Pew Report – The Internet and Democratic Debate.* 2004.
http://www.pewinternet.org/pdfs/PIP_Political_Info_Report.pdf
Katz, I. "Introduction". *The Baghdad Blogger.* By Salam Pax. London: Atlantic, 2003.
Kitzmann, A. "That Different Place: Documenting the Self within Online Environments". *Biography* 26.1. (2003): 48-65.
Kline, D. and D. Burnstein. *Blog! How the Newest Media Revolution is Changing Politics, Business and Culture.* New York: CDS, 2005.
Lenhart, A. and S. Fox. *Pew Report – Bloggers: A Portrait of the Internet's New Storytellers.* 2006.
http://www.pewinternet.org/pdfs/PIP%20Bloggers%20Report%20july%2019%202006.pdf
Miller C. R. and D. Shepherd. "Blogging as Social Action: A Genre Analysis of the Weblog". *Into the Blogosphere: Rhetoric, Community and Culture of Weblogs.* 2004.
http://blog.lib.umn.edu/blogosphere/blogging_as_social_action_a_genre_analysis_of_the_weblog.html
Pax, S. *The Baghdad Blog.* London: Atlantic, 2003.
— ."Baghdad Blogger/Salam Pax: Video Reports from Iraq". *CBC Zed Gallery.* 2004.
http://zed.cbc.ca/go;jsessionid=aHLiZhWi8ofa?POS=5&CONTENT_ID=186317&c=contentPage
Pepys, S. *The Diary of Samuel Pepys.* http://www.pepysdiary.com/
Encyclopædia Britannica Online. 2006. http://search.eb.com/eb/article-5596
Reporters Without Borders. *Handbook for Bloggers and Cyber-Dissidents.* 2005.

http://www.rsf.org/IMG/pdf/handbook_bloggers_cyberdissidents-GB.pdf

Riverbend. *Baghdad Burning*. London: Marion Boyars, 2005.

Said, E. "The Clash of Ignorance". *The Nation.* 2001. http://www.thenation.com/docprint.mhtml?i=20011022&s=said

Stark, M. "You, Me, Celebrity". *Saatchi and Saatchi 2003: Ideas from Trends*. 2003. http://www.saatchikevin.com/workingit/myra_stark_2003ideastrends.html

Van Dijck, J. "Composing the Self: Of Diaries and Lifelogs". *Fibreculture* 3. 2004. http://journal.fibreculture.org/issue3/issue3_vandijck.html

CHAPTER TWENTY

FROM HYPERTEXTS TO BLOGS:
EL PRIMER VUELO DE LOS HERMANOS WRIGHT
AND *MÁS RESPETO, QUE SOY TU MADRE*

PERLA SASSÓN-HENRY

Latin American hyperfiction has been emerging and developing since the mid-nineties. Advances in technology have provided authors with new approaches to portray and explore the intricate relationship between the content of their Latin American hyperfictions and the technical means used to convey their messages. *Extreme Conditions* (1996) by Juan B. Gutiérrez is a landmark in Latin American hyperfiction, and one of the only Latin American hyperfictions that has been the subject of an in-depth scholarly critical analysis.[1] There are, however, other pioneering Latin American hyperfictions that also deserve critical attention, such as *El Primer Vuelo de los Hermanos Wright* (1996-2006) by Juan B. Gutiérrez and *Más respeto, que soy tu madre* by Hernán Casciari (2003-2005), recipient of the Deutsche Welle International Weblog Awards 2005. Whereas the former uses adaptive hypertext to explore what its author calls "the social vices of our 'America Latina'" (Gutiérrez, 2005), the second inaugurates the *blogonovela* genre[2] to portray a variety of issues present in contemporary Argentina.

Thematically, *El primer vuelo de los hermanos Wright* and *Más respeto, que soy tu madre* refer to social, political, economic and moral

---

[1] "*Condiciones extremas*: Digital Science Fiction from Colombia" by Susana Pajares Tosca in *Latin American Literature and Mass Media*, ed. Edmundo Díaz Soldán and Debra Castillo, 2001.
[2] According to Casciari the word *blogonovela* appeared for the first time in a technological dictionary published in Portugal in 2003. For further reference see Hernán Casciari: "El *blog* en la literatura. Un acercamiento estructural a la blogonovela".

issues which reveal aspects of an early twentieth century Colombian society and of a more contemporary Argentine society respectively. Whereas the former relies on the dynamics of the inhabitants of a small Colombian town to describe what is typical of a small, isolated Colombian village, the latter uses the Bertottis, an Argentine family of Italian descent, to portray the relationships between the members of Mirta Bertotti's family, and to bring to the fore the most commonly discussed topics at the core of a middle-class Argentine family. Gutiérrez's town of Villapintada takes us back in time to a small Colombian town which transcends time and space.[3] Here, the author portrays man's nature via a thorough description of the characters and the intricate relationships between them, a style which is reminiscent of Gabriel Garcia Marquez's *A Hundred Years of Solitude*. The universality of the topics developed reminds the reader of the Borgesian claim that "[w]hat one man does is something done, in some measure, by all men" (Borges, 120). In Gutiérrez's novel, what happens in Villapintada and the interactions between its inhabitants echo the social dynamics in Latin America, which seem to be rooted in long established traditions that have enhanced the gap between rich and poor. In reference to Villapintada Gutiérrez states:

> Caminatas en Villapintada eran el principal acto social de sus habitantes. Primero estaban las caminatas, luego las invitaciones a tomar chocolate, luego la misa, luego las fiestas del pueblo, luego las fiestas particulares y por último los entierros. En ese orden crecía el acartonamiento, la incomodidad y la expectación, y en orden inverso la frecuencia. Los entierros tenían especial encanto si se llevaban a cabo en la parte rica, pues usualmente había cena en casa del difunto. El cementerio estaba dividido por un muro y cada parte tenía entradas independientes. Pero era el mismo lote, porque el párroco de la época de la fundación se negó a santificar dos terrenos por el precio de uno. (Los paseantes)[4]
>
> (Taking walks in Villapintada was the main social activity among its inhabitants. First were the walks, then the invitations to have chocolate, then Mass, then the town parties, then individual parties, and lastly the funerals. Social rigidity, discomfort and expectations increased, in this order, whereas frequency was in reverse order. Funerals had a special charm if they took place in the rich part of town because there was usually a dinner at the house of the deceased. The cemetery was divided by a wall and each part had independent entrances. It was the same lot, because when

---

[3] According to Juan B. Gutiérrez, Villapintada was modelled on the town of Salamina, Caldas, Colombia.
[4] To cite a paragraph, I will refer to the name of the lexia cited in the hypertext.

they were inaugurated, the priest refused to bless two lots for the price of one.)

Gutiérrez's characters fill the town of Villapintada with a polyphony of voices that underscores the characters' social class and status. Life in Villapintada goes on with almost no dramatic changes until the arrival of Amadeo Artemoso, an intriguing character who awakens curiosity among the *villapintanos*. It is his positive and adventurous personality that takes him to this remote location where he is considered a strange outsider. He is an engineer who arrives in town and settles down in Doña Severa Alegría's inn with the prospect of developing and implementing a pioneering technological project. Amadeo's plan is to build a cable car that will put an end to Villapintada's isolation from the rest of the world and at the same [time] develop the transportation of local products to other areas. According to Gutiérrez, Amadeo Artemoso is the "middle class representative, literate, trying to survive and sometimes doing questionable things" (2006).

Traditions, beliefs and stereotypes abound in Gutiérrez's hypernovel, where each character stands for a specific group in Latin American society. The López family stands for the aristocracy; as Villapintada's town mayor, Godofredo López is respected in his community. He and his wife Eulalia form the core of aristocratic social gatherings, many of which are offered at their home. The Lópezs have a single twenty year-old daughter named Clara and two young sons, Alfredo and Maurizio, who, in order to show a certain degree of independence from their father, do not hesitate to poison a whole town for fun.

Gutiérrez includes several meta-narratives in his hypernovel. His use of this technique results in a very rich environment that brings about parallel stories within the narrative. This sophisticated and delicately interwoven literary fabric allows the author to bring to the fore issues such as the role of the philosopher, the Church and the women in the town of Villapintada. It is on these three roles that I will focus. In *El primer vuelo de los hermanos Wright*, the author relies on the character of Sócrates Lorenzo, a writer, to narrate most of the meta-narratives. Sócrates stands for the intellectuals in Latin America. Like a story within a story, the lexia "El reflexista" takes the reader to a writer's world and creative process where Socrates envisions the character of Rosita, an independent woman, as implemented by Gutiérrez in his novel. According to Gutiérrez, "intellectuals in Latin America devote more time to intellectual activities than to action" (Gutiérrez 2006). By "intellectual activities" Gutiérrez means the act of writing, which he believes is a way of influencing society. Nevertheless, such an activity "can be totally ineffective in a region of the world with high rates of illiteracy" (Gutiérrez, 2006).

Gutiérrez also refers in his hypernovel to the long-standing and powerful presence of the Catholic Church in Latin America. In one of his stories, Sócrates writes about a friar called Leonardo Baz. The story highlights the constant struggle between good and evil among the members of the Church: *"Fray Leonardo Baz tuvo una mente aguda, inquisitiva, y mucho más adelantada que las de sus contemporáneos" (Leonardo Baz, el notable maestro)*. ["Friar Leonardo Baz had a sharp, inquisitive mind that was more advanced that those of his contemporaries."] Friar Leonardo's charismatic personality and love of the outdoors leads him to teach publicly in Calle de los Comerciantes, where he finds both his unhappiness and happiness among his audience. In the end, Friar Leonardo is expelled from the Church for his eloquent speeches to women and sentenced to die at the stake; however, he finds a way to vindicate himself and escape with his beloved.

In another section of this hypernovel (*Invitación a tomar chocolate*), Gutiérrez draws attention to the figure of Father Mateo Apóstol to remind the reader of the powerful role of the Church in all issues pertaining to Villapintada. Here, Father Mateo allows Amadeo Artemoso to present his ground-breaking ideas during the mass homily, thus almost guaranteeing the success of Amadeo's project.

The role of women plays a prominent part in Gutiérrez's hyperfiction. Rosita is new to the town of Villapintada. She is a school teacher and rents a room in Doña Severa Alegría's inn. It is here where the dialogue and interaction among its inhabitants give the reader a glimpse of the dynamics of the middle class. In reference to Rosita, Gutiérrez states, "Rosita is independent and symbolizes the advance of women in Latin American society, from not having the right to own property at the beginning of the twentieth century to becoming presidents of several Latin American countries" (Gutiérrez, 2006). Her character is also important because she is a catalyst figure in two meta-narratives as well as in the main story. In all three cases her beauty and intelligence lead to situations that raise relevant social and moral issues.

Hypernovels for the Twenty-first Century

Juan Gutiérrez envisioned and designed the first version of *El primer vuelo de los hermanos Wright,* the first Latin American hypernovel, in 1995. This literary piece, written between 1996 and 1997 was on the Web for a very brief period of time until its author removed it from public access until October 2005. Since then, to take advantage of the technological developments of his time, Gutiérrez has regarded *El primer vuelo de los hermanos Wright* as a digital narrative that deserves to grow and develop to convey the possibilities of Latin American electronic literature in the twenty-first century. In so doing, Gutiérrez's piece has evolved from a traditional hypernovel designed in Macromedia Dreamweaver to a sophisticated literary piece which relies on an innovative adaptive hypertext authoring system called Literatronic.

According to Gutiérrez, "Literatronic is an artificial intelligence engine that designs a fiction book specific to every reader based on her or his interaction with the system" (2006b). This adaptive hypertext system informs readers of the percentage of lexias they have read, thus avoiding that "helpless feeling of not knowing when a piece will end" (Marino, 2006). A recent review of this authoring system informs us that "Literatronic is a dynamic authoring system which, instead of relying solely on static hypertext links (for the system allows these as well), uses an AI engine to recommend the three next best lexias based on what you have already read" (Marino, 2006). Literatronic allows authors to input their lexias and determine which lexias should be linked to each other. "Authors assign a numeric *distance* between lexias. A passage which follows easily, or without much interpretative work, might be assigned a 5, while a passage that is distantly related might be a 25" (Marino, 2006). From the readers' perspective, Literatronic provides clearly defined multiple possibilities that lead to unique readings. In Literatronic "the computer is between the author and the reader to become one more element (that did not exist before) in the literary exchange. The system has a certain level of autonomy. It seems to be a follow-up of Marshall McLuhan's claim that "the medium is the message". In this case "the medium acts on the message" (Gutiérrez, 2006).

As a testimony to the possibilities that technology has provided for the development of digital literature in Spanish, Hernán Casciari started his blog novel *Más respeto, que soy tu madre (*also known as *Weblog de una mujer gorda)* on September 26, 2003. Casciari, an Argentine journalist and writer, developed his blog novel while living in Barcelona as a way "to channel his nostalgia" for his native country (Fajardo). The author's native town of Mercedes, its people and its places were his sources of inspiration for this blog novel, which relies on first person narrative to add vividness to the daily entries. Similarly, this first person narrative also causes the author to almost vanish under the provocative roles of the characters.

Even though Casciari's style and use of the digital medium is quite different from Gutiérrez's, there is no doubt that Casciari's work brings a unique contribution to Latin American electronic literature. In the first place, it is the first blog in Spanish which was remediated into a print version.[5] Nowadays, many print works are transformed from print into a new digital rendition, but *Weblog de una mujer gorda* became the first blog to transcend the digital realm and become the book *Más respeto, que soy tu madre*.[6] As the creator of the *blogonovela* Casciari claims:

> La blogonovela es un género literario porque necesariamente debe cumplir unas determinadas reglas. Como, por ejemplo, que el protagonista hable permanentemente en primera persona; que sea consciente del formato que está utilizando (en este caso el blog); que se enfoquen temas de actualidad, pero en el momento preciso en que ocurren; y que nunca dentro del formato se diga que es ficción. (Casciari, 2005)

> (The blog novel is a literary genre because it has to abide by certain rules; for example, the main character always speaks in the first person, he or she is aware of the format he or she is using (in this case the blog), the blogs bring into focus current events at the very moment they take place, and the fact it is fiction is never disclosed.)

Más respeto, que soy tu madre: Diario de Mirta Bertotti narrates the everyday life of Mirta Bertotti and her family. The Bertottis represent a typical middle-class Argentine family. The leading and narrative force of this blog novel is Mirta Bertotti, a fifty-two year- old housewife who recently lost her job as a shop assistant and whose son has suggested that she start a daily journal on the Internet. Mirta's grumpy husband is unemployed, but in spite of this, he is, in her own words, "a saint" (*"Quién es Zacarías Estanislao Bertotti: La familia uno por uno"*). Nacho, Caio and Sofi are the Bertotti's children; each of them stands for one aspect of the diverse Argentine society of today. Nacho used to be

---

[5] I use the term *remediated* in reference to Jay Bolter's and Richard Grusin's definition of *remediation*. According to Bolter and Grusin "[they] call the representation of one medium in another remediation, and [they] will argue that remediation is a defining characteristic of the new digital media. What might seem at first to be an esoteric practice is so widespread that we can identify a spectrum of different ways in which digital media remediate their predecessors, a spectrum depending on the degree of perceived competition or rivalry between the new media and the old (45). In *Más respeto que soy tu madre*, Casciari has performed what I called a reversed traditional remediation, whereby the digital literary text paves the way for the creation of its printed counterpart.

[6] *Más respeto que soy tu madre: Una novela sobre la mujer que nos parió* was published in October 2005 by Plaza & Janés, Spain.

gay. He is the eldest and most educated member of the family. Caio and Sofi are two typical adolescents. Whereas Caio has dropped out of high school, does nothing all day and gets along well with his grandfather for a soon-to-be disclosed reason, Sofi is an attractive fifteen year-old girl who has discovered the Internet as a way to meet boyfriends who "double her in age" (*"Quién es Sofía Mirta Sofí Bertoti: La familia uno por uno"*).

No Italian-Argentine family could exist without a Nonno (Italian for grandfather). In the Bertottis' case, the Nonno has "severe regression" and believes he is "a misunderstood adolescent" (*"Quién es Américo Nonno Bertotti: La familia uno por uno"*). A hint of hyper-realism is added to the story when the reader finds out about the Nonno's Chinese girlfriend and his marihuana liaison with Caio, his grandson. At the other end of the generational spectrum, the reader encounters Zacarías junior, Mirta's adorable baby grandson.

Language deserves special attention because of its diversity and its role in the narrative as a catalyst for communication among readers. When asked if readers play a special role in the creation of the Bertottis, Casciari explains that each chapter concludes with a section where readers express their opinions and write to the characters. These readers' comments helped him to determine the upcoming entries to Mirta's journal. (Friera)

Since the Bertottis use Argentine colloquial language, which is not always understood by all Spanish speakers, Casciari implemented a hypertextual glossary for readers. As the blog novel developed, he realized that the actual discussion on colloquialisms among his blog readers was much more useful than his original glossary (Friera). In this way, Mirta's journal became not only a literary reading piece but a catalyst that led to linguistic interaction among Spanish-speaking readers from around the world.

There is no doubt that even though the origins of Casciari's blog novel can be traced back to the popular instalment novels of the early twentieth century, which were published by newspapers to increase readership among the working classes, in its digital form *Más respeto, que soy tu madre* provides a unique and mesmerizing approach to a contemporary portrayal of Argentina in the twenty-first century. Similarly, thanks to the technological advances of our times, Gutiérrez's hypernovel *El primer vuelo de los hermanos Wright* recreates itself from the first original Latin American hypernovel to the first original Latin American adaptive hypertext fiction. If in its original version this hypernovel was a groundbreaking literary piece showcasing "some of the vices of Latin America," in its recent form, this latest generation hypertext is a clear example of how advances in technology can lead readers to rediscover and create their unique interpretation of the perpetual moral vices and virtues of Latin America. From this perspective, *El primer vuelo de los hermanos Wright* and *Más respeto, que soy tu madre* mark a promising future for Latin American digital literature in Spanish and comparative literature.

Bibliography

Bolter, J and R. Grusin. *Remediation: Understanding New Media,* 45. Cambridge, MA: MIT Press, 1998.
Borges, J. L. *Ficciones.* New York: Grove Press. 1962.
Casciari, H. *Más respeto, que soy tu madre.* 2003.
  http://mujergorda.bitacoras.com/archives.php
—. "El *blog* en la literatura. Un acercamiento estructural a la blogonovela." *Telos, 65,* 2005.
  http://www.campusred.net/telos/articulocuaderno.asp?idarticulo=5&rev=65
—. Interview with Terra. "Hernán Casciari, creador de la blogonovela: 'En España no se puede vivir de los blogs, a no ser que tengas una idea absolutamente revolucionaria'." 2005b.
  http://www.terra.es/tecnologia/articulo/html/tec13202.htm
—. *Más respeto, que soy tu madre.* Spain: Plaza & Janés Editores, S.A., 2005.
Fajardo, D. Interview with Hernan Casciari. "Hernán Casciari, autor del 'Mejor Blog del Mundo': 'Ojalá que muchos escritores se atrevan'."
  http://www.edicionesespeciales.elmercurio.com/destacadas/detalle/index.aspidnoticia=0129122005021X0060028&idcuerpo=402
Friera, S. Interview with Hernán Casciari. "Entrevista a Hernán Casciari, autor de la popular y premiada blogonovela "Los Bertotti": "No sé cómo llegué al segundo capítulo"
  http://www.pagina12.com.ar/diario/suplementos/espectaculos/2-1213-2005-12-07.html
García Márquez, G. *One Hundred Years of Solitude.* New York: Harper Collins, 2004.
Gutiérrez, J. B. *El primer vuelo de los hermanos Wright* (Version1), 1996.
  http://www.literatronica.com/wright/el_primer_vuelo.htm
—. *Condiciones extremas.* 1998-2000.
  http://www.literatronica.com/condex_ver_2/condiciones.htm
—. E-mail to the author. 11 Oct. 2005.
—. E-mail to the author. 29 Aug. 2006.

—. *El primer vuelo de los hermanos Wright* (Version 2), 2006. http://www.literatronica.com/src/Pagina.aspx?lng=HISPANIA&opus=11&pagina=1

—. "Literatronic: Adaptive Hypertext." 2006b. http://www.literatronica.com/src/Initium.aspx?lng=BRITANNIA&opus=12&pagina=&nuntius=&artifex=

Marino, M. "Literatrónica: The Next Generation of Hypertext Authoring." 2006. http://writerresponsetheory.org/wordpress/2006/05/22/literatronica

Pajares Tosca, S. "Condiciones Extremas: Digital Science Fiction from Colombia" in *Latin American Literature and Mass Media*, E. Díaz Soldán and D. Castillo (ed.). New York: Garland Publishing, (2001) 271-287.

CHAPTER TWENTY ONE

SPANISH LITERATURE IN THE DIGITAL DOMAIN: CULTURE, NATION AND NARRATIONS

DOLORES ROMERO LÓPEZ

> "For the last twenty years the technology of writing has been overdue for a *paradigm shift*"
> —Stuart Moulthrop (1989)

Introduction

Until now, new digital formats have affected at least three aspects of literature: 1.- The publication of literary texts . 2.- The teaching of literature via the Internet and 3.- New critical contributions based on hypertext theory[1] .

There is also a fourth aspect that transcends Information and Communication Technology (ICT) to situate the virtual within the sphere of the cultural. I refer to literature that is both conceived and written on the Net, which develops interdisciplinary narrative structures and codes. Today, digital literature is a nascent reality in Hispanic circles. Digital culture does not comprise only the internationalization of spaces that have to do with work, leisure, education and commerce; these very spaces generate virtual communities, where technology is converted into a powerful agent of exchange with new frontiers. Cyberculture is not only a cyberspace in which the genuine is subordinate to the power of virtual relativization, where social conscience blurs identity and the local

---

[1] See references: Amat, Borrás, Cano, Pajares, Romero-Sanz, Sánchez Mesa, Sanz-Romero, Soldán, Vega, Vilariño-Abuín, Vouillamoz.

becomes globalized. I agree with the Czech, Jakub Maceb (2005) (see the attached table) that virtual communities are incorporating the dynamics of production and consumption of new technologies, and that they advance from information and communication (Morse, 1998 and Manovich, 2001) towards spaces that are more utopian (Hawk, 1993, and Lévy, 1997), more anthropological (Escobar, 1994, and Hakken, 1999) and more epistemological (Manovich, 2003, and Lister, 2003), spaces in which the creation of a cultural and literary identity is possible.

	Utopian concepts of cyberculture	Information concepts of c.	Anthropological concepts of c.	Epistemological concepts of c.
Concept	- cyber-culture as a form of utopian society changed through ICT - anticipating futuro-logism	- cyber-culture as cultural (symbolical)codes of the information society - analytical, partly anticipating	- cyberculture as cultural practices and life styles related to ICT - analytical, oriented to the present state and to history	- cyber-culture as term for social and anthropological reflection of new media
Authors	Andy Hawk – Future Culture Manifesto (1993) Pierre Lévy – Kyberkultura (1997, česky 2000)	Margaret Morse – Virtualities: Television, Media Art and Cyberculture (1998) Lev Manovich – The Language of a New Media. (2001)	Arturo Escobar – Welcome to Cyberia: Notes on the Atrhopology of Cyberculture (1994, zde 1996) David Hakken – Cyborgs@Cyberspace (1999)	Lev Manovich – New Media from Borges to HTML (2003) Lister a spol. – New Media: A Critical Introduction (2003)

Figure 1.- Jakub Macek:"Defining Cyberculture"
http://macek.czechian.net/defining_cyberculture. Retrieved on 15-07-2007

The aim of this chapter is to try and throw some light, insofar as this is possible, on the diabolical game that exists in digital literature, between universal literary principles and cultural differences that would corroborate the need to discuss digital literatures in relation to each of our own particular literary nations (Romero, 2006). This objective arises from a double need at professional level (which is no less diabolical). On the one hand, we should decide when and how to integrate these new creative digital texts into the curricula of university arts faculties, where any new subject matter is usually required to fit in with institutional principles that encourage tradition. On the other hand, it is our duty as historians, literary critics and theorists to give this sort of literature its own living space in order to justify the expectations of it becoming the avant-garde expression of a new cultural identity appropriate for the 21st century.

Hyper-Universals

Generally, Digital Literature refers to literary issues related to cyber-literature, for example, hyperfiction, hyperpoetry, hyperperformance, etc. The Electronic Literature Organization offers the following definition of digital literature:

> Works with important literary aspects that take advantage of the capabilities and contexts provided by the stand-alone or networked computer. Within the broad category of electronic literature are several forms and threads of practice, some of which are:
> • Hypertext fiction and poetry, on and off the Web.
> • Kinetic poetry presented in Flash and using other platforms.
> • Computer art installations which ask viewers to read them or otherwise have literary aspects.
> • Conversational characters, also known as chatterbots.
> • Interactive fiction,
> • Novels that take the form of emails, SMS messages, or blogs,
> • Poems and stories that are generated by computers, either interactively or based on parameters given at the beginning.
> • Collaborative writing projects that allow readers to contribute to the text of a work.
> • Literary performances online that develop new ways of writing. (URL: http://www.eliterature.org/about/)

In other words, almost everything can pass for electronic literature as long as "important literary aspects" are perpetuated. At the present time, we have to ask ourselves: Are these "important literary aspects" an exact replica of literary principles belonging to the printed tradition? Or do they assume a change in the definition of the very concept of literature? For some critics, digital literature implies a new literary genre, while for others it is merely a new way of experimenting with literature—indeed, the only way in which literature can currently experience new forms of creation.

Specialized criticism has added a series of clichés to this very global definition of digital literature, which are constantly repeated in digital text analysis. Thus, taking as a reference the definition of hypertext based on the analysis of a few experimental works , hypertext theorists have concerned themselves with five aspects: collectivity , the death of the author (Toschi, 2004), the break-up of linearity (Aarseth, 1993 y 1997), the demythification of the canon and the democratization of art (Gómez

Trueba, 2005). Digital literary text has to be multilinear, multimedia, multiple in form and content, interactive and dynamic (Pajares, 1997). Adjectives such as these describe different postmodern theoretical contributions, based on Julia Kristeva's intertextuality, Roland Barthes' lexias, Mikhail Bakhtin's textual polyphony, Foucault's networks of power, Pilles Deleuze and Félix Guattari's rhizomes, Derridean expansive tests and Wolfgang Iser and Stanley Fish's evolution of communication systems.

The transposing of theoretical postmodernism to the digital medium, and the appeal of prestigious international writers (Sterne, Joyce, Cortazar and Borges) whose creativity motivated them to offer more than one way of reading their texts, are the two great pillars sustaining those who look favourably on digital literature; at the same time, they can use it to combat techno-phobic criticism and an entire generation of 'chalk and talk' teachers. Digital versatility is used to attack the tyranny of the line, the rigidity of the canon, patriarchy, imperialism and logocentrism. Moreover, in their desire for innovation and cybernetic perpetuation, critics talk of digital literature as establishing a useful parallel with the avant-garde movements of the early twentieth century, because of the convergence of artistic codes and the wish of the creators to redefine things literary, giving them new cultural, technological and scientific connotations.

From my point of view, literary hypertext theory is way ahead of digital literary praxis, and is providing this with both ideas on construction and historical justification. Indeed, the research I'm presenting now has arisen from the need to take stock of the digital literary praxis written in Spanish so far in the Hispanic world.

Hyper-Nations

A further step in this ordeal I'm subjecting you to is the 'linking' of two concepts that are in themselves already separately 'in conflict': digital literature and literary nationalism. The way I see it, these two concepts are the new signs of historical identity in twenty-first century literary theory. As far as I know, it hasn't yet occurred to any critic to establish a link between them. This is because until now digital literature has been a sample of what the last International Congress of the ICLA has predicted: the breaking up of binarism, the discontinuity and displacement of things literary, the standardization of taste, the universalization of criticism, and on top of this, cultural and political liberalism. It seems as if digital literature were a sublimation of the theoretical desire that critics have been seeking: the 'uncorseting' of linear thought spawned in the era of print.

From the moment we focus research on digital literature not only on text analysis or a particular technique, but also on its ontology (definition, limits and functions) within the institution and the teaching discipline, other elements appear (in addition to the universal ones mentioned above), related to linguistic, territorial and cultural determination. It is at this moment that the universal passes to the particular and the theoretical to the empirical in the historical context. The theorists Benedict Anderson (in his *Imagined Communities* [1983]) and Homi Bhabha (in *Nation and Narration* [1990] and *The Location of Culture* [1994]) define the nation as a narrative. The idea of nation/narrative in the print era was space, race, religion, language and soul. Since the advent of the new digital rhizomatic narrativity, however, it has been a dissemination of complex dialogues, of relationships that move like a shuttle back and forth across the loom, from the universal to the particular and vice versa, from prose to poetry and vice-versa, from letters to images and vice-versa, from Spanish to English and vice-versa, creating a network of international, intercultural and transliterary links that give rise to the hyper-nation, which is always on the move, always in universal chaos and with its own particular order.

Hyper-Hispanisms

I can't begin an approach of this topic without referring to a quotation from the book *De la grammatologie* (1967) by Jacques Derrida :

> Il faut commencer quelque part où nous sommes et la pensée de la trace, qui ne peut pas ne pas tenir compte du flair, nous a déjà enseigné qu'il était impossible de justifier absolument un point de départ. Quelque part où nous sommes: En un texte déjà où nous croyons être (1967: 233).

If we follow Derrida's indications just this once, we will first have to situate the "text" we believe we are in, which is none other than the context of early twenty-first century Spain, a country with concerns relating to nationalism but at the same time internationally open, especially towards Western Europe and Latin America.

Over the last year, I have been investigating the Net in search and capture of digital literature. The only limitation I put on my search was linguistic: texts had to be written in Spanish. As a basis of the creation, the Spanish language brings Literary Nations together. I can only offer here a few very brief and perhaps rather disjointed conclusions. As digital literature is found on the channel of communication that is the Web, I thought it would be interesting to analyse four fundamental aspects of this process: firstly, we will comment on the cultural context supporting the emergence of digital literature in Spanish; secondly, we will determine from the poster's perspective who the authors of these texts are and why they write digital literature; thirdly, respecting the message, we will establish a repertory of texts we have come across; and finally, with regard to reception, we will analyse who these texts are aimed at.

A. Context

Digital literature is promoted in a context that is provided with a network of directories or portals. The most important of these are:
- The one directed by José Luis Orihuela from the University of Pamplona (http://mccd.udc.es/orihuela/hyperfiction/) dedicated to hyperfiction in Spanish
- The Hipertulia magazine of the Complutense University of Madrid (http://www.ucm.es/info/especulo/hipertul/)
- The Web of the Hermeneia group (Universidat Oberta de Catalunya, http://www.uoc.edu/in3/hermeneia/cat/)
- The hyperfictions portal of the Pompeu Fabra University (http://www.iua.upf.es/~berenguer/recursos/narr/portada.htm)
- The Open Directory Project (http://dmoz.org/World/Espa%c3%b1ol/Artes/)
- The portal on the digital story of the University Javeriana in Colombia.

B. Authors

Most of the authors are unknown , but they always leave some interesting trails in the work they publish online. Authorship is generally shared: the story's inventors collaborate with the technicians who develop it into a hypertextual format. Quite a few hypertextual digital writing projects are done by students of journalism, who undertake this sort of university work under the guidance of their teachers. Perhaps because of this, the texts they create are in a style that, to a large extent, is adapted to the taste of the young people of today: There are collages of chats and e-mails; images are mixed with words and music; the influence of the comic is strongly felt. The favourite themes of these recent creations are adventures and diaries. The characters are, for the most part, young people with young people's problems, involving identity, falling in and out of love, social conflict, etc.

It is no trivial matter that the rise in new digital literature has links to the university world. I would remind you that this has been customary throughout the history of literature; think back to the medieval clerics in their monasteries, which gave rise to the first universities, or to the humanists during the Renaissance, the eighteenth century innovators, or the many intellectuals of the twentieth century. In this sense, literary history repeats itself: we are confronted with a form of literature associated with educated creators, and behind each educated creator there is a library established by virtue of the programmes of studies taught at universities. These generally consist of books from Anglo-Saxon universities or versions translated into Spanish.

C. Repertory

While tracking down hyperliterature in the directories referred to, we find that we can already count on a repertory of twenty-eight examples (see the Anexo at the end of the chapter).

Although the boundary between different literary genres in electronic virtuality is very imprecise, criticism continues to offer similarities between these texts and the three great classical genres: poetry, prose and theatre .

In the sphere of so-called hyperpoetry, we find a gradation from the simplest digitalization of the poem to hypertextuality and the creation of holopoetry, which is the most complex form of hypertextual poetry. This is the case in *Un relato de amor/desamor* by Ainara Echaniz, a story about love and the absence of love between adolescents, in which the reader selects the texts according to two versions: happy times and unhappy times. Part of the story is made up of the love poems of the Chilean poet, Pablo Neruda, around which the theme of this narrative revolves .

The multilingual text *El idioma de los pájaros* by Belén Gache, deserves a paragraph of its own. In this, birds sing and recite in unison poems by well-known poets, in which the main characters are themselves birds: Accordingly, we hear: "Volverán las oscuras golondrinas" by Gustavo Adolfo Bécquer, "Leda" by Rubén Darío,"The raven" by Edgar Allan Poe, "Le paon" by Guillome Apollinaire and "Le cygne" by Charles Baudelaire.

There are two other poems that embody the tradition of experimental poetry and what is currently called holopoetry. These are two texts by Santiago Ortiz. The first, created in 2004, is entitled *Bacterias* and consists of moving words and phrases linked up to each other that reproduce as if they were bacteria when one of the node-lexias is clicked on. The centre of the false lexical bacteria is coloured, depending on the type of food they eat. The thickness of their centre determines the energy of their relations. The different terms seem to be taken straight from chaos theory or deconstruction. The second text created by Santiago Ortiz is *Diorama*, made up of a relational network of concepts, texts, images, interactive applications, links and references in a navigable space. The contents consist of a collection of information and a reflection on the language and codes. Three forms and uses of code in particular are identified, operating in very different surroundings while at the same time being closely connected: the code generating life [genetic code], the code generating narrative [languages], and the code generating models and systems of representation [computer code]. When we are immersed in this mechanized universe, it seems as if we are actually inside artificial intelligence, where philosophy, science and technology are finally united and 'paradise lost' is regained .

In hyperfiction, I have come across two novels. One of them, which is well-known and has been well-studied, is *Condiciones extremas*, by the Colombian author, Juan B. Gutiérrez. The plot is based on intrigue, quests, persecutions, kidnappings and enigmas, set against a background of hunger for power, ambition, social climbing, racism and fear; it is also a critical reflection on the levels of contamination on our planet and to what extremes these can go. The same plot is further developed in his latest work: *The First Flight of the Wright Brothers*, which, despite its title is in Spanish only. Another hypernovel is *Como el cielo los ojos* by the Sevillian writer, Edith Checa, based on intertextual links and relationships. Once we press access to the novel, a grid appears with an eye in each square. On the vertical axis are three names and on the horizontal one the numbers one to thirteen: three characters, thirteen time frames and one novel, triggered by one single event: "Isabel is dead..."

The diversity in the short stories we have found enables us to classify them into subdivisions:

1.- Firstly, in the subcategory of "intrigue fiction", the hyperstory *Puntos de vista* by Libe Otegui y Andrés Salaberri is worthy of mention, about some fringe characters who frequent a bar in "Puesamonyola" Street. Pello Gutiérrez Peñalba's text *¿Quién es Luis Durán?* belongs to the crime category and offers us two ways of reading the story, one linear and the other interactive. A search is being carried out for a missing man by an inspector and the man's ex-wife who does not trust the inspector.

2.- A second subcategory in hyperfiction is the autobiography. An example of this is the text by Isabel Ara and Iñaki Lorenzo, *Nada tiene sentido*, which was conceived as the digital diary of a narrator who is desperate because he cannot leave his room; the only thing he can do is write how he feels on his computer screen. The text is highly original and the plot progresses until we realize that we are reading the reflections of a schizophrenic who ends up completely losing the logical order of words and who literally goes mad. What is more, if we go a bit further, we may well think that the madman in front of the machine is our own ego.

This autobiographical subcategory is the hypertextual representation of identity related to the history of mentalities in which it is not only the ego that is the centre of beliefs in modern autobiography; we not only have to confront the disintegration of the ego but the annulment of human identity proscribed by the machine—a solipsism that produces schizophrenia, the fragmentation of the real ego to dissolve in virtual space

D. Public

In all the cases mentioned, the creator gives the reader the power to direct the text wherever he or she wants, but always has a hand in marking out the course. This semi-organization relates to the realization of an old dream: that of making the reader participate in production of the work. Reading can be understood as a path, a route along which each reader progresses though the text by paving a way through fragmented units. This is an established characteristic.

Conclusions

After writing these reflections, I seem to have more unanswered questions now than when I began this short treatise:
- With which theoretical criteria ought we to interpret digital texts? With traditional ones? Or ought we to create a new critical theory using the Web itself?
- Is digital literature a subdivision within Spanish literature? Or do we have to take into account other principles that make it "different" and consider it as net art?
- Should we already be commenting on these texts in class? Or should we wait until the examples are more conclusive?

The LEETHy Research Group at Complutense University of Madrid (http://www.ucm.es/info/leethi//nav/somos_00.php) is particularly interested in examining all these theoretical apories more closely and at a more practical level as digital literatures in Spanish-speaking communities. Now we have created the 1st *UCM-Microsoft Award Literatures in Spanish: From Text to Hypermedia* . The call for awards will be published each year in three modalities: Modality A: Electronic Editions of Literary Works in Spanish; Modality B: Online Teaching of Literatures in Spanish.

Modality C: Creative Digital Literature in Spanish. A workshop will be held every year in spring to bring together those who have received the awards and attract other people interested in our research field. All the materials will be available on the LEETHy site for the e-community.

In any case, digital literature in Spanish is still in its infancy; it is still at the defining stage and it isn't at all clear what will survive and what will eventually be forgotten, which tendencies are truly innovative and creative and which are nothing more than a lot of nonsense inflated by a media greedy for novelty and companies eager to publicize the very latest technology. Where digital literature is concerned, one can be a pioneer but we still don't know who the geniuses will be.

Bibliography

Aarseth, E. (1993). "Nonlinearity and Literary Theory". In G. P. Landow, ed., *Hypertext and Literary Theory*. Baltimore: Johns Hopkins Press: 51-86.
— . (1997). "No linealidad y teoría literaria". In P. Landow (comp.) *Teoría de Hipertexto*. Barcelona, Paidós.
Anderson, B. (1991). *Imagined Communities: Reflections on the Origin and Spread of Nationalism*. London and New York: Verso.
Amat, Núria (1994). *El libro mudo*. Madrid: Anaya & Mario Muchnik.
Bhabha, H. (ed.). (1990). *Nation and Narration*. London; New York: Routledge.
— . (1994). *The Location of Culture*. London; New York: Routledge.
Blanco, E. (2003). "El canon en la literatura electrónica". In M.J. Vega ed., *Literatura hipertextual y teoría literaria*. Madrid: Marenostrum: 63-72.
Bernstein, M. (1988). "The Bookmark and the Compass: Orientation Tools for Hypertext Users", *SIGOIS Bulletin*, 9: 34-45.
— . (1990). "An apprentice that discovers hypertext links". In A. Rizk *et. al.*, (eds.). *Hypertexts: Concepts, systems and applications*. Cambridge: Cambridge University Press: 212-223.
— . (1991), "Storyspace and the process of writing". In E. Berk y J. Devlin, (eds.). *Hypertext/Hypermedia Handbook*. New York: McGraw-Hill.
Cano Ballesta, J. (1999). *Literatura y tecnología: las letras españolas ante la revolución industrial (1890-1940)*. Valencia: Editorial Pre-Textos.
Casacuberta, D. (2003). *Creación colectiva. En Internet el creador es el público*. Barcelona: Gedisa.
Derrida, J. (1967), *De la Grammatologie*. Paris: Editions de Minuit.

Escobar, A. "Welcome to Cyberia: Notes on the Atrhopology of Cyberculture". *Current Anthropology*. 35.3 (1994): http://www.unc.edu/~aescobar/text/eng/arturowelc.pdf

Hakken, D. (1999). *Cyborgs@Cyberspace?: An athnographer looks to the future*. New York: Routledge.

Hawk, A (1993). *Future Culture Manifesto*: http://project.cyberpunk.ru/idb/future_culture_manifesto.html

Landow , G. (1995). *Hipertexto. La convergencia de la teoría crítica contemporánea y la tecnología*. Barcelona: Paidós.

Lévy, P. (2001). *Cyberculture*, Minneapolis, University of Minnesota Press.

Lister, M. *et al.* (2003). *New Media: A Critical Introduction*. New York: Routledge.

Macek, J. (2005). "Defining Cyberculture": http://macek.czechian.net/defining_cyberculture.htm.

Manovich, L. (2001). *The Language of a New Media*. Cambridge, Mass: MIT Press.

— . (2001). *New Media from Borges to HTML*: http://mrl.nyu.edu/~noah/nmr/book_samples/nmr-intro-manovich-excerpt.pdf.

Morse, M. (1998). *Virtualities: Television, Media Art and Cyberculture*. Bloomington : Indiana University Press.

Moulthrop, S. (1989) "In the Zones: Hypertext and the Politics of Interpretation": http://iat.ubalt.edu/moulthrop/essays/zones.html

Moulthrop, S, and Kaplan, N. (1991), "Something to Imagine: Literature, Composition, and Interactive Fiction". *Computers and Composition*, 9, pp. 7-23.

Orihuela, J. L. (1997). "Narraciones interactivas: el futuro no-lineal de los relatos en la era digital", *Palabra-Clave*, 2,2: 37-45.

Pajares Tosca, S. (2004). *Literatura Digital. El Paradigma Hipertextual*. Cáceres: Universidad de Extremadura.

— . "Las posibilidades de la narrativa hipertextual". *Espéculo*, 6 (1997): http://www.ucm.es/info/especulo/numero6/s-pajare.htm.

Paz Soldán Ávila, E. (2001). *Sueños digitales*. Madrid: Ediciones Alfaguara.

Romero, D. (eds.) (2006). *Naciones literarias*. Barcelona: Anthropos.

Romero D., Sanz, A. (eds.). *Literaturas del texto al hipermedia*. Barcelona: Anthropos (forthcoming in 2008).

Sánchez-Mesa, D. (ed.). (2004). *Literatura y cibercultura*. Madrid: Arco/Libros S.A.

Sanz A., Romero D., (eds.). (2007). *Literatures in the Digital Era: Theory and Praxis*. Newcastle, Cambridge Scholar Publishing.
Toschi, L. (2004), "Hipertexto y autoría", en Geoffrey Numberg (ed.), *El futuro del libro ¿Esto matará eso?* Barcelona, Paidós: 173-211.
Vega, M. J. ed. (2003). *Literatura hipertextual y teoría literaria*. Madrid: Marenostrum.
Vouillamoz, N. (2000). *Literatura e hipermedia. La irrupción de la literatura interactiva: precedentes y crítica*. Barcelona: Paidós.

Index: Spanish Digital Literature

ACOSTA, X., M.	Un mar de	http://mccd.udc.es/unmardehistorias/
ARA, Isabel &	Nada	http://www.unav.es/digilab/proyectosenl/2002/nada_ti
CHECA, Edith	Como el	http://www.badosa.com/bin/obra.pl?id=n052
ECHANIZ,	Un relato	http://www.unav.es/digilab/proyectosenl/0001/final/a
ECHEVERRIA,	Ana	http://www.unav.es/digilab/proyectosenl/0001/final/an
GACHE, Belén	El idioma	http://www.findelmundo.com.ar/pajaros/index.htm
GACHE, Belén	Púrpureas	http://www.findelmundo.com.ar/gache/Default.htm
GARCÍA, Dora	Heartbeat	http://aleph-arts.org/art/heartbeat/index.html
GONZÁLEZ,	Sabines	http://mccd.udc.es/orihuela/sabines
GUTIÉRREZ	¿Quién es	http://www.unav.es/digilab/proyectosenl/0001/final/lu
GUTIÉRREZ,	Condicion	http://www.condicionesextremas.com/hipernovela.ht
HEREDIA,	Navega en	http://www.unav.es/digilab/proyectosenl/2002/navega
JIMÉNEZ, Pedro	Casi 2000	http://www.zemos98.org/nntt/casi/
LABBE, Carlos	Pentagon	http://www.ucm.es/info/especulo/hipertul/pentagonal/i
MARTÍN	La señora	http://www.imaginando.com/lasenora/senora.html
MARTÍNEZ	La hora	http://www.unav.es/digilab/proyectosenl/0001/final/la
MONTES,	Desde	http://www.ucm.es/info/especulo/hipertul/desdeaqui/i
ORTIZ, Santiago	Bacterias	http://moebio.com/santiago/bacterias/
ORTIZ, Santiago	Diorama	http://moebio.com/santiago/diorama/
OTEGUI, Libe &	Puntos de	http://www.unav.es/digilab/proyectosenl/2002/puntos
PRILL, Richard	Mentiras	http://mccd.udc.es/orihuela/lies/
RODRÍGUEZ	Gabriella	http://www.javeriana.edu.co/gabriella_infinita/
RUBIO, Mariana	Memorias	http://www.unav.es/digilab/proyectosenl/0001/final/m
SÁNCHEZ,	El	http://www.unav.es/digilab/proyectosenl/0001/final/ap
SAVITSKAIA,	El reino	http://www.unav.es/digilab/proyectosenl/0001/final/es
SUAREZ	Navegació	http://mccd.udc.es/navegacionemocional
SIERRA I	Literactiv	http://www.literactiva.net/
VALDEOLMILL	Epímone	http://www.epimone.net/

LIST OF CONTRIBUTORS

Marie-Therese Abdel-Messih is Professor of English and Comparative Literature at Cairo University. Her field of work covers critical theory, comparative cultural studies in literature and art and the translation of creative and critical texts from Arabic and English. Her authored books in Arabic are *A Transcultural Reading of Literature* (1997; 2004),*Visual and Verbal Cultural Representations* (2002) and *National Culture: Global or International Options* (forthcoming). She is editor and co-translator of *The Cambridge History of Literary Criticism: From Formalism to Poststructuralism* (2006). E-mail: matermessih@yahoo.co.uk

Ziva Ben-Porat is Director of the Porter Institute for Poetics and Semiotics at Tel Aviv University, where she taught in the Department of Poetics and Comparative Literature until her retirement. She has published extensively on various forms of rhetorical intertextuality, such as allusion, parody and imitation, as well as on cultural representations and cultural memory. She is currently working on the construction of cultural threads, consisting of multimedia textual segments explicitly linked on the basis of their intertextual relations, and on researching the validity of such threads for cultural heritage, literary research and formal and informal teaching. E-mail: zivabp@post.tau.ac.il

Laura Borrás is working at the Languages and Cultures Department of the Universitat Oberta de Catalunya. She also teaches Comparative Literature and Literary Theory at the Universitat de Barcelona. She is Director of the "Hermeneia: Literary Studies and Digital Technologies" research group and leader of the Spanish Government-sponsored project "Texto, hipertexto, cibertexto: literatura ergódica y práctica crítica en el paradigma digital". She has published several articles on literary studies and e-learning as well as two relevant books: *Textualidades electrónicas:Nuevos escenarios para la literatura* (2005) and *Testualità elettroniche* (2006). E-mail: lborras@uoc.edu

Alckmar L. Dos Santos is graduated in Electronic Engineering and has a Masters in Literary Theory from the State University of Campinas, Brazil and a Ph.D. in Literary Studies from Paris 7 University. He is Professor of Brazilian Literature at the Federal University of Santa Catarina, Brazil, and a researcher at the CNPq (National Council for Technological and Scientific Development). His main research project is concerned with literature and the digital medium. He is also an essayist, novelist and poet. E-mail: alckmar@cce.ufsc.br

María Goicoechea studied English Philology at the University Complutense of Madrid (UCM). She has studied at the University of East Anglia (UK), and at the University of Maryland Baltimore County (USA), where she obtained a Master's Degree in Intercultural Communication. Her doctoral dissertation is entitled *The Reader in Cyberspace: A Literary Ethnography of Cyberculture* (2004). Her research interests include literary theory, ethnography, and cyberculture. Currently, she is a teacher of the English Department at the University Complutense of Madrid. She also teaches Mediterranean Literature and Cinema at American University in Madrid . Dr. Goicoechea is a member of LEETHI (Literaturas Españolas y Europeas del Texto al Hipermedia) Research Group (UCM), and of Hermeneia (Open University of Catalonia, UOC), two interdisciplinary research groups dedicated to the study of literature and computers. E-mail: mgoico@filol.ucm.es

Juan B. Gutiérrez belongs to the Department of Mathematics at Florida State University. His publications include *Extreme Conditions* (electronic novel), *The First Flight of the Wright Brothers* (electronic novel), *Seven Curious Ways to Die*, (story book), short stories published in compilations and magazines and several scholastic articles in the fields of electronic literature and biomathematics. E-mail: jgutierr@math.fsu.edu

Florian Hartling is currently working on his doctorate in Media and Communication Studies, due for completion in early 2008, at the University of Halle-Wittenberg. His research interests include digital literature, authorship, online journalism and Internet theory. He is also working at the University of Halle-Wittenberg on research and curriculum development with the European School of Journalism (Alfred Neven DuMont), and on the M.A. programme "MultiMedia und Autorschaft" in the Department of Media, Communication & Sports. He has published numerous articles on literature and technology.
E-mail: florian.hartling@medienkomm.uni-halle.de

Marko Juvan is Professor of Literary Theory at the University of Ljubljana and researcher at the Scientific Research Centre of the Slovenian Academy of Sciences and Arts. He studies literary and cultural theory, European romanticism, and twentieth century Slovene literature. Among his recent publications are: *Intertekstualnost* (2000), *Vezi besedila* (2000), *Romantična pesnitev* (2002) *Writing Literary History* (co-editor, with D. Dolinar, 2006), *Hybridizing Theory and Literature* (co-editor, with J. Kernev Štrajn, 2006), *Literarna veda v rekonstrukciji* (2006). E-mail: Marko.Juvan@guest.arnes.si

Apostolos Lampropoulos studied Linguistics at the University of Athens and Literary Theory at the Université Paris III - Sorbonne Nouvelle. He is interested in narratology, reception theories, hermeneutics, cultural studies, cybercriticism, literary geographies, body and space studies, the Greek and French novel in the nineteenth and twentieth centuries and film studies. He currently teaches Comparative Literature and Literary Theory at the University of Cyprus. His publications include a monograph entitled *Le Pari de la description : l'effet d'une figure déjà lue* (2002), several articles on literary theory and cultural studies, and translations into Greek of A. Compagnon's *Le Démon de la théorie* (2003) and Jonathan Culler's *On Deconstruction* (2006). E-mail: aplampro@ucy.ac.cy and aplampro@club-internet.fr .

George Landow holds a Ph.D. from Princeton University and is currently Professor of English and the History of Art at Brown University. He has taught at Columbia, Cornell and Oxford Universities and the National University of Singapore, where he held a chaired professorship in Computer Science and English and was the founding dean of an honours programme based on the paradigm of hypertextuality. His half dozen books on nineteenth-century British painting, literature and critical theory have been followed by an equal number on digital textuality, most recently *Hypertext 3.0: New Media and Critical Theory in an Era of Globalization* (2006). E-mail: george@landow.com

Anastasia Natsina holds a doctorate from Oxford University in Modern Greek Literature. She has recently completed her post-doctoral research at the Hellenic Open University, where she currently works as a tutor of Modern Greek Literature. Her research interests include modern Greek literature, contemporary prose, the short story as a genre, hypertext, critical theory, the postmodern and the teaching of literature. She has published several articles, her most recent publication being *Literary*

Studies in Open and Distance Learning: A Collection of Essays (2006). E-mail: natsina@eap.gr

Maria Clara Paixão de Sousa studied History at the University of São Paulo and Linguistics at the University of Campinas, Brazil. She obtained a Ph.D. in Linguistics in 2004, with a dissertation on the area of Historical Linguistics. Her research interests include grammatical theory, historical syntax, Portuguese language and literature, and corpus linguistics. Her involvement with text technologies and corpus construction dates back to 1998, when she joined the research team dedicated to the formation of the Tycho Brahe Annotated Corpus of Historical Portuguese. Since 2004, she has been coordinating a restructuring project for the same Corpus. Her current research project, "Memories of the Text", focuses on developing text processing technologies for scholarly editions.
E-mail: mariaclara.ps@gmail.com

Susana Pajares Tosca is Associate Professor at the IT University of Copenhagen, where she is a member of the Centre for Computer Games Research. Her Ph.D. on *Digital Literature* was awarded the *summa cum laude* distinction at the Complutense University of Madrid and has appeared in book form. Her forthcoming book, to be published by Routledge, is *Understanding Videogames: The Essential Introduction*. She is an editor of *Gamestudies*, the first peer-reviewed academic journal for computer games research, which she co-founded with Espen Aarseth. She is also board director of the Electronic Literature Organization, and an editor of the *Journal of Digital Information*. E-mail: tosca@itu.dk

Ana Pano holds a Ph.D. in European Literatures from the University of Bologna (2006). Her research interests include contemporary literature, linguistics, new media, the pedagogical aspects of hypertext, and digital archives. She has published several articles on literature and new media, linguistics and pragmatics. She also teaches Spanish Linguistics at the University of Bologna. E-mail: ana.pano@unibo.it

Priscilla Ringrose is a post-doctoral research fellow at NTNU, the Norwegian University of Science and Technology. Her research interests include post-colonial francophone literature, feminist theory and popular culture. Her book *Assia Djebar: In Dialogue with Feminisms* was published by Rodopi in 2006. E-mail: priscilla.ringrose@hf.ntnu.no

Dolores Romero studied Spanish Philology at the University of Salamanca, Spain, where she obtained her Ph.D. in Spanish Contemporary Poetry and then went on to study Critical Theory and Comparative Literature at the University of Nottingham in the U.K. She currently teaches Spanish Literature at the Complutense University in Madrid. She has published the following books: *Orientaciones en Literatura Comparada* (1998), *Una relectura del fin de siglo en el marco de la Literatura Comparada* (1998), *Naciones literarias* (2006) and *Seis siglos de poesía española escrita por mujeres* (2006). (UCM). She is Chair of the Research Committee on "Comparative Literature in the Digital Age" (CLDA) of the International Comparative Literature Association (ICLA). E-mail: dromero@filol.ucm.es

Alexandra Saemmer holds a Ph.D. in Arts and teaches at the University of Lyon 2, France. Her research focuses on textual and film versions of Margarit Duras' works and the relations between text and the visual arts. She is co-director of the Seminar E-Formes ("Ecritures visuelles sur support numérique") at the Centre Interdisciplinaire d'Etudes et de Recherche sur l'Expression Contemporaine (CIEREC) de l'Université de Saint-Étienne. She has published the following books: *Les lectures de Marguerite Duras* (2005) and *Matières textuelles sur support numérique* (2007). E-mail : Alexandra.Saemmer@univ-lyon2.fr

Amelia Sanz has a Ph.D. in Philology from the Complutense University of Madrid, where she teaches in the French Department of the Faculty of Arts. Her work focuses on comparative literature, particularly the study of transference processes between French and Spanish literatures from the seventeenth to the nineteenth centuries. She has developed theoretical reflections on key concepts of twentieth century critical theory, such as intertextuality, systemic approaches, interculturality and hypertextuality. She is coordinator of the research group "Literaturas Españolas y Europeas del Texto al Hipertexto" (LEETHI) and director of the E-learning Programme at the Faculty of Arts of the Complutense University of Madrid. E-mail: amsanz@filol.ucm.es

Perla Sassón-Henry is Associate Professor at the United States Naval Academy where she teaches Spanish Language, Literature and Culture. Her areas of interest include the works of Jorge Luis Borges and their intimate relationship with science, digital literature and net-art. Sassón-Henry's recent publications include several articles on Borges, hyperfiction and cybertext. Her book *Borges 2.0: From Text to Virtual Worlds* is scheduled for publication by Peter Lang Publishing in autumn, 2007. E-mail: sasson@usna.edu

Lee Scrivner is a doctoral student at the London Consortium, University of London. His Ph.D. thesis *The Insomnia of Modernity: Cultures of Sleeplessness 1870-1930* investigates the conditions of insomnia in modern culture, primarily in the poetry of James Thomson (B.V.), and T.S. Eliot. E-mail: leescrivner@gmail.com

Jola Skulj is a senior research fellow at the Scientific Research Centre of the Slovene Academy of Sciences and Arts. Her research focuses on the theoretical and methodological aspects of literature (textuality, novel, narrativity, historicity, cross-national and cross-cultural issues as dialogism) as well as on historical studies of the twentieth century. She has published extensively on electronic media and literature. She is a member of the Executive Bureau and Research Committee on Eastern and South-Eastern Europe of the ICLA/AILC, and of the Executive Committee of REELC/ENCLS (European Network of Comparative Studies /Réseau Européen d'études comparatistes). She is also on the editorial board of the Slovenian Comparative Literature periodical *Primerjalna književnost*. E-mail: jsk@zrc-sazu.si

Steven Tötösy de Zepetnek is interested in areas of scholarship related to comparative cultural studies, including comparative media and communication studies, comparative literature, postcolonial and ethnic minority studies, films and literature, audience studies, English, French, German, Central European, US-American, and Canadian cultures and literatures, history, bibliographies, new media and knowledge management, and editing. He is Professor of Comparative Literature at the University of Alberta and the University of Halle-Wittenberg. His recent books include *Imre Kertész and Holocaust Literature* (2005), *Comparative Cultural Studies and Michael Ondaatje's Writing* (2005), *Comparative Cultural Studies* (forthcoming in 2008).
E-mail: clcweb@purdue.edu

Dirk Van Hulle is associate Professor of Literature in English at the University of Antwerp. He is editor of *Genetic Joyce Studies* and maintains the Beckett Endpage. His publications include *Textual Awareness: A Genetic Study of Late Manuscripts by Joyce, Proust and Mann* (2004), *Joyce and Beckett, Discovering Dante* (2004), *Samuel Beckett's Last Bilingual Works* (2007). He is executive editor of the series of genetic editions of Samuel Beckett's bilingual works and is currently working with Mark Nixon and Vincent Neyt on a digital manuscript edition of four works by Beckett. E-mail: dirk.vanhulle@ua.ac.be